STRATEGY FORMULATION AND IMPLEMENTATION

Tasks of the General Manager

STRATEGY FORMULATION AND IMPLEMENTATION

Tasks of the General Manager

ARTHUR A. THOMPSON, Jr.
A. J. STRICKLAND, III

both of
The University of Alabama

1980

BUSINESS PUBLICATIONS, INC.
Dallas, Texas   75243
Irwin-Dorsey Limited
Georgetown, Ontario   L7G 4B3

ISBN 0-256-02277-1
Library of Congress Catalog Card No. 79-53966

Printed in the United States of America

2 3 4 5 6 7 8 9 0 ML 7 6 5 4 3 2 1

PREFACE

This book is intended for both senior-level and MBA courses in business policy. It contains a thorough survey of strategy/policy concepts and a set of contemporary readings. Although the text material parallels our *Strategy and Policy: Concepts and Cases* published earlier, this version constitutes a fresh, up-dated, and expanded treatment of the role and tasks of the general manager in directing the total enterprise.

We envision this book being used successfully in several different pedagogical formats. First, and perhaps foremost, it can serve as a basic text for those courses where the instructor wishes to emphasize case analysis but feels that the time has come to devote class time to formal coverage of the significant concepts and analytical techniques of strategic management which have come to prominence during the past decade. Exposing students to this literature and its managerial implications not only illustrates the power and practicality of systematic strategic evaluation but it also gives them a stronger foundation for doing a better job of case analysis. We think a concise, paperback text which covers the essential strategy/policy ideas is an ideal text supplement for instructors who prefer to build their course around their own cases or a selection of ICCH cases or a casebook (such as one of the Harvard casebooks published by Richard D. Irwin, Inc.). The textual material can be assigned either as additional reading to support the instructor's own lectures or it can be used as a supplementary resource for class discussion of cases.

In addition, we see this book as being well-suited as a basic text in conjunction with a management simulation game. It is a useful resource for executive development seminars on strategic management. Both the textual material and the readings offer ample opportunities for lively discussions of strategy/policy concepts and how these apply to actual company situations.

Orientation and content

In recent years, the field of business policy has made significant strides in becoming a discipline of its own with a distinctive literature of its own. This literature aims at analyzing a company's overall situation and assessing the enterprise as a whole, using a framework focused on strategy formulation and strategy implementation. While the concept of corporate strategy and the attendant methods of formal strategic analysis do not constitute a "theory" of how to manage, they very definitely do represent a "way of thinking" that illuminates the fundamental economics of a business and that addresses whether a firm is doing the right things. The literature of strategic analysis highlights the managerial importance of (1) a creative, insightful determination of a firm's overall strategic game plan and (2) putting the company's game plan into effect in ways that will make it both effective and efficient.

We think it is extremely valuable for students to be exposed to the prevailing views and ideas about the manager as an architect and implementer of strategy. Strategic decisions can be pivotal in their impact on a firm's future success and they certainly impact managers and employees at every level. Hence, even though many business school graduates may never reach positions of *top* management or have a general manager type job, they will be in a better position to contribute to the organization as staff specialists, department heads, and lower and middle managers if they have an accurate sense of their organization's purpose, its character, and the direction it is heading—in other words, if they better understand the overall company point of view. This perspective is the unique contribution of the business policy course.

The book's focus throughout is therefore on strategic management— the process of defining business purpose and setting objectives, deciding which set of businesses to enter, to continue in, and to get out of, formulating and implementing a viable strategic plan, monitoring performance and results, and all of the subactivities that these entail. We have endeavored to present a complete picture of management's functions and responsibilities in charting the course of a business and to indicate why these are essential in shaping an organization's character and future success.

Making the conceptual material relevant

Special pains have been taken to illustrate the use of strategic management concepts in actual practice. All six chapters of text are laced with concrete examples of the triumphs and failures of companies and their managements—what has worked, what hasn't, and why. However, to further highlight application and use of the concepts presented, we have included a series of in-depth illustration capsules. These are intended to keep the bridge between concept and application always open to the reader without disjointing the discussion. The ways in which managers and companies rely upon the concepts of strategic management cannot always be meaningfully presented in a passing sentence, footnote, or brief paragraph. We have endeavored to circumvent this difficulty by boxing off in capsule form a number of relatively detailed and extended illustrations which give the reader a full flavor and intuitive feel for how strategy/policy concepts are applied in real-world management circumstances. None of the capsules are "trumped-up" or "cute attention grabbers"; rather, they are no-nonsense, practical applications of concepts discussed in the text. We think students will find the illustration capsules worthwhile, enjoyable, and informative; most involve companies or people which the student will have heard of previously and several are suitable for use as case incidents. The liberal use of examples and the illustration capsules, together with the conceptual framework, should give students a useful package of ideas and tools for the case analysis part of the course.

Added pedagogical features

Two additional features of the text deserve special mention. Appendix A contains a chapter-length discussion of the case method and suggestions for case analysis. We have included it to help give students some positive direction in how to size up and evaluate a company's situation. Appendix A is intended to lessen any student uncertainties about case analysis by focusing their attention on the traditional analytical sequence of (1) identify, (2) evaluate, and (3) recommend. We have specifically included a thorough checklist of areas to probe in sizing up a company's strategic position, what to look for in identifying company strengths and weaknesses, how to prepare a case for oral class discussion, and guidelines for written case analyses. These discussions should be particularly useful for students who want assistance in making the transition from the lecture method to the case method of teaching/learning.

Appendix B contains a listing and brief description of some freshly written cases which you may wish to consider using in your course. We have grouped these cases so that the central issues and problems conform as much as possible to the sequence of chapters. However, since most of the cases embrace a variety of strategic issues, most of the cases listed can be used successfully at any of several different places in your course. Inspection copies of the suggested cases can be ordered directly from the Intercollegiate Case Clearing House (Soldiers Field Post Office, Boston MA 02163).

Acknowledgments

We have benefited from the help of many people in the evolution of this book. First are the many hundreds of students at the University of Alabama who have responded to our presentations of the subject matter in the classroom. R. C. Hauser (University of Southwestern Louisiana), R. Duane Ireland (Oklahoma State University), and John Claire Thompson (University of Connecticut—Storrs) provided thoughtful evaluations and advice on all parts of the volume.

Our intellectual debt to the writers and academicians upon whose work we have drawn is plain to any reader familiar with the literature on strategic management. We are likewise indebted to the authors and publishers of the readings for their permission to reprint their materials.

If even with all the help we received, the book is still less than perfect, then the fault is ours alone. However, if you will be kind enough to let us know what kinds of improvements you would find helpful, then we shall endeavor to make the book more suitable. Your critiques and suggestions will be warmly received; write us at P.O. Box J, University, AL 35486.

December 1979   Arthur A. Thompson, Jr.
                                             A. J. Strickland, III

CONTENTS

Combination Strategies. When Some Corporate Strategies Are More Logical than Others. The Basic Alternatives of Line of Business Strategy: *Strategies for Underdog and Low Market Share Businesses. Business Strategies for Dominant Firms. Business Strategies for Firms in Growth Markets. Strategies for Weak Businesses. Turnaround Strategies. Strategies to Be Leery of. Strategies to Avoid. Business Strategies. A Perspective View.*

READING

4. Strategic Evaluation and Strategic Choice.....................

Strategy Evaluation at the Corporate Level: *The Portfolio Approach to Corporate Strategy Evaluation.* Strategy Evaluation at the Business Level: *Developing a Strategic Profile of an Industry. Assessing Competitive Position. The Role of Competition in Strategy Evaluation. Gearing Business Strategy to the Economic Environment. Narrowing Down the List of Alternatives. Weighing the Strengths and Weaknesses of Leading Candidate Strategies.* Strategic Choice: Corporate Strategy and Business Strategy: *Risk/Reward Considerations. Timing Considerations. Contribution to Performance and Objectives. The Act of Strategic Commitment.*

READING

5. Structuring a Strategically Effective Organization..............

Strategy and Organization. Stages of Organizational Development. Guidelines for Linking Structure to Strategy. Guidelines for Assessing Structural Efficiency. Approaches to Organizational Diagnosis. Alternative Forms of Organization: *The Functional Organization Structure. Geographic Departmentation. Process, Market Channel, or Customer Departmentation. Decentralized Product Divisions. Strategic Business Units. Matrix Forms of Organization. Supplemental Methods of Organization. Perspectives on Organization Design.* Nonstructural Considerations in Organizing for Strategic Accomplishment: *Building a Distinctive Competence. Focusing Organizational Resources on Strategic Objectives.*

READING

6. Managing Organizational Processes..........................

Motivational Considerations. Instilling a Spirit of Performance. Leadership. Instituting Management Controls. Communication and Management Control. Problem Areas in Managing People. Playing "The Power Game."

READINGS

STRATEGY AND POLICY: A GENERAL MANAGEMENT OVERVIEW

"Cheshire Puss," she (Alice) began . . . "would you please tell me which way I ought to go from here?" "That depends on where you want to get to," said the cat.

Lewis Carroll

Why are some enterprises outstanding successes, while others are only moderately or marginally successful and still others are dismal failures? What is it about an organization that tends to make it a winner or a loser? These are intriguing questions and they have attracted serious study. Although what we have learned to date has produced neither a proven set of step-by-step management procedures which guarantee business success nor a genuine theory of management, the studies do point directly to the conclusion that it is management and managers that make organizations perform. Some of the managerial differences between successful and unsuccessful organizations are well worth pondering:

1. The managers of successful organizations work hard at developing a clear sense of direction and at defining exactly what the organization intends to do and to become. The managers of unsuccessful organizations appear less able to escape the press of day-to-day operating problems long enough to give their organizations purposeful direction; they are so consumed with "putting out brush fires" and tending to administrative detail that they neglect the importance of assessing direction and effectiveness.

2. The managers of successful organizations formulate an astute and opportune *strategy* for accomplishing the organization's purpose and mission, then effectively implement it through unified policy actions. The managers of unsuccessful organizations have no comprehensive game plan which is being deliberately and systematically pursued.

3. The managers of successful organizations have a detailed understanding of what business they are in, who their customers are, and why buyers want or need the organization's product/service. The managers of unsuccessful organizations are less perceptive about the hows and whys of "the market" for their product/service.

4. The managers of successful organizations exhibit a skill for engineering an effective, results-oriented system for creating, performing, and delivering the organization's product/service. Less successful organizations tend to be preoccupied with various sorts of internal bottlenecks, operating problems, coordinating mechanisms, and control procedures; their activities seem to be problem-focused instead of opportunity-focused and results-focused.

Differences in sales growth, in market share, in profitability, in product innovation, in technological prowess, in quality of manufacture, in customer loyalty and satisfaction, in image and reputation, and in capacity to adapt and respond to change all seem based, to some significant degree, upon how well managers perform the related tasks of formulating an astute and timely organization strategy, then implementing and executing the strategic plan via unified policies calculated to achieve the intended performance and results.

Where Strategy and Policy Fit in

Just why managerial performance of the strategy and policy functions contributes mightily to an organization's success or failure is rooted in the familiar expression "if you don't know where you are going, any road will take you there." The point, very simply is that the management of the *total enterprise* cannot be left to circumstance, spur-of-the-moment decision, chance happenings, and whatever comes over the threshold. "Whatever will be will be" is *not* a recipe for successfully conceiving and directing the *totality* of an organization's activities.

Instead, any enterprise if it is to be successful must be *managed*. This means more than just seeing that the traditional functions of manufacturing, finance, marketing, personnel, accounting, and so on are performed efficiently, then coordinated. It means more than being concerned with the nuts and bolts of daily activities—seeing that the necessary administrative details are done on time and that operations flow smoothly. When we speak of managing the *total* enterprise, we are talking about the managerial functions and skills that bear directly upon an organization's capacity to survive, to adapt to market and environment changes, to develop and expand, and to move perhaps in new directions and become a different type of organization altogether. The focus is not so much on everyday operations and temporary crises as on sustaining and enhancing the growth and development of the organization over time. It is on the direction-setting decisions: making or ratifying a choice among strategic alternatives, establishing long-range and short-range objectives, allocating resources among the enterprise's various divisions and activities, evaluating merger and acquisition possibilities, deciding what new businesses to get into, which ones to continue, and which ones to abandon. It is on the ability of the enterprise to develop the staying power to survive and win out over competition, product-market-technological changes, and the winds of economic uncertainty.

How an organization goes about dealing with these real-life aspects of its present and future existence is the core of what managerial strategy and policy are all about. In a general sense, then, the terms *strategy* and *policy* are used to embrace the managerial activities associated with giving an organization purposeful direction, formulating a comprehensive strategy for accomplishing the chosen objectives, marshalling and allocating the resources requisite for strategic accomplishment, and directing pursuit of the strategic plan so to produce the desired performance and results. The concern of strategy and policy is, therefore, with the management of the *total enterprise*. It is with the nature of the forest, not with the trees.

Taking a balanced, overall look at how a particular event, situation, problem, or proposal will impact the *total* organization is commonly referred to as a *general management* point of view. In fact, the term *general management* has become synonomous with the management of the total enterprise and with the particular managerial perspective and skills associated with evaluating factors in terms of their impact upon the *whole* organization. Further, a person who is charged with overall responsibility for the activities and results of an organization (or organization subunit) is known as a *general manager*. Because of their position, general managers are necessarily concerned with strategy-policy issues; that is, with the performance of the organization as a whole and with defining, deciding, and putting into effect a conscious purpose and direction appropriate to emerging opportunities, threats, and internal capabilities.

Obviously, strategy-policy decisions are matters of "top" management concern. But the strategy-policy domain does not belong exclusively to a small group of senior executives. Most large organizations and many medium-sized organizations now have general management positions at the product group level, the division level, and the departmental level—a direct outgrowth of the corporate movement toward decentralization. Furthermore, the strategy-policy pronouncements of higher-level managers are seldom definitive enough to provide unambiguous guidance through an uncertain future and the one-of-a-kind situations that constantly crop up. At the very least, lower-level managers are expected to interpret, clarify, and fine-tune organizational strategies and policies to meet the circumstances of daily operations. This means that a significant amount of strategy-policy discretion resides below the top management and general manager levels. Consequently, whether in a line or a staff position, lower and middle managers influence the strategy-policy process through their everyday activities, and how they deal with problems posed by day-to-day operations contributes to keener strategy-policy definition.

The point here is that *all* managers need to be acquainted with strategy-policy problems and how to view and deal with them. Strategy and policy are not just a top management concern. They relate directly to the performance of the entire management function and go to the heart of organization success or failure. The study of strategy, policy, and general management is thus not as remote from the immediate realm of lower-level managers and students of management as might first appear.

Our discussion should make it clear that the managerial roles, skills, and functions which relate to strategy and policy are vital to all types of organizations, whether they be large or small, profit or not-for-profit. The study of managerial strategy and policy is fundamentally as applicable to a local real estate firm, a small manufacturer of chemicals, or chain of drugstores, or the Pittsburgh Steelers as to IBM or U.S. Steel. It speaks to the problems of managing hospitals, educational institutions, a local YMCA, the National Organization for Women, a state department of public safety, the Ford Foundation, Sigma Chi Fraternity, the Roman Catholic Church, and the U.S. Postal Service just as much as to privately-owned, profit-motivated enterprises.

In succeeding pages a serious attempt will be made to elaborate on the *general* applicability of the strategy-policy discipline to all sizes and types of organizations (although the major emphasis will focus on profit-seeking enterprises operating in a competitive market environment). We shall endeavor to stress how and why the study of strategy and policy is important, how it relates to the problems of general managers, and how it represents a way of thinking and a perspective view that zeroes in on what and where an organization is now, where it is headed, and how its performance might be improved.

KEY CONCEPTS AND TERMINOLOGY

It will prove useful if, at the outset, we get a firmer grip on some of the key concepts and terminology that serve as the foundation for this text. This is especially important because throughout the literature of management such terms as purpose, objectives, goals, strategy, and policy have been defined and interpreted in a variety of ways.

Organization Purpose and Mission

Simply stated, an organization's *purpose* and *mission* consist of a long-term vision of what it seeks to do and the reasons why it exists. Purpose is management's concept of the organization and its service mission to customers and to society. An organization's purpose, when expressed in managerially meaningful terms, indicates exactly what activities the organization intends to engage in now and in the future. It says something specific about what kind of organization it is and is to become and, by omission, what it is not to do and not to become.[1] It depicts an organization's business character and does so in ways that tend to distinguish the organization from other organizations. In this sense, a purpose sets forth the principles and conceptual foundation upon which the organization rests and the nature of the business or businesses in which it plans to participate.

Rogers cites Westinghouse Electric Corporation in 1969 as having the following purpose and mission statement:

> It is the basic purpose of Westinghouse, in all of its decisions and actions, to attain and maintain the following:
>
> 1. A continuous high level of profits which places it in the top bracket of industry in its rate of return on invested capital.
>
> 2. Steady growth in profits, sales volume and high turnover investment at rates exceeding those of the national economy as a whole.
>
> 3. Equitable distribution of the fruits of continuously increasing productivity of management, capital and labor among stockholders, employees and the public.
>
> 4. Design, production and marketing, on a worldwide basis, of products and services which are useful and beneficial to its customers, to society and to mankind.
>
> 5. Continuous responsiveness to the needs of its customers and of the public, creating a current product line which is First in Performance and a steady flow of product improvements, new products and new services which increase customer satisfaction.
>
> 6. A vital, dynamic product line by continuous addition of new products and businesses and prompt termination of old products and businesses when their economic worth, as measured by their profit performance, becomes substandard.
>
> 7. The highest ethical standards in the conduct of all its affairs.
>
> 8. An environment in which all employees are enabled, encouraged and stimulated to perform continuously at their highest potential of output and creativity and to attain the highest possible level of job satisfaction in the spirit of the Westinghouse Creed.
>
> These eight points are indivisible. Together, as a unit, they state the fundamental management philosophy of the Westinghouse Electric Corporation.[2]

---

[1] C. Roland Christensen, Kenneth R. Andrews, and Joseph L. Bower, *Business Policy: Text and Cases*, 4th ed. (Homewood, Illinois: Richard D. Irwin, 1978), p. 125.

[2] Westinghouse Electric Corporation, *Guide to Business Planning* (Pittsburgh, 1969), p. 1, as cited and quoted in David C. D. Rogers, *Business Policy and Planning: Text and Cases* (Englewood Cliffs, N.J.: Prentice-Hall, Inc., 1977), p. 84.

Professor George A. Steiner has reported that the purposes of Lockheed Aircraft during the late 1960s were:

1. To be the major company satisfying in the highest technical sense the national security needs of the United States and its allies in space, air, land, and sea.

2. To employ technical resources in meeting the nondefense needs of governments and the requirements of commercial markets.

3. To achieve continuous growth of profits at a rate needed to attract and retain stockholder investment.

4. To recognize and appropriately discharge our responsibilities for the welfare of our employees, the communities in which we do business, and society as a whole.

5. To maintain a large proportion of sales in advanced technical products bearing the Lockheed name.

6. To maintain continuity of the enterprise by holding relatively low rates of change of ownership, management and employees.[3]

On occasions, managers resort to platitudes and all-inclusive language in describing organization purpose. An umbrella-like statement that "our purpose is to serve the food needs of the nation" can mean anything from growing wheat to operating a vegetable cannery to delivering milk to manufacturing farm machinery to running a Kentucky Fried Chicken franchise. Such sweeping statements of purpose are mostly rhetoric and are certainly *too broad to guide management action.* They do not establish direction nor do they *narrow* down and focus management attention on what the firm is to do.[4] They offer no guidance to managers in developing sharply focused, results-oriented objectives, strategies, and policies. A detailed understanding of organization purpose is thus the starting point for rational managerial action and for the design of organization structure, processes, and procedures. Put another way, managerial effectiveness tends to begin with clarity of purpose—with an accurate, carefully delineated concept of just what the organization is trying to do and why.

A key feature of organization purpose is that its focus must be external rather than internal. Purpose is ultimately defined by the satisfying of customer wants. In this regard, Peter Drucker, in *Management: Tasks, Responsibilities, Practices,* maintains:

---

[3] George A. Steiner, *Top Management Planning* (New York: Macmillan Co., 1969), p. 146.

[4] Any "danger" of an organization "locking itself in" with an overly narrow concept of its purpose is contrived rather than real. Organization purpose is always subject to revision and is not something "carved in stone." Many, if not most, organizations fundamentally change the scope of their activities (and hence their purposes) from time to time. This is particularly true of firms which, for one reason or another, diversify into activities well outside their original business (as when a cigarette manufacturing company diversifies into brewing beer). But even without broad diversification an organization's actual purpose and direction seldom remain rigidly fixed for more than a decade or two.

To know what a business is we have to start with its *purpose*. Its purpose must lie outside of the business itself. In fact, it must lie in society since business enterprise is an organ of society. There is only one valid definition of business purposes: *to create a customer*.[5]

Drucker's view, which in effect makes profit necessary but not sufficient as the underlying purpose and motive of enterprise, correctly emphasizes that unless an organization can develop a sufficiently large clientele for its product/service, it is destined to wither and die. The customer is the foundation of an organization and keeps it in existence.[6]

Organization Objectives

Objectives refer to the specific kinds of results which an organization seeks to achieve in pursuing its purpose and mission.[7] Typically, organizational objectives relate to (1) the desired impacts upon the organization's customers in terms of satisfaction, product performance, and meeting individual and societal wants and needs, and (2) the desired internal performance and results; i.e., market share, growth, profitability, cash flow, return on investment, and so on. By delineating the results which are to be achieved, objectives give concrete meaning to the general direction indicated in a statement of purpose and mission.

Unless an organization's purpose is converted into *specific* targets and *specific* actions, there is risk of it remaining a statement of good intentions and unrealized achievement. When the desired results are made concrete

---

5 Peter Drucker, *Management: Tasks, Responsibilities, Practices* (New York: Harper and Row Publishers, 1974), p. 61.

6 Ibid. Moreover, according to Drucker, every organization, profit-seeking or not-for-profit, has an implied contract with society that calls not only for the organization's purpose to be ratified by its customers but also for the organization's activities to be consistent with the expectations of society at large. Society has, after all, entrusted a portion of its pool of scarce, productive resources to the organization and thus has a right to expect they not be misused. For this reason, failure to act in socially responsible ways or to perform socially useful functions quite properly tends to trigger serious societal scrutiny of an organization's activities and, usually, a reevaluation by the organization of its purpose and behavior.

7 The literature of management is filled with references to *goals* and *objectives*. These terms are used in a variety of ways, many of them conflicting. Some writers use the term goals to refer to the *long-run* results which an organization seeks to achieve and use the term objectives to refer to intermediate, *short-run* performance targets. Other writers reverse the usage, referring to objectives as the desired long-run results and goals as the desired short-run results. Still other writers use the terms interchangeably, as synonyms. In our view, the semantical confusion over the usage of the terms goals and objectives is secondary; the important thing is to recognize that the results a firm seeks to attain can have a time perspective. In nearly every instance, those organizations which are results-oriented will tend to establish both long- and short-range performance targets. Practically speaking, it makes no difference what labels one attaches to the long-range targets and the short-range targets. Thus we have deliberately chosen to use the single term *objectives* to refer to the performance targets and results which an organization seeks to attain. We will use the adjectives long-range (or long-run) and short-range (or short-run) to identify the relevant time frame.

and measurable through managerial objectives, it is more likely that (1) resources can and will be allocated to their attainment, (2) priorities can be agreed upon and deadlines set, and (3) responsibility can be assigned and somebody held accountable for producing the desired results. Consequently, the managerial role of objectives is, first and foremost, to serve as a vehicle for transforming broad direction into *concrete, measurable action commitments*.[8] The specifications for properly formulated objectives include the following:

- □ They must give explicit direction (and not take the form of vague abstractions and pious platitudes).
- □ They must set forth organizational priorities.
- □ They must be the basis for management action and the guidelines for management decisions.
- □ They must act as the cornerstones for designing jobs and for organizing the activities to be performed.
- □ They must become the measure of achievement.
- □ They must serve as the standards against which actual performance is measured and against which individuals and groups are judged in terms of having done a good job or not.[9]

Illustration Capsule 1 contains a number of possible organizational objectives, some clearly, and some poorly defined, exemplifying properly and improperly formulated objectives.

Since the role of objectives is to guide the concentration of resources and efforts toward the desired ends, objectives should be selective as opposed to all-encompassing. Nonetheless, management rarely can rely on

---

ILLUSTRATION CAPSULE 1
Examples of "Good" and "Bad" Organizational Objectives

Examples of "Good" (clearly-defined) Objectives — *Remarks*

1. "We plan to make Product X the number one selling brand in its field in terms of units sold." — Leaves little doubt as to the intended sales objective and market standing.

2. "We strive to be a leader, not a a follower, in introducing new products and in implementing new technologies by spending no less than 5 percent of sales revenue for R&D." — Indicates an attempt to remain on or near technological frontiers and says how this attempt is to be financed.

---

[8] Drucker, *Management*, p. 99.
[9] Ibid., pp. 99–102.

ILLUSTRATION CAPSULE 1 *(continued)*

3. "Our profit objective is to increase earnings per share by a minimum of 8 percent annually and to earn at least a 20 percent aftertax return on net worth."

Clear, concrete, and readily measured.

4. "We seek to produce the most durable, maintenance-free product that money can buy."

An obvious focus on being the leader with respect to high quality.

5. "It is our objective to help assure that the wood products needs of this country are met by planting two seedlings for every tree we cut and by following exemplary forest management practices."

A specific commitment.

Examples of "Bad" (poorly-phrased) Objectives

Remarks

1. "Our objective is to maximize sales revenue and unit volume."

Not subject to measurement. What dollar figure constitutes maximum sales? Also, may be inconsistent; the price and output which generate the greatest dollar revenue is almost certainly not the same as the combination which will yield the largest possible unit volume.

2. "No new idea is too extreme and we will go to great lengths to develop it."

Too broad. No firm has the money or capability to investigate any and every idea that it comes across. To even try is to march in all directions at once.

3. "We seek to be the most profitable company in our industry."

Vague. By what measures of profit —total dollars? earnings per share? return on sales? return on equity investment? all of these?

4. "In producing our products we strive to minimize costs and maximize efficiency."

What are the standards by which costs will be said to be minimum and efficiency maximum? How will management know when the objective has been achieved?

5. "We intend to meet our responsibilities to stockholders, customers, employers, and the public."

In what respects? As determined by whom? More a platitude than an action commitment.

just a single organizational objective. In general, objectives are needed in *all areas* on which the *survival* and *success* of the organization depend.[10] Moreover, it is normally desirable to develop both long-range objectives and short-range objectives. *Long-range objectives* keep management alert to what has to be done *now* to attain the desired results later. *Short-range objectives* serve to indicate the speed and momentum which management seeks to accomplish longer range objectives and purpose; they direct the attention of managers and organizational subunits toward the desired standards of performance and behavior in the near term.

As concerns the long-run, most organizations have need for:

1. *Marketing objectives,* to create a viable, sustainable customer base and market for its products/services;

2. *Technology-innovation objectives,* to keep products/services up-to-date and competitive (thereby avoiding obsolescence);

3. *Profitability objectives,* to cover the risks of economic activity, test the validity of the organization's contributions, and generate the financial capital requisite for preserving (and enhancing where desirable) the organization's productive capability;

4. *Efficiency objectives,* to remain cost competitive and to make judicious use of the economic resources entrusted by society to its care;

5. *Resource supply objectives,* to conserve whatever human, capital, and natural resources are needed for continuing to supply customers (society) with the organization's products/services; and

6. *Social responsibility objectives,* to keep a watchful eye on how well the organization performs in accord with societal expectations, and to take full responsibility for and justify the impact which its activities have on the environment at large.

The foregoing list is, of course, by no means exhaustive. An organization may wish, for example, to have long-run objectives relating to future growth, industry leadership, competitive position, overall size and degree of diversification, technological capability, the financial payoffs it seeks to provide stockholders in the form of dividends and capital gains, and reduced vulnerability to recession.

Because long-run objectives relate to the ongoing activities of an organization, their achievement tends to be open-ended in the sense of not being bounded by time. For example, the objective of survival is never completely attained since failure and bankruptcy are always future possibilities. A long-run objective of 10 percent growth in sales and profits continues into the future even though it may have been successfully reached in the past.

---

[10] Ibid., p. 100. See also Charles H. Granger, "The Hierarchy of Objectives," *Harvard Business Review,* vol. 42, no. 3 (May-June 1963), pp. 63–74.

An organization's short-run objectives act as the intermediate quantitative and qualitative performance targets which management wishes to attain in moving toward long-run objectives. Because short-run objectives are inherently keyed to the pursuit of longer-run objectives, they should: (1) relate to some specific long-run objective or set of long-run objectives; (2) measure the progress being made in achieving long-run objectives; (3) specify a time frame for accomplishment; (4) be internally consistent to avoid conflicts between objectives; and (5) be realistic in the sense of being within the reach of organizational capability and within what market and competitive conditions will allow. Once the set of short-run objectives is established, they should be ranked according to priority. For reasons to be discussed later, short-run objectives should be established not just for the overall organization but also for each of the specific products and lines of business in which the organization has an interest and, further, for each subunit within the organization structure.

The following statements are illustrations of short-run objectives:

1. We have set our sights on a target market share of 15 percent this year and 17.5 percent next year.
2. Our objective every year is the same—to win the national championship.
3. The company's immediate objective is to open up at least two new sales territories each year for the next five years to boost our market coverage to eight states.
4. We intend to reduce new store openings by 10 percent this year.
5. Our immediate target is to increase donations and contributions by 20 percent.
6. Our aim is to cutback staffing requirements by 5 percent each of the next three years.
7. We seek to gain enough new accounts this year to reach our interim goal of $50 million in deposits.
8. We aim to reduce infant mortality rates to less than 1 per 1000 births within 12 months.
9. The plant's annual production objective is an output rate close to 95 percent of rated capacity.
10. The objective of this year's rush is to get 20 new pledges.

Observe that the statements all reflect a short-range target level of achievement. Contrast this with the longer term focus of the stated objectives in Illustration Capsule 1.

In summary, objectives can be used as rallying points for coordinating the activities of organizational subunits and as a basis for establishing common purpose in the performance of diverse tasks. Acceptance of organizational objectives by the people concerned promotes teamwork and a united approach to achieving the organization's purpose and mission.

ILLUSTRATION CAPSULE 2
The Role and Function of Objectives

The following remarks of a vice president of marketing for a small candy manufacturer illustrates the internal role and function of objectives (Observe that the manager uses the terms goals and objectives interchangeably whereas we distinguish between short-run objectives and long-run objectives—see footnote 6.)

Basically I'm trying to operate so my people will grow along with the company. I set high standards. I know they won't all be met, but at least people will know what I'm looking for. I expect a subordinate to have ideas and to have plans on what he wants to do and how. I may differ with him, and I'll explain why I think another way is better, but I don't penalize people for doing things their own way. What I want is results, and if a man has his own way, that's O.K.

Our regional men and brokers have quotas and also specific goals to reach in each market. I ask them to set a quota for themselves, partly to get their appraisal of a market and partly so I can appraise their motivation and judgment. I don't want them to promise pie in the sky, but neither do I want to see them aiming low to be sure of hitting it and getting a bonus.

We give each regional manager a discretionary fund to spend as he pleases. It's only $5,000, but it is important in a couple of ways. For one thing the way a man uses it helps me appraise his judgment. Second, it makes him a much more important part of the organization. The brokers look to him to use some of the money for promotions in their territory—so it helps the regional man get the broker's cooperation. And don't forget that it's the strength of our distribution that has let us grow rapidly on so little money.

All this field work is done within the general framework of corporate marketing objectives. We write these up and send them out to each broker and regional man. Each month we send him a rundown on how he is doing compared to the objectives (based on information from the IBM reports). At the end of the year we go over the plan and each unfulfilled objective with every man. We try to determine if we were unrealistic, if it was unavoidable, or if it was a lack of something on his part. It isn't done to crucify someone; we want our objectives and quotas to be realistic or they are worse than useless. We want each man to believe he can hit them, so it's important that we all understand why they weren't reached.

SOURCE: George A. Smith, Jr., C. Roland Christensen, Norman A. Berg, and Malcolm S. Salter, *Policy Formulation and Administration*, 6th ed. (Homewood, Ill.: Richard D. Irwin, 1972), pp. 363–64. © 1972 by Richard D. Irwin, Inc.

Where objectives are stated in quantitative terms, they can serve as criteria for measuring and evaluating performance of (1) the organization as a whole, (2) organizational subuits, and (3) individual managers. Illustration Capsule 2 provides an inside look at the managerial role and function of organizational objectives.

Organization Strategy

In almost every case, an organization will have several viable options for going about what it is trying to do—as the old adage goes "there's more than one way to skin a cat." *Strategy* serves the function of indicating how management has chosen to reach organizational objectives. It is a blueprint of the organizational game plan. It says in specific terms how the organization intends to get where it wants to go. It indicates what management's program of action will be over both the short-term and the long-term. It is the guide for the enterprise's development and indicates how management intends to shape and align the organization's activities to take into account both the external environment and internal constraints.

It should be obvious from this brief description that the concept of strategy bears directly on how the *total* enterprise is to be managed. In particular, strategy embraces four areas of management concern:

1. The choice of products, markets, and types of businesses the organization will enter, stay in, and get out of.
2. How an organization's perhaps diverse range of activities will be integrated, coordinated, and otherwise fit together to make a workable whole.
3. What priorities and guidelines are to be observed in allocating organizational resources among various products, divisions, and activities, and what, if any, *distinctive competence* management will try to build into the organization's range of capabilities.
4. How the organization intends to compete in each one of the businesses in which it engages.

General Electric, one of the pioneers in the development and use of the concept of strategy, has simplified these areas of strategic concern into the following capsule definition: strategy is a statement of how what resources are going to be used to take advantage of which opportunities to minimize which threats to produce a desired result. This view of strategy emphasizes that for organizations to survive, and certainly for them to succeed, management must seek to position an organization in its environment such that it can be effective in utilizing internal competencies and resources to take advantage of external opportunities and reduce the impact of externally imposed threats.

One example of how strategy is used to guide an enterprise's development is given by Beatrice Foods' transformation from a local dairy operation into a $5 billion company:

> Beginning as a local butter and egg company in Beatrice, Nebraska, the company began an effort to diversify its product line and reduce its dependence on local conditions. It started by acquiring a string of small dairies. From the outset, Beatrice followed two key principles—diversification and decentralization. Only firms headed by independent-minded entrepreneurs were brought into the fold. Although Beatrice found that the dairy business had the disadvantage of low profit margins, it had the advantage of generating a lot of excess cash (mainly because inventories of milk are provided by nature and do not require endless financing). Thus, having acquired dairies coast to coast and grown into a $200 million dairy company, Beatrice began to invest some of its cash in higher-margin food companies. LaChoy Food Products was the first acquisition and, when it worked out well, Beatrice began to push into other food lines at an accelerating rate. In the 1960's Beatrice acquired some nonfood firms and by the 1970's owned several different kinds of manufacturing operations, a warehousing division, and an insurance company. Among its products are such brands as Samsonite (luggage), Meadow Gold (dairy products), Martha White (flour), Dannon (yogurt), Clark (candy bars), Eckrich (meats), Gebhardt's (chili and tamales), and LaChoy (Chinese foods).
>
> Beatrice's acquisition strategy followed some strict guidelines. Commodity-oriented firms were excluded because of the unpredictable price swings. Companies in head-on competition with such powerhouses as Kellogg's and Campbell Soups were avoided. In the nonfood areas, Beatrice shied away from labor-intensive companies because of the risks of inflation of labor costs. Industries like steel and chemicals were avoided because of their heavy capital demands.
>
> The basic acquisition strategy was to go after companies with at least five years of sales and profit increases, and to eliminate from consideration any firm so large that failure could seriously damage Beatrice's overall profitability. Between 1952 and 1962 most of the acquired firms had sales of about $2 million. While Beatrice sought companies with a growth rate higher than its own, it insisted on a purchase price keyed to a price-earnings multiple about one-third below Beatrice's own current price-earnings ratio. Beatrice was generally successful in buying firms it wanted at a "discount" because the Beatrice stock it was offering in return had performed so very well over the years.

In 1977, Beatrice Foods overtook Kraft and Esmark to become the nation's largest food processor.[11] Another example of the use of strategy to accomplish objectives is given in Illustration Capsule 3.

---

[11] For a more complete discussion of Beatrice's strategy and operating philosophy, see Linda Grant Martin, "How Beatrice Foods Sneaked Up On $5 Billion," *Fortune* (April 1976), 118–29.

ILLUSTRATION CAPSULE 3
Northwest Industries' Strategy for Coping with
Inflation and Producing Real Growth

In November 1978, Northwest Industries explained what its strategies were to lessen the impact of inflation on its operations and its stockholders:

No company can control or even completely foresee the rate of inflation. But at Northwest Industries we're always trying to lessen its influence on our operations. We do this by sticking with longstanding management strategies that are particularly helpful in uncertain times.

Our goal is to produce real growth. And that means to maximize the total return to our stockholders—including dividend income.

Vertical Integration

One tool we use is vertical integration. It doesn't just provide cost efficiencies. It also helps insulate our operating companies from price volatility in purchased materials and services. For instance, our General Battery Corporation's integrated production processes include everything from secondary lead smelting and plastic case manufacturing to the delivery of batteries by the company's own truck distribution system. This kind of control helps keep our product costs both reasonable and comparatively predictable.

We also have a conscious policy of making forward commitments on key raw materials well into the future—far longer than many of our competitors. Occasionally we guess wrong and miss out on falling prices. But we like the advantage of having known costs for an extended period of time. For instance, by settling now on future cotton costs, Union Underwear Company can stabilize an important cost element. This helps Union plan production and price its goods sensibly. But be sure of this: we are *not* speculators or commodity traders. We are manufacturers.

Efficient Production

Efficient production also helps us fight inflation. Almost all of our companies are industry leaders. That allows us advantages many competitors do not have, so we can make good products at lower costs. And when it comes to maintaining or increasing margins in an inflationary environment, our companies frequently do the job through cost reduction rather than by relying simply on price increases.

Another way our companies maintain margins without price increase is by upgrading product mix. They drop lower margin goods to concentrate on more profitable items. This ensures our facilities are utilized for maximum profitability. An example is Acme Boot Company getting out of the manufacturing of golf and dress shoes to make and sell more western boots. A simple move, but effective.

ILLUSTRATION CAPSULE 3 *(continued)*

Acquisition Criteria

That we seek stability in an unstable economy is also evident in our acquisition criteria. These criteria generally rule out companies subject to unusually large cyclical swings. We avoid companies that are dependent on a single supplier or customer. We never want to be in a position where a customer or supplier can control our bottom line. Also, we avoid highly labor intensive businesses. We believe we can control the availability of capital more easily than the availability of labor.

U.S. Orientation

Another way we have tried to insulate our stockholders from uncertainty is by keeping Northwest's earnings coming essentially from the U.S., and for good reason. With 95 percent of our earnings U.S. based, we have avoided the comparatively high rates of inflation and the unstable economies of many countries, not to mention the damaging effects of fickle policy changes by foreign governments. In so doing, we have largely avoided the vagaries of foreign currency fluctuations.

Every policy we follow—whether it pertains to management, manufacturing, or marketing—seeks to add stability to our rates of growth. And not just growth at the rate of inflation, but at a considerably higher rate.

SOURCE: Ad appearing in *Business Week*, November 20, 1978, pp. 168–69.

Organization Policy

Whereas strategy depicts how the organization's purpose and objectives are to be accomplished, it is the role of policy to guide and channel the implementation of strategy and to prescribe how internal organization processes will function and be administered. Thus, the term *policy* refers to the organizational methods, procedures, rules, and practices associated with implementing and executing strategy.[12] In this sense, policies are

---

[12] In management literature, definition and actual use of the term *policy* is far from uniform. In years past, it was common and customary to refer to "policy" to describe company purpose, company direction, and ways of doing business—a usage which makes policy and strategy indistinguishable. This overlap in usage is giving way to a conceptual difference between strategy and policy much like we have used and defined the terms here. Nonetheless, there are times when both academicians and practitioners use the term policy to refer to top management pronouncements on what course of action a company will follow (it is our "policy" not to diversify into markets where we lack technological proficiency) and on statements of management intent (it is our "policy" to pay dividends equal to 50 percent of net earnings per share). It is important for the reader to be alert, therefore, to the fact that policy is sometimes used in a much broader sense than we have defined it here; our definition is a relatively narrow one. The definition we presented tends to equate "policy" with those managerial actions and decisions relating specifically to strategy implementation and execution. We think this

guides to carry out strategy; they set boundaries and limit the kinds and directions of actions which are to be taken. They are the result of institutionalizing and operationalizing the chosen strategy and of getting the organization into a position of being able to execute the strategic plan effectively and efficiently.

Plainly, in the managerial scheme of things, policy is (or should be!) subordinate to and supportive of strategy and purpose, since it signals what should and should not be done to further achievement of the desired performance and results. Examples of policies which an organization might adopt in support of its overall purpose and strategy include:

1. A retail grocery chain giving store managers authority to buy fresh produce locally when they can get a better buy, rather than ordering from the regional warehouse.

2. An oil company's deciding to lease the properties and buildings for its service station operations so to minimize long-term capital requirements.

3. A graduate school of business deciding not to admit to its MBA program any applicant who does not have at least two years of business experience as well as a B average on all undergraduate coursework.

4. A firm's requiring each of its product divisions and profit centers to file weekly sales and profit reports with headquarters as a means of monitoring and evaluating progress toward corporate goals.

5. A hospital's requiring all patients to make a $100 cash deposit on being admitted, as part of its plan for maintaining financial solvency.

Policy may take the form of written statements, or it may consist of unwritten understandings of past actions (which may or may not be intended to establish precedents or frames of reference for future action). The need for both major and minor policy guides exists at all levels in the management structure. Thus, the scope of policy statements may range widely from such lofty principles as "It is company policy to give our customers complete satisfaction or their money back" and "We are an equal opportunity employer" down to such mundane matters as "It is company policy not to accept personal checks for more than the amount of purchase" and "It is the policy of this organization to pay one half the tuition fees of employees who wish to further their education."

Some policies concern operating procedures and amount to little more than work rules, as in the case of statements specifying the length of coffee breaks and the methods for obtaining reimbursement for travel

---

is advantageous since it permits a sharper conceptual distinction to be made between those actions and decisions relating primarily to strategy formulation and those relating to strategy implementation. In practice, as we shall later point out, strategy and policy decisions blur and shade into one another.

expenses. Yet, others may provide vital support to an organization's strategic plan. For example, General Motor's policy of trying to standardize as many parts as possible in producing its many different models of Chevrolets, Pontiacs, Buicks, Oldsmobiles and Cadillacs was aimed at achieving greater mass production economies and minimizing the working capital tied up in parts inventories.

Whatever the scope and form, the managerial thrust of policy is to set organizational mechanisms in place that will support strategic success.

THE INTERRELATIONSHIPS AMONG PURPOSE, OBJECTIVES, STRATEGY AND POLICY

Taken together, an organization's purpose and objectives set forth *exactly what the organization intends to do and to accomplish*—in both the short-run and long-run. Purpose delineates an organization's service mission to customers and to society; long- and short-run objectives serve to indicate the organization's priorities and commitments to specific results. Strategy, then, addresses the issue of precisely how the desired results are to be accomplished: it is the means to the end, the game plan, the outline of how things are to be done, the blueprint for getting the organization where it wants to go. Policy refers to strategy implementation —the organizational procedures, practices, and structure associated with administering and operating the organization on a day-to-day basis. In conjunction, organizational purpose, objectives, strategy, and policy define an overall grand design for the organization and indicate the guidelines and principles by which it is to be managed. Figure 1–1 depicts these relationships.

It should be emphasized at this point that in actual situations it is not always easy to distinguish sharply between purpose and objectives, objectives and strategy, and strategy and policy. We have tried to maintain a fairly clear-cut separation in our definitions and conceptual descriptions, so to better expose the elements inherent in charting and following an organization's course and path of development. But, unfortunately, definitions are not always well-settled nor are they strictly adhered to in practice. Words like purpose, objectives, strategy, and policy are "accordianlike" in the sense they include statements which can span the spectrum from broad to narrow, very important to comparatively unimportant, and general to specific. Moreover, statements of purpose and mission shade into objectives, objectives into strategies, and strategies into policies. An indication of the possibility for overlap and blurring is given by the statement "Our major objective is to be a diversified, growing, and profitable company with emphasis on manufacturing electronic products and components for worldwide use in industry, government, and the home." This statement, which is not unusual, contains an indication of what the com-

FIGURE 1-1

A Schematic of the Relationships among Purpose, Objectives, Strategy, and Policy

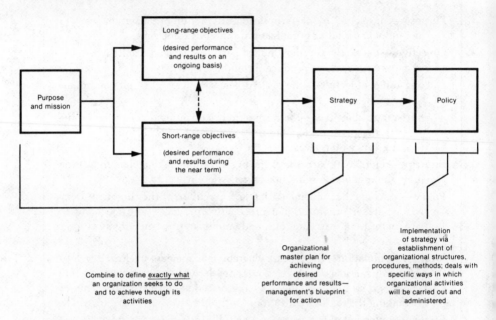

pany is trying to do (its purpose and mission); it suggests the existence of several objectives (diversification, growth, profitability); and it has hints of strategy (the emphasis on manufacturing electronic products and its identification of target markets).

The blurring and overlap among purpose, objectives, strategy, and policy suggest, however, an even more important point. The sequence of steps from purpose to objectives to strategy to policy implied in Figure 1–1 is not something that managers actually do sequentially. In practice, the steps are interrelated and can be undertaken more or less simultaneously. This is particularly true of the three direction-setting components: purpose, objectives, and strategy. Strategy is plainly predicated on and intertwined with an organization's purpose and objectives; at the same time, though, strategy (especially a highly successful one) bends back to influence objectives and purpose. There is two-way cause and effect. Thus, to consider purpose, objectives, and strategy as interconnected and integral parts of an overall strategic plan accurately lumps together the key direction-setting components of an organization's activities.

In ensuing discussions, therefore, we shall use the term strategy broadly to embrace and include the whole process whereby management (in no set order) interprets market needs, analyzes threats and opportunities, decides what the organization should and should not do, establishes specific objectives, develops strategy, and positions the firm in its environment. This

---

SUMMARY DEFINITIONS OF TERMS

Purpose—consists of a long-term vision of what an organization seeks to do and what kind of organization it intends to become.

Objectives—define the specific kinds of performance and results which the organization seeks to produce through its activities.

    Long-range objectives—the desired performance and results on an ongoing basis.

    Short-range objectives—the near-term organizational performance targets the organization desires to reach in progressing toward its long-range objectives.

Strategy—refers to a blueprint of the organizational game plan, indicating how the organization intends to get where it wants to go.

Policy—concerns the implementation and execution of the chosen strategy via whatever organizational procedures, practices, and mechanisms are helpful in carrying out and administering the organization's activities.

Strategy formulation—the process whereby management in effect develops an organization's purpose and mission, derives specific objectives, and chooses a strategy; includes all the direction-setting components of managing the *total* organization.

Strategy implementation—embraces the full range of managerial activities associated with putting the chosen strategy into motion and supervising its pursuit.

---

broad view of strategy as a process shall be referred to as *strategy formulation*. It is intended to include all of the direction-setting activities and decisions undertaken by management. Those remaining activities, which revolve around carrying out and monitoring the pursuit of the chosen strategy, we shall designate as *policy* and *strategy implementation*. The strategy-policy framework, or its counterpart of strategy formulation/ strategy implementation, offers a conceptual way of approaching the management of the total enterprise and of gaining a general management perspective. It is the approach we will take throughout this text.

Let us turn now and get a bird's eye view of the strategy-policy roles of the general manager. A more complete discussion of these will follow in succeeding chapters.

TASKS OF THE GENERAL MANAGER: STRATEGY FORMULATION AND STRATEGY IMPLEMENTATION

As the preceding discussion of terminology suggests, general management can be divided conceptually into two distinct, albeit closely related, tasks. One is the task of formulating a strategy for the organization; the other is implementing and managing pursuit of the strategic plan.

The managerial task of strategy formulation is primarily *entrepreneurial* in character and focus. The key activities are in such entrepreneurial areas as identifying opportunities to create and enter new markets, developing new and improved products and services, devising better ways to meet customer needs and wants, evaluating how to meet emerging environmental or competitive threats, deciding upon when and how to diversify, and, ultimately, choosing which businesses to get out of, which to continue with, and which new ones to enter. Of equal importance is an entrepreneurial alertness for opportunities to redirect resources away from areas of low or diminishing results toward areas of high or increasing results. The managerial posture in strategy formulation is not so much one of "how can we do better what we're already doing?" as one of "what sorts of *new* or *different* activities should we undertake?" The keynote is on insightful, timely, and creative opportunism.

In effect, then, the general management task of strategy formulation consists of an entrepreneurial size-up of whether the organization is *doing the right things* and how it can be *more effective* in what it does. It entails working at being shrewd and perceptive enough to establish the right directions and priorities and to fund their pursuit. The whole managerial thrust is (or should be) to devise a game plan for producing *extraordinary* results, generating *superior* organization performance, and keeping the organization responsive to change and capable of future success.

The second general management task—that of implementing and executing the strategic plan—is essentially *administrative* in charatcer. A manager always has to administer: to structure and organize the necessary daily activities, to set policy and monitor how well it functions, to deal with a wide assortment of "people problems," to make sure that schedules and timetables are met, to be clever at increasing the accomplishments from available funds and staff personnel, to try to do better what is already being done, to initiate corrective action when actual performance does not measure up to expectation. Administrative efforts typically aim at increased *efficiency* and at *doing things right*. Specifically, *administrative efficiency* is understood to mean getting more accomplished with the same budget allocation, being well organized and meeting deadlines, seeing that daily operations flow smoothly, being able to supervise people in a capable manner, and keeping overhead and operating costs to an efficient minimum. A good administrator is a person who is good at doing these kinds of things.

Of these two general management tasks—strategy formulation (entrepreneurship) and strategy implementation (administration)—strategy formulation ranks as the more important and more crucial determinant of organizational success.[13] Why? Because when it comes to a choice of being effective (doing the right things) or being efficient (doing things right), *the first requirement for organizational success is effectiveness.* An organization simply cannot be successful or outstanding or a winner if it is doing the wrong things—irrespective of how efficient and well-administered it may be. A simple example illustrates the point. An automobile manufacturer may be an extremely efficient producer of internal combustion engines; but if a growing scarcity of gasoline makes the widespread use of internal combustion-powered cars impractical, then the effectiveness and long-run success of the automobile manufacturer is rightfully suspect. It is fair to say that the most efficient organization cannot survive, much less succeed, if it is efficient doing the wrong things. Hence, while efficiency may keep an enterprise alive for a time, it takes *entrepreneurial effectiveness* and a strategy predicated on doing the right things at the right time to generate *superior* performance and results over the long-term. Or, to put it a bit differently, the foundations of organizational success rest *first* on an entrepreneurially astute strategy keyed to doing the right things. Administrative efficiency and doing things right are optimal conditions once effectiveness is demonstrated.

It follows that any manager of an organization (or major subunit) is well advised to take time for periodic strategy review and reappraisal. It is always appropriate to ask: Are we doing the right thing? Are we headed in the right direction? Are we in the right business (or mix of businesses)? How does our actual performance compare with what we might be doing in some other set of activities? When the answers to such questions come up short of satisfactory, it is time for management to evaluate whether the organization's strategy is entrepreneurially effective.

Let's look now at the job of the general manager in more depth.

The Job of the General Manager: Strategy Formulation and Entrepreneurship

In fulfilling their entrepreneurial responsibilities, general managers quickly confront the entire range of direction-setting components of management: defining organization purpose and mission, seeing that appropriate objectives are set, identifying and evaluating strategic alternatives, arriving at a strategic plan to achieve the desired objectives, clarifying and defending objectives and strategies against external attack or internal erosion, installing purposeful action in place of improvisation or expediency, and replacing organization drift with measurable performance targets.[14] Of these, perhaps the most crucial, insofar as long-term entre-

---

[13] Drucker, *Management*, pp. 45–48; Chester I. Barnard, *The Functions of the Executive* (Cambridge, Mass.: Harvard University Press, 1938), pp. 26–32, 55–61.

[14] Christensen, Andrews, and Bower, *Business Policy*, p. 20; Kenneth Andrews, *The Concept of Corporate Strategy* (Homewood, Ill.: Dow Jones-Irwin, 1971), chap. 1.

preneurial performance is concerned, is that of searching out new strategic opportunities made valid by changing market outlooks, emerging societal wants and needs, and organizational capabilities. A constant probing for fresh strategies nurtures an organization's entrepreneurial spirit and capacity for successful response to changing circumstances. By keeping the potential of product-market changes high on the organization agenda, a manager increases the likelihood that the organization will remain alert and well-positioned to capitalize upon new opportunities.

In close conjunction with the task of new strategy identification, however, a general manager has to undertake an insightful, unbiased assessment of the internal pros and cons of strategic options. A carefully reasoned analysis of organizational capabilities is essential to sensible strategy design for the simple reason that without the necessary skills and resources the most appealing strategy cannot be executed effectively.

One of the hardest-to-come-by skills useful to the managerial strategist is that of investing the organization's strategy with a magnetic and cohesive quality. The value of an inspiring strategy (and the unity and commitment which results) becomes clear when pressures and temptations to deviate from it set in, as surely they will. Internal conflicts over objectives, strategy, and values are certain to occur, and it falls to the general manager's responsibility to see that they are resolved or, at least, kept within bounds. Moreover, from time to time events and changes in the external environment will raise some questions as to the appropriateness of the prevailing strategy. It is no small job for the managerial strategist to know when to defend a successfully focused strategy against superficially attractive alternatives (faster growth, merger opportunities), and when emerging factors have rendered a once viable strategy obsolete, thereby making strategy reformulation propitious. This is why continuous monitoring of strategies and policies is the only prudent procedure for a general manager to follow. And it accounts for why the process of strategy formulation is never-ending. Change is certain and changing circumstances, in turn, will prompt the course of strategy to turn not only in new directions but also at new speeds.

The Job of the General Manager: Strategy Implementation and Administration

Once the creative and analytical aspects of strategy formulation have been settled for the time being, the managerial priority is one of converting the strategic plan into something operationally effective. Indeed, a strategy is never complete, even as a formulation, until it gains a commitment of the organization's resources and becomes embodied in organizational activities.[15] Putting the strategy into place and building an organization

---

[15] Christensen, Andrews, and Bower, *Business Policy*, p. 593.

which is capable of executing the chosen strategy—with acceptable results —entails a variety of functions and activities the most important of which can be summarized as follows:

1. Structuring and organizing the available resources in ways that are supportive of strategic accomplishment.
2. Attempting to develop internal proficiency and a distinctive competence in carrying out the organization's activities.
3. Focusing organizational resources and energies on achieving the desired objectives and overall organizational performance.
4. Developing measures of effective performance and using these measures to set up feedback and internal controls for monitoring progress toward organizational objectives.
5. Using the established performance measures as the basis for evaluating actual performance and taking corrective action.
6. Exercising whatever leadership posture and managerial style is appropriate for the situation at hand.
7. Setting policies and monitoring how well they function. Some brief comments on each of these is in order.

Structuring the Organization. A primary general management consideration in organizing and administering the technical tasks of research and development, production, finance, marketing, personnel, and so on, is to try to make the organization strategically successful. From a structural standpoint one way of doing this is to gear the whole organizational structure around those key activities upon which strategic success or failure depends. Clearly, successful execution of strategy is assisted when an organization's structure is *supportive* of strategy and serves its peculiar needs.[16] When a general manager fails to shape the formal organization scheme, its informal relationships, and the task-reward structure to the specific requirements of the organization's strategic plan, then the chances for internal wheel-spinning and erosion of purpose become

---

[16] The strength of the case for strategy being the controlling factor in designing organizational structure and administrative processes is partly indicated by examining some of the factors which in the past have shaped an organization's design. In some organizations the chief determinant of design appears to have been chance occurrences or historical accidents occasioned by the particular experiences and personalities of the organization's leaders, the position of a company in its industry, and the economic circumstances surrounding an organization's development (war, depression, sudden technological change). In other instances, organization design seems to have been influenced mainly by a conviction that one form of organization is intrinsically better than another, or by the recommendations of consultants, or by alleged principles of organization as depicted in textbooks on the subject. None of these, as a general rule, seem overly compelling as a guide to organization when compared to the needs of strategy. See Alfred D. Chandler, *Strategy and Structure* (Cambridge, Mass.: The M.I.T. Press, 1962); and Christensen, Andrews, and Bower, *Business Policy*, p. 595.

decidedly greater. And as soon as departmental and/or individual goals begin to usurp those of the total organization, then cohesion is jeopardized and the organization's ability to respond consistently as an entity is impaired.

At the same time, though, a manager is wise to be sensitive to the power structure existing in the organization and to relate strategic plans to the human side of organization. It does not take long to learn that the organization and the people who comprise it are, at once, the major constraint to strategy implementation and the vehicle through which the strategy must be made successful. Thus, a good general manager must be adept in figuring out how hard the organization can be pushed and just what it is capable of doing and not doing.

Developing a Distinctive Competence. In most high-performing organizations, management will be found to have worked hard at figuring out how the organization can be not only just good at what it does but also how it can be *better* than rival organizations. Management may accomplish this by hiring technical talent to give the organization technical superiority, striving to be more innovative, focusing energies on some neglected but important facet of furnishing a product/service and translating this into a competitive edge, figuring out ways to make good employees perform over their heads, or maybe even by out-managing other organizations. Whatever the approach, the importance of managers trying to build and develop a *distinctive competence* rests with the unique capability it gives the organization for being both effective and efficient in achieving the desired performance and results.

It is difficult to overstate the contribution which a well conceived distinctive competence can make to organization success. IBM's distinctive competences in computer software and service have given the company a major competitive edge over other computer manufacturers even though IBM computer hardware is not generally viewed as "superior." McDonald's distinctive competence in its system of controls and procedures for operating hamburger and french fry outlets produce profit margins which are the envy of the fast food industry. Thus, it is clear that an instinctive understanding of the role and importance of a distinctive competence is one of the traits of entrepreneurially effective management. To the extent that management can identify and develop a distinctive competence in the way the organization creates, produces, and delivers its products/services, then the task of strategy implementation and execution is made more certain of success.

Focusing Resources on Achieving Objectives. At this juncture, the value and usefulness of objectives comes to fore. If management is to keep the organization results-oriented and pointed in the direction of strategy accomplishment, then the organization's set of strategic objectives should become the basis for work and for assignments. In some fundamental sense, it is objectives which point to the key activities of the organization and, thus, to an allocation of people to specific assignments. Hence, from a general management perspective, objectives indicate directly where the resources and energies of the organization should be mobilized. This is why objectives should be formulated and stated in such a way that they degenerate into work, specific tasks, assignment of responsibility, and deadlines.

Such an approach suggests one of the guides a general manager can follow in figuring out who should do what: jobs and tasks should be defined in terms of the desired strategic results and performance, not just in terms of the functions to be performed. Why? Because it puts the emphasis on what is to be accomplished (the strategic plan), not on what activities are to be performed.

Managing by objectives (with the implied aim of implementing and executing the chosen strategy) starts with the questions, "What results do we want to produce?" and "What do we want to accomplish?" Next, it is asked, "What key activities, what organization units, what jobs need to be set up and organized to generate these results?" And then: "What skills, expertise, staffing, and funding are needed to allow the various organizational units to accomplish the agreed upon, assigned results?" This sort of managerial mindset helps to keep the focus of the general manager trained on implementing and executing strategy, rather than letting attention drift towards that of "caretaker and administrator of the status quo."

Developing Measures of Effective Performance. A basic element in the job of every general manager is measuring performance. Measurement and evaluation are essential to knowing where the organization is in terms of its strategic plan. The starting point is to define what sorts of results constitute effective strategy execution. From these, specific performance measures can be developed for the organization as a whole, for each major subunit, and, ultimately, through the efforts of lower-level managers, for each job. The job of each manager in the organization, from the "big boss" on down to the first-level supervisor needs to be spelled out in terms of expected results and the objectives to be achieved. Usually, a number of performance criteria will be used, most of which typically are quantifiable but some of which may be subjective; rarely will a single standard suffice. For obvious reasons, the objectives and performance standards attached to each job and each organizational unit should always derive from those objectives stressed and implied in the strategic plan.

To the extent that management properly defines the performance expected at each organizational level, the entire organization will tend to be performance and results oriented. Otherwise some degree of confusion and misdirection is guaranteed. Indeed, when managers *fail* to (1) devise ways to measure performance, (2) set standards of accomplishment, (3) indicate minimum acceptable results, (4) assign responsibility for results, and (5) fix deadlines, the stage is set for a shortfall in strategy execution and strategic accomplishment.

Evaluating Actual Performance. The performance standards, once established, must become the *real* basis for evaluating individual efforts and the performance of organizational units. Managers must insist that contributions and results be documented and rigorously compared against standards and objectives. They must be informed and ready to intervene when actual performance falls short of the performance targets specified in the overall strategic plan. Appropriate corrective actions are an obvious general management responsibility whenever negative deviations from plan are encountered. It is not, however, possible to generalize about the form these actions should take, since they ought to be tailored to fit the specifics of the situation. But one precaution can be urged. General managers need to guard against a tendency to acknowledge all activities/products/services as virtuous, worthy of more funding, and essential to continue. When the results and performance of a product/division/activity are unsatisfactory (because it is out-of-date, poorly conceived, or ineffective), it should be scrutinized for ways to overhaul it; or if circumstances demand, to phase it out or abandon it at once. It is in such instances that timely opportunity may exist to shift resources and energies into more productive endeavors. In addition, general managers should use the time for evaluating actual performance also as a time for regularly reviewing and appraising whether the organization is doing the right things.

Leadership Role and Management Style. As head of an organization or organization subunit, the general manager is called upon to play numerous leadership roles: taskmaster, crisis-solver, policymaker, decision maker, motivator, inspirationist, and so on. No one leadership style or managerial approach stands out as uniquely correct. For example, sometimes it is useful to be authoritarian and hardnosed; at other times a participative, collegial approach may work best. There is good reason to believe that different leadership approaches are needed to cope with different situations and that it is the manager's job to be prepared to gear his style to fit the circumstances. Yet, there are two personal traits which should always be in evidence: honesty and integrity. Without these, a manager is not destined to enjoy the respect of subordinates, an outcome which can be personally and organizationally debilitating.

It goes almost without saying that one of the chief leadership responsibilities of the general manager is securing ample commitment of subordinates and members of organizational subunits to established objectives. In getting organizational members to accept the priorities of strategy, a general manager will find it useful to be a visible and effective communicator. Besides being familiar with varied viewpoints and having a good sense of timing, this includes the skills to persuade, to inspire confidence, to propose, to explain, to project empathy, to remain poised under fire, and to stay in command of difficult situations. On occasions, a general manager will have to be tough in a showdown and an astute practitioner of organizational politics.

The functions that attach to the communication of strategy and policy give the general manager an opportunity to infuse flair and distinction into the organization and its activities.[17] It also provides a chance to influence the organization with one's own ideas. But there will only be a limited number of personal ideas that a manager can get adopted. So one useful managerial trait is that of knowing how to stimulate the organization through the ideas of subordinates and how to encourage a flow of good proposals. Then the trick is to become skillful in arousing enough support for those ideas and proposals that are deemed worthy.

Finally, it should be emphasized that whether the general manager's leadership style is visionary, charismatic, or lackluster, his or her energy, personality, and integrity will rub off on the organization and help set the tone of enthusiasm and motivation that go into making up an organization's personality. Thus, by personal character and example, the general manager keynotes the moral, ethical, and personal behavior that is expected of others.

Setting and Monitoring Policy. Policies are not only necessary for efficiently managing an organization, they also make the job easier. Day-to-day operations can be managed largely by policy and most routine problems solved by reference to "standard operating procedures." Such an outcome is the cardinal intent of policy. The managerial functions of policy are noteworthy:

1. Policy promotes *uniform handling of similar activities*—a uniformity which facilitates better coordination of work tasks and helps reduce friction arising from favoritism, discrimination, and disparate handling of common functions.

---

[17] Machiavelli in his famous classic *The Prince* offers a number of guidelines as to how a manager should conduct himself to acquire a reputation and become a distinctive leader. Although Machiavelli's advice was to heads of state (or princes as he referred to them), it is readily evident that his suggestions apply to managers of any kind of organization:

... a wise man should ever follow the ways of great men and endeavor to imitate only such as have been most eminent; so that even if his merits do not quite equal theirs, yet that they may in some measure reflect greatness. ... Nothing makes a prince so much esteemed as the undertaking of great enterprises and the setting a noble example in his own person. ... It is also important for a prince to give striking examples of his interior administration ... when an occasion presents itself to reward or punish any one ... so that it may be much talked about. But, above all, a prince should endeavor to invest all his action with a character of grandeur and excellence.

See N. Machiavelli, *The Prince* (New York: Washington Square Press, 1963), pp. 20, 98–99.

2. Policy introduces *continuity of action and decisions* throughout an organization, thereby minimizing zigzag behavior and conflicting actions and establishing some degree of order, regularity, stability, and dependability in both the organization's internal and external dealings.

3. Policy acts as an *automatic decision maker* by formalizing organization-wide answers to previously made management decisions about how particular questions and problems should be resolved; policy thus becomes a guide for handling future such problems or issues as they recur without them being passed up repeatedly through higher management echelons again and again.[18]

4. Policy offers a *predetermined answer to routine problems* and gives managers more time to cope with nonroutine matters; in this way decisions pertaining to both ordinary and extraordinary problems are greatly expedited—the former by referring to established policy and the latter by drawing upon a portion of the manager's time.

5. Existing policies afford managers a mechanism for insulating themselves from hasty and ill-considered requests for a policy change. The prevailing policy can always be used as a reason (or excuse) for not yielding to emotion-based, expedient, or temporarily valid arguments for policy revision.[19]

6. Policy serves as *a major communication link* to an organization's several constituents. External policy statements aid outsiders in appraising organization behavior and performance; internal policy pronouncements not only illustrate to employees what sort of actions and decisions are appropriate but also assist in casting the organization's character and personality.[20]

---

[18] The automatic decision-making function of policy should not be interpreted as advocating all matters be settled by searching through an omnibus policy manual for the proper policy to apply to a situation, and if a suitable one is not found, forcing the application of something close. Policies are not designed to be rigidly applied without the exercise of judgment. Exceptions and situations with unique twists always arise, and all who apply policies are expected to recognize when a policy should be bent to fit the circumstances.

See also the views of H. Edward Wrapp, "Good Managers Don't Make Policy Decisions," *Harvard Business Review*, vol. 45, no. 5 (September-October 1967), p. 95.

[19] The value of a healthy skepticism of policy change unless and until sufficient evidence in support of revision has been accumulated is illustrated by the experience of the manufacturers of Florsheim shoes. According to a top executive for Florsheim:

When DuPont was introducing Corfam, its marketing organization placed extreme pressure on quality shoe manufacturers, such as us, to incorporate the plastic material into our lines. This was a key factor in marketing strategy for Corfam: get the material associated with quality before trading down to popular priced lines. All types of pressure and persuasion were employed to try to get us (Florsheim) to make some Corfam shoes. But our policy to make only quality leather shoes automatically made our decision for us in spite of the heavy pressure on us to change it. In this case we are quite glad to note that we escaped the problems that our competitors encountered with the material.

This quotation is reported in Richard H. Buskirk, *Business and Administrative Policy* (New York: John Wiley & Sons, 1971), pp. 147–48.

[20] The above listing was developed and adopted by the authors from Ibid., pp. 145–50.

Ideally, policies flow from an organization's strategy; they can relate either to administrative matters or to operating procedures. Policies can be written or oral, stated or unstated, implicit or explicit, open or covert, firm or flexible, well-defined or deliberately vague.

Whatever the specifics, the strategy-implementing features of policy relate primarily to developing methods and procedures conducive to internal efficiency and to an operating mode supportive of the desired organizational performance. They include counteracting any tendency for parts of the organization to resist or reject strategy and objectives by instituting an effective system of rewards and incentives. A network of management controls with clear reporting channels and ample information feedback will almost certainly have to be designed and installed so that strategic progress can be monitored. Reviewing current performance and reassessing specific aspects of strategy require a flow of timely, reliable information. It is the general manager's responsibility to see that such information exists and to keep in touch with what is happening.

Is the General Manager's Job Too Demanding?

Our sketch of the general manager as entrepreneur and administrator may seem to require more of a person than is humanly possible. Admittedly, the job of a general manager is complex, but it is not an impossible job, nor does it require Herculean qualities. One reason is that the general manager is not forced to perform each of the roles and functions outlined above on a daily basis. A good manager knows how to conserve time and energy for those few particular issues, decisions, and problems where personal attention is absolutely required. He knows the distinction between staying fully informed and being drawn into participating in lower-level decisions or, even worse, making them. Hence, he is by no means put in the position of constantly having to be all things to all people on all issues. Second, many managerial matters can be effectively handled by policy, thereby freeing the manager to deal personally only with the exceptions rather than the rule and to devote adequate time to those areas having the greatest long-term strategic impact on the organization.

A Capsule Summary of the General Management Process

Our introductory survey of general management has stressed the basic elements involved in managing the total enterprises and, in particular, what it takes to make an organization successful and effective in what it does. The job of the general manager as portrayed is comprised of two related tasks. The first is giving direction to the organization, the outcome of which is a comprehensive, detailed strategic plan. The second task is implementing and executing the strategic plan, along with monitoring how well the chosen strategy is working.

In more specific terms, the job of the general manager in trying to make an organization entrepreneurially effective and results-focused embraces the following functions and tasks:

1. Start with developing a clear, carefully thought out concept of exactly what the organization seeks to do—its purpose and mission.
2. Derive specific, measurable objectives from the definition of purpose. (In the case of multiproduct, multimarket, multinational enterprises, objectives will be needed for each product, market, and line of business, as well as for the whole organization.)
3. Develop a detailed strategy for achieving organizational objectives and purpose and set priorities for concentrated effort.
4. Assign responsibility and accountability for all of the organization's activities, and most especially for those activities crucial to strategic success.
5. Set policies and administer the organization on a day-to-day basis.
6. Devise measures of performance; set standards of accomplishment; indicate minimum acceptable results; fix deadlines.
7. Use the performance measures to set up an information system for monitoring strategy implementation and organization activities.
8. Undertake periodic comparisons of strategy and actual performance so to

    a. Identify any need for strategy change.
    b. Pinpoint areas of unsatisfactory results and their causes.
    c. Zero in on inefficient activities and areas of low performance.
9. Demand that contributions be spelled out and documented and that results be rigorously appraised against established objectives.

Items 1, 2, and 3 constitute the organization's direction-setting components and, taken together, make up what we call the *process of strategy formulation*. The remaining six items are the essential ingredients of the *process of strategy implementation*. If the two processes are done properly, then chances are good the organization will be one which is effective, which performs, which is engaged in doing the right things, and which is successful. This is what management of the *total* enterprise is all about. In the succeeding chapters and readings, we shall add flesh to this skeletal outline of general management and the strategy-policy discipline.

SUGGESTED READINGS

Andrews, Kenneth R. *The Concept of Corporate Strategy.* Homewood, Ill.: Dow Jones-Irwin, Inc., 1971, chap. 1.

Barnard, Chester I. *The Functions of the Executive.* Cambridge, Mass.: Harvard University Press, 1938, chap. 15, 16, and 17.

Boettinger, Henry M. "Is Management Really an Art?" *Harvard Business Review,* vol. 53, no. 1, January-February 1975, pp. 54–64.

Drucker, Peter F. *Management: Tasks, Responsibilities, Practices.* New York: Harper and Row, Publishers, Inc., 1974, chaps. 2, 4, 30, 31, and 50.

Granger, Charles H. "The Hierarchy of Objectives." *Harvard Business Review,* vol. 42, no. 3, May-June 1964, pp. 63–74.

Katz, Robert L. "Skills of an Effective Administrator." *Harvard Business Review,* vol. 33, no. 1, January-February 1955, pp. 33–42.

Koontz, Harold "Making Strategic Planning Work." *Business Horizons,* vol. 19, no. 2, April 1976, pp. 37–47.

Livingston, J. Sterling "Myth of the Well-Educated Manager." *Harvard Business Review,* vol. 49, no. 1, January-February 1971, pp. 79–87.

Machiavelli, N. *The Prince.* New York: Washington Square Press, Inc. 1963.

Mintzberg, Henry "The Manager's Job: Folklore and Fact." *Harvard Business Review,* vol. 53, no. 4, July-August 1975, pp. 49–61.

Ross, Joel, and Kami, Michael *Corporate Management in Crisis: Why the Mighty Fall.* Englewood Cliffs, N.J.: Prentice-Hall, Inc., 1973.

Tilles, Seymour "The Manager's Job: A Systems Approach." *Harvard Business Review,* vol. 41, no. 1, January-February 1963, pp. 73–81.

Wrapp, H. Edward "Good Managers Don't Make Policy Decisions." *Harvard Business Review,* vol. 45, no. 5, September-October 1967, pp. 91–99.

READING

The Manager's Job: Folklore and Fact*

HENRY MINTZBERG
McGill University, Montreal, Canada.

If you ask a manager what he does, he will most likely tell you that he plans, organizes, coordinates, and controls. Then watch what he does. Don't be surprised if you can't relate what you see to these four words.

When he is called and told that one of his factories has just burned down, and he advises the caller to see whether temporary arrangements can be made to supply customers through a foreign subsidiary, is he planning, organizing, coordinating, or controlling? How about when he presents a gold watch to a retiring employee? Or when he attends a conference to meet people in the trade? Or on returning from that conference, when he tells one of his employees about an interesting product idea he picked up there?

The fact is that these four words, which have dominated management vocabulary since the French industrialist Henri Fayol first introduced them in 1916, tell us little about what managers actually do. At best, they indicate some vague objectives managers have when they work.

The field of management, so devoted to progress and change, has for more than half a century not seriously addressed *the* basic question: What do managers do? Without a proper answer, how can we teach management? How can we design planning or information systems for managers? How can we improve the practice of management at all?

Our ignorance of the nature of managerial work shows up in various ways in the modern organization—in the boast by the successful manager that he never spent a single day in a management training program; in the turnover of corporate planners who never quite understood what it was the manager wanted; in the computer consoles gathering dust in the back room because the managers never used the fancy on-line MIS some analyst thought they needed. Perhaps most important, our ignorance shows up in the inability of our large public organizations to come to grips with some of their most serious policy problems.

Somehow, in the rush to automate production, to use management science in the functional areas of marketing and finance, and to apply the skills of the behavioral scientist to the problem of worker motivation, the manager—that person in charge of the organization or one of its subunits —has been forgotten.

My intention in this article is simple: to break the reader away from Fayol's words and introduce him to a more supportable, and what I believe to be a more useful, description of managerial work. This description derives from my review and synthesis of the available research on how various managers have spent their time.

In some studies, managers were observed intensively ("shadowed" is the term some of them used); in a number of others, they kept detailed diaries of their activities; in a few studies, their records were analyzed. All kinds of managers were studied—foremen, factory supervisors, staff managers, field sales managers, hospital administrators, presidents of companies and nations, and even street gang leaders. These "managers" worked in the United States, Canada, Sweden, and Great Britain.

A synthesis of these findings paints an interesting picture, one as different from Fayol's classical view as a cubist abstract is from a Renaissance painting. In a sense, this picture will be obvious to anyone who has ever spent a day in a manager's office, either in front of the desk or behind it. Yet, at the same time, this picture may turn out to be revolutionary, in that it throws into doubt so much of the folklore that we have accepted about the manager's work.

I first discuss some of this folklore and contrast it with some of the discoveries of systematic research—the hard facts about how managers spend their time. Then I synthesize these research findings in a description of ten roles that seem to describe the essential content of all managers' jobs. In a concluding section, I discuss a number of implications of this synthesis for those trying to achieve more effective management, both in classrooms and in the business world.

Some Folklore and Facts about Managerial Work

There are four myths about the manager's job that do not bear up under careful scrutiny of the facts.

1. *Folklore: The manager is a reflective, systematic planner.* The evidence on this issue is overwhelming, but not a shred of it supports this statement.

Fact: Study after study has shown that managers work at an unrelenting pace, that their activities are characterized by brevity, variety, and discontinuity and that they are strongly oriented to action and dislike reflective activities. Consider this evidence:

□ Half the activities engaged in by the five chief executives of my study lasted less than nine minutes and only 10 percent exceeded one hour.[1] A study of 56 U.S. foremen found that they averaged

---

[1] All the data from my study can be found in Henry Mintzberg, *The Nature of Managerial Work* (New York: Harper & Row, 1973).

583 activities per eight-hour shift, an average of 1 every 48 seconds.[2] The work pace for both chief executives and foremen was unrelenting. The chief executives met a steady stream of callers and mail from the moment they arrived in the morning until they left in the evening. Coffee breaks and lunches were inevitably work related, and ever-present subordinates seemed to usurp any free moment.

◻ A diary study of 160 British middle and top managers found that they worked for a half hour or more without interruption only about once every two days.[3]

◻ Of the verbal contacts of the chief executives in my study, 93 percent were arranged on an ad hoc basis. Only 1 percent of the executives' time was spent in open-ended observational tours. Only 1 out of 368 verbal contacts was unrelated to a specific issue and could be called general planning. Another researcher finds that "in *not one single case* did a manager report the obtaining of important external information from a general conversation or other undirected personal communication."[4]

◻ No study has found important patterns in the way managers schedule their time. They seem to jump from issue to issue, continually responding to the needs of the moment.

Is this the planner that the classical view describes? Hardly. How, then, can we explain this behavior? The manager is simply responding to the pressures of his job. I found that my chief executives terminated many of their own activities, often leaving meetings before the end, and interrupted their desk work to call in subordinates. One president not only placed his desk so that he could look down a long hallway but also left his door open when he was alone—an invitation for subordinates to come in and interrupt him.

Clearly, these managers wanted to encourage the flow of current information. But more significantly, they seemed to be conditioned by their own work loads. They appreciated the opportunity cost of their own time, and they were continually aware of their ever-present obligations—mail to be answered, callers to attend to, and so on. It seems that no matter what he is doing, the manager is plagued by the possibilities of what he might do and what he must do.

When the manager must plan, he seems to do so implicitly in the context

2 Robert H. Guest, "Of Time and the Foreman," *Personnel*, May 1956, p. 478.

3 Rosemary Stewart, *Managers and Their Jobs* (London: Macmillan, 1967); see also Sune Carlson, *Executive Behaviour* (Stockholm: Strombergs, 1951), the first of the diary studies.

4 Francis J. Aguilar, *Scanning the Business Environment* (New York: Macmillan, 1967), p. 102.

of daily actions, not in some abstract process reserved for two weeks in the organization's mountain retreat. The plans of the chief executives I studied seemed to exist only in their heads—as flexible, but often specific, intentions. The traditional literature notwithstanding, the job of managing does not breed reflective planners; the manager is a real-time responder to stimuli, an individual who is conditioned by his job to prefer live to delayed action.

2. *Folklore: The effective manager has no regular duties to perform.* Managers are constantly being told to spend more time planning and delegating, and less time seeing customers and engaging in negotiations. These are not, after all, the true tasks of the manager. To use the popular analogy, the good manager, like the good conductor, carefully orchestrates everything in advance, then sits back to enjoy the fruits of his labor, responding occasionally to an unforeseeable exception.

But here again the pleasant abstraction just does not seem to hold up. We had better take a closer look at those activities managers feel compelled to engage in before we arbitrarily define them away.

Fact: In addition to handling exceptions, managerial work involves performing a number of regular duties, including ritual and ceremony, negotiations, and processing of soft information that links the organization with its environment. Consider some evidence from the research studies:

□ A study of the work of the presidents of small companies found that they engaged in routine activities because their companies could not afford staff specialists and were so thin on operating personnel that a single absence often required the president to substitute.[5]

□ One study of field sales managers and another of chief executives suggest that it is a natural part of both jobs to see important customers, assuming the managers wish to keep those customers.[6]

□ Someone, only half in jest, once described the manager as that person who sees visitors so that everyone else can get his work done. In my study, I found that certain ceremonial duties—meeting visiting dignitaries, giving out gold watches, presiding at Christmas dinners—were an intrinsic part of the chief executive's job.

□ Studies of managers' information flow suggest that managers play

[5] Unpublished study by Irving Choian, reported in Mintzberg, *The Nature of Managerial Work.*

[6] Robert T. Davis, *Performance and Development of Field Sales Managers* (Boston: Division of Research, Harvard Business School, 1957); George H. Copeman, *The Role of the Managing Director* (London: Business Publications, 1963).

a key role in securing "soft" external information (much of it available only to them because of their status) and in passing it along to their subordinates.

3. *Folklore: The senior manager needs aggregated information, which a formal management information system best provides.* Not too long ago, the words *total information system* were everywhere in the management literature. In keeping with the classical view of the manager as that individual perched on the apex of a regulated, hierarchical system, the literature's manager was to receive all his important information from a giant, comprehensive MIS.

But lately, as it has become increasingly evident that these giant MIS systems are not working—that managers are simply not using them—the enthusiasm has waned. A look at how managers actually process information makes the reason quite clear. Managers have five media at their command—documents, telephone calls, scheduled and unscheduled meetings, and observational tours.

Fact: Managers strongly favor the verbal media—namely, telephone calls and meetings. The evidence comes from every single study of managerial work. Consider the following:

□ In two British studies, managers spent an average of 66 percent and 80 percent of their time in verbal (oral) communication.[7] In my study of five American chief executives, the figure was 78 percent.

□ These five chief executives treated mail processing as a burden to be dispensed with. One came in Saturday morning to process 142 pieces of mail in just over three hours, to "get rid of all the stuff." This same manager looked at the first piece of "hard" mail he had received all week, a standard cost report, and put it aside with the comment, "I never look at this."

□ These same five chief executives responded immediately to 2 of the 40 routine reports they received during the five weeks of my study and to four items in the 104 periodicals. They skimmed most of these periodicals in seconds, almost ritualistically. In all, these chief executives of good-sized organizations initiated on their own —that is, not in response to something else—a grand total of 25 pieces of mail during the 25 days I observed them.

An analysis of the mail the executives received reveals an interesting picture—only 13 percent was of specific and immediate use. So now we have another piece in the puzzle: not much of the mail provides live, current information—the action of a competitor, the mood of a government

---

[7] Stewart, *Managers and Their Jobs;* Tom Burns, "The Directions of Activity and Communication in a Departmental Executive Group," *Human Relations* 7, no. 1 (1954): 73.

legislator, or the rating of last night's television show. Yet this is the information that drove the managers, interrupting their meetings and rescheduling their workdays.

Consider another interesting finding. Managers seem to cherish "soft" information, especially gossip, hearsay, and speculation. Why? The reason is its timeliness; today's gossip may be tomorrow's fact. The manager who is not accessible for the telephone call informing him that his biggest customer was seen golfing with his main competitor may read about a dramatic drop in sales in the next quarterly report. But then it's too late.

To assess the value of historical, aggregated, "hard" MIS information, consider two of the manager's prime uses for his information—to identify problems and opportunities,[8] and to build his own mental models of the things around him (e.g., how his organization's budget system works, how his customers buy his product, how changes in the economy affect his organization, and so on). Every bit of evidence suggests that the manager identifies decision situations and builds models not with the aggregated abstractions an MIS provides, but with specific tidbits of data.

Consider the words of Richard Neustadt, who studied the information-collecting habits of Presidents Roosevelt, Truman, and Eisenhower:

> It is not information of a general sort that helps a President see personal stakes; not summaries, not surveys, not the *bland amalgams*. Rather . . . it is the odds and ends of *tangible detail* that pieced together in his mind illuminate the underside of issues put before him. To help himself he must reach out as widely as he can for every scrap of fact, opinion, gossip, bearing on his interests and relationships as President. He must become his own director of his own central intelligence.[9]

The manager's emphasis on the verbal media raises two important points:

First, verbal information is stored in the brains of people. Only when people write this information down can it be stored in the files of the organization—whether in metal cabinets or on magnetic tape—and managers apparently do not write down much of what they hear. Thus the strategic data bank of the organization is not in the memos of its computers but in the minds of its managers.

Second, the manager's extensive use of verbal media helps to explain why he is reluctant to delegate tasks. When we note that most of the manager's important information comes in verbal form and is stored in his head, we can well appreciate his reluctance. It is not as if he can hand a

---

[8] H. Edward Wrapp, "Good Managers Don't Make Policy Decisions," HBR September-October 1967, p. 91. Wrapp refers to this as spotting opportunities and relationships in the stream of operating problems and decisions; in his article Wrapp raises a number of excellent points related to this analysis.

[9] Richard E. Neustadt, *Presidential Power* (New York: John Wiley, 1960), pp. 153–54; italics added.

dossier over to someone; he must take the time to "dump memory"—to tell that someone all he knows about the subject. But this could take so long that the manager may find it easier to do the task himself. Thus the manager is damned by his own information system to a "dilemma of delegation"—to do too much himself or to delegate to his subordinates with inadequate briefing.

4. *Folklore: Management is, or at least is quickly becoming, a science and profession.* By almost any definitions of *science* and *profession*, this statement is false. Brief observation of any manager will quickly lay to rest the notion that managers practice a science. A science involves the enaction of systematic, analytically determined procedures or programs. If we do not even know what procedures managers use, how can we prescribe them by scientific analysis? And how can we call management a profession if we cannot specify what managers are to learn? For after all, a profession involves "knowledge of some department of learning or science" (*Random House Dictionary*).[10]

Fact: The managers' programs—to schedule time, process information, make decisions, and so on—remain locked deep inside their brains. Thus, to describe these programs, we rely on words like *judgment* and *intuition*, seldom stopping to realize that they are merely labels for our ignorance.

I was struck during my study by the fact that the executives I was observing—all very competent by any standard—are fundamentally indistinguishable from their counterparts of a hundred years ago (or a thousand years ago, for that matter). The information they need differs, but they seek it in the same way—by word of mouth. Their decisions concern modern technology, but the procedures they use to make them are the same as the procedures of the nineteenth-century manager. Even the computer, so important for the specialized work of the organization, has apparently had no influence on the work procedures of general managers. In fact, the manager is in a kind of loop, with increasingly heavy work pressures but no aid forthcoming from management science.

Considering the facts about managerial work, we can see that the manager's job is enormously complicated and difficult. The manager is overburdened with obligations; yet he cannot easily delegate his tasks. As a result, he is driven to overwork and is forced to do many tasks superficially. Brevity, fragmentation, and verbal communication characterize his work. Yet these are the very characteristics of managerial work that have impeded scientific attempts to improve it. As a result, the management scientist has concentrated his efforts on the specialized functions of

---

10 For a more thorough, though rather different, discussion of this issue, see Kenneth R. Andrews, "Toward Professionalism in Business Management," *HBR* (March-April 1969), p. 49.

the organization, where he could more easily analyze the procedures and quantify the relevant information.[11]

But the pressures of the manager's job are becoming worse. Where before he needed only to respond to owners and directors, now he finds that subordinates with democratic norms continually reduce his freedom to issue unexplained orders, and a growing number of outside influences (consumer groups, government agencies, and so on) expect his attention. And the manager has had nowhere to turn for help. The first step in providing the manager with some help is to find out what his job really is.

Back to a Basic Description of Managerial Work

Now let us try to put some of the pieces of this puzzle together. Earlier, I defined the manager as that person in charge of an organization or one of its subunits. Besides chief executive officers, this definition would include vice presidents, bishops, foremen, hockey coaches, and prime ministers. Can all of these people have anything in common? Indeed they can. For an important starting point, all are vested with formal authority over an organizational unit. From formal authority comes status, which leads to various interpersonal relations, and from these comes access to information. Information, in turn, enables the manager to make decisions and strategies for his unit.

The manager's job can be described in terms of various "roles," or organized sets of behaviors identified with a position. My description, shown in *Exhibit* 1, comprises ten roles. As we shall see, formal authority gives rise to the three interpersonal roles, which in turn give rise to the three informational roles; these two sets of roles enable the manager to play the four decisional roles.

Interpersonal Roles. Three of the manager's roles arise directly from his formal authority and involve basic interpersonal relationships.

1. First is the *figurehead* role. By virtue of his position as head of an organizational unit, every manager must perform some duties of a ceremonial nature. The president greets the touring dignitaries, the foreman attends the wedding of a lathe operator, and the sales manager takes an important customer to lunch.

The chief executives of my study spent 12 percent of their contact time on ceremonial duties; 17 percent of their incoming mail dealt with acknowledgments and requests related to their status. For example, a letter to a company president requested free merchandise for a crippled school-

---

[11] C. Jackson Grayson, Jr., in "Management Science and Business Practice," *HBR* (July-August 1973), p. 41, explains in similar terms, why, as chairman of the Price Commission, he did not use those very techniques that he himself promoted in his earlier career as a management scientist.

EXHIBIT 1
The Manager's Role

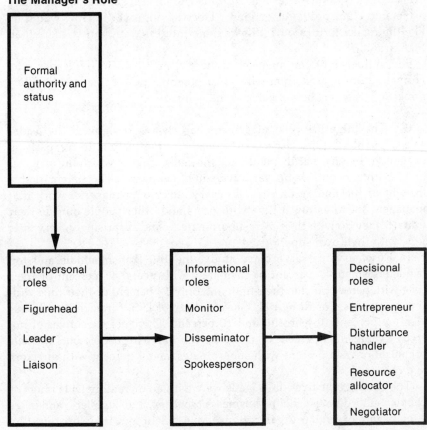

Formal
authority and
status

Interpersonal
roles

Figurehead

Leader

Liaison

Informational
roles

Monitor

Disseminator

Spokesperson

Decisional
roles

Entrepreneur

Disturbance
handler

Resource
allocator

Negotiator

child; diplomas were put on the desk of the school superintendent for his signature.

Duties that involve interpersonal roles may sometimes be routine, involving little serious communication and no important decision making. Nevertheless, they are important to the smooth functioning of an organization and cannot be ignored by the manager.

2. Because he is in charge of an organizational unit, the manager is responsible for the work of the people of that unit. His actions in this regard constitute the *leader* role. Some of these actions involve leadership directly—for example, in most organizations the manager is normally responsible for hiring and training his own staff.

In addition, there is the indirect exercise of the leader role. Every manager must motivate and encourage his employees, somehow reconciling their individual needs with the goals of the organization. In virtually every contact the manager has with his employees, subordinates seeking leadership clues probe his actions: "Does he approve?" "How would he like the report to turn out?" "Is he more interested in market share than high profits?"

The influence of the manager is most clearly seen in the leader role. Formal authority vests him with great potential power; leadership determines in large part how much of it he will realize.

3. The literature of management has always recognized the leader role, particularly those aspects of it related to motivation. In comparison, until recently it has hardly mentioned the *liaison* role, in which the manager makes contacts outside his vertical chain of command. This is remarkable in light of the finding of virtually every study of managerial work that managers spend as much time with peers and other people outside their units as they do with their own subordinates—and surprisingly, very little time with their own superiors.

In Rosemary Stewart's diary study, the 160 British middle and top managers spent 47 percent of their time with peers, 41 percent of their time with people outside their unit, and only 12 percent of their time with their superiors. For Robert H. Guest's study of U.S. foremen, the figures were 44 percent, 46 percent, and 10 percent. The chief executives of my study averaged 44 percent of their contact time with people outside their organizations, 48 percent with subordinates, and 7 percent with directors and trustees.

The contacts the five CEOs made were with an incredibly wide range of people: subordinates; clients, business associates, and suppliers; and peers —managers of similar organizations, government and trade organization officials, fellow directors on outside boards, and independents with no relevant organizational affiliations. The chief executives' time with and mail from these groups is shown in *Exhibit* 2. Guest's study of foremen shows, likewise, that their contacts were numerous and wide ranging, seldom involving fewer than 25 individuals, and often more than 50.

As we shall see shortly, the manager cultivates such contacts largely to find information. In effect, the liaison role is devoted to building up the manager's own external information system—informal, private, verbal, but, nevertheless, effective.

Informational Roles. By virtue of his interpersonal contacts, both with his subordinates and with his network of contacts, the manager emerges as the nerve center of his organizational unit. He may not know everything, but he typically knows more than any member of his staff.

Studies have shown this relationship to hold for all managers, from street gang leaders to U.S. presidents. In *The Human Group*, George C. Homans explains how, because they were at the center of the information

EXHIBIT 2
The Chief Executives' Contacts

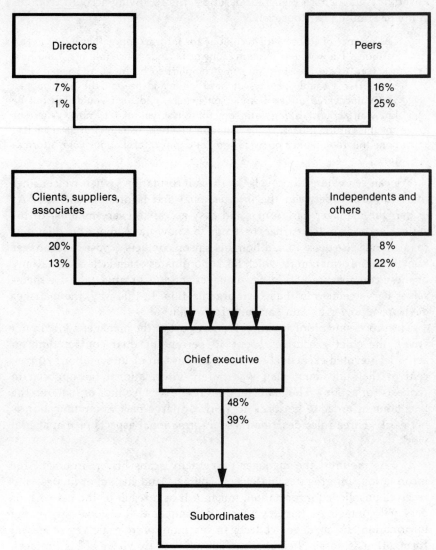

NOTE: The top figure indicates the proportion of total contact time spent with each group and the bottom figure, the proportion of mail from each group.

flow in their own gangs and were also in close touch with other gang leaders, street gang leaders were better informed than any of their followers.[12] And Richard Neustadt describes the following account from his study of Franklin D. Roosevelt:

> The essence of Roosevelt's technique for information-gathering was competition. "He would call you in," one of his aides once told me, "and he'd ask you to get the story on some complicated business, and you'd come back after a couple of days of hard labor and present the juicy morsel you'd uncovered under a stone somewhere, and *then* you'd find out he knew all about it, along with something else you *didn't* know. Where he got this information from he wouldn't mention, usually, but after he had done this to you once or twice you got damn careful about *your* information."[13]

We can see where Roosevelt "got this information" when we consider the relationship between the interpersonal and informational roles. As leader, the manager has formal and easy access to every member of his staff. Hence, as noted earlier, he tends to know more about his own unit than anyone else does. In addition, his liaison contacts expose the manager to external information to which his subordinates often lack access. Many of these contacts are with other managers of equal status, who are themselves nerve centers in their own organization. In this way, the manager develops a powerful data base of information.

The processing of information is a key part of the manager's job. In my study, the chief executives spent 40 percent of their contact time on activities devoted exclusively to the transmission of information; 70 percent of their incoming mail was purely informational (as opposed to requests for action). The manager does not leave meetings or hang up the telephone in order to get back to work. In large part, communication *is* his work. Three roles describe these informational aspects of managerial work.

1. As *monitor*, the manager perpetually scans his environment for information, interrogates his liaison contacts and his subordinates, and receives unsolicited information, much of it as a result of the network of personal contacts he has developed. Remember that a good part of the information the manager collects in his monitor role arrives in verbal form, often as gossip, hearsay, and speculation. By virtue of his contacts, the manager has a natural advantage in collecting this soft information for his organization.

2. He must share and distribute much of this information. Informa-

---

[12] George C. Homans, *The Human Group* (New York: Harcourt, Brace & World, 1950), based on the study by William F. Whyte entitled *Street Corner Society*, rev. ed. (Chicago: University of Chicago Press, 1955).

[13] Neustadt, *Presidential Power*, p. 157.

tion he gleans from outside personal contacts may be needed within his organization. In his *disseminator* role, the manager passes some of his privileged information directly to his subordinates, who would otherwise have no access to it. When his subordinates lack easy contact with one another, the manager will sometimes pass information from one to another.

3.   In his *spokesman* role, the manager sends some of his information to people outside his unit—a president makes a speech to lobby for an organization cause, or a foreman suggests a product modification to a supplier. In addition, as part of his role as spokesman, every manager must inform and satisfy the influential people who control his organizational unit. For the foreman, this may simply involve keeping the plant manager informed about the flow of work through the shop.

The president of a large corporation, however, may spend a great amount of his time dealing with a host of influences. Directors and shareholders must be advised about financial performance; consumer groups must be assured that the organization is fulfilling its social responsibilities; and government officials must be satisfied that the organization is abiding by the law.

Decisional roles.   Information is not, of course, an end in itself; it is the basic input to decision making. One thing is clear in the study of managerial work: the manager plays the major role in his unit's deicsion-making system. As its formal authority, only he can commit the unit to important new courses of action; and as its nerve center, only he has full and current information to make the set of decisions that determines the unit's strategy. Four roles describe the manager as decision maker.

1.   As *entrepreneur*, the manager seeks to improve his unit, to adapt it to changing conditions in the environment. In his monitor role, the president is constantly on the lookout for new ideas. When a good one appears, he initiates a development project that he may supervise himself or delegates to an employee (perhaps with the stipulation that he must approve the final proposal).

There are two interesting features about these development projects at the chief executive level.

First, these projects do not involve single decisions or even unified clusters of decisions. Rather, they emerge as a series of small decisions and actions sequenced over time. Apparently, the chief executive prolongs each project so that he can fit it bit by bit into his busy, disjointed schedule and so that he can gradually come to comprehend the issue, if it is a complex one.

Second, the chief executives I studied supervised as many as 50 of these projects at the same time. Some projects entailed new products or processes; others involved public relations campaigns, improvement of the cash position, reorganization of a weak department, resolution of a morale problem in a foreign division, integration of computer operations, various acquisitions at different stages of development, and so on.

The chief executive appears to maintain a kind of inventory of the development projects that he himself supervises—projects that are at various stages of development, some active and some in limbo. Like a juggler, he keeps a number of projects in the air; periodically, one comes down, is given a new burst of energy, and is sent back into orbit. At various intervals, he put new projects on-stream and discards old ones.

2.   While the entrepreneur role describes the manager as the voluntary initiator of change, the *disturbance handler* role depicts the manager involuntarily responding to pressures. Here change is beyond the manager's control. He must act because the pressures of the situation are too severe to be ignored: strike looms, a major customer has gone bankrupt, or a supplier reneges on his contract.

It has been fashionable, I noted earlier, to compare the manager to an orchestra conductor, just as Peter F. Drucker wrote in *The Practice of Management:*

> The manager has the task of creating a true whole that is larger than the sum of its parts, a productive entity that turns out more than the sum of the resources put into it. One analogy is the conductor of a symphony orchestra, through whose effort, vision and leadership individual instrumental parts that are so much noise by themselves become the living whole of music. But the conductor has the composer's score; he is only interpreter. The manager is both composer and conductor.[14]

Now consider the words of Leonard R. Sayles, who has carried out systematic research on the manager's job:

> [The manager] is like a symphony orchestra conductor, endeavouring to maintain a melodious performance in which the contributions of the various instruments are coordinated and sequenced, patterned and paced, while the orchestra members are having various personal difficulties, stage hands are moving music stands, alternating excessive heat and cold are creating audience and instrument problems, and the sponsor of the concert is insisting on irrational changes in the program.[15]

In effect, every manager must spend a good part of his time responding to high-pressure disturbances. No organization can be so well run, so standardized, that it has considered every contingency in the uncertain environment in advance. Disturbances arise not only because poor man-

---

[14] Peter F. Drucker, *The Practice of Management* (New York: Harper & Row, 1954), pp. 341–42.

[15] Leonard R. Sayles, *Managerial Behavior* (New York: McGraw-Hill, 1964), p. 162.

agers ignore situations until they reach crisis proportions, but also because good managers cannot possibly anticipate all the consequences of the actions they take.

3. The third decisional role is that of *resource allocator*. To the manager falls the responsibility of deciding who will get what in his organizational unit. Perhaps the most important resource the manager allocates is his own time. Access to the manager constitutes exposure to the unit's nerve center and decision maker. The manager is also charged with designing his unit's structure, the pattern of formal relationships that determines how work is to be divided and coordinated.

Also, in his role as resource allocator, the manager authorizes the important decisions of his unit before they are implemented. By retaining this power, the manager can ensure that decisions are interrelated: all must pass through a single brain. To fragment this power is to encourage discontinuous decision making and a disjointed strategy.

There are a number of interesting features about the manager's authorizing others' decisions. First, despite the widespread use of capital budgeting procedures—a means of authorizing various capital expenditures at one time—executives in my study made a great many authorization decisions on an ad hoc basis. Apparently, many projects cannot wait or simply do not have the quantifiable costs and benefits that capital budgeting requires.

Second, I found that the chief executives faced incredibly complex choices. They had to consider the impact of each decision on other decisions and on the organization's strategy. They had to ensure that the decision would be acceptable to those who influence the organization, as well as ensure that resources would not be overextended. They had to understand the various costs and benefits as well as the feasibility of the proposal. They also had to consider questions of timing. All this was necessary for the simple approval of someone else's proposal. At the same time, however, delay could lose time, while quick approval could be ill considered and quick rejection might discourage the subordinate who had spent months developing a pet project.

One common solution to approving projects is to pick the man instead of the proposal. That is, the manager authorizes those projects presented to him by people whose judgment he trusts. But he cannot always use this simple dodge.

4. The final decisional role is that of *negotiator*. Studies of managerial work at all levels indicate that managers spend considerable time in negotiations: the president of the football team is called in to work out a contract with the holdout superstar; the corporation president leads his company's contingent to negotiate a new strike issue; the foreman argues

a grievance problem to its conclusion with the shop steward. As Leonard Sayles puts it, negotiations are a "way of life" for the sophisticated manager.

These negotiations are duties of the manager's job; perhaps routine, they are not to be shirked. They are an integral part of his job, for only he has the authority to commit organizational resources in "real time," and only he has the nerve center information that important negotiations require.

The Integrated Job. It should be clear by now that the ten roles I have been describing are not easily separable. In the terminology of the psychologist, they form a gestalt, an integrated whole. No role can be pulled out of the framework and the job be left intact. For example, a manager without liaison contacts lacks external information. As a result, he can neither disseminate the information his employees need nor make decisions that adequately reflect external conditions. (In fact, this is a problem for the new person in a managerial position, since he cannot make effective decisions until he has built up his network of contacts.)

Here lies a clue to the problems of team management.[16] Two or three people cannot share a single managerial position unless they can act as one entity. This means that they cannot divide up the ten roles unless they can very carefully reintegrate them. The real difficulty lies with the informational roles. Unless there can be full sharing of managerial information— and, as I pointed out earlier, it is primarily verbal—team management breaks down. A single managerial job cannot be arbitrarily split, for example, into internal and external roles, for information from both sources must be brought to bear on the same decisions.

To say that the ten roles form a gestalt is not to say that all managers give equal attention to each role. In fact, I found in my review of the various research studies that

. . . sales managers seem to spend relatively more of their time in the interpersonal roles, presumably a reflection of the extrovert nature of the marketing activity;

. . . production managers give relatively more attention to the decisional roles, presumably a reflection of their concern with efficient work flow;

. . . staff managers spend the most time in the informational roles, since they are experts who manage departments that advise other parts of the organization.

Nevertheless, in all cases the interpersonal, informational, and decisional roles remain inseparable.

---

[16] See Richard C. Hodgson, Daniel J. Levinson, and Abraham Zaleznick, *The Executive Role Constellation* (Boston: Division of Research, Harvard Business School, 1965), for a discussion of the sharing of roles.

Toward More Effective Management

What are the messages for management in this description? I believe, first and foremost, that this description of managerial work should prove more important to managers than any prescription they might derive from it. That is to say, *the manager's effectiveness is significantly influenced by his insight into his own work.* His performance depends on how well he understands and responds to the pressures and dilemmas of the job. Thus managers who can be introspective about their work are likely to be effective at their jobs.

Let us take a look at three specific areas of concern. For the most part, the managerial logjams—the dilemma of delegation, the data base centralized in one brain, the problems of working with the management scientist—revolve around the verbal nature of the manager's information. There are great dangers in centralizing the organization's data bank in the minds of its managers. When they leave, they take their memory with them. And when subordinates are out of convenient verbal reach of the manager, they are at an informational disadvantage.

1. *The manager is challenged to find systematic ways to share his privileged information.* A regular debriefing session with key subordinates, a weekly memory dump on the dictating machine, the maintaining of a diary of important information for limited circulation, or other similar methods may ease the logjam of work considerably. Time spent disseminating this information will be more than regained when decisions must be made. Of course, some will raise the question of confidentiality. But managers would do well to weigh the risks of exposing privileged information against having subordinates who can make effective decisions.

If there is a single theme that runs through this article, it is that the pressures of his job drive the manager to be superficial in his actions—to overload himself with work, encourage interruption, respond quickly to every stimulus, seek the tangible and avoid the abstract, make decisions in small increments, and do everything abruptly.

2. *Here again, the manager is challenged to deal consciously with the pressures of superficiality by giving serious attention to the issues that require it, by stepping back from his tangible bits of information in order to see a broad picture, and by making use of analytical inputs.* Although effective managers have to be adept at responding quickly to numerous and varying problems, the danger in managerial work is that they will respond to every issue equally (and that means abruptly) and that they will never work the tangible bits and pieces of informational input into a comprehensive picture of their world.

As I noted earlier, the manager uses these bits of information to build models of his world. But the manager can also avail himself of the models of the specialists. Economists describe the functioning of markets, operations researchers simulate financial flow processes, and behavioral scientists explain the needs and goals of people. The best of these models can be searched out and learned.

In dealing with complex issues, the senior manager has much to gain from a close relationship with the management scientists of his own organization. They have something important that he lacks—time to probe complex issues. An effective working relationship hinges on the resolution of what a colleague and I have called "the planning dilemma."[17] Managers have the information and the authority, analysts have the time and the technology. A successful working relationship between the two will be effected when the manager learns to share his information and the analyst learns to adapt to the manager's needs. For the analyst, adaptation means worrying less about the elegance of the method and more about its speed and flexibility.

It seems to me that analysts can help the top manager especially to schedule his time, feed in analytical information, monitor projects under his supervision, develop models to aid in making choices, design contingency plans for disturbances that can be anticipated, and conduct "quick-and-dirty" analysis for those that cannot. But there can be no cooperation if the analysts are out of the mainstream of the manager's information flow.

3. *The manager is challenged to gain control of his own time by turning obligations to his advantage and by turning those things he wishes to do into obligations.* The chief executives of my study initiated only 32 percent of their own contacts (and another 5 percent by mutual agreement). And yet to a considerable extent they seemed to control their time. There were two key factors that enabled them to do so.

First, the managers has to spend so much time discharging obligations that if he were to view them as just that, he would leave no mark on his organization. The unsuccessful manager blames failure on the obligations; the effective manager turns his obligations to his own advantage. A speech is a chance to lobby for a cause; a meeting is a chance to reorganize a weak department; a visit to an important customer is a chance to extract trade information.

Second, the manager frees some of his time to do those things that he— perhaps no one else—thinks important by turning them into obligations. Free time is made, not found, in the manager's job; it is forced into the schedule. Hoping to leave some time open for contemplation or general

---

[17] James S. Hekimian and Henry Mintzberg, "The Planning Dilemma," *The Management Review*, May 1968, p. 4.

planning is tantamount to hoping that the pressures of the job will go away. The manager who wants to innovate initiates a project and obligates others to report back to him; the manager who needs certain environment information establishes channels that will automatically keep him informed; the manager who has to tour facilities commits himself publicly.

CONCEPTS OF ORGANIZATION STRATEGY

. . . a business enterprise guided by a clear sense of purpose rationally arrived at and emotionally ratified by commitment is more likely to have a successful outcome, in terms of profit and social good, than a company whose future is left to guesswork and chance.

Kenneth R. Andrews

Without a strategy the organization is like a ship without a rudder, going around in circles. It's like a tramp; it has no place to go.

Joel Ross and Michael Kami

It matters little whether one prefers to view strategy as (1) the game plan for the organization, (2) a set of directional signals, (3) a blueprint for where an organization is trying to go and how it is going to get there, or (4) the composite of an organization's purpose, objectives, plans, and policies describing what businesses an organization is in or is to be in and the kind of organization it is or is to be. All these shorthand definitions convey compatible notions of strategy and do so in language which makes the basic meaning of strategy easy enough to grasp.

But it is one thing to understand the concept of strategy in its most elemental form and another thing to understand fully what is required to forge a full-blown strategic plan of action. This chapter explores the many facets of a comprehensive concept of strategy in an effort to make the substance and scope of strategy formulation operationally useful.

The Value of a Consciously Formulated Strategy

Every organization can be said to have a strategy, however imperfect or unconscious it may be. Its strategy may be explicit or it may have to be deduced from its actions and operating patterns. The strategy may have been carefully calculated and regularly assessed from every angle or it may have emerged haphazardly and be mainly a product of chance and circumstance. Or, most frequently, it may have evolved gradually over time, standing as a result of trial and error and market feedback regarding what worked and what didn't.

The key question, though, is whether a consciously formulated strategy is better than one which has been arrived at by "muddling through." Can better strategies and better performance result if management takes the time and trouble to do a thorough strategic review and analytically arrive at a carefully formulated strategy? After all, organizations have been known to succeed by relying mainly on ownership of key raw materials, superior finances and/or manpower skills, good products (or services), key patents and unique technical knowhow, outstanding location, clever ads, the luck and circumstance of having been in the right place at the right time, and so on. Based on current research evidence to date, the answer seems to be that strategic planning and formal strategy analysis do have a positive impact on performance.[1]

The advantages of an organization having a consciously formulated strategy, rather than one which just evolves from drift and circumstance, include: (1) the guidance it provides to lower-level general managers, (2) the contribution it makes to identifying strategic issues and to coordinating management's direction-setting decisions, (3) the rationale it provides top management in deploying organizational resources among various activities and in evaluating competing requests from business units for corporate funds; and (4) the desirability of trying to *influence* rather than merely *respond* to product-market-technological-environmental change.[2] The fourth advantage is of acute importance. A well-managed enterprise will always seek to *impact* the market with a timely, perceptive, and opportunistic strategy. Indeed, a major thrust of corporate strategy formulation revolves around how to *initiate* and *influence* rather than just *respond* and *react;* although, obviously, it is sometimes useful to employ adaptive and defensive strategies as well as offensive strategies. But it

---

[1] For a representative sample of studies, see Stanley Thune and Robert House, "Where Long-Range Planning Pays Off," *Business Horizons,* vol. 13, no. 4 (August 1970), pp. 81–87; Joseph O. Eastlack and Philip R. McDonald, "CEO's Role in Corporate Growth," *Harvard Business Review,* vol. 48, no. 3 (May-June 1970), pp. 150–63; David M. Herold, "Long-Range Planning and Organizational Performance: A Cross-Validation Study," *Academy of Management Journal,* vol. 15, no. 1 (March 1972), pp. 91–102; Dan Schendel, G. R. Patton, and James Riggs, "Corporate Turnaround Strategies," *Journal of General Management,* vol. 3, no. 3 (Spring 1976), pp. 3–11; and S. Schoeffler, Robert Buzzell, and Donald Heany, "Impact of Strategic Planning on Profit Performance," *Harvard Business Review,* vol. 52, no. 2 (March-April 1974), pp. 137–45.

[2] Kenneth R. Andrews, *The Concept of Corporate Strategy* (Homewood, Ill.: Dow Jones-Irwin, Inc., 1971), pp. 36, 41; and Seymour Tilles, "How to Evaluate Corporate Strategy," *Harvard Business Review,* vol. 41, no. 4 (July-August 1963).

can be fairly said that *the acid test of a powerful strategy is the extent to which it successfully impacts markets, buyers, rival firms, and the directions of product-market-technological changes.* The desired outcome is one in which the firm's strategy becomes the *trend-setter* for the whole industry, with the added benefit that its products/services become differentiated and strong buyer preferences for them are created.

In the final analysis, of course, the value of conscious strategy formulation and careful strategy analysis hinges on whether and how much organizational performance is improved. Whether better performnce is realized depends on how much is learned from the process of developing a full-blown organizational strategy, the quality of the strategy (the assumptions, predictions and business savvy on which it is based), and the skill with which it is implemented. By itself, strategy formulation—while clearly a step forward—is still only a useful prelude to action.

Where Strategy Formulation Begins—With a Concept

The necessary and logical starting point of strategy formulation is with the concept of what the business will be, now and in the future, that is, with organizational purpose and mission. The following questions are fundamental: What should the business character of our organization be like? Should it have any distinctive features? What products or services do we want to provide? What functions will they serve and are these functions marketable? Who will our customers be? Why should they buy our product? How will we compete? How does our intended purpose and mission mesh with competitive and market realities? What should we continue to do and what should we plan to abandon? And, in the case of diversified firms: Should our several lines of business be related? If so, in what ways? Not infrequently, the answers to these kinds of questions are far from clearcut, even for established or successful enterprises. Nor are the answers ever final—changing circumstances can and do cause firms to redefine their business scope and to reorient organization purpose.

In actuality, there are several ways for an organization to approach the the question of "what is our business, what will it be, and what should it be?" Some organizations build the concept of their businesses around the dominant characteristics of their products or services. Thus, a trucking company may think of itself as being in the trucking business, a chemical company in the chemicals business, and a shoe manufacturer in the shoe business. Similarly, in the nonprofit sector a university may think of itself as being in the business of higher education; an agricultural extension service may think of its business as agriculture-related technical assistance and information; and the local fire department may view its business as fire fighting and fire prevention. Other organizations describe their businesses by the principal ingredient in their products, as with steel companies, aluminum companies, and paper companies. Technology can also serve as the basis for conceptual definition, an example being General Electric, whose thousands of products are related in varying degrees to the technology of electricity.

Still other organizations prefer a concept based on a *broad* view of the customers or markets they serve. Thus, rural electric cooperatives often construe their business as one of supplying electrical service to residents of less-populated rural areas. A community college may view its mission as one of furnishing two-year college programs to graduates of high schools within a 50-mile radius of its campus. An agricultural machinery manufacturer may define its business as supplying farm equipment to farmers. The business of home appliance manufacturers may be thought of as one of offering effort-saving and time-saving devices to households.

Yet another alternative is for a firm to define its business in terms of a product aimed at a specific *market segment* or distinguishable group of customers having some common (and strategically relevant) characteristic: location, usage of product, timing of purchase, volume bought, service requirements, and so forth. For instance, typewriters sold as office equipment define a buyer segment quite distinct from portable typewriters sold to individuals through retail channels. Likewise the clientele of a major state university is fundamentally different from that of a small private liberal arts college. And the business of a neighborhood convenience food mart is different from that of a large supermarket. In such cases, an organization's concept of its business combines a definition of its product with a definition of the class of customer or market segment to which that product is sold. This approach to defining the business seeks a strategic match between a particular product (or service) and the more narrowly focused target market for which it is primarily intended.

Finally, an enterprise may have a concept of itself that is predicated on the scope of its operations. For a small company, just part of an industry may constitute its sole field of endeavor; such would be the case of a firm whose business consists, say, of drilling offshore oil wells. This type of firm is often labeled as "specialized," and such a firm may well perceive its economic mission as none other than a specialty-type enterprise performing a limited service. Larger firms may, for reasons of scale economies, have activities extending across several stages of the process of getting a product to the final consumer (mining, manufacturing, distribution) and are thus said to be "integrated." An example would be an oil company which drills its own oil wells, pipes crude oil to its own refineries, and sells gasoline through its own network of branded distributors and service station outlets. Still other firms, large or small, are said to be "diversified" because their operations extend into several different industries, either related or unrelated.

Strictly speaking, most organizations are in a variety of distinct businesses. Either they sell the same product to different types of customers in distinctly different ways, or they utilize a number of different distribution channels in gaining access to customers and markets, or they have a diversified product line. Consequently, to arrive at the *total* organization's concept of its purpose and mission, it may be necessary to look at each line of business and judge how the *overall* purpose and corporate strategy relate to specific products or product groups, markets or market segments, technology, end-uses and needs, scope of activity in an industry, narrow diversification, or broad diversification. However, in the case of true conglomerate organizations which, by design, are in a number of *unrelated* businesses, the overall definition or organizational concept tends to relate more to issues of risk, financial objectives of the owners, growth, and earnings stability than to a unifying fit among its numerous product-market-technology activities.[3]

"What Is Our Business and What Should It Be?"

For many years Peter Drucker has been the most noted and perceptive authority on the whys and hows of an organization clearly defining its purpose and mission. According to Drucker, while nothing may seem simpler or more obvious than "What is our business?", a neglect of this question is the most important single cause of organization frustration and failure. He argues quite forcefully, therefore, that the theory of an organization's business should be thought through and spelled out clearly; otherwise the organization will lack a solid foundation for establishing realistic objectives, strategies, plans, and work assignments.[4] Drucker offers the following approach to defining "What is our business?":

> A business is not defined by the company's name, statutes, or articles of corporation. It is defined by the want the customer satisfies when he buys a product or a service. To satisfy the customer is the mission and purpose of every business. The question "What is our business?" can, therefore, be answered only by looking at the business from the outside, from the point of view of customer and market. What the customer sees, thinks, believes, and wants, at any given time, must be accepted by management as an objective fact. . . .
> . . . to the customers, no product or service, and certainly no company, is of much importance. . . . The customer only wants to know what the product or service will do for him tomorrow. All he is interested in are his own values, his own wants, his own reality. For this reason alone, any

---

[3] See, for example, Richard F. Vancil and Peter Lorange, "Strategic Planning in Diversified Companies," *Harvard Business Review*, vol. 53, no. 1 (January-Februray 1975), pp. 81–90.

[4] Peter F. Drucker, *Management: Tasks, Responsibilities, Practices* (New York: Harper and Row, Publishers, 1974), pp. 77–79.

serious attempt to state "what our business is" must start with the customer, his realities, his situation, his behavior, his expectations, and his
values.[5]

Following up on this rationale, Drucker advocates a searching inquiry into
such questions as: Who is our customer and what are his needs? Where is
the customer? What does the customer buy? Is it status? Comfort? Satisfaction of a physical need? An ego need? Security? What is value to the
customer? Is it price? Function? Quality? Service? Economy of use? Durability? Styling? Convenience?

These questions plainly need to be posed and answered at the inception
of a business and whenever it gets in trouble. But every so often a successful operation should also ask them.[6] Sooner or later, even the most
successful response to "What is our business?" becomes obsolete. Therefore, in periodically addressing the question of "What is our business?",
management is well-advised to add "and what will it be?"[7] This latter
question forces the organization to look ahead and try to anticipate the
impact of environmental changes on the organization's business. It lays
the basis for conscious redirection of the organization. It reduces the
chances of becoming smug and complacent. Answering it also means doing
some serious thinking about "What are the customer's *unsatisfied* wants?",
the response to which may suggest the direction of changes in products,
markets, and technologies. The clues thus uncovered should help in
modifying, extending, and developing the organization's existing business
concept.

Finally, it is pertinent to inquire "What *should* our business be?"[8] How
can innovations be converted into new businesses? What other opportunities are opening up or can be created that offer attractive prospects
for transforming the organization into a *different* (and more desirable)
business? Which things should the organization continue doing and which
should it plan to abandon? Should, for example, Exxon consider itself as
primarily an oil company or an energy company? Should IBM's concept of
its business be computers or information processing? Should the business
of hospitals remain one of curing those persons who are sick enough to be
patients or should they seek to become comprehensive centers for all types
of medical and health care?

By and large, if an organization follows Drucker's prescribed methodology for periodically thinking through its definition of purpose and
mission, the outcome will be a clearer and more perceptive understanding
of how the enterprise should be managed.

---

[5] Ibid., pp. 79–80.
[6] Ibid., pp. 87–88.
[7] Ibid., pp. 88–89.
[8] Ibid., p. 82.

Strategic Fit—Is It Necessary?

In defining its purpose and mission, an organization should be alert to the problems of arriving at a concept of its business which is too broad to be operationally useful.[9] While the widespread tendency of organizations to diversify has rendered the traditional identification of firms with particular industries obsolete and overly narrow, there is equal danger in establishing a statement of purpose that is so encompassing as to obscure what an organization is and where it is headed. For example, a hospital may perceive its mission broadly as one of "providing comprehensive health care to the residents of the surrounding community." But is this to include filling cavities and pulling teeth, examinations for eyeglasses, nursing of the aged, annual checkups, and rehabilitation services for the handicapped—all of which are often performed by medical professionals outside hospitals? A state university is unquestionably in the business of "higher education," but does this mean it should offer the *full* range of programs in "higher education"—including technical training, associate degrees similar to those of junior colleges, adult and continuing education, as well as undergraduate and graduate programs in *all* disciplines and professions? A railroad company may decide to view itself as a "transportation company," but does this mean it should get into long-haul trucking or air-freight services or fleet car leasing or intercity busing or rapid transit?

Generally speaking, an organization's concept of its business should (1) avoid the ambiguity of organizational direction that comes with an overly broad concept, (2) give *specific guidance* as to objectives and strategy, and (3) not be so confining as to foreclose growth and adaptation to environmental change. There is some dispute, however, over whether an organization's concept of itself should provide a "common thread," or unifying theme, for its several activities.

The prevailing view seems to be that it is desirable for an organization's activities, however diversified, to contain some form of *strategic fit*. Strategic fit is a measure of the joint effects, or mutually reinforcing impacts, that engaging in different activities have on an organization's overall effectiveness and efficiency.[10] To put it more simply, strategic fit is a $2 + 2 = 5$ phenomenon. The fit can take several forms. *Product-market fit* exists when different products follow common distribution channels, utilize the same sales promotion techniques, are bought by the same customers, and/or can be sold by the same sales force. *Operating fit* results from purchasing and warehousing economies, joint utilization of plant

---

[9] H. Igor Ansoff, *Corporate Strategy* (New York: McGraw-Hill Book Co.), pp. 105–8.

[10] David T. Kollat, Roger D. Blackell, and James F. Robeson, *Strategic Marketing* (New York: Holt, Rinehart and Winston, Inc., 1972), pp. 23–24.

and equipment, overlaps in technology and engineering design, carryover of R&D activities, and/or common manpower requirements. *Management fit* emerges when different kinds of activities present managers with comparable or similar types of technical, administrative, or operating problems, thereby allowing the accumulated managerial know-how associated with one line of business to spill over and be useful in managing another of the organization's activities. The value of having strategic fit in a diversified organization is the unifying focus and rationale it gives to management in planning and administering the organization's activities.

On the other hand, the conglomerate movement is by design characterized by lack of product-market-technology fit and a common thread concept. Textron, for example, has built a successful sales-profit record with activities as diverse as Bell helicopters, Gorham silver, Homelite saws, Sheaffer pens, Fafnir bearings, Speidel watchbands, Polaris snowmobiles, Sprague gas meters and fittings, Bostitch staplers, air cushion vehicles, iron castings, milling machines, rolling mills, industrial fasteners, insurance, and missile and spacecraft propulsion systems—among others. (Illustration Capsule 4 describes the logic underlying Textron's diversity.) Using an aggressive acquisition-merger strategy quarterbacked by Harold Geneen, International Telephone and Telegraph (ITT) in the short span of 15 years grew from a medium-sized telecommunications company in 1959 into the nation's largest industrial corporation with annual sales exceeding $11 billion in 1975. A Congressional committee hearing in 1969 revealed that ITT's aggressive acquisition-merger strategy made "the world of ITT" a conglomerate structure of some 350 companies having an additional 700-plus lower-tier subsidiaries of their own. ITT products and companies run the gamut, including telephone equipment, Sheraton hotels, Wonder Bread, Avis Rent-a-Car, Smithfield Hams, Bobbs-Merrill Publishing Co., Hartford Insurance Co., Aetna Finance Co., Jabsco Pump Co., Gotham Lighting Co., Speedwriting Inc., Transportation Displays, Inc., Rayonier chemical cellulose, Bramwell Business School, South Bend Window Cleaning Co., and Scott lawn care products.

Textron and ITT, along with several other conglomerates, have been successful enough to cast doubt upon the *necessity* of a unified theme and strategic fit. But the final verdict is not yet in.[11] Managing widely diverse companies effectively has proved to be something many corporate managements are not able to do. Acquisition-minded conglomerates have had serious difficulties in profitably operating so many diverse subsidiaries— chiefly because corporate managers have found themselves short on the experience and grassroots product/market knowledge requisite for pro-

---

[11] For an interesting discussion of some of the issues involved, see Lewis Meman, "What We Learned from the Great Merger Frenzy," *Fortune* (April 1973), pp. 70–73, 144–50.

ILLUSTRATION CAPSULE 4
How One Conglomerate Views the Concept of Its Business

In its 1976 and 1977 *Annual Reports,* Textron made the following statements about its corporate purpose, objectives, and strategy:

Textron is founded on the principle of balanced diversification, designed on the one hand to afford protection against economic cycles and product obsolescence and on the other to provide a means for participating in new markets and new technologies. The key elements are balance and flexibility in a rapidly changing world.

Textron, . . . , has established a versatile business organization with a presence in many markets, geographic areas and technologies, and a management style and philosophy that has generated a proven record.

Textron seeks to be distinctive in its products and services—distinctive as to technology, design, service and value. Superior performance will be achieved by way of excellence and quality. These, plus motivated people of high standards, are the essential ingredients for achievement of an overall goal of superior performance on a continuing basis.

Through more than two dozen Divisions in five Groups—Aerospace, Consumer, Industrial, Metal Product, and Creative Capital—Textron's decentralization of day-to-day operations is coupled with corporate coordination and control to assure consistency of standards and performance. The operating Divisions are provided with the capital and planning assistance to meet demonstrated needs for growth. This business structure combines the enthusiasm and quick response of moderate-sized enterprises with the planning and financial resources available on a consolidated basis.

Textron has three important priorities: *People development. Internal profit growth. New initiatives.* Emphasizing these priorities, Textron seeks to accomplish quantitative objectives set in 1972 for the ten-year period ending 1982. These specific targets for compound rates of growth are:

Sales: 8 percent per year, to $3.5 billion in 1982.
Progress, 1972 to date: 11 percent to $2.8 billion in 1977.

Net income: 10 percent per year, to $200 million in 1982.
Progress, 1972 to date: 11 percent to $137 million in 1977.

Net income per common share: 10 percent per year, to $6.00 in 1982.
Progress, 1972 to date: 9 percent to $3.65 in 1977.

viding guidance on the enormous number of unrelated problems being encountered at the division and operating levels.[12]

Consequently, while it is not *absolutely essential* for a common thread or strategic fit to run through each of an organization's several activities, experience seems to indicate that few organizations have managed to build a successful organization concept and strategy without finding a common denominator for at least most of its business. The reason, simply enough, is that from the standpoint of managerial know-how the problems of managing diversification tend to get out of hand when an organization's range of operation spans many unrelated product markets and technologies.[13] The conglomerate's penchant for rate-of-return criteria as *the* decisive strategic guide thus runs the risk of deteriorating into mediocre long-run performance unless a conglomerate's managers are exceptionally good at using "management by the numbers" as a substitute for firsthand knowledge of the business.

The Levels of Strategy

Once an enterprise has gotten a firm grip on the kind of organization it wants to become, the direction-setting task turns toward the development of a strategic plan. Four major levels of organizational strategy are distinguishable: (1) *corporate strategy,* (2) *line of business* (or just *business*) *strategy,* (3) *functional area support strategy,* and (4) *operating-level strategy.*

Corporate strategy refers to the comprehensive strategic plan for the organization as a whole. It embraces all of the organization's product lines, operating divisions, and business interests. Corporate strategy is the umbrella under which an organization's perhaps diverse activities are linked, and it tackles head on the gut issue of "what *set* of businesses should we be in—now and in the future?" In effect, corporate strategy is composed of two main elements: (1) the firm's scope of activities and (2) how internal resources will be allocated among these activities. The strategic importance of a firm's scope of activities is that it determines how the organization will be positioned in the external environment— whether it is well-situated to capitalize on opportunities and how vulnerable it may be to emerging threats. Scope may be described in terms of products, markets, service to customers, technology, distribution channels,

---

[12] The confusion and uncertainty over corporate purpose, corporate objectives, and corporate strategy that is engendered by conglomerate diversification is evidenced by the number of firms which now designate themselves by initials—LTV, FMC, ACF Industries, SCM, NLT, MCA, AMAX, CPC International, AMP, A-T-O, TRW, GAF, NVF, DHJ Industries, UMC Industries, SCOA Industries, RLC, and NL Industries.

[13] As an illustration of some of the difficulties a conglomerate company may encounter see Dan Cordtz, "What Does U.S.I. Do? Why, Almost Everything," *Fortune* (February 1973), pp. 73–77.

geographic coverage, degree of vertical integration, degree of diversification, or any other relevant factor. The second element of corporate strategy—the priorities and patterns for internal resource deployment—is crucial because it supplies a much-needed rationale for management to use in evaluating competing requests for corporate resources. Furthermore, it forces some management consideration of how to develop the kind of match between internal resource capability and scope of operations that will yield high performance and results.

The concept of corporate strategy has classic application in multiproduct, multiindustry, multitechnology organizations since their top managements are continually under the gun to make a workable whole out of numerous activities, some or many of which are not related. But it also applies to single-business enterprises which are contemplating some kind of diversification and/or shift in corporate direction. In either case, the task of corporate strategy is heavily focused on what new businesses (if any) to get into, which current businesses to stay in, and which existing activities to divest or close down. Necessarily then, corporate strategy is concerned with whether and to what extent different lines of business should be related or unrelated. It is concerned with how much and what kind of diversification to pursue. It is concerned with the whys and hows of acquisition and divestiture and, more generally, with a strategic rationale for evaluating a portfolio of businesses. Then, too, it is concerned with the criteria and priorities to be used in allocating financial capital and organizational skills among the chosen lines of business. This last concern is an important one because if a high level of performance is to be achieved, both the availability of internal resources and the patterns with which they are deployed must be in close alignment with the success requirements of each line of business.

Line of business (or *business*) *strategy* focuses on how a firm plans to conduct its activities in a single market or market segment. It addresses most particularly the issues of (1) how the organization intends to compete in that specific business and (2) how organizational resources will be allocated to various facets of that business to give the organization a viable competitive advantage and, if possible, a unique and distinctive competence in creating, producing, and delivering the product or service. The external aspects of line of business strategy deal with how the organization can be entrepreneurially effective in that particular business and with the specifics of adapting to the evolutionary aspects of both products and markets. The internal character of line of business strategy suggests how the different pieces of the business (manufacturing, marketing, finance, R&D, and so on) ought to be aligned and coordinated so to be responsive to those market factors upon which competitive success depends. In this regard, line of business strategy provides guidance for organizing and funding the performance of subactivities within the business in ways which speak directly to what is needed for strategic success. Obviously, for a single-product, single-business enterprise, corporate strategy and business strategy are one and the same—except for when new diversification is being contemplated. Our distinction between corporate and business strategy is most relevant for multiproduct, multiindustry firms; that is, for firms which are sufficiently diversified to have more than one line of business or more than one strategy for each of its several products/businesses.

Functional area support strategy deals with how the key functional areas of the business should be managed and how the resources allocated to each functional area are to be made effective and efficient in their contribution to the accomplishment of the overall business strategy. Each of the activities within a single business, most especially the key activities, ought to be integrated and fit together to form a smoothly functioning and mutually reinforcing unit. Thus, functional area support strategies are major corollaries of the line of business strategy—they give it substance, completeness, and concrete meaning as applied to a specific function in the business (production, marketing, finance, R&D, personnel). They indicate how each subactivity in the business is to be managed for the accomplishment of the strategy of the overall business unit. Because of the close tie between line of business strategy and functional area support strategies, major decisions regarding the latter tend to be ratified in the higher echelons of the management structure of that business unit.

Operating-level strategies refer to the strategic guidelines operating-level managers develop and use in managing their areas of responsibility. They indicate the *day-to-day kinds of action* which the business unit (or one of its departments) intends to take in competing in the marketplace, producing its products, financing its operations, securing needed resources, organizing and administering the business, and carrying out the *daily* strategic requirements of the business. In general, operating-level strategies deal with the nuts and bolts of how various activities of the functional area strategies will be carried out (pricing approaches, discounts, credit arrangements, inventory levels, amount of promotional activity, raw material purchasing, and the like). Thus, the differences between functional area strategy and operating-level strategy pertain to matters of role and scope in the overall business strategy and to the level of management where the respective strategic actions tend to be taken.

Ideally, corporate strategy, business strategy, functional area support strategy, and operating-level strategy will be developed in sufficient detail that the managers in the organization have a confident understanding of how to manage their areas of responsibility in accordance with the total game plan. This is why many layers of strategy typically are needed (especially in large, diversified organizations), each layer being progressively more detailed to provide strategic guidance for the next level of subordinate managers. In addition, the separate pieces and layers of strategy should be consistent and interlock smoothly, like the pieces of a puzzle. When the elements of corporate strategy are in harmony and mutually supportive, strategy can be a useful source of organizational cohesiveness. An effectively articulated strategy helps weld an organization's activities together and promotes a shared commitment among managers to accomplishing the game plan. It assists in keeping functional perspectives from blurring larger strategic priorities.[14]

Figure 2–1 provides examples of some "good" and "bad" strategy statements. Observe that the more specific and detailed the strategy statement is, the more clear it is what kind of organization is being described, where it is headed, and how it is going to get there. Unless strategy reveals these

FIGURE 2–1
Examples of "Good" and "Bad" Strategy Statements

Strategy Statement	*Remarks*
1. "The strategy of Company A is to become a growth company and to emphasize fast-growing product lines."	This statement is more an expression of an objective and some intentions rather than a delineation of how growth is to be achieved and what set of businesses that Company A seeks to engage in.
2. "Our strategy is to become the most efficient firm in the industry."	The statement is explicit as compared to statement 1, but it still describes an objective. No mention is made of how the enterprise intends to become the most efficient firm.
3. The strategy of Ajax Corporation is to become a fully integrated steel producer over the next five years.	This strategy statement indicates the direction the company will be moving and its intended scope of operations, but it is incomplete because it says nothing about resource allocation among the stages of vertical integration nor does it address how the firm intends to compete successfully and how a distinctive competence will be achieved.

---

[14] The ease with which functional areas can get at cross purposes with business strategy is illustrated by the following example. A company trying hard to build up a new customer base for industrial castings found that work orders for castings were given the lowest priority in the milling and shipping departments because they were a new item and required different handling procedures; the strategic importance of the castings had simply not found its way to these two functional subunits.

FIGURE 2-1 *(concluded)*

Strategy Statement	Remarks
4. PWB Company's strategy is to retain all of its profits to finance diversification into the leisure time industry and thereby raise its annual growth rate of sales and profits from 5 to 10 percent. Diversification will emphasize acquiring young, rapidly-growing companies which have proven management and which have demonstrated the ability to manufacture and market a quality product.	Although the strategy suggests a wider scope of operation and the means to finance it, as well as relating strategy to specific objectives, it omits mention of PWB's existing business. Also the notion of "leisure time industry" needs to be pinned down more specifically.
5. Our strategy for the next two years is to compete in the low price segment of the women's apparel business, with a limited line of fashion conscious items that can be sold on the basis of style and low price to national retail chains catering to budget-conscious women. During this period, no diversification efforts will be undertaken and all available internal funds will be allocated to debt retirement, increased marketing efforts, and improved production methods —in that order of priority.	This strategy statement is the most complete and detailed of the five statements. It describes the intended scope of operations, the deployment of resources, and the competitive approach to the market. Yet it could be improved by adding references to distinctive competence, sought-for competitive advantages, and how the strategy relates to corporate objectives.

things about an organization, it is too vague to be of managerial value.

Figure 2-2 depicts a hypothetical composite strategy and the several levels of directional actions and decisions requisite for making it operationally complete. Note the logical flow from business strategy to functional support strategies to operating-level strategies. It should be evident from an examination of this figure why an organization's strategic plan is the sum total of the directional actions and decisions it must make in trying to accomplish its objectives.

One final word about the levels of strategy. No matter how layered and specific a given strategy is, it should still be regarded as dynamic

FIGURE 2–2
The Levels of Strategy for a Hypothetical Petroleum Company

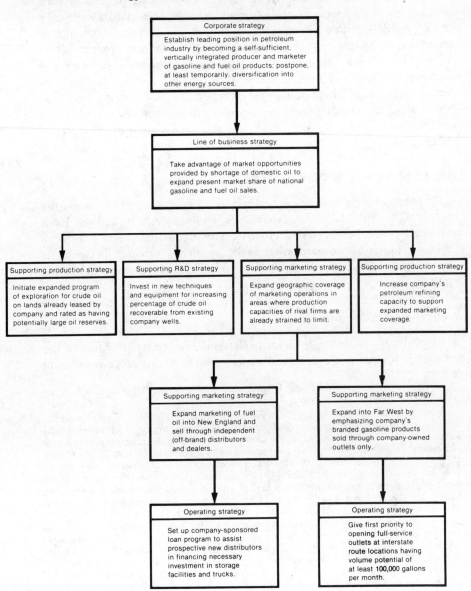

and temporal.[15] While an organization's fundamental purpose and long-term objectives may not change significantly over long periods of time (particularly if they were carefully drawn), the strategic nature and scope of its product-market-technological activities are certain to change in material ways in response to a fairly constant flow of new environmental circumstances. As a consequence, fine-tuning the elements of strategy, and an occasional major change in strategic thrust, will be a normal and expected occurrence. The *inevitability of an evolving strategy* means that any strategy statement should be viewed as only *currently* useful, a fact which speaks loudly for regular review and revalidation of all levels of strategy.

THE DETERMINANTS OF STRATEGY

An astute, timely strategy is typified by "goodness of fit" between the organization's internal skills, capabilities, and resources on the one hand and on the other, the external environment it confronts. The evaluative process whereby an organization seeks an effective match between its internal and external environments highlights the factors which determine strategy.

Product-Market Opportunities

Opportunity is always a factor in determining strategy.[16] Most of the time it is a pivotal strategic consideration, for unless one perceives that an

---

[15] Richard F. Vancil, "Strategy Formulation in Complex Organizations," *Sloan Management Review*, vol. 17, no. 2 (Winter 1976), pp. 2–5.

[16] As cogently pointed out by Philip Kotler, there is a difference of opinion in the literature of management regarding whether the strategy formulation process should begin with the identification of opportunities or with the defining of purpose and objectives. Those who say the first step should be to identify opportunities argue that (1) many organizations have gotten their start because they recognized the existence of a major opportunity (Xerox, Polaroid, Holiday Inns, IBM, and Coca-Cola, among others); (2) many organizations which lack sharply-defined objectives and are unable to articulate what they are really trying to do have nonetheless compiled a good record of seizing opportunities; and (3) a number of organizations have changed their objectives when their opportunities changed (as did the March of Dimes in shifting to the problem of birth defects when the Salk vaccine virtually eliminated polio). Those who argue that the setting of purpose and objectives should logically precede a search for opportunity point out that (1) a number of organizations have been observed to look for opportunities that will allow them to achieve sales, profit, and growth objectives, (2) the environment is simply too full of opportunities for companies to look merely for opportunities without a guiding purpose and set of objectives, and (3) organizations can and do, from time to time, change their objectives—an event which, subsequently, leads them to search for new and different opportunities.

Both viewpoints have merit in theory and in practice. Quite clearly there is a close two-way link between an organization's search for opportunity and its definition of purpose and objectives. As long as this is recognized, there is little need to become embroiled in a "chicken or egg-which came first" type of controversy.

See Philip Kotler, *Marketing Management: Analysis, Planning, and Control*, 3d ed. (Englewood Cliffs, N.J.: Prentice-Hall, Inc., 1976), p. 46.

opportunity exists there is little point in proceeding. But on occasions, opportunity is just a necessary presence. For instance, when market demand is growing rapidly, it is virtually certain that an organization will pursue the opportunity for increased sales and profits; the gut issue here is how best to approach the market and outcompete rival organizations pursuing the same opportunity.

In viewing the role of opportunity in the strategy formulation process, it is important to distinguish between *environmental opportunities* and *company opportunities.*[17] It is fair to say that there are always product-market opportunities in an economy as long as there are unsatisfied needs and wants backed up by adequate purchasing power. But none of these necessarily represent opportunities for a specific company. New forms of health care delivery are probably not an opportunity for Texaco, nor is a growing popularity of tennis an opportunity for General Motors. The environmental opportunities that are most likely to be relevant to a particular company are those where the company in question will be able to enjoy some kind of strategic fit or competitive advantage.

A number of companies have been observed to pursue product/market growth opportunities in a particular strategic sequence. Starting from a single-product, limited-market base, a firm first seeks to increase its sales volume, improve its market share, and build customer loyalty. In essence, this step represents a more intensive implementation of the existing strategy. Price, quality, service, and promotion are fine-tuned to respond more precisely to a detailed market need, often including the introduction of a full product line to meet minor variations in customer tastes and preferences. As this strategy approaches its full exploitation, a growth-minded company next will begin to assess the opportunities for geographical market expansion. Normally, the strategy of wider geographical coverage proceeds from local to regional to national to international markets, though the degree of penetration may be uneven from area to area because of varying profit potentials and may, of course, stop well short of global or even national proportions. When the opportunities for profitable market area expansion start to peter out, the organization's strategy may shift toward opportunities for vertical integration—either backward to sources of supply or forward to the ultimate consumer. For some companies this is a natural strategic move, owing to the close relationships to the organization's main product line and to the potential for realizing economies of scale.

Once a firm has reached the limits of geographical market expansion for its original product line and also has come to terms with the possibilities of forward and backward integration, the strategic options are either to continue in the same lines of business and attempt a more intensive implementation or to shift the focus to diversification opportunities.

---

[17] Ibid., p. 47.

Organizational Competence and Resources

No matter how appealing or how abundant product-market opportunities may be, the strategist is forced to validate the viability of each "opportunity" by inquiring into whether, given the opposing forces of competition and organizational circumstance, the organization has the means to capitalize upon it. Opportunity without the organizational competence to capture it is an illusion. An organization's strengths (demonstrated and potential) may make it particularly suited to seize some opportunities; likewise, its weaknesses may make the pursuit of other sorts of opportunities excessively risky or else disqualify it entirely. The strategist is thus well-advised to seek out a match between opportunity and competence which exploits or extends organizational strengths and which contains or minimizes dependence upon its weaknesses.

An organization's skills and strengths derive primarily from gradually accumulated experience and sustained success in its business. Unique and occasional flashes of skill or strength are rarely as dependable as those built up over a period of time and subjected to the tests of competitive pressure. It takes more than a year or two of experience and success to develop a level of expertise in which much confidence can be placed.

In practice, one finds that the strengths and capabilities of rival organizations vary significantly. Firms in the same industry ordinarily will be found to have different financial resources, marketing skills, degrees of technical know-how, costs, morale, images and market standing, managerial depth—in short, different internal capabilities. Whether the internal differences prove to be important strengths or important weaknesses depend on how they relate to the chosen strategy. But clearly, significant differences between one organization and its major rivals have the potential for being the cornerstone of strategy.

Because of the strategic relevance of organizational strengths and weaknesses, it is always worthwhile for an organization to ponder what *distinctive* skills and capabilities it can bring to bear that will allow it to draw business away from rival organizations. Some organizations excel in manufacturing a "quality product," others in creative approaches to marketing, still others in innovation and new product development. An organization's *distinctive competence* is thus more than just what it can do—it is what it can do *especially well* as compared to rival enterprises.[18] The importance of distinctive competence to strategy rests with the unique capability it gives an organization in developing a comparative advantage in the marketplace.

Typically, a key element in successful business strategy formulation is

---

[18] Philip Selznick, *Leadership in Administration* (Evanston, Ill.: Row, Peterson & Company, 1957), p. 42.

the ability to build into the strategic plan a product-market approach that will set the organization apart from others and give it some kind of strategic advantage. Generally, this means (1) following a different course from rival firms, (2) conceiving a plan which will have quite different (and more favorable) consequences for one's own organization than for competitors, and (3) making it hard for other organizations to imitate the strategy should it succeed.[19] Obviously enough, these guidelines are easier to follow when an organization has some kind of distinctive competence around which to build its strategy. It is always easier to develop strategic advantage in a market where the success requirements correspond to the organization's distinctive competence, where other organizations do not have these competences, and where potential rivals are not able to attain these competences except at high cost and/or over an extended period of time.[20] But if an organization has no particular distinctive competence on which to try to capitalize, the next best bet is to focus on ways to exploit existing differences between the organization and those of its competitors.

Environmental Threats

Very often, certain factors in the environment (existing or potential) present *threats* to an organization's current or contemplated strategy. These environment-related threats may concern possible new technological developments, the advent of new substitute products, recession, inflation, government action, changing consumer values and lifestyles, projections of natural resource depletion, unfavorable demographic shifts, and the like. Such threats can be a major determinant in shaping organizational strategy, and a wise strategist is as much alert to the threats of environmental change as to the opportunities that it presents.

An example of the technological threat which solid-state digital watches presented to Timex is described in Illustration Capsule 5. Other examples of environmental threats which have produced major strategic implications include:

◻ the possibility of nationalization and government takeover which transnational corporations face if they locate facilities in less-developed nations where there is a record of political instability.

◻ the rapidly developing technology of copying equipment, which soon led to the use of plain paper and thereby ruined the business of the coated paper manufacturers.

---

[19] Bruce D. Henderson, "Construction of a Business Strategy," reprinted in Daniel J. McCarthy, Robert J. Minichiello, and Joseph R. Curran, *Business Policy and Strategy: Concepts and Readings* (Homewood, Ill.: Richard D. Irwin, 1975), p. 290.

[20] David T. Kollat, Roger D. Blackwell, and James F. Robeson, *Strategic Marketing,* p. 24.

ILLUSTRATION CAPSULE 5
Strategic Implications of the Solid-State Technology Threat to Timex

In 1975, Timex ranked as the world's largest maker of finished watches. Its sales of some 40 million watches a year gave it a commanding 50 percent of the U.S. mechanical watch market and 70 percent of the electric watch market. The core of Timex's strategy was (1) to mass-produce a simple pin-levered movement watch in highly efficient plant facilities, and (2) to market them at rock-bottom prices through some 150,000 outlets—drugstores, variety stores, department stores, and even auto supply dealers. With eye-catching point-of-sale displays and skillful television advertising (the "torture test ads" narrated by John Cameron Swazy) to go with its low prices, Timex watches made steady market inroads to become the leading brand.

But, unexpectedly in 1975, Timex found itself confronted with a major technological challenge to its market position: how to develop a strategic response to the digital watch and the technology of solid-state electronics —a technology that was on the verge of sweeping the watch industry and undermining the cost advantage Timex enjoyed with its simple pin-levered mechanical watches. To complicate matters, Timex had little, if any, digital technology capability of its own.

The solid-state revolution in digital display watches was spearheaded not by established watch companies (Timex, Bulova, Benrus, Gruen, and others), but by semiconductor companies, including Texas Instruments, National Semiconductor, Litronix, Hughes Aircraft, and Fairchild Camera & Instrument. These firms, although newcomers to the watch industry, moved aggressively to dominate the market. Accustomed to competing in an industry where technological breakthroughs change things almost overnight, they quickly began to ignore traditional watch business practices (such as financing the watch inventories of retail jewelers and considering a 50 percent margin of selling price over cost as standard). They initiated bold price cuts even though demand seemed to be outstripping supply. Whereas the strategy of several semiconductor firms was, originally, to seek to enter into joint ventures with the traditional watchmakers, when the latter reacted so slowly, the strategy was changed to one of beating them head-on in the marketplace. Developments were so fast-paced that by mid-1975 jewelers were worried about the digital watch killing their watch business—not only because of the sharply lower profit margins but also because the semiconductor companies planned to furnish what little service or repair was needed on digitals from the factory, rather than at the point of sale.

Digital watch technology represented a radical departure from the Timex pin-levered watch. The digital watch had no moving parts to wear out and was far more accurate (within a minute per year) than even the most expensive mechanical watch. It operates with just four components: a battery, quartz crystal, an integrated circuit, and a digital display. The

ILLUSTRATION CAPSULE 5 *(continued)*

battery causes the quartz crystal to vibrate at 32,768 cycles per second (in most watches). The integrated circuit divides the vibrations into one pulse per second, accumulates the pulses to compute minutes, hours, days, and months, and transmits signals to the display to illuminate the digits showing the time and date.

When the first digital watches appeared in 1972, Timex was not unduly alarmed. It, together with most other watch manufacturers, viewed digitals as a fad or at most a specialty watch. Moreover, the first digitals were poorly designed, big and ugly, and experienced 60 percent defective returns. The biggest problem was in the digital time displays which were unreliable and often unreadable. Within three years, however, the semiconductor firms had made rapid progress in making the displays dependable and easy to read; styling was much sharper; and components had been made much smaller. Then in a move reminiscent of their strategy in the calculator business, the semiconductor firms in early 1975 slashed the prices of components in half—to as low as $20 per watch. Lower digital watch prices quickly followed (about half of what prices were in 1974). The move caught Timex and other traditional watch manufacturers off-guard. The apparent pricing strategy of the semiconductor firms was based on the "cost learning curve" whereby the prices of watches and component modules were to be lowered as production efficiency increased. But, at the same time, the digital watch firms were finding ways to reduce the number of parts in the module, ways to squeeze more of the electronic circuitry onto the main circuit, and ways to cut assembly costs. These savings permitted large price cuts to be made even sooner than planned.

As late as 1975, Timex had done little more than dip its toe into the digital market, with mediocre results. Solid-state technology was new to Timex. The company had no in-house capacity to produce such components as integrated circuits and digital displays, although it had introduced a digital watch line back in 1972.

Previously, Timex had rejected several contractual offers from semiconductor firms to supply it with digital-watch components. Hughes Aircraft Company, for example, which produced integrated circuits for Timex analog quartz watches, offered in 1971 to build a digital watch to sell under the Timex label if Timex would guarantee a minimum production run of 1 million units. The Hughes offer was for watches with light-emitting diode readouts which have to be turned on by pushing a button. Timex rejected the offer. Meanwhile, Timex's own efforts to develop in-house electronic watch capability progressed slowly. The head of its program to develop both digital and analog quartz watches left in 1973 to become director of watch operations at Rockwell International Corporation; his departure reportedly was due to Timex's failure to move rapidly in building up a digital capability.

The solid-state technology threat thus raised several strategy issues of vital concern to Timex's future:

ILLUSTRATION CAPSULE 5 *(concluded)*

1. Was the digital watch just a fad or was solid-state circuitry the wave of the future in watchmaking technology? (In 1974, digital watch sales totaled 650,000; some forecasts called for digital sales of 2.5 million units in 1975, and as much as 10 million in 1976.)

2. How quickly and to what extent would the rapidly falling prices of digital watches begin to create strong competitive pressures for Timex? (The prices of digital watches fell from $125 in 1974 to $50 in 1975, and to as low as $20 in early 1976.)

3. When and to what extent should Timex begin to push its own line of digital watches?

4. Should it purchase digital watch components from suppliers or should it develop its own digital component manufacturing capability? If the latter, then should the capability be developed internally or should Timex seek to acquire a firm with the technological know-how and experience?

In the minds of many observers, there was little doubt that Timex would soon have to offer a wide range of digital watches and, because of its carefully nurtured image as a producer of economy-priced watches, that the new digital watches would also have to be low priced. Otherwise, its market position would be in serious jeopardy.

SOURCE: Based on information in "The Electronics Threat to Timex," *Business Week*, August 18, 1975, pp. 42 ff; "Digital Watches: Bringing Watchmaking Back to the U.S.," *Business Week*, October 27, 1975, pp. 78 ff; "Timex Corporation" in H. Uyterhoeven, R. W. Ackerman, and J. W. Rosenblum, *Strategy and Organization: Text and Cases in General Management* (Homewood, Ill.: Richard D. Irwin, Inc., 1973), pp. 309–20; and "The $20 Digital Watch Arrives a Year Early," *Business Week*, January 26, 1976, pp. 27–28.

□ the approved use of gasohol as a lower-priced substitute for gasoline, which threatened to alter the market demand for both alcohol and gasoline in major ways.

□ the scientific discovery that various flurocarbons in aerosol sprays damage the ozone layers in the earth's atmosphere and the likelihood of future government bans on their use in aerosols, which caused both the aerosol chemical manufacturers and the manufacturers of items sold in aerosol cans to initiate a high priority search for substitute forms of technology and packaging.

□ the widespread public concern over the safety aspects of nuclear-powered generation of electricity, which caused electric utilities companies to order no new nuclear power plants in 1978 and cast doubt over the future of nuclear energy—indeed, GE decided to withdraw from the business of selling nuclear power plants.

For the most part, organizations appear to *react* to environmental threats rather than plan for or anticipate them. Actually, this is not a strong criticism of managers; a great portion of the environmental changes having major strategic implications are not readily subject to prediction. Some occur without warning and with few, if any, advance clues; others are "bound to happen" but the uncertainty is when. Moreover, even when threatening signals are detected early, it is not always easy to assess the extent of their strategic significance. Trying to forecast those future events which have strategic significance is scarcely an exact science. But this is not sufficient to provide excuses or alibis; it is management's function and responsibility to stay keenly tuned to the possibilities of adverse environmental change and to have strategic plans for any contingencies.

Personal Values and Aspirations

Strategy formulation is rarely so objective an analytical process that the personal values and aspirations of managers are excluded. On the contrary, both casual observation and systematic studies indicate that personal values and aspirations are important determinants of strategy.[21]

Most managers have personal concepts of what their organization's strategy is or ought to be. These concepts are certain to reflect, in part, a manager's own personal values and commitments—especially when he or she has had a hand in formulating the strategy. There is a natural tendency for managers to draw upon their own personal values and preferences when choosing among alternative strategies and interpreting the strategic plan. Sometimes the influence of one's own values and aspirations is conscious and deliberate, at other times it may be unconscious.

The following examples illustrate how personal values and aspirations can influence strategy:

□ A minister aspires to be the pastor of the largest congregation in town so he launches a well-organized campaign to attract new members and, in turn, a fundraising drive to build the biggest church in the area.

□ A corporate president has unswerving bias against dealing with unions, so he deliberately insists on locating plant facilities in geographical areas where workers have traditionally been indisposed toward unionism. In turn, he uses the ability to pay subunion wages as a tactic for gaining a competitive edge on costs and selling price.

□ A division manager in a diversified corporation wishes to make the business unit she heads "number one in sales and in the industry" so she pushes for a marketing strategy that calls for increasing volume

[21] See, for instance, William D. Guth and Renato Tagiuri, "Personal Values and Corporate Strategy," *Harvard Business Review*, vol. 43, no. 5 (September-October 1965), pp. 123–32; Kenneth R. Andrews, *The Concept of Corporate Strategy* (Homewood, Ill.: Dow Jones-Irwin, Inc., 1971), chap. 4; and Vancil, "Strategy Formulation in Complex Organizations," pp. 4–5.

and sales revenue even at the expense of slightly smaller (though acceptable) profit margins and returns on investment.

Societal Constraints and Social Responsibility

The ethical, political, social, and economic aspects of the external environment obviously enter into strategy formulation. Although the interaction between strategy and societal factors is a two-way street, here we wish to focus on how societal values, expectations, and constraints impinge on strategy. That consumerism, truth-in-packaging, equal opportunity employment, antitrust regulation, occupational health and safety, open housing, product safety, shifts in foreign policy, import quotas and tariffs, inflation, changes in national economic policy, tax reform, ethics and moral values, and other similar societal-based factors have an impact on organization strategies requires no discussion. Adapting strategy to accommodate these factors is commonplace and generally accepted. Some firms, since they exercise little control over external developments, view the social-economic-governmental dimension of strategy formulation as a constraint and sometimes as a threat. This view is not without some justification; external changes can indeed be potentially threatening to an organization's business (see Illustration Capsule 7 in Chapter 3). But, what is threatening to one enterprise may, at the same time, open new doors to another organization. For instance, while dwindling crude oil supplies pose obvious long-run strategic threats to the oil companies, there arises simultaneously major new market opportunities for organizations with expertise in energy research and for manufacturers of energy efficient devices.

Irrespective of whether changes in societal values and requirements destroy or create strategic opportunities, constant monitoring of the societal aspects of the external environment is now an essential ingredient of effective strategy formulation. Indeed, the desirability (if not the imperative) of relating the organization to the needs and expectations of society has come to be a standard feature of strategy formulation and strategy implementation, falling under the heading of *social responsibility*. The concept of social responsibility, as it affects strategy and policy, entails (1) adapting the organization to the changing requirements and expectations of society, (2) endeavoring to keep organizational activities in tune with what is generally perceived as the public interest, (3) responding positively to emerging societal priorities, (4) demonstrating a willingness to take needed action ahead of confrontation, and (5) balancing stockholder interests against the larger interest of society as a whole. Being "socially responsible" has both carrot and stick aspects. There is the positive appeal for all organizations to pursue strategies and policies that will enhance their own performance opportunities—these are always inexorably tied to the healthy economic well-being of society.[22] And there is the negative burden of public criticism and onerous regulation if they come up short.

Strategy and Organizational "Personality"

Every organization has a personality and modes of behavior which are somewhat unique to itself. Some organizations are noted for being aggressive and exhibiting leadership; others are clearly more complacent and slow-moving, often quite content to assume a follow-the-leader role. A few older, long-established family-dominated firms display the characteristics of paternalism toward employees or toward long-standing customers. Companies may be variously noted for their conservatism, or their pervasive preoccupation with technological virtuosity, or their financial wheeling and dealing, or their hard-hitting competitive style, or their emphasis on growth, or their social consciousness, or their desire to avoid risk. Quite clearly, these traits can spill over into, and even dominate, organization strategy at all levels.

How the Determinants of Strategy Combine to Affect Strategic Choice

Our discussion of the determinants of strategy raises the question of how the determinants interact with one another and in due course work their way into an organization's choice of strategy. Figure 2–3 presents a simple model of the strategy formulation process and indicates the role of the major strategy determinants in this process. As Figure 2–3 implies, we think it is appropriate to view strategy formulation as a special kind of problem-solving *process* for choosing an organization's strategy. The strategy formulation process entails five main steps or phases:

1. *Current strategy identification*—an assessment of where the company is now (in terms of purpose, objectives, and strategy) and how its present position has been shaped by personal aspirations and values of owners/managers, competition, opportunities and threats, societal expectations and government regulations, internal resources, and so on.

---

[22] Those who doubt the general principle that high levels of organization performance are closely tied to the general well-being of society should take note of the remarkable good correlation between changes in the levels of business profits and changes in the level of economic activity. Comparatively few businesses will be found to enjoy higher levels of performance during periods of social and economic decline. There is more truth to the view that "what's good for General Motors is good for the U.S.A." than it is currently fashionable to admit.

2. *External environment/market analysis*—an evaluation of product-market opportunities, competition, environmental threats, and other relevant external factors.

3. *Evaluation of internal resources, skills, and competences*—an assessment of what the organization can do, how hard it can be pushed, and an inventory of its base of skills, competences, and capabilities.

4. *Analysis of strategic alternatives*—identification and evaluation of each of the options around which a new strategy can be devised, taking into account the need to closely align the organization's responses to opportunities/threats with its internal resource capabilities.

5. *Selection of strategy*—arriving at a choice of one or more of the strategic options, after factoring in all of the considerations which are deemed relevant (specifically, opportunities, threats, values and aspirations, societal expectations, government regulations, competitive and market realities, and internal capabilities).

Except for organizations that are highly diversified and also experienced in the use of complex strategy formulation techniques, the model depicted in Figure 2–3 is a reasonably sufficient portrayal of what is in-

FIGURE 2–3
A Simple Model of the Determinants of Strategy and the Strategy Formulation Process

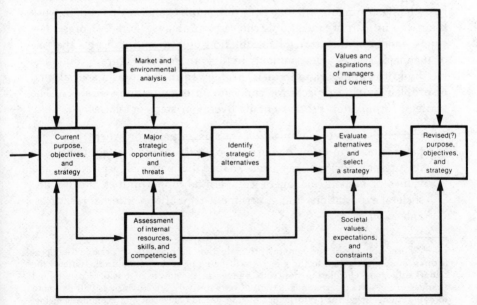

SOURCE: Adapted by the authors from Kenneth R. Andrews, *The Concept of Corporate Strategy* (Homewood, Illinois: Dow Jones-Irwin, Inc., 1971).

volved in choosing the right organization strategy.[23] In our view, the *methodology* of strategy formulation and an elaborate *modeling* of the strategy formulation process are not as important to the practicing manager and to organization success as is a strong orientation toward creative, perceptive, insightful, and opportunistic entrepreneurship. The substance underlying good strategy is astute entrepreneurship, not a detailed schematic of the steps to be followed.

Characteristics of an Effective Strategy

The effectiveness of a particular strategy can be appraised from two angles.[24] One is from the perspective of whether the strategy is right for the organization in its particular situation. Does it offer a viable and potentially effective fit between the organization's internal and external environments? Does it allow the enterprise to exploit attractive product-market opportunities and/or to escape the impact of externally imposed threats? Is it compatible with the organization's perceived strengths and weaknesses? Does it fully utilize internal competences and resources? Is it timely? In short, does the strategy exemplify "goodness of fit" among the relevant external/internal considerations?

The second angle involves the more subtle issue of whether the strategy has been sufficiently delineated. Is the strategy complete enough to allow managers to proceed confidently in managing their areas of responsibility according to the game plan? Has the strategy been developed and articulated in sufficient detail, beginning at the corporate level and continuing in ever more detailed layers down to the operating level? The whole of an organization's strategy is always a compound of many distinct actions and decisions, rather than a single point of attack.

An effective and complete concept of strategy says a great deal about the organization involved—its present and future character. It reconciles the organization-wide response to the questions of: What might we do? What can we do? What do we want to do? What should we do? It supplies an answer to "what set of businesses should we be in?" Ultimately, it defines the organization's business in terms of products, markets, and geographic coverage. At the competitive level, these definitions are clear-cut enough to pinpoint product functions and uses, as well as the precise customer classes for which these products are intended. Strategy provides direction and guidance for administrative process and policies, and for internal resource allocation. It speaks to whether and how the organization seeks a distinctive competence. It points toward the criteria for operating

---

[23] For more elaborate strategy formulation models, see Ansoff, *Corporate Strategy*, p. 202; and Charles W. Hofer and Dan Schendel, *Strategy Formulation: Analytical Concepts* (St. Paul, Minn.: West Publishing Co., 1978), Chapter 3.

[24] Vancil, "Strategy Formulation in Complex Organizations," p. 3.

the organization on a day-to-day basis. It indicates organizational priorities and, because of its close relationship to the organization's long-run and short-run objectives, it is indicative of the kinds of performance and results to be achieved.

A Concluding Point

As Professor Vancil has said, strategy is the conceptual glue that binds an organization's activities together.[25] Yet it is doubtful whether one can speak accurately of *the* strategy, except in very simple types of organization. In most organizations, and especially in diversified firms of some size, it is more correct to think of strategy as a collection of strategies— one for each facet of the organization's activities and perhaps one for each manager. These strategies form a hierarchical network, linked together by analysis and soul-searching as well as by an interactive, iterative process of negotiation and agreement on objectives, plans, policies, and constraints. To be effective, strategy must personally affect each manager, guiding what is to be done but in a manner which gives the manager enough elbow room to devise his/her unit's strategy within the broader context.[26]

Management from time to time may attempt to express strategy (or some parts thereof) in a written statement, but it is rare for such statements to be developed at the same time for every organization unit and every facet of the organization's activities. Consequently, the web of an organization's strategy is rarely delineated and written down as explicitly and comprehensively as has been described in this chapter. Much of strategy consists of verbal agreements and implied understandings between managers. Some pieces of strategy are readily deduced from visable management actions (acquisitions, divestiture, competitive behavior). Other pieces may appear in the forms of annual reports, speeches of top executives before meetings of securities analysts, internal memoranda, in-house studies and reports, minutes of meetings, and the like. Consequently, one should not expect an organization's strategy to be laid out boldly and regularly in some document called "the strategic plan." But, irrespective of whether an organization's strategy is written or oral, explicit or implicit, open or covert, the foregoing discussion should suffice to indicate that managers' alertness to the role of strategy and their understanding of existing strategy are of prime importance in the management of the total organization. In this regard, we would urge that the concept of strategy is neither an empty academic box nor a managerially moot activity with little or no bottom-line impact.

---

[25] Ibid., p. 18.
[26] Ibid.

SUGGESTED READINGS

Andrews, Kenneth R.   *The Concept of Corporate Strategy.* Homewood, Ill.: Dow Jones-Irwin, Inc., 1971, chaps. 2, 3, 4, and 5.

Ansoff, H. Igor   *Corporate Strategy.* New York: McGraw-Hill Book Co., 1965, chap. 6.

Cannon, J. Thomas   *Business Strategy and Policy.* New York: Harcourt, Brace, and World, Inc., 1968, chaps. 1 and 2.

Drucker, Peter F.   *Management: Tasks, Responsibilities, Practices.* New York: Harper & Row, Publishers, Inc., 1974, chaps. 6 and 7.

Hall, William K.   "Strategic Planning, Product Innovation, and the Theory of the Firm." *Journal of Business Policy,* vol. 3, no. 3, Spring 1973, pp. 19–27.

Hanan, Mack   "Reorganize Your Company Around Its Markets." *Harvard Business Review,* vol. 52, no. 6, November-December 1974, pp. 63–74.

Hofer, Charles W., and Schendel, Dan.   *Strategy Formulation: Analytical Concepts.* St. Paul, Minn.: West Publishing Co., 1978, chap. 2.

Levitt, Theodore   "Marketing Myopia." *Harvard Business Review,* vol. 38, no. 4, July-August 1960, pp. 45–56.

Newman, William H.   "Shaping the Master Strategy of Your Firm." *California Management Review,* vol. 9, no. 3, Spring 1967, pp. 77–88.

Tilles, Seymour   "Making Strategy Explicit." In *Business Strategy,* edited by H. Igor Ansoff. New York: Penguin Books, Inc., 1970, pp. 180–209.

Vance, Jack O.   "The Anatomy of a Corporate Strategy." *California Management Review,* vol. 13, no. 1, Fall 1970, pp. 5–12.

Vancil, Richard F.   "Strategy Formulation in Complex Organizations." *Sloan Management Review,* vol. 17, no. 2, Winter 1976, pp. 1–18.

Vancil, Richard F., and Lorange, Peter   "Strategic Planning in Diversified Companies." *Harvard Business Review,* vol. 53, no. 1, January-February 1975, pp. 81–90.

READING

Strategy Formulation in Complex Organizations*

RICHARD F. VANCIL

Richard F. Vancil is professor of business administration at the Harvard Business School.

The primary source of cohesiveness in an organization is strategy. To be effective, however, strategy must be more than just a ringing statement of purpose or objectives. It must also provide guidance that will assist subordinate managers in deciding how to proceed toward achieving the objectives. Furthermore, strategy should help to weld an organization together by developing among the members of the management team both a shared belief in the efficacy of major action programs and a shared commitment to execute those programs successfully. The purpose of this article is to discuss how strategy can be formulated in such a way that it will be more than simply a statement of purpose but will have an active role in shaping decision making in a complex organization.

Some Definitions

Before we proceed we must define three words—*strategy, objectives,* and *goals.* This is necessary because these words will be used in this article to convey a specific meaning which is not always synonymous with their common use in business.

Strategy. The strategy of an organization, *or of a subunit of a larger organization,* is a conceptualization, *expressed or implied by the organization's leader,* of (1) the long-term objectives or purposes of the organization, (2) the broad constraints and policies, *either self-imposed by the leader or accepted by him from his superiors,* that *currently* restrict the scope of the organization's activities, and (3) the *current* set of plans and near-term goals that have been adopted in the expectation of contributing to the achievement of the organization's objectives.

This definition is intended to be read twice. Reading it first and ignoring the italicized words, the definition is not significantly different from the several that already exist in the literature.[1] The second reading, focusing on the italicized words, emphasizes three important additional aspects of this definition of strategy. First, the definition applies not only to the

---

* Richard F. Vancil, "Strategy Formulation in Complex Organizations," *Sloan Management Review,* Winter 1976, pp. 1–18. Reprinted by permission.

[1] See K. R. Andrews, *The Concept of Corporate Strategy* (Homewood, Ill.: Dow Jones-Irwin, Inc., 1971), p. 28.

organization as a whole but to every major component of the organization. The "broad constraints and policies," which is what most businessmen mean by the term "strategy," may be either self-imposed or handed down from above. Strategy in a complex organization is conceived in a hierarchy and there are many levels of strategy in such an organization. Second, the strategy of an organizational component is never really "handed down"; it is conceived by an individual, the leader of the organizational unit, and this definition makes his role explicit. Third, the strategy of an organizational unit is dynamic. At any point in time, it expresses the *current* constraints, policies, and plans, but the likelihood of change in these statements is widely recognized throughout the organization. These three characteristics of strategy, as noted above, have major implications for the development of management systems in the organization.

Objectives and Goals. These two words, often used interchangeably by businessmen, can be differentiated to convey two quite different concepts, as implied in the definition of strategy above. The distinction between these two concepts is important, because a statement of strategy needs them both. The delineation of objectives and goals serves two different management purposes.

An *objective* is an aspiration to be worked toward in the future. A *goal* is an achievement to be attained at some future date. However, these short definitions fail to convey the essence of the difference between these two concepts, that is the distinction between "reach" and "grasp." For example, one of John F. Kennedy's *objectives* in 1960 was to reestablish and maintain this country's position as a leader in the fields of science and technology. One of his *goals* was to land a man on the moon and return him safely before the end of the decade.

The difference between objectives and goals may be drawn in terms of the following four dimensions.

1. *Time Frame.* An objective is timeless, enduring, and unending; a goal is temporal, time-phased, and intended to be superceded by subsequent goals. Kennedy's goal for the '60s was achieved, and it did contribute toward his objective, but new goals for the '70s are needed for the "maintenance of leadership" objective.

2. *Specificity.* Objectives are stated in broad, general terms, dealing with matters of image, style, and self-perception; goals are much more specific, stated in terms of a particular result that will be accomplished by a specified date. It is because of their open-endedness that objectives can never be achieved while goals can. We may believe that landing the first man on the moon did reestablish our scientific leadership, but that perception may not be universally shared. To shift the analogy, we clearly won a battle, but not necessarily the war.

3. *Focus.* Objectives are usually stated in terms of some relevant environment which is external to the organization; goals are more internally

focused and carry important implications about how the resources of the organization shall be utilized in the future. Objectives are frequently stated in terms of achieving leadership or recognition in a certain field. A goal implies a resource commitment, challenging the organization to use those resources in order to achieve the desired result.

4. *Measurement.* Both objectives and goals frequently can be stated in terms that are quantifiably measurable, but the character of the measurement is different. Quantified objectives are stated in relative terms. For example, the managers of one growth company have stated that their objective is "to achieve a compound rate of growth in earnings per share sufficient to place its performance in the top 10 percent of all (relevant) corporations." This objective may be achieved in any one year, but it is timeless and externally focused, providing a continuing challenge for the management of that company. A quantified goal is expressed in absolute terms. Several years ago, the president of a diversifying aerospace corporation stated that the company would "achieve 50 percent of its sales revenue from non-government customers by 1970." The achievement of that goal can be measured irrespective of environmental conditions and competitors' actions.

In order to prepare an effective statement of strategy in a complex organization, the distinction between objectives and goals must be recognized. Objectives are the first element in a statement of strategy; goals are the last. In the time that elapses between the delineation of these two statements, there must be a great deal of interplay between the managers at various levels in the organization's hierarchy. This complex process of starting with a statement of objectives and working toward the development of more specific goals will be discussed at length later in this article. First, however, we will discuss the three major elements of effective strategy.

Characteristics of Effective Strategy

The effectiveness of a particular strategy can be appraised from two different perspectives. First, of course, is the question of whether or not the strategy is right for the organization in its particular situation. Does it provide a proper match between environmental opportunities and organizational resources? Second is the more subtle question of whether or not the strategy has been constructed in such a way that it facilitates the management processes of the organization. Evaluated from this second point of view, an effective statement of strategy has three characteristics that are not commonly recognized.

Operational Guidance. The guidance that a statement of strategy provides for subordinate managers is usually cast in the form of what *not* to do rather than in the form of *what* to do. Such guidance, then, is really a set of constraints on appropriate organizational actions. These constraints are usually not stated explicitly both because it would be impractical to do so (the list would be too long) and because constraints have a negative connotation. Thus, an airline, for example, does not say that its strategy is *not* to be in the chemical business or *not* to be in the textile business, but rather that it is "to be a leader in the air transportation industry." The value of such a statement is not what it says explicitly, but the implicit message that a great many other activities which do not fall under the "air transportation industry" umbrella are to be ignored.

The guidance provided by a statement of strategy must be pervasive and operational. The statement must provide guidance to all the managers in the organization in sufficiently explicit terms to allow each manager to proceed with his tasks in the knowledge that his actions are consistent with the objectives of the organization. No single statement of strategy will suffice to provide this kind of guidance in a complex organization. Instead, many layers of strategy are needed, each layer being progressively more detailed to provide strategic guidance for the next level of subordinate managers. As the diversity and complexity of the organization increase, the degree of specificity of strategic guidance provided by corporate-level management appears to decrease. The strategy of a conglomerate corporation cannot be stated nearly as crisply as that of an airline. Nevertheless managers at lower levels of the conglomerate need guidance analogous to that provided to airline managers, and they receive it through a progressive delineation of the strategy of each major operating unit.

Personal Commitment.   Another characteristic of an effective statement of strategy is that it is drafted by the manager who must carry it out. This is obviously true for a corporate president who has no superior officer to tell him what the limits should be on the scope of the corporation's activities. Surprisingly perhaps, it is equally true for several levels of subordinate managers in a well-run corporation.

A personalized strategy is feasible in a complex organization if the statement of strategy is drafted carefully. As discussed earlier, the superior manager devises his strategy and expresses it in the form of constraints on the scope of the activities of his subordinates. However, he should take care to leave them some discretion as to how they operate within those constraints. Each subordinate manager will then accept (or challenge) those constraints, devise "his" strategy within them, and in turn express his strategy to his subordinates in the form of constraints on their activities. The resulting series of progressively detailed statements of strategy are personalized, in the sense that each manager can see his imprint on his part of the series. Furthermore, they are integrated throughout the organization as a whole, because each statement is consistent with the constraints imposed by higher authority.

Two of the several advantages of personalized strategies deserve mention here. First, encouraging each manager to use his imagination to devise the best strategy he can increases the vitality and creativity of the organization. In a complex organization, no one man, not even the president, can identify all the opportunities that exist, and a framework of progressive constraints that elicits personalized strategies multiplies the sources of initiative in the corporation. Second, a personalized strategy engenders a personal commitment. As Andrews says, in discussing the relevance of personal values in the determination of strategy, "Somebody has to have his heart in it."[2]

Expectation of Change. Finally, an effective statement of strategy should recognize explicitly that it is a temporal document. Whereas the objectives of the organization, particularly if carefully drawn, may not change perceptibly over time, the scope of its activities is likely to change in an expansionist fashion and the organization's major plans are almost certain to change as it continues to adapt to its dynamic environment. The inevitability of an evolving strategy does not mean that managers should not take the trouble to make the current strategy explicit or that the task should be done in a casual manner; it does mean that any such explicit statement should be viewed as only currently useful. The implication of this is that provision must be made in the management process for a periodic review and revalidation of all levels of strategy.

Tradeoffs in Strategy Formulation

It is now necessary to look briefly at some of the problems which plague any individual manager in developing his own statement of strategy. Even if we ignore, for the moment, the complexities that arise because his organization is a part of a larger complex, his task is a difficult one. His approach to this task must be both rational and emotional, his analysis of his situation both coolly analytic and unabashedly subjective. As Professor Andrews has described so well, the strategist seeks to reconcile conflicting forces. He must deal simultaneously with four questions: What *might* we do?, What *can* we do?, What do we *want* to do?, and What *should* we do? Obviously, the strategy that results from this analysis is based on the manager's personal perception of opportunities, his personal assessment of the strengths and weaknesses of his organization, and his personal aspirations and values.

In terms of the definition given earlier, strategy consists of three elements: (1) objectives, (2) constraints and policies, and (3) plans and goals. While these three elements are not determined independently in a neat, chronological sequence, it is convenient to discuss them as though they were.

---

[2] See K. R. Andrews, *The Concept of Corporate Strategy* (Homewood, Ill.: Dow Jones-Irwin, Inc., 1971), p. 117.

Objectives. The most personal element of an individual manager's strategy is the setting of objectives for his organization. If the task is difficult (and it need not always be), the trouble is frequently caused by a conflict between the manager's personal aspirations and values on the one hand and his professional or positional obligations on the other. Although the nature of the professional obligation varies with the level in the organization, even the highest officer must recognize that the organizational objectives he sets are not the same as his individual objectives. For the chief executive officer, the restraints imposed by his position are primarily external; his objectives for the organization must attempt to relate it to the broader society in which it exists. For a manager at a lower level, personal aspirations must be balanced off against the obligations inherent in his position as the leader of a subunit within a larger organization. For any manager, this tradeoff is essentially subjective; his aim is to frame a set of objectives for his organization which acknowledges his positional responsibilities and which is consistent with his own desires and beliefs.

Constraints and Policies. Determining the scope and balance of an organization's activities is a somewhat more analytical process and is always difficult. In simplistic terms, this task consists of finding the most appropriate match between environmental opportunities and organizational resources; the best set of activities to engage in are those which take best advantage of the organization's strengths, thus permitting the most progress toward achieving the organization's objectives. However, because the time frame involved is so long, this description of the task is insufficient. Stated more realistically, the task is to find a match between opportunities that are still unfolding and resources that are still being acquired. Substantial uncertainty exists on both counts. Opportunities may not develop in the direction or at the rate expected, and the organization may not be able to acquire new resources as effectively as the manager had hoped. Thus, determining the boundaries on an organization's sphere of activities is best conceived of as positioning the organization so that it will be able to capitalize on future opportunities. The choice that this presents for a manager is not simply the result of a neat, economic analysis. It is true that the choice needs to be wrapped in the cloak of rationality, if only to make it more communicable and to engender the commitment of subordinate managers. However, the choice is inevitably influenced, and appropriately so, by the manager's own perceptions and assessments as well as by the aspirations and obligations that he recognized in framing the organization's objectives.

Plans and Goals. The most specific element of strategy, that is the tangible plans for near-term actions and the results expected from those actions, is the most amenable to rational analysis. Here again the manager's task is to match opportunities and resources, but the choice must be based on the current situation or on what the situation will be in the very near future. The limitations on a purely rational solution occur because of the familiar tradeoff between short-term goals and long-term objectives. A manager's plan of action may be optimal, in the sense that he believes he has achieved the best balance across the time dimension, but that is still a personal belief. He may even attempt to prove the validity of his plan quantitatively, but it is almost inevitable that any such proof will ultimately rely on premises drawn from the broader elements of strategy discussed above.

A statement of strategy, then, is highly situational for two reasons. First, the strategy must reflect the organization as it now exists, its current activities, and its current set of resources. Second, and at least as important, the strategy for an organizational unit is determined by an individual; it bears the mark of his character, perceptivity, and personality. The process of permitting each manager in a complex organization to develop his own unique strategy is the topic to which we now turn.

Three Levels of Strategy

Generalizations about strategy are difficult, not simply because any statement of strategy is situational, but also because strategy in a complex organization is so detailed. Most literature on the subject stops short of exploring this detail because it is so messy. We will take the other tack here in order to provide a description that may be useful to practicing managers and more specifically to designers of long-range planning systems.

Even this first attempt at a detailed look at strategy must be simplified to some extent. In this article, we shall deal with a crude stereotype of a diversified corporation. Such a corporation, as shown in Figure 1, is conventionally organized into product divisions each with its own general manager which we will call the business manager. The principal subordinates of the business manager will be called activity managers.

Strategy, even in this simplest of all complex organizations, is an intricate web of personal statements by managers at each of the three levels in the hierarchy. Figure 2 displays the elements of strategy for each of the three types of managers. In order to understand that figure, it must be read both horizontally and vertically. The horizontal reading is the most appropriate to discuss first; it will permit us to examine each statement of strategy from the point of view of the individual manager who enunciates it. Viewed from this perspective, the strategy for this illustrative organization may be conceived of as an amalgam of about three dozen individual strategies: one corporate strategy, five divisional strategies, and perhaps six activity strategies within each division. If properly prepared, these individual statements form an interrelated set. However,

FIGURE 1

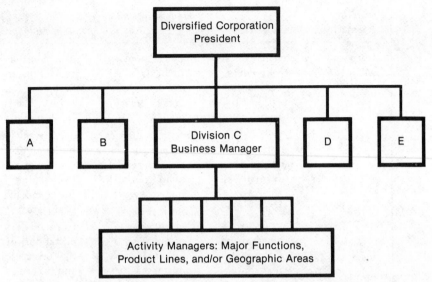

it is important to realize that each such statement must be capable of standing alone.

Corporate Managers. The statement of strategy expressed by the top manager of a diversified corporation can be broken into the three elements shown in Figure 2. Corporate objectives consist of two broad types: financial and nonfinancial. Financial objectives recognize the corporation's obligation to its shareholders and express management's aspirations for fulfilling shareholder expectations. It is increasingly rare, however, for corporate presidents to endorse the simplistic objective of "maximizing earnings over the long run." Instead, by stating the financial objectives in terms relative to what the managers of other corporations are able to achieve, the president recognizes that the performance of his company must be evaluated in the context of the economy as a whole.

In addition to setting financial objectives, many presidents today find it desirable to make explicit the social and ethical obligations of their corporation. Nonfinancial objectives may go beyond mere statements of the corporation's intention to be a good citizen; a corporate "creed" or some similar statement of the personal values shared by individuals in the organization is not uncommon. For example, such statements have been used for decades in large retailing organizations, such as J. C. Penney, Avon Products, and the Jewel Companies. The ability of these objectives to provide a set of ethical guidelines for a large number of employees dealing with an even larger group of customers would suggest that their value need not be restricted to retailing organizations.

FIGURE 2   Elements of Strategy in a Hierarchical Organization

Level in the Hierarchy	Objectives	Constraints and Policies	Plans and Goals
Corporate Managers	Stated in terms for stockholders, other identifiable constituencies, society at large. Examples: Financial performance of the corporation Corporate citizenship and "personality" characteristics	Financial policies (debt structure, dividends, diversity of risk, etc.). Specific industries to be in, or characteristics of appropriate industries. Criteria for approving new resource commitments to businesses.	Prospective magnitude of discretionary resources to be utilized by the corporation. Prospective distribution of resources in order to affect the future mix of businesses. Performance expectations for the corporation and for each business over the next 5–10 years.
Business Managers	Stated in terms for corporate management. Examples: Financial performance of the business Position of the business in the industry	Definition of niche in the industry; relative importance of, and interrelationships between, each activity. Priorities for changing the relative contribution from each activity.	Prospective patterns of resource allocation intended to affect the future contribution from each activity. Performance expectations for the business and for each activity over the next 3–7 years.
Activity Managers	Stated in terms for business management. Examples: Contribution of the activity to the business Position of the activity in the industry	Delineation of limits on the scope of the entire activity. Criteria for optimizing the use of resources available to the activity.	Prospective sequence of resource utilization intended to affect the future contribution from the activity. Performance expectations for the activity for each subactivity over the next 1–3 years.

The constraints and policies segment of corporate-level strategy consists of two types of statements. One type, statements of financial policy, may not always be critical to the success of the enterprise. Nevertheless, these statements are necessary because there are some elements of financial management, such as dividend policy, which corporate management cannot delegate to subordinates.

The other type of constraints/policies statement deals with the most crucial element of corporate strategy—the diversity of corporate activities. At a minimum, this statement identifies the industries in which the corporation is currently involved and revalidates an intention to restrict corporate activities to those industries over the long term. The top managers of corporations that are continuing to diversify have a somewhat more difficult problem. One useful way of specifying a constraint on the scope of corporate activity in such situations is to identify the major types of business opportunities which seem to capitalize on the resource capabilities of the corporation. Because the opportunities and the resources must be stated in rather general terms, the resulting statement lacks specificity. Still, this sort of statement provides a great deal more guidance for subordinates than a simple statement of the prospective financial performance that is required before a corporation will enter a new business. With the exception of only a few "pure" conglomerates, diversification actions rarely are based solely on financial criteria, and a thoughtful statement of corporate strategy can make the other criteria more explicit.

Finally, a corporate-level statement of strategy must specify the current set of major plans that are to be pursued in the years immediately ahead. In very crude terms, the feasibility of such plans must be related to corporate financial policies. The financial resources necessary to execute the plans need not be in hand, but their availability must be foreseeable. Despite the fact that the prospective distribution of funds across the range of corporate activities is highly tentative, subordinate managers must be given some idea of this distribution so that they plan in sufficient detail. Similarly, though the prospective effects of such allocations are even more tentative, such goals must be stated in order to provide corporate management with a crude test of the feasibility of all of the elements of its strategy.

Business Managers. In terms of the hypothetical organization cited in Figure 1, the manager of a product division is a business manager. He has been delegated the responsibility for formulating and implementing strategy in one of the industries in which a diversified corporation is engaged. Given that set of responsibilities, the statement of strategy which the business manager enunciates contains the same three elements noted above for corporate managers, but the scope and substance of the strategy are different.

Long-term objectives for a business manager in a hierarchical corporation must acknowledge the limitations in scope that are inherent in his position. The range of his activities is usually proscribed within the natural boundaries of an externally definable industry. Accordingly, his objectives for the business may be stated in terms relative to the performance of other companies in the same industry. Objectives need not be limited to financial performance; statements expressing an aim to achieve (or retain) a position as the industry leader in, for example, product development or customer service are also highly desirable. Such statements serve both to express the manager's aspirations to his subordinates and to encapsulate the essence of his strategy.

The cornerstone of business strategy is the concept which Professor Andrews and his colleagues refer to as "niche." Except in the case of a total monopoly, each company in an industry seeks to find a place for itself among its competitors. A niche may be a small nook or cranny in the marketplace where the winds of competition blow with somewhat less force, or it may be the top of the mountain which is occupied by a company with a commanding market share, while the storms of competition rage below. But even staying on the mountaintop, or finding a larger and somewhat more comfortable cave higher up the slope, requires a clear understanding of the relationship between a company and its competitors who are seeking to serve the same set of customers.

The constraint/policy element of a statement of business strategy is an attempt to delineate that competitive relationship. Here the manager's task of analyzing and matching opportunities with resources can be somewhat more specific than the task of his corporate counterpart. His major competitors are unlikely to change substantially over the next decade, and the thrust of technological and market development can be foreseen, however, dimly. Some would say that delineating this crucial element of a business strategy is more challenging, and more personally rewarding, than the equivalent corporate-level task of determining the strategy of diversification.

Once a business manager has determined the broad constraints that will guide his competitive approach to the marketplace, the remaining element of his strategy is to develop implementation plans and short-term goals for achievement. Figure 2 refers to these plans as *prospective patterns of resource allocation*. This compact phrase is intended to encompass both the expected magnitude of resources that the corporation may be able to make available to the business and the currently intended distribution of those resources among the alternative action programs which the business might pursue. Naturally, such a pattern is highly tentative. Nothing ever happens precisely as forecast, least of all such critical planning factors as the rate of market change and the nature of competitor response. Nevertheless, the performance results must also be forecast in order to permit the business manager to evaluate the cohesiveness and effectiveness of all elements of his strategy.

Activity Managers. The strategy for an activity manager, the third level in the hierarchy shown in Figure 1, is more difficult to generalize about because complex corporations organize their businesses in diverse ways. The principal subordinates of a business manager may be responsible for a major functional area such as manufacturing or sales, a portion of the product line, a geographical area, or some combination of the three. We will use two examples, a product line manager and a functional manager, to illustrate the elements of strategy at the activity manager level.

The first thing to be said about an activity manager of either sort is that his job is where the action is. The scope of his position is, of course, even more proscribed than that of the business manager to whom he reports and the statement of strategy that he drafts as a guide to his activities is accordingly more specific. However, it is the activity manager who must devise and execute the set of actions that will serve to implement the business strategy and, ultimately, the corporate strategy. The need for an activity manager to have a strategy of his own, to develop and maintain his own sense of perspective, is every bit as great as it is for his higher-ranking counterparts.

The objectives of an activity manager must be stated in terms that are appropriate to the nature of his assigned task. A product line manager's objectives might include market share, the rate of growth in sales and profitability, profit margins, and/or the image of the product in the market place. A functional manager's objectives might include costs and productivity, quality and customer service, and/or performance along these dimensions vis-à-vis competitors. For either type of activity manager, the critical characteristics of objectives defined earlier still apply; objectives are externally focused and stated in terms of the relative performance of this activity compared to similar activities performed by others.

For the activity manager the constraints/policies element of strategy is, as it was for the corporate and business managers, the most challenging aspect of strategy formulation. The product line manager's responsibility is to analyze the opportunities and to pick those that are best suited to achieve his objectives. He does this by developing a statement of constraints or priorities concerning the breadth of his product line. In it, he delineates the current and future scope and balance among the various products for which he is responsible.

Similarly, a functional manager also needs to develop a set of self-imposed constraints and policies concerning the scope of his activity. A useful concept here is that of "value added." For a functional manager, the essential question is, "What is the strategically optimal degree of vertical integration within my activity?" A manager in charge of manufacturing must worry about the strategic question of backward integration: can he capture some of the profits of his suppliers efficiently enough to increase the contribution of the manufacturing function to the business? The sales manager's analogous question concerns forward integration: to what extent could the contribution from his activity increase if he attempted to perform some of the functions now performed by others in the distribution chain between him and the ultimate consumer? Careful analysis of opportunities against resources is required to answer these questions and lead to a strategic determination of the limits on the scope of a functional activity.

Finally, the third element of every activity manager's strategy is the set of action programs that he would propose to undertake in order to implement his strategy. The necessary resources are always scarce. Therefore, priorities must be established and, in order to determine a rational sequence of actions, the performance implications of alternative sequences must be examined. Priorities will surely change as events and new opportunities unfold but, for the time at which it is made, the activity manager's strategy expresses both what he is trying to do and how he proposes to do it.

Each of the descriptions above describes the process of strategy formulation by an individual manager as though it were a neatly chronological, three-step sequence. As a practical matter, delineating a strategy is not as pedestrian as outlined, but neither is it cataclysmic in the sense of leaping full-blown from the manager's mind in one great surge of creative insight. However, the elements of a manager's strategy are related to each other, and Figure 3 is an attempt to illustrate that schematically.

FIGURE 3
Strategy for an Individual Manager

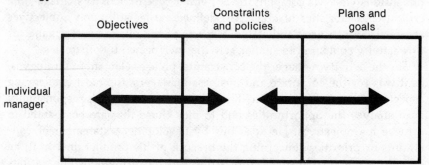

As noted above, the most critical element in strategy formulation is that of constraints/policies. Objectives are rarely specified without recognizing their implications on the scope of a manager's activities. Similarly, the availability of an attractive action plan may lead to a modification of strategic constraints in order to legitimatize pursuing that action. Thus, we can see that constructing a cohesive statement embracing all three elements of strategy is a creative, evolutionary process. Plans and goals are expected to change over time; major policies, constraints on scope, and even objectives for the activity will also change, although the rate of evolution should be somewhat slower.

The discussion thus far has emphasized the fact that strategy must be a personalized statement enunciated by an individual manager. The fact that there may be hundreds of such managers in a complex organization does not diminish the need for personal analysis and strategic choice within the confines of each manager's positional responsibility. At the same time one would hope that the strategy of a large corporation is something more than a simple melange of independently derived statements by individuals. It is, in fact, the need to coordinate and integrate these individual statements that makes the task of strategy formulation in a complex organization so difficult.

Strategic Interrelationships

Referring back to Figure 2 and reading it vertically this time, a different picture of strategy in a complex organization emerges. Each manager, working individually, should develop his own statement of strategy, but it is quickly obvious that these statements must still make sense when they are arranged hierarchically. Figure 4 is a schematic attempt to represent the nature of these interrelationships.

The cells depicted in Figure 4 have been numbered for easy reference in correspondence to the sequence of discussion in the preceding section. It is important to point out here that constructing such a strategic grid for a complex organization is not a chronological sequence involving nine steps. The grid is actually put together like a mosaic and, in order to see how the pieces fit together, we will examine the major elements of strategy within this context.

Objectives.   The citizenship and personality objectives of a corporation in Cell 1 are the only free-standing element of strategy in the entire grid, and yet even corporate management does not have carte blanche. Articulating objectives of this sort will be effective only if they represent a codification of the values shared by most members of the organization. The value of a statement of strategy under these conditions is two-fold: (1) it reinforces and crystallizes the nature and extent to which values are shared in the organization, and (2) it makes it somewhat easier for a prospective new member of the organization to decide whether he wishes to join it or not. Generally, as the range of diversity of a corporation's activities increases, the breadth of the values shared by all members of the corporation will decrease. Thus, a highly diverse conglomerate may not state corporate-level objectives of this sort, although such statements might be quite appropriate in some of the businesses in that corporation.

The determination of corporate financial objectives, on the other hand,

FIGURE 4
Hierarchical Strategic Relationships

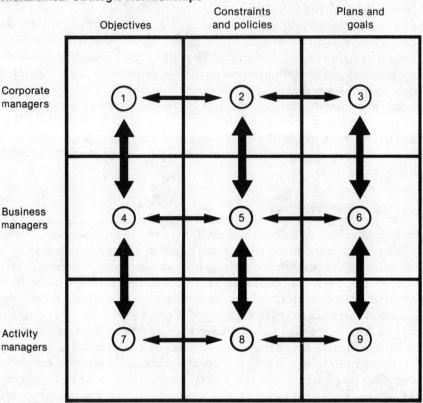

is clearly not independent of other elements in the strategic grid. The relationship between Cells 1 and 2 has already been noted but, as Figure 4 makes clear, there is also a relationship between Cells 1 and 4. The financial performance objectives for a diversified corporation must relate to the performance objectives for each of the underlying businesses. Perhaps less obvious is the link between Cells 2 and 4, but the importance of that link becomes clear when the problem is viewed from the perspective of one of the business managers in the corporation. He cannot set performance objectives for his business without knowing something about corporate-level constraints and policies regarding diversification. How important is his business in the eyes of corporate managers? How tightly constrained should he expect to be in expanding the scope of his business? He answers these questions by defining the industry and his niche in it (Cell 5), but the delineation of his objectives is directly affected by both of the first two elements of corporate-level strategy.

Similarly, the objectives for any one of the activity managers reporting to a business manager are affected by their hierarchical relationship. The direct link between Cells 4 and 7 is only part of the story; an activity manager's objectives must recognize the constraints and policies that the business manager has specified in Cell 5. An activity manager uses his superior's constraint/policy statement for guidance in drafting an analogous statement of the limits on the scope of his own activity (Cell 8), but that same guidance is also a direct input to the activity manager's thinking as he attempts to enunciate his long-run, externally-oriented objectives.

Constraints and Policies. The difficulty of preparing an integrated set of statements of strategy is compounded when we turn to the critical task of delineating a progressive series of constraints on the scope of the organization's activities. At first glance, the integration of this element of strategy in a complex organization might appear to be as simple as following the vertical arrows in the center column of Figure 4. As a practical matter, tying these elements of strategy together is much more involved than that.

The focal point in preparing an integrated strategy is the statement in which each business manager defines his industry and his niche in it. This is the center cell in the strategic grid in Figure 4. It affects, and is affected by, many other elements of strategy. The corporate-level statement of the types of industries that the corporation will participate in (Cell 2) cannot be prepared in a vacuum; corporate managers must understand what opportunities exist in their current businesses before they can decide how to affect the future mix of businesses. Those decisions, set forth tentatively as corporate plans and goals (Cell 3), have an important, and not unintended, side effect. A business manager, trying to delineate his current and future niche in an industry, must have some idea of the magnitude of corporate resources that can be made available to his business over time. Thus, there is a direct link between Cell 5 and Cell 3, which affects the business manager's thinking about the potential scope of his business. The determination of his own plans and goals (Cell 6) also helps him to determine a reasonable set of constraints on his business.

In a similar fashion, the constraints and policies adopted by an activity manager are affected not only by the scope of the business as a whole but also by his superior's tentative plans for the utilization of resources available to the business (Cell 6). Thus, there is a direct relationship between Cell 8 and Cell 6 with regard to the availability of resources for the activity, as well as a relationship between Cells 8 and 9 which concerns how those resources might be used.

Plans and Goals. Finally, the last and most tangible element of strategy, the plans and goals at each level in the hierarchy, must also be integrated. Compared to the complex interrelationships described above, the task of integrating plans is relatively straightforward. The vertical

98

arrows in the last column of Figure 4 point in both directions; the tentative allocation of corporate resources cannot be made without knowing how those resources would be used in each of the businesses, and a business manager cannot plan the use of his resources without knowing what his activity managers expect to accomplish. An activity manager's planning horizon is shorter than that of his superiors. His plans are more action-oriented and definitive, and his performance goals are frequently treated as personal commitments that can and will be achieved. At the business and corporate levels, plans and goals beyond the next year or two are more fluid; tentative plans are needed to express the other elements of strategy in a more tangible form and thus to provide guidance to subordinates. Still, all the managers involved must know that the plans will change over time.

The Strategy Formulation Process. Figure 5 is a graphic representation of the interrelationships discussed above. The heavy, lateral arrows in that chart are intended to emphasize the complex way that the various elements of each manager's strategy are tied together. Even so, the chart

FIGURE 5
The Strategy Formulation Process

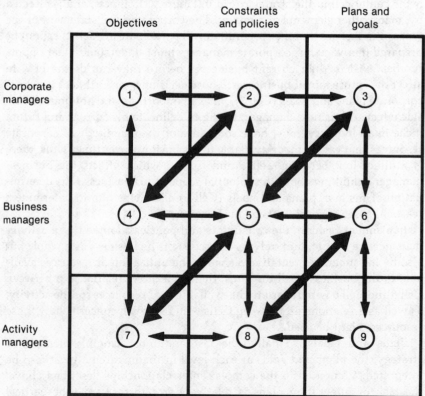

understates the extent of the interrelationships. There are several business managers and perhaps several dozen activity managers in a complex organization. Thus, a three-dimensional chart would really be required to express all the interrelationships.

Formulating, revising, or revalidating strategy is more than a task of individual economic analysis and personal soul-searching. In a complex organization, it is also an interactive, iterative process. Dozens, literally hundreds, of two-person agreements must be negotiated, many of them almost simultaneously. The process is never completed because the agreements continue to change and evolve. Each manager, from time to time, may attempt to express his strategy in a written statement, but it is a rare, and very temporary, event for all the managers in a complex organization to develop such statements at the same point in time. On the other hand, organizing the efforts of all managers in the organization to attempt such an undertaking can be extremely valuable, and this is really the primary purpose of formal planning systems.

Summary

Strategy is the conceptual glue that binds the diverse activities of a complex organization together. To be effective, strategy must personally affect each manager, constraining the scope of his activities to some extent yet providing him with enough elbow room to devise his own strategy within the broader context. In such organizations it is not very useful to think about *the* strategy. Rather, one should think of the strategy as a collection of strategies, one for each manager, linked together by a progressive series of agreements on objectives, constraints and policies, and plans and goals. Each manager must have *a* strategy in which he believes and which is compatible with the strategies of his superiors, his peers, and his subordinates.

This complex web of strategies is rarely enunciated as explicitly and comprehensively as has been described here. Most of the two-party hierarchical agreements that are required take the form of an implicit understanding between a manager and one of his subordinates. The value of explicit strategies goes beyond the simple fact that a conscious choice among strategic alternatives is likely to be better than an intuitive choice. The process of formulating explicit strategies affects both the quality of the resulting choice and the likelihood that the chosen strategy will be implemented successfully. A good formal planning system is designed to provide orderly processes that permit complex organizations to achieve all three of these benefits.

3

IDENTIFYING STRATEGIC ALTERNATIVES

Markets are not created by God, nature, or economic forces but by businessmen.

Peter F. Drucker

Every organization ought to be wary of becoming a prisoner of its present strategy. Sooner or later all strategies grow stale or obsolete. They need either fine-tuning, major overhaul, or radical surgery. Thus, while it is by no means necessary for the incumbent strategic plan to be shoved aside in favor of new, "creative" alternatives each time the issue of strategy review arises, an alert management will guard against letting strategic reevaluation be little more than a time for finding clever variations to what it is already doing.

The real purpose behind regular reappraisal of strategy is to help avoid the complacency of viewing the prevailing strategy as too much of a given rather than only one among several viable, and perhaps more attractive, possibilities. True, taking an entrepreneurial approach to strategy reformulation raises a possibility that the existing strategy will be deemphasized; this may threaten those in the organization who have vested interests in the current strategic plan. But for an enterprise which aspires to continued success and high performance, this is the way things must be. Imaginative strategy formulation and reformulation is virtually a prerequisite for sustained high performance. Nostalgic and inopportune adherence to existing strategy merely paves the way for other organizations which, lacking a strategy, will surely be less reluctant to formulate one if they view the entrenched firm's strategy as vulnerable to attack. For this reason alone, a strong commitment to regular strategic reappraisal and, further, to creative identification of strategic alternatives is an essential ingredient of entrepreneurially effective management.

As we have indicated, corporate strategies and business strategies are two very different animals. Business strategy relates to how an enterprise intends to conduct its business for a particular product, product line, or group of related products. It specifically is concerned with how to compete effectively and profitably in a distinct, identifiable, and strategically relevant line of business. On the other hand, corporate strategy is most relevant to diversified organizations whose activities cut across several lines of business and thus pose to management the ever-present issue of "what set of businesses should we be in—what should we continue to do, what existing businesses should we get out of, and what new businesses should we get into?" Corporate strategy aims at making a workable whole out of diverse activities and at giving directions to the total mix of organizational activities. For a single-product, single-market, single-technology enterprise, corporate strategy and business strategy turn out to be the same, because there is only one line of business to be managed and directed. But today many organizations, and certainly most medium and large corporations, are diversified, thereby making the distinction between corporate and business strategy managerially relevant. In identifying and discussing the various strategic alternatives open to an enterprise, it is therefore desirable to consider two levels of strategic alternatives: those of corporate strategy and those of business strategy. We begin with corporate strategy.

THE BASIC ALTERNATIVES OF CORPORATE STRATEGY

In trying to decide on an overall strategy to accomplish its chosen purpose and objectives, an organization has essentially nine basic corporate strategy options to select from (either singly or in combination):

1. Concentration on a single business.
2. Vertical integration.
3. Concentric diversification.
4. Conglomerate diversification.
5. Merger and acquisition.
6. Joint ventures.
7. Retrenchment.
8. Divestiture.
9. Liquidation.

Each of these merits discussion.

Concentration on a Single Business

The number of organizations which have made their mark parlaying a single-product, single-market, or single-technology strategy is impressively long. The power and achievement which attaches to concentrating on the right business at the right time is testified to by the blue-chip strategic performance of such familiar companies as McDonald's, Holiday Inn, Coca-Cola, BIC Pen Corp., Campbell Soup Co., Anheuser-Busch, Xerox, Dr. Pepper, Gerber, and Polaroid.[1]

A concentration strategy offers numerous strengths and advantages. To begin with, a specialized business is more manageable. Simplicity breeds clarity and unity of purpose. With the efforts of the *total* organization aimed at successfully catering to a clearly identified target clientele, objectives can be made precise and results appraised more easily. Managers can have first-hand, in-depth knowledge of the business, the market, the organization, its customers, its technology, and major competitors. As a consequence, there is a better chance that the organization's productivity and overall efficiency can become above average, if not superior. The outcome of a concentration strategy, therefore, can be an organization with good ability to:

1. Focus on doing *one* thing *very well,* thereby building a distinctive competence.
2. Zero in on specific markets and market segments, thus gaining greater market visibility and even a leadership position.
3. Avoid the temptation to spread limited organizational resources over many different activities.
4. Detect changes and trends in customer purchasing behavior and market conditions at an early stage and respond quickly to them.
5. Achieve a high degree of efficiency in meeting stiffer competition and in reacting to new market opportunities.
6. Create a differential strategic advantage via the market reputation and the competitive strength that come from having a distinctive competence.

The advantages of a concentration strategy cannot be taken lightly. That they are well recognized and important is acknowledged by the widespread attempt of diversified firms to decentralize their activities into well-defined lines of business so that a concentration strategy can be successfully pursued. The market viability of a concentration strategy is also suggested by the fact the managers of large diversified companies often view their strongest competitors as being smaller, specialized enterprises with concentrated, in-depth expertise in particular products and market segments. When a given product or customer group is only one among many of a company's interests, it may not receive the same degree of attention and management priority as when it is the organization's sole business.

---

[1] In the nonprofit sector the specialist strategy has proved successful for the Boston Pops Orchestra, the Red Cross, the Girl Scouts, Phi Beta Kappa, and the American Civil Liberties Union.

It is important to recognize that a concentration strategy does not require an enterprise to continue doing the same thing in the same ways. There are numerous options for varying and fine-tuning a concentration strategy. One option is to pursue ways to gain greater market penetration of the present product line. This could include one or more of the following:

1. Trying to increase current customers' usage of the product by
   a. Increasing the size of units offered for sale,
   b. Incorporating more features into the basic unit,
   c. Creating and promoting more uses for the product,
   d. Using innovation to shorten the time span for the product to become obsolete, and
   e. Giving price discounts for increased use.
2. Endeavoring to attract customers away from rival firms via
   a. Increased advertising and promotional efforts,
   b. Sharper product differentiation and brand identification, and
   c. Lower prices.
3. Attracting nonusers to buy products by
   a. Inducing trial use through free samples, cents-off coupons, and low introductory price offers,
   b. Advertising new or different product uses and features, and
   c. Repricing the product—up or down.

A second option is to expand into additional geographic markets—regional, national, or international. A third approach is to improve product quality, convenience of use, customer services, and the like. A fourth set of options entails developing new product features and catering to distinct buyer preferences via any of the following:

1. Offering a wider variety of models and sizes.
2. Distributing the product line through other types of distribution channels.
3. Advertising in different kinds of media.
4. Developing new or different product features (by making the item shorter, lighter, smaller, stronger, thicker, longer, or more durable; or by changing the item's color, odor, taste, sound, components, styling, design, or packaging—as may be appropriate).

The corporate strategy of concentrating on a single business does pose a major business risk, however. By specializing, an enterprise puts all of its eggs in one basket. If the market for the enterprise's product or service declines, so does the enterprise's business. Changing customer needs, technological innovation, or new products can undermine or virtually wipe out a highly specialized, single-business firm in short order. One has only to recall what television did to the profitability and markets of the once-powerful Hollywood movie producers and what IBM electric typewriters did to the manual typewriter business formerly dominated by Royal-McBee, Underwood, and Smith Corona. And if the product/service is particularly vulnerable to recessionary influence in the economy, then the enterprises's fortunes are subject to wide swings and, consequently, a normally lower stock market appraisal.

Furthermore, by concentrating its expertise in a narrow area, an organization may find itself without the competence and know-how to break out of its shell and develop alternatives if and when the time arrives to cast off a fast-obsolescing strategic plan. Every product, every service, every technology eventually loses its market grip.[2] Sales volume may still be there, but profitability and growth opportunities shrivel. If the specialist firm is to escape stagnation, it must keep some fresh options open. And like any habit, doing something new and different must be kept sharp by practice. Otherwise the capacity for shifting to new strategies and new businesses either never develops or withers away.

Vertical Integration[3]

Two factors tend to trigger serious corporate-level consideration of a vertical integration strategy: (1) diminishing profit prospects associated with further expansion of the main product line into new geographic markets and (2) being the wrong size to realize scale economies and performance potentials. Market saturation and the impracticalities of an oversize market coverage give rise to the first factor cited. A variety of causes underlie being the wrong size but the symptom is easy enough to spot: one (or a few) of the organization's production or distribution activities are out of proportion to the remainder, thereby making it difficult for the organization to support the volume, the product line, or the market standing requisite for economical operations and long-run competitive survival.[4]

Vertical integration has much to recommend itself as a strategy for dealing with these two factors. Consider first the benefits of integrating backward. To begin with, backward integration offers the potential for converting a cost center into a profit producer. This potential may be very attractive when suppliers have wide profit markets. Moreover, inte-

---

2 It has been estimated that eighty percent of today's products will have disappeared from the market ten years from now and that eighty percent of the products which will be sold in the next decade are as yet unknown. See E. E. Scheuing, *New Product Management* (Hinsdale, Ill.: The Dryden Press, 1974), p. 1.

3 This section draws heavily from Arthur A. Thompson, *Economics of the Firm: Theory and Practice*, 2d ed. (Englewood Cliffs, N.J.: Prentice-Hall, Inc., 1977), chap. 2.

4 Peter F. Drucker, *Management: Tasks, Responsibilities, Practices* (New York: Harper and Row Publishers, 1974), pp. 666–67.

grating backward allows a firm to supercede market uncertainties associated with supplies of raw materials. Where a firm is dependent on a particular raw material or service furnished by other enterprises, the door is always open for requisite supplies to be disrupted by strikes, bad weather, production breakdowns, or delays in scheduled deliveries. Furthermore, the cost structure is vulnerable to untimely increases in the prices of critical component materials. Stockpiling, fixed-price contracts, or the use of substitute inputs may not be feasible ways for dealing with such market uncertainties. When this is the case, bringing supplies and costs under its own wings may be an organization's most profitable option for securing *reliable deliveries* of essential inputs at *reliable prices*. In short, sparing itself the uncertainties of being dependent on suppliers permits an organization to coordinate and routinize its operating cycle, thereby (1) avoiding the transient, but upsetting, influences of unreliable suppliers and wide swings in supply prices, (2) realizing the cost efficiencies of a stable operating pattern, and (3) insulating itself from the tactical maneuvers of other firms regarding raw material sources. In so doing, an organization can become more a master of its own destiny than a slave to fortuitous market circumstances beyond its control.

While backward integration may be justified by an economic need to assure sources of supply, it may also be the best and most practical way to obtain a workable degree of commitment from suppliers. The case of Sears offers a prime example.[5] A large portion of the merchandise which Sears sells is made by manufacturers in which Sears has an ownership interest. While this may be due to Sears' desire to "control" its suppliers, it is as probable that Sears found it could not get reputable suppliers to commit themselves to making goods especially for Sears unless assured of a long-term relationship. The reason is simple: for a firm to become the chief supplier of one of Sears' big-ticket or volume items is likely to make Sears the supplier's main customer and major channel of distribution. For a supplier to allow itself to become a "captive company" of Sears without some sort of guarantee that the relationship would be a continuing one would be foolhardy and unduly risky. Thus for Sears to get major suppliers to forgo their independence and agree to orient most or all of their business of manufacturing products to Sears' specifications, to be sold under Sears' brand names, and to be delivered according to Sears' demands very likely meant in some cases that Sears had to go beyond the offering of a "long-term" contract. Without ties as permanent as those of ownership, some key suppliers would surely have balked and Sears would have found itself with unwanted gaps in its product line. Given Sears' merchandising strategy, being the "wrong size" to assure itself of ample suppliers at constant quality and reasonable cost would have been a serious strategic flaw.

---

[5] Ibid., p. 686.

The strategic impetus for forward integration has much the same roots. Undependable sales and distribution channels can give rise to costly inventory pileups and frequent production shutdowns, thereby undermining the economies of stable production operations. Loss of these economies may make it imperative for an organization to gain stronger market access in order to remain competitive. Sometimes even a few percentage point increases in the average rate of capacity utilization can make a substantial difference in price and profitability.

For a raw materials producer, integrating forward into manufacturing may help achieve greater product differentiation and thus allow for increased profit margins. In the early phases of the vertical product flow, intermediate goods are "commodities," that is they have essentially identical technical specifications irrespective of producer (wheat, coal, sheet steel, cement, sulfuric acids, newsprint). Competition is extremely price-oriented. Yet, the closer the production stage is to the ultimate consumer, the greater are the opportunities for a firm to differentiate its end product via design, service, quality features, packaging, promotion, and so on. Marketing activities become more critical and the importance of price shrinks in comparison to other competitive variables.

For a manufacturer, integrating forward may take the form of building a chain of closely supervised dealer franchises or it may mean establishing company-owned and operated retail outlets. Alternatively, it could entail simply staffing regional and district sales offices instead of selling through manufacturer's agents or independent distributors. Whatever its specific format, forward integration is usually motivated by a desire to realize the higher profits that come with stable production, large-scale distribution, and product differentiation and to enjoy the security that comes with having one's own capability for accessing markets and customers.

There is, however, one other aspect of vertical integration which warrants mention. The large size that accompanies full integration puts a firm in a position to exert a measure of monopolistic control over its costs, its selling prices, its production technology, and its customers' buying propensities and attitudes. Size breeds power, and power gives management latitude in making decisions and setting policies. For instance, to the degree that an integrated firm is self-sufficient at each of the intermediate stages of the production process, it is also partially insulated from the impacts of competition and short-run price-quantity adjustments in the intermediate goods markets. Such freedom is not without design or social import. Max Weber, years ago, observed how complex organizations, moved by an instinct for self-protection and risk avoidance, acted to construct devices that would shield them from unwanted change while, at the same time, promoting a degree of order and stability conducive to achieving peak efficiency and profitability. Needless to say, the competitive latitude and discretion conferred on management by large size and market power merit close social scrutiny, if not outright attack, for it is a virtual certainty that an organization will have occasions to use them to serve its own interests.

Aside from the obvious social disadvantages that *may* accrue from extensive vertical integration, there are internal organizational shortcomings as well. The large capital requirements of vertical integration may place a heavy strain on an organization's financial resources. Second, integration introduces more complexity into the mangement process. It requires new skills and the assumption of additional risks since the effect is to extend the enterprise's scope of operations. It means bearing the burdens of learning a new business and coping with the problems of a larger organization. While this may all be justified if it remedies a disparity between costs and profits, it can so increase a firm's vested interests in its technology and production facilities that it becomes reluctant to abandon its heavy fixed investments. Because of this inflexibility a fully integrated firm is vulnerable to new technologies and new products. Either it has to write off large portions of its fixed investments or else it must endure a competitive disadvantage with innovative enterprises having no proprietary interests to protect.

Moreover, integration can pose problems of balancing capacity at each production stage. The most efficient sizes at each phase of the vertical product flow can be at substantial variance. Exact self-sufficiency at each interface is the exception not the rule. Where internal capacity is deficient to supply the next stage, the difference will have to be bought externally. Where internal capacity is excessive, customers will need to be found for the surplus. And if by-products are generated, they will require arrangements for disposal.

All in all, vertical integration strategy has both important strengths and weaknesses. Which direction the scales tip on integration depends on (1) how compatible it is with organization purpose and objectives, (2) whether it strengthens an organization's position in its primary business, and (3) whether it permits fuller exploitation of an organization's technical talents. Unless these issues are answered in the affirmative, vertical integration is likely to be an unattractive corporate strategy option.

Corporate Diversification Strategies

A number of wide-ranging factors account for the appeal of corporate diversification:

1. An organization may consider diversification because market saturation, competitive pressures, product line obsolescence, declining demand, or fear of antitrust action no longer allow performance goals to be met solely through an expansion of its current product-market activities.

2. Even if appealing expansion opportunities still exist in its current busi-

ness, an organization may diversify because its free cash flow exceeds the cash needs of expansion.

3. An organization's diversification opportunities may have a greater expected profitability than that of expanding its present business.

4. An organization may consider diversification because of a desire to spread risk and increase the stability and security of its operations. This desire may stem from uneasiness about "overspecialization" in particular products or technologies, the risks of having a disproportionately large fraction of sales to a single customer, dwindling supplies of a key raw material, the threat of new technologies, or vulnerability to swings in the economy.

5. A firm may diversify because of a perceived financial serendipity associated with certain kinds of acquisitions. This search for financial-related advantages is said to account for (a) attempts by firms with depressed earnings to diversify into areas of higher average earnings performance level, (b) the pursuit of "instantaneous profits" whereby an acquiring firm buys out firms having lower pre-merger price-earnings ratios in an effort to immediately realize a higher stock price and earnings per share, and (c) the attempt to increase one's access to capital by acquiring enterprises with large cash flows and/or low debt to equity ratios. In such instances, the market and technology aspects of an acquisition appear secondary to the financial considerations.

6. An organization may pursue diversification because owners/managers enjoy the challenges of something new and something different.[6]

One viewpoint even goes so far as to make diversification a condition of survival: "In the long run an organization must diversify or die."[7] The argument here is that a concentration strategy easily falls victim to the new obsoleting the old. Be that as it may, the wealth of organizational experiences with diversification strategies clearly demonstrates that there is *right* diversification and *wrong* diversification.[8] Drucker's analogy to the musician illustrates the point well:

> An accomplished and well-established concert pianist will as a matter of course, add one new major piece to his repertoire each year. Every few years he will pick for his new piece something quite different from the repertoire through which he has made his name. This forces him to learn again, to hear new things in old and familiar pieces, and to become a better pianist altogether. At the same time, concert pianists have long known that

---

[6] H. Igor Ansoff, *Corporate Strategy* (New York: McGraw-Hill, 1965), pp. 129–30; Drucker, *Management*, p. 684; George A. Steiner, "Why and How to Diversify," *California Management Review*, vol. 6, no. 4 (Summer 1964), pp. 11–17; J. F. Weston and S. F. Mansinghka, "Tests of the Efficiency of Performance of Conglomerate Firms," *Journal of Finance*, vol. 26, no. 4 (September 1971), pp. 919–36; and Ronald W. Melicher and David F. Rush, "Evidence on the Acquisition-Related Performance of Conglomerate Firms," *Journal of Finance*, vol. 29, no. 1 (March 1974), pp. 141–49.

[7] George A. Steiner, "Why and How to Diversify," p. 12.

[8] Peter F. Drucker, *Management*, p. 692.

they slough off an old piece as they add on one new major one. The total size of the repertoire remains the same. There are only so many pieces of music even the greatest pianist can play with excellence.[9]

If and when corporate diversification appears on the strategy agenda, the question of what kind of diversification—how exactly to apply the musician's rule—becomes paramount.

There are two basic kinds of corporate diversification: *concentric* and *conglomerate*. Concentric diversification is *related* diversification; that is, the organization's lines of business, although distinct, still possess some meaningful kind of strategic fit. In concentric diversification, the related nature of the various lines of business can be keyed to common technology, customer usage, distribution channels, methods of operation, managerial know-how, or product similarity—virtually any strategically meaningful facet. In contrast, conglomerate diversification is *unrelated* or *pure* diversification; there is no common thread or element of true strategic fit among the organization's several lines of business.

Concentric Diversification Strategies. Concentric diversification tends to be an attractive corporate strategy. It allows an enterprise to preserve a common core of unity in its business activities, while at the same time spreading the risks out over a broader product base. But more importantly, perhaps, concentric diversification has the advantage of allowing an organization to make the most out of its distinctive competence in related areas.

Specific types of concentric diversification include:

1. Moving into closely related products (a bread bakery getting into saltine crackers).
2. Building upon company technology or know-how (a synthetic fibers manufacturer diversifying into the production of carpets).
3. Seeking to increase plant utilization (a coarse paper bag manufacturer deciding to utilize excess paper-making capacity by adding corrugated paperboard boxes to its product line).
4. Utilizing available sources of raw materials (a lumber products firm elects to devote some of its timberland to plywood production).
5. Making fuller utilization of the firm's sales force (a wholesaler of electrical supplies adds electric heating and cooling equipment to its line of products.
6. Building on the organization's brand name and goodwill (a successful coffee firm diversifies into tea).

Numerous actual examples abound. Procter & Gamble has been eminently successful in building a diversified product line (Crest toothpaste,

---

[9] Ibid., p. 685.

Ivory Snow, Tide, Duncan Hines cake mixes, Folger's coffee, Pringles potato chips, Head and Shoulder's shampoo, Crisco shortening, Comet cleanser, Charmin toilet tissue, to mention a few) around its expertise in marketing household products through supermarket channels. Pepsi-Cola practiced concentric diversification when it bought Frito-Lay, Pizza Hut, and Taco Bell, as did Coca-Cola in purchasing Minute Maid orange juice and Taylor wine, and Lockheed in encircling the needs of the Department of Defense with its product lines of airframes, rocket engines, missiles, electronics, defense research and development, and shipbuilding. Sears learned that the diverse nature of TV sets, auto repair centers, men's suits, draperies, refrigerators, paint, and homeowner's insurance posed no difficulty to its corporate strategy because the same customer buys them, in very much the same way, and with the same value expectations, thereby providing the essential link for its version of customer-based concentric diversification.

Technology-based concentric diversification has proven successful in process industries (steel, aluminum, paper, and glass), where a single processing technique spawns a multitude of related products. The same paper machines which produce newsprint are equally adept at turning out stationery, notebook paper, and specialty printing paper for books and magazines. The line of products emerging from a single steel mill might include sheet steel, steel rails, reinforcing rods, I-beams, metal door frames, and wire products.

Other firms (in chemicals and electronics particularly) have pursued a technology-linked diversification strategy because their expertise in a given scientific area led to the discovery of new technological branches having practical market application. Often, in the early stages of a major technology, it is not feasible to exploit an innovation fully by concentrating on just one of a few product markets. Simultaneous, or else closely-sequenced, R&D efforts into several product areas may be optimal.[10]

A further indication of the use and preference for concentric diversification strategies is shown in Illustration Capsule 9.

Conglomerate Diversification Strategies. While one might expect an

---

[10] However, beyond some stage the progressive branching out of a common technology can spread an enterprise so thin and push it in so many different directions that further technological-based diversification dilutes what once was clear advantage. According to Peter Drucker:

> That this might be the case is indicated by the fact that most of these giant extended technological families have a few areas in which they have strength and maintain their leadership position: GE and Westinghouse in heavy electrical apparatus, Philips in consumer electronics, Union Carbide in metallurgical chemistry, DuPont in textile fibers and so on. In these areas they also maintain their innovative capacity. The reason for the relative sluggishness and vulnerability of these companies is not "poor management" but "spotty management." It is not that they are in too few "good" businesses but that they are in too many that do not "fit."

See Drucker, *Management*, p. 705.

overwhelming majority of organizations to favor concentric diversification because of the greater likelihood of good strategic fit, the conglomerate strategy has nonetheless attracted some important companies. A simple criterion of "will it meet our minimum standard for expected profitability?" captures the essence of the corporate strategy of such firms as Textron, Whittaker, ITT, Litton, Gulf and Western, U.S. Industries, Fuqua Industries, and Northwest Industries.

However, other organizations have opted for the conglomerate approach because their distinctive competence either was so narrow as to have little in common with other businesses or was so lacking in depth that any diversification move was inherently conglomerate in nature. Still others have viewed a conglomerate approach as the optimal way of escaping a declining industry or overdependence on a single product-market area. Possible options for conglomerate diversification strategies include:

1. Seeking a match between a cash-rich, opportunity-poor company and an opportunity-rich, cash-poor firm.

2. Diversifying into areas with a counterseasonal or countercyclical sales pattern so as to smooth out sales and profit fluctuations.

3. Attempting to merge an opportunity-poor, skill-rich company with an opportunity-rich, skill-poor enterprise.

4. Seeking out a marriage of a highly leveraged firm and a debt-free firm so as to balance the capital structure of the former and increase its borrowing capacity.

5. Gaining entry into new product markets via licensing agreements or purchase of manufacturing or distribution rights.

6. Acquiring any firm in any line of business so long as the projected profit opportunities equal or exceed minimum criteria.

Aside from the pros and cons of being in businesses not having either a common thread or strategic fit, a purely conglomerate diversification strategy has several other advantages and limitations which should be set forth. First, a conglomerate strategy can lead to improved sales, profits, and growth when an organization diversifies into industries where the economic potential is stronger than its existing businesses. However, an organization should beware of being blinded by promising opportunities. Sooner or later every business gets into trouble. Thus, whenever management contemplates either acquisition or grass-roots diversification it should ask "If the new business got into trouble, would we know how to bail it out?" If the answer is no, it is surely diversification of the wrong kind even though the lure of above-average profitability seems to exist.[11]

---

[11] Of course, management may be willing to assume the risk that trouble will not strike before it has had time to learn the business well enough to bail it out of most any difficulty. See Drucker, *Management*, p. 709.

Second, despite the fact that its consolidated performance may improve, the price which a conglomerate pays to buy its way into a growth industry may impair stockholder earnings. This holds whether diversification takes place from within or through acquisition since some kind of $2 + 2 = 5$ effect is frequently needed to offset the premium price paid to get into the business. The high price-earnings multiples which many conglomerates have paid for their acquisitions, as well as the millions of dollars of purchased "goodwill" which appear on corporate financial statements, are ample evidence of the added costs of "buying in."

Third, unless some kind of $2 + 2 = 5$ benefits can be developed, the consolidated performance of a conglomerate enterprise will tend to be no better than if its divisions were independent firms, and it may be worse to the extent that centralized management policies hamstring the operating divisions. This implies that the best which conglomerates can generally expect is to be at no cost/efficiency disadvantage in trying to compete against nonconglomerates.[12] Fourth, although in theory a conglomerate strategy would seem to offer the potential of greater sales-profit stability over the course of the business cycle, in practice the attempts at counter-cyclical diversification appear to have fallen short of the mark. Conglomerate profits have evidenced no propensity to suffer milder reversals in periods of recession and economic stress.[13] In fact, during times of adversity, the staying power of conglomerates appears to be weaker than that of concentrically-diversified firms.[14] Finally, the "financial synergism" of a marriage between businesses with a high cash throw-off and those with a large cash appetite is more often than not an illusion. For a conglomerate strategy to be truly successful, a great deal more strategic fit is needed than money alone (see Illustration Capsule 6).[15]

A Perspective View on Corporate Diversification Strategies. Diversification—whether concentric or conglomerate—can be neither recommended nor condemned per se. Many organizations are actively pursuing diversification strategies of some sort, and doing so for what they view as good and sufficient business reasons. It plainly makes sense for a firm to *consider* diversification when its existing business has been expanded to its

---

[12] Evidence to this effect is given in Stanley E. Boyle, *Economic Report on Conglomerate Merger Performance: An Empirical Analysis of Nine Corporations,* Staff Report to the Federal Trade Commission, reprinted in *Mergers and Acquisitions,* vol. 8, no. 1 (Spring 1973), pp. 5–41; Ronald W. Melicher and David F. Rush, "The Performance of Conglomerate Firms: Recent Risk and Return Experience," *Journal of Finance,* vol. 28, no. 2 (May 1973), pp. 381–88; and Robert L. Coun, "The Performance of Conglomerate Firms: Comment," *Journal of Finance,* vol. 28, no. 3 (June 1973), pp. 754–58.

[13] Drucker, *Management,* p. 767.

[14] See H. I. Ansoff and J. F. Weston, "Merger Objectives and Organization Structure," *Quarterly Review of Economics and Business,* vol. 2, no. 3 (August 1962), pp. 49–58.

[15] Drucker, *Management,* pp. 707–8.

ILLUSTRATION CAPSULE 6
Pillsbury's Shift in Diversification Strategy

During the sixties many companies initiated strategies for broadly diversifying their activities. During the seventies, when it became painfully apparent that many of the newly-acquired businesses were not performing up to expectations or else did not "fit in" very well, a sizeable number of these very same companies changed their strategies from pure diversification to one of related diversification. Pillsbury was one of the companies which retreated from a conglomerate approach to a conceptual approach to diversification.

When William H. Spoor became chairman of the board of Pillsbury in January 1973, he moved quickly to narrow Pillsbury's product base to the area he felt the company knew best—food. In short order Pillsbury moved to divest its low-growth, cyclical business in poultry, its minority housing unit (Pentom Builders), its interest in magazine publishing (*Bon Appetit*), its computer services business, and its money-losing wine business (Souverain Winery). Mr. Spoor was quoted as saying, "I am only interested in businesses that fall into three categories. We should only be in consumer foods, food away from home, and agriproducts."

Pillsbury's original base of businesses from which it first launched its diversification efforts consisted of flour milling (it is the largest miller in the U.S.), producing bakery mixes (some 300 varieties), commodity merchandising, grain exports, and grocery items for consumers (including flour, cake mixes and frostings, pancake mix, quick bread mixes, and a wide assortment of refrigerated dough products). Most of these businesses generated healthy profits and cash flows but were in markets where growth was slower. Volume gains, particularly in the consumer products categories, were largely dependent on taking business away from rival brands—a costly process with little prospect of major gains in profitability. This was what motivated the original diversification strategy.

Under its new chairman, Pillsbury's acquisitions took on a more focused direction and reflected the decision to become an international food company participating in the three major areas of agribusiness, household food items, and restaurants. Recent acquisitions bear this out:

1. Wilton Enterprises, Inc. (acquired in 1973)—the nation's leading marketer of cake decorating products.
2. Totino's Pizza (acquired in 1976)—the second largest maker of prepared pizzas, with just over a 20 percent market share.
3. Fox Deluxe Foods (acquired in 1976)—operator of a pizza manufacturing plant in Joplin, Missouri.
4. American Beauty Macaroni Company (acquired in 1977)—manufacturer of a broad line of quality pasta products.

ILLUSTRATION CAPSULE 6 *(continued)*

5. Speas Company (acquired in 1978)—a manufacturer of apple juice, cider vinegar, and pectin.
6. Green Giant Co. (acquired in 1978)—maker of frozen and canned foods.

The Green Giant acquisition represents a major strategic effort by Pillsbury to gain a product mix that would put the company on a par with Kellogg Co. and H. J. Heinz, and to prepare it for a later capability to compete more broadly with General Mills and General Foods. By acquiring Green Giant, Pillsbury gained some strategic leverage in capturing shelf space in supermarkets for Pillsbury's less widely distributed lines (cake decorating sets, Funny Face and Squoze powdered drink mixes, Erasco food products, American Beauty pasta, and Sprinkle Sweet artificial sweetner). Green Giant's canned and frozen foods lines are popular and thus attractive lines for supermarkets to carry. A key to success in gaining distribution through supermarkets is for a manufacturer to have products with dominant first or second positions in fast-growing sales areas—something Pillsbury had not been able to accomplish as well as some other manufacturers. Green Giant products were tagged to fill this gap.

Besides its new acquisitions, Pillsbury has been active for some time in expanding its interests in the restaurant business. In 1967, Burger King Corp. was acquired; this unit is now the company's main revenue producer. When Burger King failed to keep pace with its fast-growing market, Spoor hired the No. 3 man at McDonald's, Donald Smith, to revitalize the chain, specifically, to double the number of outlets and triple earnings by 1983. During the 1973–1978 period, 70 percent of Pillsbury's capital improvement budget, or $385 million, was allocated to the Burger King division. Expansion has also occurred in Pillsbury's Steak and Ale restaurants (some of which operate under the names of Jolly Ox and Bennigan's) where the number of outlets rose from 52 in 1973 to 165 in 1978. At the same time, Pillsbury has pushed forward in expanding its Poppin Fresh Pie Shops business; the number of units open increased from 6 in 1974 to 45 in 1978. The pie shops are mid-priced family restaurants, seating about 135 persons, featuring 27 varieties of pies and offering a limited menu of sandwiches, soups, and salads.

In its *1977 Annual Report*, Pillsbury announced that the current corporate strategy and diversification program were aimed at producing a "repetitive, predictable, and growing" stream of earnings. The company's quantitative targets are (1) an average annual sales growth rate of 10 percent, (2) a minimum annual earnings per share growth rate of 10 percent, (3) a pretax return on average invested capital of 20 percent, (4) an aftertax return on stockholders' equity of 16 percent, and (5) an "A" credit rating.

practical limits and/or when it is severely threatened by outside forces; it may or may not make sense to diversify before this occurs.

In addition, the pros and cons of what kind and how much diversification an organization needs to get the best performance and results weigh differently from case to case. A logical place for an organization's management to begin its evaluation of diversification alternatives is with a consideration of "What is the least diversification we need to attain our objectives and remain a healthy, viable entity, capable of competing successfully?" At the other extreme, though, management is equally obliged to examine the question of "What is the most diversification we can manage, given the complexity it adds?"[16] In all likelihood, the optimal answer lies in between. And after deciding what to include and what to exclude, the next step is to make the diversification strategy specific enough to define the role of each line of business within the total organization. The reverse approach of letting corporate strategy be merely an aggregation of each line of business strategy is risky—it can quickly deteriorate into marching in too many directions at once. Illustration Capsule 7 indicates how Cooper Industries has put together its multi-industry strategy.

The investor disfavor which conglomerates have acquired, the poor performance of several prominent conglomerates, and the serious issue of how to manage a diverse number of businesses effectively have caused many highly diversified firms to avoid or discard the conglomerate label by developing "corporate unity themes." Multiproduct firms have come up with broad labels like leisure-time, high technology, consumer products, materials processing, communication systems, and total service to mask the variety of distinct businesses they operate. The idea seems to be to convey the image of being diversified around a concept ("a conceptually oriented conglomerate") rather than projecting the image of a "pure" or "free-form" conglomerate.

Merger and Acquisition Strategies

A given merger or acquisition can reflect any or all of the three types of strategies previously discussed: it can be motivated by a desire to concentrate on a single business, by a move to integrate vertically, or by an effort at diversification. In this sense, merger/acquisition is not so much a fundamental strategy in its own right as a specific technique for accomplishing the larger target of entry into other businesses. But it is still a distinctive strategic act and one which is often used, sometimes with drama, stress, and marketwide impact. Some firms use merger/acquisition as the exclusive means for entering the business they want to be in. Indeed,

---

[16] Ibid., pp. 692–93.

ILLUSTRATION CAPSULE 7
Strategic Realignment at Cooper Industries

Until 1967, Cooper Industries was basically a one-product, one-market company making engines and compressors for energy-producing companies. Its business was very cyclical and Cooper's economic forecast indicated that the next downward cycle would be especially steep. As a consequence, Cooper's management decided to put some of the company's eggs into a second basket in an effort to help smooth out the cyclical fluctuations in its main business.

Cooper decided on hand tools as its first diversification move, reasoning that all kinds of people use hand tools—wrenches, pliers, files—year in and year out so that the demand is steady and not very sensitive to major ups and downs of the company. The first hand tool company Cooper acquired was the Lufkin Rule Company, a leading maker of measuring tapes and rules. Interestingly, Lufkin's own strategic plan was to build one strong hand tool company from several smaller, complementary companies. The new company would offer hardware dealers a variety of tools from a single source.

When Cooper acquired Lufkin, two more criteria were set up as a basis for building a well-rounded tool company. In addition to helping Cooper smooth out its earning cycle, any candidates for acquisition would have to:

1. Have a quality image and a first-class brand name, and
2. Be just as interested in joining Cooper as Cooper was in acquiring them.

In going multiindustry, it was Cooper's plan to continue to be an operating company, not just a holding company.

Within a very short time, the Cooper group of tool companies grew to include Lufkin; Crescent wrenches, pliers, and screw drivers; Weller soldering equipment; Nicholson files and saws; and Xcelite Electronics Tools. The sales strategy for Cooper's tool groups became "a single source for five great brands." By 1975 the Cooper tool division was an established leader in the hand tool industry with sales of $164 million.

Not long after Nicholson File became a division of Cooper Industries the decision was made by Nicholson to drop 90 percent of its files from its product line. The reason? As long as Nicholson depended solely on files for its business, it felt it had to offer customers every kind of file imaginable; the strategy was "we've got 'em all." But when Nicholson joined forces with Cooper and became part of a group of companies boasting several top brand names in hand tools, the strategy of carrying every file under the sun became obsolete. Nicholson continues to manufacture almost 2,000 different types of files, including many specialty items. And despite dropping 90 percent of its files, Nicholson's sales and profits increased.

The same principle was applied to all the Cooper Industries' tool companies. Low-margin and low-turnover items were dropped, averaging a 50 percent cut. All the emphasis went behind the bread and butter of the line; sales rose to new heights. Profits also went up for dealers and distrib-

ILLUSTRATION CAPSULE 7 (continued)

utors, owing to a higher turnover of fewer items. At the same time, sales force economies were taken advantage of; five independent hand tool companies needed five salesmen to call on one customer. But when the five companies were put together, only one salesman per customer was required, thereby lowering the cost of selling. Besides combining sales forces, Cooper also combined warehousing, distribution, advertising, merchandising, and paperwork flows. Customers also benefited because they found it more convenient and less expensive to deal with one supplier instead of five.

In addition to the selling advantage of five companies in one, the tool companies benefited from becoming part of a multiindustry organization. For instance, the Energy Services Division of Cooper provided the tool companies with more than $50 million for modernization. Then, in 1975–76, the tool companies returned the favor, providing cash to take advantage of a sharp upswing in the markets for Cooper's energy products.

1971 was a bad year for Cooper's energy divisions and prompted a hard look at each product and each market to make sure it was worth staying in them. One of the decisions Cooper faced was especially tough: whether to keep making centrifugal compressors for certain process industries—mainly ammonia, ethylene, and methanol plants—or to drop out of that market and concentrate on natural gas compression. There were strong arguments on both sides. On the one hand, process industries were growing; to drop out would be to leave an expanding market. In addition, Cooper was a recognized quality leader in the market and Cooper felt that this gave prestige to the Cooper Industries name and professional pride to its engineers.

On the other hand, compressors for these plants required almost total custom design which meant high engineering costs. It also meant that Cooper found it hard to hold down costs by building several identical units, the way they did for the natural gas compression units. Moreover, Cooper Industries did not have as dominant a position in the process market as it had in natural gas compression. So when sales slacked off in the process market, Cooper was among the first companies to feel the squeeze. After a lot of soul-searching, Cooper decided to pull out of its business of making centrifugal compressors for the process industries. It was a controversial decision, but Cooper felt its commitment had to be to the long-term profitability of the company.

The earnings of its energy division went up in 1972 despite the fact that sales fell even lower because of the decision to get out of centrifugal compressors. In 1976, Cooper boasted that the changes that were made in 1971 were really beginning to pay off. In 1976, almost 40 percent of the centrifugal horsepower used in natural gas was built by Cooper-Bessemer— worldwide. In addition, the company found that the excess capacity created by pulling out of the weak markets in 1971 was being gradually brought back into production as market penetration in natural gas energy services

ILLUSTRATION CAPSULE 7 *(concluded)*

increased. This meant that Cooper Industries did not have to invest heavily in new facilities to keep pace with mushrooming energy demand.

The company's strategy also included one of emphasizing products that generate follow-on sales. More than one third of its energy-related revenue in 1976 was estimated to come from parts and services, steadier revenue sources than the sale of original equipment.

In 1976, Cooper Industries was touting itself as a "very well-balanced company with leadership positions in three different markets: hand tools, aircraft services, and energy services. This combination will help us ride out the economic ups and downs."

By business category the Cooper Industries companies as of 1976 were:

1. In hand tools—The Cooper Group (Lufkin, Crescent, Weller, Nicholson, Xcelite, Rotor tool).
2. In aircraft services—Cooper Airmotive.
3. In energy services—Cooper Energy Services (Cooper-Bessemer, Ajax, Penn Pump).

SOURCES: Cooper Industries *Annual Reports* and full page advertisements placed by Cooper Industries in *The Wall Street Journal*, February 12, 1976, p. 17; March 11, 1976, p. 15; and March 24, 1976, p. 15.

entire companies (nearly all of the large conglomerates) have been put together by mergers and acquisitions. For this reason, we think merger and acquisition strategies deserve separate mention as a basic type of corporate strategy.[17]

A *merger* can be thought of as combining two (or more) firms into one. An *acquisition* is when one firm (the parent) acquires another and absorbs it into its own operations, often as an operating subsidiary or division. Obviously, the difference is mainly one of semantics, and the terms are commonly used interchangeably.

From the standpoint of corporate strategy, there are several types of mergers and acquisitions. *Horizontal merger* is when one firm acquires or merges with another firm in the same industry. Examples are National Steel's acquisition of Granite City Steel, Honeywell's acquisition of General Electric's computer division, and Atlantic Richfield's (ARCO) acquisition of Sinclair Oil Corporation. Horizontal mergers are an offshoot of a concentration strategy since the acquiring firm remains in much the same business (unless the firm which is acquired has other business interests as

---

[17] An excellent source of information on mergers and acquisitions is the periodical *Mergers and Acquisitions: The Journal of Corporate Venture*, published quarterly.

well). The chief constraint in employing a horizontal merger strategy is staying clear of Section 7 of the Clayton Act which forbids acquisition of competitors where the effect "may be substantially to lessen competition, or to tend to create a monopoly." Horizontal mergers tend to raise issues of market power because they eliminate side-by-side competition between the two firms. Normally, the Antitrust Division of the Justice Department will challenge a horizontal merger when the firms involved have a combined market share greater than 10 percent. Obviously, this limits the use of horizontal merger as a corporate strategy.

A second type of merger is the *vertical merger*, aimed at creating a more vertically integrated enterprise. An example of vertical merger is U.S. Plywood's merger with Champion Paper to form U.S. Plywood-Champion Paper Corp. Although vertical mergers do not generally entail anticompetitive effects, there are instances where they have been held to raise barriers to entry, to produce unfair control over sources of critical inputs, and to allow vertically integrated firms to put a profit squeeze on nonintegrated firms. As a consequence, vertical mergers combining 10–20 percent market shares at both levels will usually be given close scrutiny by antitrust officials.

The third type of mergers are those involving market extension. A *market extension merger* involves two firms selling the same product in different *geographical* areas. This type of merger is a commonly used strategy since many firms seek to enter new geographical areas by acquiring a firm (young or mature, large or small, successful or not so successful) which operates in the desired location. Examples include Winn-Dixie's acquisition of a retail grocery chain in Texas, Standard Oil of California's acquisition of Standard Oil of Kentucky, and Philips' acquisition of Magnavox.

A fourth merger type is that involving related product diversification or *product extension* mergers. A product extension merger occurs when Firm A adds a product related to its existing product line by acquiring Firm B. According to the Federal Trade Commission, these are the most common types of mergers and represent a form of concentric diversification.[18] Examples include Pepsico's acquisitions of Pizza Hut, Rheingold Beer, and Taco Bell, Colgate-Palmolive's acquisition of Helena Rubenstein, and American Motors' acquisition of Kaiser Jeep Corporation.

The remaining type of merger is the *conglomerate merger*. Conglomerate mergers are typically used to accomplish an organization's attempt at pure diversification. Roughly 30 percent of the merger activity of the 1960s and 1970s has consisted of conglomerate mergers—a direct reflection

---

[18] Federal Trade Commission, Bureau of Economics, *Statistical Report on Mergers and Acquisitions*, November 1977 (Washington, D.C.: U.S. Government Printing Office, 1977). This document contains statistical breakdowns on various types of mergers and acquisitions since 1946.

of the use of conglomerate diversification strategy. Some of the more prominent examples include Beatrice Food's acquisition of Samsonite, United Technologies' acquisition of Otis Elevator, Philip Morris' acquisition of Miller Brewing Co., American Tobacco's acquisition of Sunshine Biscuits, and Illinois Central's acquisition of Midas International.

Pros and Cons of Acquisition Strategies. There are several reasons why an organization may prefer acquisition of an existing enterprise to launching its own grassroots development of a new business. The factors involved are those implicit in any "buy or build" situation, but often the most important considerations are time and money. Acquiring existing organizations, products, technologies, facilities, or talent and manpower has the strong advantage of much quicker entry into the target market while, at the same time, detouring such barriers to entry as patents, technological inexperience, lack of raw material supplies, substantial economies of scale, costly promotional expenses requisite for gaining market visibility and brand recognition, and establishment of distribution channels. Internally developing the knowledge, resources, and reputation necessary to become an effective competitor can take years and entails all the problems of startup. Internal entry can also result in oversupply conditions in the market. For instance, if existing firms already have the production capability to supply customers' needs and/or if entry must be on a large scale to take advantage of scale economies, then the added presence of a new, large supplier can produce an acute surplus of capacity. The likely outcome would be a spirited and profitless battle for market share. The prospect of such situations effectively reduces the number of viable options to two: entry via acquisition versus no entry at all.

Yet, acquisition is not without its own drawbacks. Finding the right kind of company to acquire can sometimes present a problem. Conceivably, an acquisitive-minded firm may face the dilemma of buying a successful company at a high price or a struggling company at a low price. In the first case, the seller is in position to demand a general compensation for the risks that have been faced and for the effort expended in putting together a successful product, technology, market, organization or whatever key feature (distinctive competence) is being acquired. If the buying firm has very little knowledge about the industry it is seeking to enter but has ample capital, then it may be better off acquiring a capable firm—irrespective of the higher price. On the other hand, it can be advantageous to acquire a struggling firm at a bargain price when the new parent sees promising ways for transforming the weak firm into a strong one and has the money and know-how to back up its turnaround strategy.

Mergers and acquisitions can be accomplished via any of several financial strategies: purchase of stock on the open market, tender offers, an exchange of stock, a purchase of assets, or a pooling of interests. They can occur amicably or with conflict and tension, intermingled with proxy fights, bidding wars, and complex legal maneuvering. One of the most dramatic of these is the takeover.

Takeover Strategies. A *takeover* is the surprise attempt of one firm to acquire ownership or control over the management of another firm against the wishes of the latter's management (and perhaps some of its stockholders). In recent years, takeover strategies have been used increasingly as a means of acquisition. The motives for takeover and the types of takeover mergers (horizontal, vertical, conglomerate, etc.) are the same as for any kind of merger/acquisition; what makes takeover unique is its unfriendly nature and the mechanics by which it is carried out.

A takeover strategy can follow many different paths and sequences. Typically, the acquiring firm or its investment banker conducts a search for likely takeover candidates which meet management's criteria: hundreds or even thousands of firms may be looked at via computerized procedures. When the takeover target is selected, an offer price is chosen—usually 20–30 percent above the current stock price—and other specific details are worked out. The takeover target may be approached openly at this point (in hope of a friendly merger or a quiet surrender) or the tender offer may be sprung publicly as a surprise. The terms of the tender offer are frequently announced at a news conference, followed up quickly with newspaper ads and personal contacts with known large shareholders of the target firm.

The takeover target may initiate a vigorous defensive strategy: denouncing the offer as too low, urging all shareholders not to accept the tender offer, making special attempts to convince major stockholders to reject the bid for their stock, requesting the Justice Department or other government agencies to intervene to stop the merger, seeking out a more attractive merger partner, filing lawsuits to block the takeover, and trying quickly to arrange some acquisitions of its own—to force a revision of the takeover offer. In launching its defense, top management is usually trying both to get better offer terms and to protect its own jobs and independence.

The struggle may last a few days, a few weeks, or a few months. The original tender offer may be raised one or more times; especially if another bidder enters the fray, attracted by the action and seeing interesting takeover possibilities of its own. The market price of the target firm's stock will generally fluctuate as the tender offer changes and prospects of merger brighten or darken. The stock market's response to the takeover attempt will be watched closely. Speculators may trade heavily in the stock, buying, selling, or selling short according to their estimates of the situation. An actual takeover attempt is described in Illustration Capsule 8.

The outcome can go either way and depends on many factors. If the takeover target escapes, its management is likely to make numerous changes in strategy and internal operations to avert future takeover attempts and, especially, to improve performance and results. Dividends

ILLUSTRATION CAPSULE 8
Strategic Responses to a Takeover Bid: To Fight or to Bargain?

When W. R. Grace & Co. announced a takeover bid of $3.75 a share for the stock of Daylin, Inc., a West Coast health services and specialty retailing firm, Daylin's management wasted little time in developing a strategy to preserve its independence. Daylin was unimpressed with the Grace offer even though Daylin's stock was selling at $2.38 before the Grace bid. Daylin had cash on hand equal to $1.30 a share ($46 million); and it had a net tax-loss carryforward of $88 million of which $66 million expired in 1980 (worth an estimated $1.35 per share). This meant that Grace was offering barely over $1 per share for Daylin's basic business, at a time when earnings were expected to be nearly 40 cents a share.

Just eleven days after the Grace announcement, Daylin simultaneously filed suit to block Grace's takeover (on grounds that Grace had violated federal securities laws and had not disclosed possible antitrust implications with respect to Grace's and Daylin's home improvement centers) and proposed a tender offer of its own of $38 per share for the 1.8 million shares of Narco Scientific Inc., a communication and health care concern. Only five days before, Narco had agreed in principle to accept a $28 per share offer to be acquired by Rorer Group Inc., a maker of pharmaceutical and surgical products. Both Narco and Rorer are based in Fort Washington, Pennsylvania. Narco viewed Rorer's offer of $28 as fair, since the book value of Narco's stock was roughly $15.65 and since the market price of Narco's stock had recently traded in the $12.75–$14.00 range. Needless to say, Narco's management was surprised by the size of the Daylin offer, since the $38 bid was not only 36 percent higher than Rorer's but also represented a price 18 times Narco's 1978 earnings per share and 2.4 times its book value.

Daylin justified the $38 offer price as necessary "to demonstrate our sincerity and ensure a high probability of success." (Daylin failed on two acquisition attempts in 1978). Daylin's management further expressed the view that Narco's medical products complemented Daylin's and that Narco had proprietary and patented products with sufficient growth potential beyond 1980 to warrant a hefty price-earnings multiple.

Three days after the Daylin offer, Narco's board of directors announced it might be willing to support a takeover bid from Daylin if Daylin were serious rather than using the bid to fight Grace's takeover of Daylin, if Daylin could give assurance of its ability to finance the proposed purchase of Narco, and if Daylin would clear up certain other reservations (one of which was that if the Grace takeover of Daylin was successful, Grace might cancel Daylin's offer for Narco and, perhaps, foul up the chance for Narco's stockholders to benefit from the Rorer offer). Daylin immediately reaffirmed its position that the offer for Narco "really had nothing to do with Grace. We've been looking at the Narco acquisition for a long period of time, and the offer isn't being done for defensive purposes." Meanwhile, W. R. Grace officials offered no immediate public comment and adopted a wait-and-see posture on the Daylin-Narco deal.

ILLUSTRATION CAPSULE 8 *(continued)*

Epilogue

Within a matter of days after these developments, W. R. Grace's management upped the offer bid for Daylin's stock from $3.75 to $4.065 a share. Daylin's management and board of directors agreed to support the offer, which was subject to stockholder approval. Daylin then promptly withdrew its offer to purchase Narco Scientific. Rorer Group, Inc. and Narco Scientific quickly agreed in principle to a slightly higher tender offer for Narco's shares than the $50.8 million in cash and stock which Rorer had earlier offered, but with the stipulation that Narco's three nonhealth subsidiaries be divested. Except for finalizing all the details, the strategic maneuvers among the four parties were over and the dust had settled within three weeks.

SOURCES: David G. Santry, "Staying Independent and Paying for It," *Business Week*, January 29, 1979, p. 100; and *The Wall Street Journal* issues of January 5, 1979, January 16, 1979, January 22, 1979, and February 1, 1979.

may be increased to try to solidify stockholder support of present management. The firm may become bolder, more innovative, and more competitive in outlook. If the takeover is successful, the acquiring firm may absorb the acquired firm and parcel its activities among various subunits; or it may operate the acquired firm as a separate and fairly autonomous division, keeping the original management or replacing all or part of top management with its own team. Either way, changes in the acquired firm can be expected in the way of revised objectives, new strategies, attempts to improve operating efficiency and profit performance, transfers of assets, closing or selling of marginal plants, expansion or pruning of the product line, new policies and procedures—in general, new direction.

The significance of takeover strategies, for our purposes, is two-fold: one, it is a new and increasingly used vehicle for accomplishing a merger/acquisition that might otherwise not occur, thereby opening up strategic opportunities for giving an organization new direction and different focus. Two, fears of takeover are prompting managements to adjust corporate strategies to make their firms less vulnerable to takeover. Examples of defensive moves being undertaken to help thwart a takeover include (1) stock splits (to broaden and splinter ownership and thereby make it harder for an outsider to gain control by secretly negotiating the purchase of large blocks of shares), (2) keeping liquidity to a safe minimum (to avoid large cash reserves which may be viewed as a desirable target in itself by "cash-poor" or "opportunity-rich" firms), (3) discarding "conservative" policies and strategies in favor of more innovative, aggressive ones, and (4) making special efforts to remain efficient and as profitable as possible (thus eliminating takeover attempts motivated by the potential for sharply higher profits).

Joint Venture Strategies

The joint venture is the right strategy for several types of situations.[19] It is, first, a device for doing something an organization is not well-suited to do alone. Entering into a "consortium" kind of arrangement is a means of making a workable whole out of otherwise undersized levels of activity. In such cases, the whole is greater than the sum of its parts because alone each part is smaller than the threshold size of effectiveness. The Alaskan pipeline, for instance, is a joint venture in raw material supply which not only is beyond the prudent financial strength of any one oil giant but which also, in its most economical size, is designed to carry more crude oil than one company could produce from its reserve holdings. For each oil company owning oil reserves on the Alaskan North Slope to build its own pipeline geared to the size of its own production capability would make little business or environmental sense. But for them all to contribute to a jointly financed and jointly operated pipeline allows the group to make economic fits out of misfits and thereby realize a profit from their Alaskan oil reserves. At the same time, the strategy of joint venturing carries the advantage that risk is shared and therefore reduced for each of the participating firms. This is no small matter in a relatively large undertaking.

A second type of joint venture emerges when the distinctive competence of two or more independent organizations is brought together to form a jointly owned business. In this joint venture format each company brings to the deal special talents which, when pooled, give rise to a new enterprise with features quite apart from the parents. The complementarity of two or more distinctive competences can create a degree of synergy that spells the difference between success and near-success. For example, when in the 1920s General Motors developed tetraethyl lead to cure engine knocking problems, it decided not to start its own gasoline production and distribution business to exploit the advantages of tetraethyl lead but, instead, chose to enter into a joint venture with Standard Oil of New Jersey (now Exxon) which already knew the gasoline business and had the missing expertise. Thus was born Ethyl Corporation which grew into a worldwide supplier of tetraethyl lead for all the large gasoline marketers. With its joint venture strategy GM, in effect, made money on every gallon of tetraethyl lead gasoline sold: an effective outcome compared to that of

---

[19] Drucker, *Management*, pp. 720–24. Information regarding the joint venture activities of firms can be found in *Mergers and Acquisitions: The Journal of Corporate Venture.*

entering the gasoline business on its own and trying to compete directly against the oil companies.[20]

Lastly, there are joint ventures created chiefly to surmount political and cultural roadblocks.[21] The political realities of nationalism often require a foreign company to team up with a domestic company if it is to gain needed government approval for its activities. At the same time there are added pressures for a foreign company to seek out a domestic partner to help it overcome language and cultural barriers. So powerful are nationalistic interests in the smaller developing nations such as Brazil, Chile, Peru, and India that it is not unusual for foreign companies to find themselves restricted to a minority ownership position. Indeed, local businesses in Brazil and India, even though deeply engaged in joint ventures with multinational corporations based in the U.S. and in Europe, have been quite vocal in demanding protection from multinational domination, advocating not just majority or at least controlling ownership but the closing off of whole economic sectors to multinationals as well.

Retrenchment Strategies

The conceptual thrust of a corporate retrenchment strategy is to fall back and regroup.[22] It is a common short-run strategy for organizations during periods of uncertainty about the economic future, recession, tight

---

[20] General Motors and Standard Oil, N.J., sold Ethyl Corporation in the 1960s largely because Ethyl had become too big and too successful to be continued as a joint venture. Likewise, when Sears decided it was time for Whirlpool not only to supply Sears but also to sell appliances under the Whirlpool brand, Sears took the company public while retaining a controlling majority interest. Gradually, then, Sears sold its holdings of Whirlpool shares as the company began to make it on its own. Such a spinning off of joint ventures into independent companies is not uncommon, either with or without the parent companies retaining an ownership interest.

To extend the life of a successful joint venture beyond some point in its development can have the effect of stunting its growth. Moreover, conflicts begin to arise between objectives of the parent company and the mission of the joint venture. Hence, at some point it becomes propitious for a successful joint venture company to begin to develop its own mission, objectives, strategy, and policies and for its management to become truly autonomous.

Alternatively, the joint venture can be liquidated by the parents splitting up the business and absorbing it into their own operations. This was the fate of Standard Vacuum, a joint venture of Standard Oil, N.J., and Mobil Oil begun in the World War I era to produce, refine, and market petroleum products in the Far East. In the 1950s Standard Vacuum's petroleum business in the Far East had expanded to a size where it was more desirable for each of the parents to proceed on their own rather than to continue a joint venture where their strategies and objectives were beginning to clash. See Drucker, *Management*, pp. 722–24.

[21] Kotler, *Marketing Management*, pp. 472–74.

[22] A retrenchment strategy can be (and is) used at both the levels of corporate strategy and business strategy. This section focuses on retrenchment at the corporate level—primarily as concerns diversified firms; business strategy retrenchment is discussed later in this chapter along with the other types of business level strategies.

money and corporate financial strain, and poor corporate performance. Retrenchment at the corporate level can assume either of two variations: one, stringent internal economies aimed at wringing out organizational slack and improving efficiency and, two, a reduction in the corporation's scope of business activities.

In the first instance, an organization which finds itself in a defensive or overextended position elects to hold onto most or all of its business activities and weather the storm with various internal economy measures. Ordinarily this type of corporate retrenchment strategy is highlighted by corporate-wide directives to reduce operating expenses, improve productivity, and increase profit margins. The specifics of retrenchment vary according to the situation but may include reducing hiring of new personnel, trimming the size of corporate staff, postponing capital expenditure projects, stretching out the use of equipment and delaying replacement purchases to economize on cash requirements, retiring obsolete equipment, dropping marginally profitable products, closing older and less efficient plants, internal reorganization of work flows, inventory reductions, revised purchasing procedures, and so on.

The second variation of corporate retrenchment is more fundamental and consists of reappraisal of the desirability of continuing in each one of the present lines of business. Reappraisal of the scope of corporate activities is nearly always a byproduct of poor overall corporate performance and/or persistently poor performance in one or more operating divisions. Many diversified firms have found it necessary to retrench because they had severe trouble managing so many different businesses which did not "fit," or because they encountered operating problems in one or more divisions which were intractable or beyond their expertise, or because they found themselves short of the cash needed to support the investment needs of all of their different lines of business.

Corporate retrenchment is a typical reaction to adversity from within or without the organization. Ordinarily, it is a temporary or short-run strategy for riding through bad times; once it becomes feasible to renew growth and pursue expansion opportunities, retrenchment strategies are usually discarded in favor of some other strategy.

Divestiture Strategies

Even a shrewd corporate diversification strategy can result in the acquisition of businesses that just do not work out. Misfits or partial fits cannot be completely avoided, if only because it is impossible to predict precisely how getting into a new line of business will actually work out. Moreover, market potentials change with the times and what once was a good diversification move may later turn sour. Subpar performance by some operating units is bound to occur, thereby raising questions of whether to continue. Other operating units may simply not mesh as well with the rest of the organization as was originally thought.

Sometimes a diversification move which originally appeared to make good sense from the standpoint of common markets, technologies, or channels turns out to lack the compatability of values essential to a *temperamental fit*.[23] The pharmaceutical companies had just this experience. When several tried to diversify into cosmetics and perfume they discovered that their personnel had little respect for the "frivolous" nature of such products as compared to the far nobler task of developing miracle drugs to cure the ill. The absence of "temperamental unity" between the chemical and compounding expertise of the pharmaceutical companies and the fashion-marketing orientation of the cosmetics business was the undoing of the pharmaceutical's diversification move into what otherwise was a business with related technology and logical product fit.

Partial misfits and poorly performing divisions can also occur, despite the presence of some strategic fit, owing to an organization's inability to manage the business or to the overload placed on internal cash resources. In still other cases, the market changes slowly but surely to where the product consumers want to buy differs from what the producer is trying to sell, thereby breaking up what once was a good strategic fit with the seller's other products. Likewise, technological branching can progress to a point where pruning becomes a wise course of action if not a necessary one.

When a particular line of business loses its appeal (for any of the preceding reasons), divestiture may be the most attractive corporate strategy for that part of the organization. Normally such businesses should be divested as fast as is practical. To drag things out in hopes of a breakthrough or a turnaround is liable to be futile and risks draining away valuable organization resources. This explains why every diversified organization needs a systematic "planned abandonment" strategy for divesting itself of poor performers, losers, and misfits. A useful guide for determining if and when to divest a particular line of business is to ask the question "If we were not in this business today, would we want to get into it now?"[24] When the answer is "no" or "probably not," then divestiture ought to become a strategic consideration.

Divestiture can take several forms. Successful misfits may be spun off into financially and managerially independent companies, with the parent company electing to maintain either a majority or minority ownership.[25]

[23] Drucker, *Management*, p. 709.

[24] Ibid., p. 94.

[25] One of the more unique approaches to divestiture involved Ling-Temco-Vought's reorganization of the Wilson Company in 1967. Shortly after it acquired Wilson, LTV split Wilson into three separate corporations: Wilson and Company

On the other hand, a business may not be able to survive as an independent operation, in which case a buyer needs to be found. This is a "marketing" rather than a "selling" problem.[26] As a rule, one should avoid approaching divestment with a view of "Who can we pawn this business off into and how much can we get for it?" Instead, it is stronger to undertake divestitute on the basis "For what sort of organization would this business be a good fit and under what conditions would it be viewed as a sound bet?" In identifying organizations for whom the business is a "perfect fit," one also finds the buyers who will pay the highest price.

Liquidation Strategy

Of all the strategic alternatives, liquidation is the most unpleasant and painful, especially for a single-product enterprise where it means terminating the organization's existence. For a multiproduct firm to liquidate one of its lines of business is much less traumatic: suffering through layoffs, plant closings, and so on, while imposing hardships, still leaves an ongoing organization, and perhaps one that eventually will turn out to be healthier after its pruning than before.

In hopeless situations, an early liquidation effort often serves owner-stockholder interests better than an inevitable bankruptcy. Prolonging the pursuit of a lost cause merely exhausts an organization's resources and leaves less to liquidate; it can also mar reputations and ruin management careers. Unfortunately, of course, it is seldom simple for management to differentiate between when a cause is lost and when a turnaround is achievable. This is particularly true when emotions and pride get mixed with sound managerial judgment, as often they do.

Combination Strategies

The nine corporate strategy alternatives discussed above are not mutually exclusive. They can be used in combination, either in whole or in part, and they can be chained together in whatever sequences may be appropriate for adjusting to changing internal and external circumstances. Moreover, there are endless variations of each of the nine "pure" alternatives themselves. These variations allow ample room for organizations to

---

(meats and food products), Wilson Sporting Goods, and Wilson Pharmaceutical and Chemical Company. LTV then sold off a substantial minority portion of the stock of each of the three new companies at price-earnings ratios higher than it initially paid for the total Wilson operation. LTV was attracted to this approach because it allowed LTV to improve its return from the Wilson acquisition by recovering part of its initial investment, while retaining control over all three of the new Wilson companies. For a more complete discussion, see Robert S. Attiyeh, "Where Next for Conglomerates," *Business Horizons*, vol. 12, no. 6 (December 1968), p. 42.

[26] Drucker, *Management*, p. 719.

ILLUSTRATION CAPSULE 9
Corporate Liquidation: A Case of Being Worth More Dead than Alive

Rarely does a healthy company pursue a liquidation strategy, especially if it is a large company listed no. 357 on the *Fortune 500*. But in early 1979 the board of directors of UV Industries, at the urging of board chairman and major stockholder Martin Horwitz, voted unanimously for a resolution to sell or distribute all of the company's assets to stockholders.

During the 1960s and 1970s UV Industries (formerly U.S. Smelting, Refining, and Mining Co.) used an aggressive acquisition strategy to increase sales from $31 million to over $600 million and profits from $2.3 million to nearly $40 million. After approval of the liquidation resolution, UV's stock price jumped from $19 a share to about $30 a share, and a successful liquidation was projected to yield shareholders $33 or more a share.

UV's business interests included copper, gold, and coal operations, oil and gas properties, a lead-refining company, and a manufacturer of electric generating equipment. The sale of the latter, Federal Pacific Electric Co.— UV's largest business (60 percent of sales and earnings), was arranged in late 1978; Reliance Electric offered UV a handsome $345 million in cash for Federal Pacific, a price which represented a price-earnings ratio of 13 at a time when UV's common stock was selling at 5 times earnings. The sale price produced a sizeable capital gain, and a tax liability of some $45 million. Liquidation offered a way to avoid this tax since under Section 337 of the Internal Revenue Code any corporation that liquidates itself in the space of one year pays no *corporate* capital gains tax on the sale of its assets (however, shareholders are subject to capital gains taxes on any appreciation in the common stock price). Liquidation was also a good defensive strategy against a takeover, given that UV would be flush with some $500 million in cash from the Federal Pacific sale and from funds generated by various other securities transactions.

Management's liquidation plan was to sell off those divisions and businesses where attractive prices could be obtained and, where the offers to buy were deemed too low, to spin the divisions off into independent companies, distributing shares to current UV stockholders. Liquidation was not expected to produce a hardship because UV only had 40 employees at its New York City headquarters and its operating divisions would presumably continue to exist—albeit under new owners and managers.

SOURCE: Peter W. Bernstein, "A Company That's Worth More Dead than Alive," *Fortune* (February 26, 1979), pp. 42–44.

create their own individualized blend of corporate purpose, objectives, and strategies. As a consequence, the difficulty of determining corporate strategy concerns not so much figuring out what options are open as evaluating the various viable alternatives.

When Some Corporate Strategies Are
More Logical than Others

A firm's market position and competitive strength is often such that some corporate strategy alternatives offer a stronger logical fit than do others.[27] Consider, for instance, Figure 3-1 where a firm's competitive position is plotted against the rate of market growth to create four distinct strategic situations. Firms which fall into quadrant I (rapid market growth and strong competitive position) are clearly in an excellent strategic position. In such circumstances a concentration strategy has powerful appeal and one can logically expect quadrant I firms to push hard to maintain or increase their market shares, to develop further their distinctive competences, and to make whatever capital investments may be necessary to continue in a leadership position. In addition, a quadrant I company may find it desirable to consider vertical integration as strategy for undergirding its market standing and protecting its profit margins. It may also make sense for an organization to look into concentric diversification as a means of spreading its business risks and capitalizing on its distinctive competence.

Firms falling into quadrant II should, first of all, direct their attention to a concentration strategy (given the high rate of market growth) and address the questions of (1) why their current approach to the market has resulted in a weak competitive position and (2) what it will take to become an effective competitor. With the market expanding rapidly, there should be ample opportunity for even a weak firm to carve out a viable market niche, provided strategic and organizational shortcomings can be overcome and the needed resource base developed. Certainly, a young, developing company has a better chance for survival in a growing market where there is plenty of new business than it does in a stable or declining industry. However, if a quadrant II firm lacks one or more key ingredients for a successful concentration strategy, then either horizontal merger with another company in the industry that has the missing pieces or else merger with an outsider having the cash and resources to support the organization's development may be the best corporate strategy alternative. Failing this, the most logical strategies would entail getting out of

27 C. Roland Christensen, Norman A. Berg, and Malcolm S. Salter, *Policy Formulation and Administration,* 7th ed. (Homewood, Ill.: Richard D. Irwin, 1976), pp. 16–18.

FIGURE 3–1
Identifying Strategic Alternatives that Fit a Firm's Market Circumstances

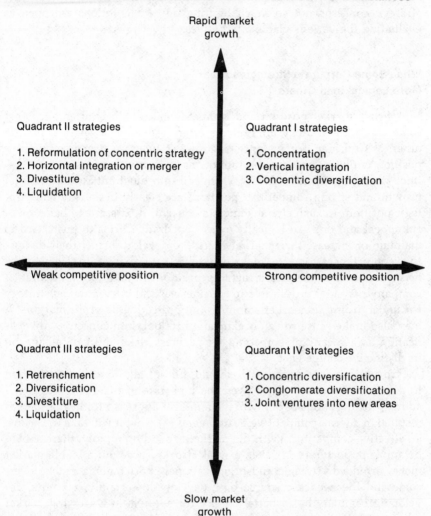

Rapid market
growth

Quadrant II strategies

1. Reformulation of concentric strategy
2. Horizontal integration or merger
3. Divestiture
4. Liquidation

Quadrant I strategies

1. Concentration
2. Vertical integration
3. Concentric diversification

Weak competitive position   Strong competitive position

Quadrant III strategies

1. Retrenchment
2. Diversification
3. Divestiture
4. Liquidation

Quadrant IV strategies

1. Concentric diversification
2. Conglomerate diversification
3. Joint ventures into new areas

Slow market
growth

NOTE: Strategies in each quadrant are listed in probable order of attractiveness.

the industry: divestiture in the case of a multiproduct firm or liquidation in the case of a single-product firm. While getting out may seem extreme, it is well to remember that a company which is unable to make a profit in a booming market probably does not have the ability to make a profit at all and has little prospect of survival—particularly if recession hits or competition stiffens.

Quadrant III companies with their weak competitive position in a more or less stagnant market would do well to consider (1) retrenchment—to free up unproductive resources for possible redeployment, (2) diversification—either concentric or conglomerate, depending on existing opportunities elsewhere, (3) getting out of the industry (divestiture of this line of business), or even (4) liquidation—if profit prospects are nonexistent and other opportunities fail to materialize.

Quadrant IV organizations, given their dim growth prospects, are likely to be drawn toward using the excess cash flow from their existing business to begin a program of diversification. A concentric approach keyed to the distinctive competence that gave it its dominant position is an obvious option, but conglomerate diversification should be considered if concentric opportunities do not appear especially attractive. Joint ventures with other organizations into new fields of endeavor are another logical possibility. Whichever, the firm will likely wish to minimize new investments in its present facilities (to do little more than preserve the status quo), thereby freeing the maximum amount of funds for new endeavors.

Comparing firms on the basis of competitive position and market growth rate (or any other two variables) is useful for the insight it provides into why companies (even those in the same industry) may have good reason to pursue different corporate strategies. The nature of a firm's market standing, its competitive capabilities, its cash flow, its capital investment requirements, its ability to respond to emerging market opportunities, its distinctive competences, and so on, all combine to shape its strategic position and its strategic alternatives. Sometimes a company's situation is such that a radical change in corporate strategy is called for; at other times, though, maintaining the status quo or just fine-tuning will suffice.

THE BASIC ALTERNATIVES OF LINE OF BUSINESS STRATEGY

The focus of strategy at the business level is "How do we compete effectively in this particular business?" Strategic analysis at the business level consists primarily of (1) assessing opportunities and threats in particular markets and for particular products, (2) determining the keys to success in that particular business, (3) evaluating the competitive strategies of rival organizations, (4) searching for an effective competitive advantage, (5) identifying organizational strengths and weaknesses, and (6) trying to match specific product-market opportunities with internal skills, distinctive competences, and financial resources. The *essential* concern is finding an approach to the market and a competitive strategy that is capable of being effective and producing the desired performance and results.

Numerous types of business strategies abound. We shall discuss the following categories and classifications:

1. Strategies for underdog and low market share businesses.
2. Strategies for dominant firms.
3. Strategies for firms in growth markets.
4. Strategies for weak or declining businesses.
5. Turnaround strategies.
6. Strategies to be leery of.
7. Strategies to avoid.

Strategies for Underdog and Low Market Share Businesses

In many cases the most important strategic concern is how a firm can increase its market share and transform a trailing position into a more profitable position, or a "middle-of-the-pack" position into a leadership position. A sizeable (10 percent or more) market share is sometimes necessary to realize scale economies, to generate an ample R&D budget, to gain good distribution, and, in general, to establish a viable long-run competitive niche in the industry. Normally, if a firm is to be "outstandingly successful" it will need some sort of differentiating strategy aimed at building a competitive advantage; rarely is real success founded upon imitating what other firms in the industry are doing.

The stage of the product-market life cycle often dictates just where the right kind of competitive advantage is likely to be located.[28] During the product development stage of a young industry, the competitive spot-

---

[28] Most discussions of product-market life cycles speak of five stages: (1) introduction and development, (2) take off and rapid growth, (3) maturity, (4) saturation, and (5) stagnation and decline. The period of introduction and development entails slow growth as initial inertia, product debugging, and start-up must all be overcome. Growth is a period of rapid market acceptance and substantial profit improvement. Many new firms may be drawn into the market to try to capitalize upon the opportunities present whereas other firms, unable to keep pace, fall by the wayside. Maturity is characterized by a slowing down in sales growth, proliferation of products, attempts at intense market segmentation, and increased competition; there is often an industry-wide *shakeout* of weak, inefficient, and ineffective firms. Saturation brings on negligible sales growth and pressure on profit margins, as price cutting and competition heat up—the struggle is much like a "survival of the fittest" type of contest. Stagnation and decline is the period where new and better substitutes begin to appear, sales erode and begin a downward drift, and profits decline rapidly toward the zero level. The point here is that the nature of competition shifts in important ways over the course of the cycle. What it takes to compete effectively in the early part of the product-market life cycle is not the same as in the latter part of the cycle. For an excellent treatment of product-market life cycles see Robert D. Buzzell, "Competitive Behavior and Product Life Cycles," in *New Ideas for Successful Marketing*, ed. by John S. Wright and Jac L. Goldstucker (Chicago: American Marketing Association, 1966), pp. 46–68; and Kotler, *Marketing Management*, pp. 231–45.

light tends to center on product design, product quality positioning, and technical capability. Later, during the maturity-shakeout phase, the keys to competitive success tend to turn to product performance features, pricing, service, effectiveness of distribution channels, and market segmentation. Even so, underdog firms must still figure out just what strategic approach to product design, product positioning, product performance, market segmentation, and so on they ought to employ. No dependable generalizations can be offered. Each situation is sufficiently unique that creativity and sensitivity to market forces will be required. In some cases, a low market share business faces only two strategic options: fight to increase its share or withdraw from the business (gradually or quickly). In other cases, though, companies having a low market share may be able to remain small, compete effectively, and earn healthy profits.

There are several business strategies which seem to work well for underdog and low market share companies:

1. *Vacant niche strategy*—search out and cultivate profitable areas of the market that larger firms are not catering to, ignoring or not as well equipped to serve. Examples include the small tire manufacturers which have managed to survive competing with Goodyear, Firestone, B. F. Goodrich, and Uniroyal.

2. *Specialist* or *concentration strategy*—attempt to compete in only a few, carefully chosen market *segments*, rather than making a broad assault on the entire industry. Sell only to segments where the company has special expertise and where the company's strengths will be highly valued by customers. Be alert to the fact that a market can be segmented by location of plants, stage of production, price-quality-performance characteristics of the product, the cost and speed of distribution, credit and service arrangements, manufacturing capability—as well as by products and customers. Companies which have successfully used a specialist or concentration approach include Control Data (which developed a better computer for scientific research), Timex (which designed a cheap, but reliable, watch), and Crown Cork and Seal (which concentrated on metal cans for hard-to-hold products and on aerosol cans).

3. *"Ours-is-better-than-theirs" strategy*—try to capitalize on opportunities to improve on the products of dominant firms and develop an appeal to quality-conscious or performance-oriented buyers. Be more innovative. Work closely with major customers to develop a better product. Some examples: Chivas Regal's approach to selling scotch, Zenith's attempt to overtake RCA with its "the quality goes in, before the name goes on" strategy, and Mercedes-Benz's appeal to luxury car buyers.

4. *Channel innovation strategy*—find a new way to distribute goods that offers substantial savings or that reaches particular groups of buyers more efficiently. Examples are Avon's door-to-door selling of cosmetics and Timex's use of drug stores and discount stores as outlets for its watches.

5. *Distinctive image strategy*—seek to develop a differential competitive advantage via some distinctive, visible, and unique appeal. Examples include Dr. Pepper's combined strategy of distinctive taste and effective advertising slogans; Miller's introduction of Lite beer; and Avis' "We're No. 2, We Try Harder" campaign to provide cleaner rental cars and more personal attention.[29]

Without a doubt, low market share companies have some serious obstacles to overcome: lack of access to economies of scale in manufacturing, distribution, or sales promotion, small R&D budgets, less opportunity to distribute through internal channels, difficulties in attracting capital, keeping good managerial and technical personnel, and low public and customer recognition.[30] But not all low share businesses are "dogs." In some cases the handicaps can be surmounted and a viable competitive position established. The most promising strategic guidelines seem to be: (1) specialize and compete only where particular strengths can be developed; that is, carefully segment the market and avoid a head-on attack of dominant firms via price cutting and increased promotional expenditure; (2) focus R&D budgets on developing a distinctive competence in new product development or technical capabilities, but only for the target market segments; (3) be content to remain small and emphasize profits rather than sales growth or market share; (4) push specialization rather than diversification (but if diversification is needed, enter closely related markets); and (5) manage the business in an innovative/"dare to be different"/ "beat-the-odds" type of mode. On the other hand, if the business is one where market share is the key to profitability, then the preceding guidelines must be modified and emphasis placed upon developing a competitive advantage that extends over many market segments. Of course, a trailing firm may be able to make major market share gains without a real competitive advantage if it makes a sudden technological breakthrough, if the leaders stumble or become complacent, or if it is willing to make major investments over long periods of time to secure incremental gains in its products and customer base.

Business Strategies for Dominant Firms

The strategic position of a dominant firm is more enviable. As a leader, it has a well-established and well-known market position. The main issue of business strategy thus tends to revolve around how best to harvest what has been achieved and how to maintain or improve upon the present position. Several different strategic postures are open:

---

[29] For more details, see Kotler, *Marketing Management*, pp. 239–40 and R. G. Hamermesh, M. J. Anderson, Jr., and J. E. Harris, "Strategies for Low Market Share Businesses," *Harvard Business Review*, vol. 56, no. 3 (May–June 1978), pp. 95–102.

[30] Hamermesh, Anderson, and Harris, "Strategies for Low Market Share Businesses," p. 102.

1. *Keep-the-offensive strategy*—refuse to be content with just being a leader. Seek to continue to outperform the industry by breaking records the firm itself has already set. Become firmly established as *the* source of new product ideas, cost-cutting discoveries, innovative customer services, and better means of distribution. In general, exercise initiative, set the pace, and exploit the weaknesses of rival firms.

2. *Fortification strategy*—surround the chief products with patents; foreclose the attractiveness of entry by introducing more of the company's own brands to compete with the already-successful company brands; introduce additional items under current brand names.

3. *Confrontation strategy*—defend the company's market base by being quick to launch massive promotional wars which underdog firms cannot hope to match; promptly meet all competitive price cuts of lesser-sized firms to neutralize any benefits to would-be price-cutters; make it hard for aggressive-minded smaller firms to grow by selling at prices so low that smaller firms are denied the profit margins and total earnings needed to make further expansion attractive.

4. *Maintenance strategy*—peg the level of reinvestment in the business sufficiently high to maintain production capacity, operating efficiency, product quality, and customer service, thus avoiding any slippage in sales, market share, and profitability. Shift extra cash flow and retained earnings to other businesses where growth and profit potential may be greater. A maintenance strategy is appropriate for a dominant firm when the business occupies an important position in the organization's overall lineup and when it generates ample cash flow to support other ventures.[31]

Business Strategies for Firms in Growth Markets

Two crucial strategic issues confront firms trying to participate in a rapidly growing market: (1) how to acquire the resources needed to grow with the market so the firm can maintain or improve its current position and (2) how to develop the sort of distinctive competence and competitive stamina that will be needed as growth slows and maturity-saturation begins.[32] Again, no neat prescriptions can be given for just how these two issues should be resolved. Strategy has to be geared to match the specifics of each growth market. Nonetheless, the following strategic guidelines can be offered:

1. Manage the business in an entrepreneurial mode with the aim of building the business for its future potential.

2. Be alert for product development opportunities keyed to product quality, performance features, styling, additional models and sizes, and improved design.

3. Search out new market segments and new geographical areas to enter.

---

[31] Kotler, *Marketing Management*, pp. 240–41.

[32] Charles W. Hofer and Dan Schendel, *Strategy Formulation: Analytical Concepts* (St. Paul, Minn.: West Publishing Co., 1978), pp. 164–65.

4. Shift the focus of advertising and promotion from building product awareness to increasing frequency of use and to creating brand loyalty.

5. Seek out new distribution channels to gain additional product exposure.

6. Watch for the right time to lower prices to attract the next layer of price-sensitive buyers into the market.

7. Although the priorities may be on growth, market share, and a strengthening of competitive position, recognize that during the growth stage, market-expanding activities usually come at the expense of higher current profits. If the profits foregone now to capture growth are to be recaptured later, then any market share or dominant position gained at the expense of profitability in the growth stage should offer the prospect of a higher than otherwise return on investment.[33]

However, one caution can be urged. The strategic imperative of how to maintain/improve competitive market position during the takeoff stage should not blind management to the longer-range strategic need to prepare for the different types of competition that will occur when the market matures and a rigorous market share struggle sets in.[34] The temptation to neglect the latter for the former can be great when current market growth is in the 15–50 percent range and management must spend much of its energies figuring out ways to continue to achieve rapid growth; that is, how to supplement internal cash flows with debt and equity capital, where to build new plants, how many personnel to add, which way to push R&D and market development efforts, how to respond to the product developments of rival firms, and so on. Moreover, it may be hard to foresee what twists competition may take as the market matures.

Nonetheless, the longer-range needs of strategy ought to be balanced against the immediate needs. This can be accomplished most easily in multiindustry enterprises that have had experience in managing young businesses through the early stages of product-market evolution. A single-business enterprise in a rapid growth situation does have some strategic substitutes for experience: it can gain guidance via wise selection of members for its board of directors; it can hire skilled management personnel from firms that have recently passed through the shakeout stage or else are in the early maturity phase; or it can try to gain functional skills via acquisition or merger.

Strategies for Weak Businesses

Management has essentially four options for handling a weak business (whether it be a division, product line, or product).[35] It can employ a *building strategy* and pour enough money and talent into the business to

---

[33] Kotler, *Marketing Management*, p. 236.

[34] Hofer and Schendel, *Strategy Formulation*, pp. 164–65.

[35] Ibid., p. 166.

make it a stronger performer. It can use a *maintenance strategy* and budget enough funds to maintain sales and profitability at present levels. It can opt for a *divestment strategy* or a *liquidation strategy* and abandon the business, quickly or gradually. Or, it can resort to a *harvest strategy* whereby investment levels are reduced and efforts are made to "harvest" reasonable short-term profits and/or maximize short-term cash flow. The first three options are self-explanatory. The fourth deserves added treatment.

A harvesting strategy steers a middle course between maintenance and abandonment. It entails a level of resource support between what is required for maintenance and a decision to divest or liquidate. It is a phasing down approach. Kotler has suggested seven indicators of when a business should become a candidate for harvesting:

1. When the business is in a saturated or declining market.
2. When the business has gained only a small market share, and building it up would be too costly or not profitable enough; or when it has a respectable market share that is becoming increasingly costly to maintain or defend.
3. When profits are not especially attractive.
4. When reduced levels of resource support will not entail sharp declines in sales and market position.
5. When the organization can redeploy the freed-up resources in higher opportunity areas.
6. When the business is not a major component of the organization's overall business portfolio.
7. When the business does not contribute other desired features (sales stability, prestige, a well-rounded product line) to the total business portfolio.[36]

The more of these seven conditions which are present, the more ideal the business is for harvesting.

The features of a harvesting strategy are fairly clearcut. The operating budget is reduced to a bare bones level—stringent cost-cutting is undertaken. The business is given little, if any, capital expenditure priority, depending on the current condition of fixed assets and whether the harvest is to be fast or slow. Price may be raised, promotional expenses cut, quality reduced, customer services curtailed, equipment maintenance decreased, and the like. The mandate, typically, is to maximize short-term cash flow, for redeployment to other parts of the organization. It is understood that sales will fall to some core level of demand, but it may be that costs can be cut such that profits do not suffer much, at least immediately. Ideally, though, sales and market share will not fall far below their pre-harvest

---

[36] Philip Kotler, "Harvesting Strategies for Weak Products," *Business Horizons*, vol. 21, no. 4 (August 1978), pp. 17–18.

level in the short-run. If the business cannot make money and/or generate positive cash flow at the lower core level of demand, then it can be divested or liquidated. A harvesting strategy thus clearly implies the sunset or twilight stage of a product or business in its life cycle.

Although a harvesting strategy calls for reduced budgets and cost-cutting, it is useful to implement these moves in ways which do not alert competitors and customers to the harvesting intention.[37] To do so merely precipitates the decline in sales and reduces the potential harvest. Generally, the first cutbacks should be in expenditures for R&D and for plant and equipment. Later, marketing expenditures can be reduced and prices raised slightly. Still later, product quality and customer services can be trimmed. Management may also elect to splash some advertising occasionally, since such sporadic bursts will recapture customer and dealer attention, thereby slowing sales decay. Such an approach may result in a smaller gain in cash flow, but one which lasts over a longer period. A fast harvest, where deep cutbacks are made across the board, produces a large cash flow increase, but it doesn't last long.

Although it may not seem so at first, harvesting strategies have much to recommend, especially in diversified companies having products in different stages of their life cycle. Different lines of business deserve different levels of resource support depending on their profit potential, their life cycle stage, and their rank in an organization's overall line of business portfolio. Businesses which are fading or on the verge of decline are logical candidates for a harvesting strategy. Reducing resource support and commitment to a line of business (or division or product) makes strategic sense when costs can be decreased without proportionate losses in sales. The result can be improved profitability and cash flow in the short-run—the very things at which a harvesting strategy aims.

Turnaround Strategies

Turnaround strategies come into play when a business worth saving has fallen into disrepair and decline. The goal is to arrest and reverse the situation as quickly as possible. Assuming that it is possible to avoid failure and/or bankruptcy, the first task of a turnaround is diagnosis. What is the cause of the decline? Is it bad strategy? Or poor implementation and execution of an otherwise workable strategy? Is it weak management? Or are the causes of decline beyond management control? One must know what is wrong before a plan for cure can be formulated. Moreover, one must learn what internal skills and resources need to be protected to preserve them as a base for launching a turnaround strategy. Generally speaking, there are five approaches to turnaround: (1) a re-

---

[37] Ibid., p. 20.

placement of top management and other key personnel, (2) revenue-increasing strategies, (3) cost-reduction strategies, (4) asset reduction/retrenchment strategies, and (5) a combination of these. Replacing key management personnel is an obvious turnaround alternative. Management is responsible for successful performance of a business. It is obliged to take whatever actions are deemed advisable to accommodate internal and external changes and to ensure efficient, effective performance. It is reasonable to infer that when decay sets into a business, management has either taken no action to ward off poor performance or else it has taken inappropriate actions. Whichever, one corrective approach is to install new management.[38] Only when the circumstances underlying decline are beyond management control should no change in management be seriously contemplated.

Revenue-increasing turnaround strategy focuses on how to increase sales volume (increased promotion, more emphasis on marketing, added customer services) and whether and how much of a price increase can be instituted. It is a necessary strategic approach when there is little or no room in the operating budget to cut back on expenses and still break even, and when the key to restoring profitability is an increased utilization of existing capacity.

Cost-reduction turnaround strategies work best when the firm's cost structure is flexible enough to permit radical surgery, when operating inefficiencies are identifiable and readily correctable, and when the firm is relatively close to its breakeven point. Accompanying a general belt-tightening can be an increased emphasis on budgeting and cost control, elimination of jobs and hirings, modernization of existing plant and equipment to gain greater productivity, and capital expenditure cutbacks.

Asset reduction/retrenchment turnaround strategies are necessary when cash flow is a critical consideration and when the most practical way to generate cash is through (1) sale of some of the firm's assets (plant and equipment, land, patents, divisions, or inventories) and (2) retrenchment—pruning of marginal products from the product line, closing or sale of older plants, a reduced work force, withdrawal from outlying markets, cutbacks in customer service, and the like. A divestment of assets may not only be needed to improve cash flow but it may also represent the best way to unload money-losing activities and restore profitability. Thus asset reduction may not signify liquidation and retrenchment as much as it does an attempt to eliminate losses and cash drains.

Combination turnaround strategies are usually the most effective, es-

[38] One study of corporate turnaround reports the occurrence of significant changes in general managers, including chief executive officers, in 39 out of 54 firms attempting to reverse a downturn in performance. See Dan Schendel, G. R. Patton, and James Riggs, "Corporate Turnaround Strategies," *Journal of General Management*, vol. 3, no. 3 (Spring 1976), pp. 3–11.

pecially in grim situations where fast action on a broad front is required. This is because the result to be gained from the best asset reduction and revenue increasing actions are greater than from the third or fourth best cost-reducing actions, and conversely.[39]

No matter which variety of turnaround strategy is chosen, attention will tend to center on those actions which have the greatest short-term cash flow impact and which will move the business toward breakeven the quickest. The urgency and limited resources of a near-bankrupt business make these considerations imperative. The key to turnaround is management action of the right kind. Specifically, it is important to diagnose whether the prevailing strategy is suitably matched to the external environment and to internal resources. If so, the difficulties probably lie in operating inefficiency and poor internal management. But if strategy is at the root of the decline in performance, the spotlight of turnaround must be on strategy reformulation.

Strategies to Be Leery of

On occasion management may be pulled toward the adoption of a strategy which is risky and lacks the potential for real success. This can occur out of desperation or poor analysis or simply lack of creativity. The following strategies are offered as examples of those which managers should be cautious about adopting:

1. *"Me too"* or *"copy-cat"* strategy—imitating the strategy of leading or successful enterprises; trying to play catch-up by beating the leaders at their own game. *Weakness:* Ignores development of firm's own personality, image, strategy and policies.

2. *Take-away strategy*—trying to achieve greater market share and market penetration by attacking other firms head on and luring away their customers via a lower price, more advertising, and other attention-getting gimmicks. *Weakness:* Invites retaliation and risks precipitating a fierce and costly battle for market share in which no one wins, including the firm trying to play take-away.

3. *Glamour strategy*—when a firm gets seduced by the prospects of a new idea for a product or technology which it thinks will sweep the market. *Weakness:* The best laid plans. . . .

4. *Test-the-water strategy*—often arises when an enterprise is engaged in developing new opportunities or is reacting to market-technological-environmental changes which call for a fundamental reformulation or redesign of strategy. In such cases, firms may "test-the-water" in venturing out into new fields of endeavor. *Weakness:* A half-way effort or "sideline stepchild" seldom succeeds for lack of adequate corporate commitment; it's usually best to get in or stay out entirely.

5. *Hit another home-run strategy*—this strategy is typified by a firm which

---

[39] Hofer and Schendel, *Strategy Formulation*, p. 174.

has hit one "home-run" (pioneering a very successful product and strategy) and which is urgently looking for ways to hit a second home-run (by getting into a new line of business either related or unrelated to its first home-run), so to continue to grow and prosper at its former rate. A second "home-run" business may be necessary because growth of the initial business is rapidly slowing down and becoming more competitive. *Weakness:* Trying to repeat the same strategy in a new business may not work out because some key ingredients are missing.

6. *Arms-race strategy*—may emerge when firms of relatively equal size enter into a spirited battle for increased market share. Commonly, such battles are waged with increased promotional and advertising expenditures and/or aggressive price cuts and/or increased R&D and new product development budgets and/or extra services to customers. As one firm pours more money into its efforts, other firms feel forced to do likewise for defensive reasons. The result is escalating costs, producing a situation much like an arms race. *Weakness:* Seldom do such battles produce a substantial change in market shares, yet they almost certainly raise costs—costs which must either be absorbed in the form of lower profit margins or else passed on to customers via higher prices.[40]

Strategies to Avoid

Experience has shown that some business strategies seldom if ever work. An alert management, for obvious reasons, will seek to avoid use of the following strategies:

1. *Drift strategy*—when strategy is not consciously designed and coordinated but rather just evolves out of day-to-day decisions and actions at the operating level.

2. *Hope-for-a-better-day strategy*—emerges from managerial inertia and tradition and is exemplified by firms which blame their subpar sales-profits-market share performance on bad luck, the economy, unexpected problems, and other circumstances "beyond their control." Such "entrepreneurial coasting" until good times arrive is a sure sign of a dim future and managerial ineptness.

3. *Losing hand strategy*—arises in companies where a once successful (and perhaps spectacularly so) strategy is fading and no longer viable. Nonetheless, management, blinded by the success-breeds-success syndrome, continues to be reluctant to begin to reformulate its strategy, preferring instead to try to rekindle the old spark with cosmetic changes, in hopes of reversing a downhill slide.

4. *Popgun strategy*—seeking to go into head-to-head competition with proven leaders when the firm has neither a differential competitive advantage nor adequate financial strength with which to do battle.[41]

---

[40] Kotler, *Marketing Management*, 2d ed., chap. 8; and Joel Ross and Michael Kami, *Corporate Management in Crisis: Why the Mighty Fall* (Englewood Cliffs, N.J.: Prentice-Hall, Inc., 1973).

[41] Ibid.

144

Business Strategies: A Perspective View

The foregoing survey of business strategy alternatives is by no means exhaustive. For example, concentration or specialist strategies, joint venture strategies, retrenchment strategies, divestiture, and liquidation, all of which were discussed under the heading of corporate strategy, also have their counterparts in line of business strategy. Moreover, as has been pointed out, whether a particular business strategy is "right" for an organization depends upon the stage of product-market evolution, the competitive position a firm has, the competitive position it seeks, the business strategies being used by rival firms, and the internal resources and distinctive competences at a firm's disposal—to mention only the more important considerations.

How a firm should try to compete—the overriding issue in line of business strategy—is therefore variable from situation to situation and from time to time. Competition is a dynamic process which assumes many forms and comes in many different shades of intensity. Thus, there can be no nice, neat package of business strategy options to choose among; just as with corporate-level strategy, line of business strategy is something which must be tailor-made to fit the situation at hand. Our sampling of strategic alternatives is intended to highlight the variety of approaches and to demonstrate the need for creative strategy formulation.

SUGGESTED READINGS

Ansoff, H. Igor *Corporate Strategy*. New York: McGraw-Hill Book Co., 1965, chap. 7.

Ansoff, H. Igor, and Stewart, John M. "Strategies for a Technology-Based Business." *Harvard Business Review*, vol. 45, no. 6, November-December 1967, pp. 71–83.

Bettauer, Arthur "Strategy for Divestments." *Harvard Business Review*, vol. 45, no. 2, March-April 1967, pp. 116–24.

Bloom, Paul N., and Kotler, Philip "Strategies for High Market Share Companies." *Harvard Business Review*, vol. 53, no. 6, November-December 1975, pp. 63–72.

Bright, William M. "Alternative Strategies for Diversification." *Research Management*, vol. 12, no. 4, July 1969, pp. 247–53.

Cooper, Arnold C., and Schendel, Dan "Strategic Responses to Technological Threats." *Business Horizons*, vol. 19, no. 1, February 1976, pp. 61–69.

Doutt, J. T. "Product Innovation in Small Business." *Business Topics*, vol. 8, no. 3, Summer 1960, pp. 58–62.

Drucker, Peter *Management: Tasks, Responsibilities, Practices*. New York: Harper and Row, Publishers, Inc., 1974, chaps. 55, 56, 57, 58, 60, and 61.

Hamermesh, R. G.; Anderson, Jr. M. J.; and Harris, J. E. "Strategies for Low

Market Share Businesses." *Harvard Business Review,* vol. 56, no. 3, May-June 1978, pp. 95–102.

Hanan, Mack "Corporate Growth through Internal Spinouts." *Harvard Business Review,* vol. 47, no. 6, November-December 1969, pp. 55–66.

Kotler, Philip "Harvesting Strategies for Weak Products." *Business Horizons,* vol. 21, no. 4, August 1978, pp. 15–22.

Mason, R. S. "Product Diversification and the Small Firm." *Journal of Business Policy,* vol. 3, no. 3, Spring 1973, pp. 28–39.

Steiner, George A. "Why and How to Diversity." *California Management Review,* vol. 6, no. 4, Summer 1964, pp. 11–17.

Vancil, Richard F., and Lorange, Peter "Strategic Planning in Diversified Companies." *Harvard Business Review,* vol. 53, no. 1, January-February 1975, pp. 81–90.

Webster, Frederick A. "A Model of Vertical Integration Strategy." *California Management Review,* vol. 10, no. 2, Winter 1967, pp. 49–58.

Woodward, Herbert N. "Management Strategies for Small Companies." *Harvard Business Review,* vol. 54, no. 1, January-February 1976, pp. 113–21.

READING

Strategic Control: The President's Paradox*

CARTER F. BALES

Carter F. Bales is a principal in the international consulting firm of McKinsey and Company, New York City.

"I call it the president's paradox—that I as chief executive can't participate in an informed way in the decisions most vital to our future. Let's face it, today those decisions are being made in the product divisions. At corporate headquarters, we don't really understand what's going on out there. We're out of touch and out of date. In fact, we're on the verge of losing control of the company—strategically anyway." Benson looked around the table at his executive group. Most of them had worked together for well on to fifteen years building the enterprise from a single, $200 million business to a multinational, multiproduct, multimarket, multitechnology multicompany—with sales nearing $2 billion.

"It's not hard to see how this situation has crept up on us," Benson went on. "Back in the sixties, our big decisions were which businesses to enter and what companies to acquire. We could work those out at headquarters, let the divisions take care of themselves, and measure them on bottom-line results. Today, we act like nothing has changed. We're still running the businesses like a financial portfolio.

"And that's crazy, given our present environment. Growth isn't the name of the game any more. We've got to reckon with economic uncertainty and greater risk for a long time to come. The board is pushing for solid earnings, market and asset protection, self-financing growth and a strong balance sheet. So we've got to make sure that our core businesses are properly managed for solid, long-term earnings. We can't just sit back and watch the numbers. We've got to know what the real issues are out there in the profit centers. Otherwise, we're not even in a position to check our managers on the big decisions. And considering the pressures they're under, that's pretty dangerous for all concerned."

Like Benson, many corporate executives find themselves too remote from their major businesses even to understand the important decisions being made down the line, much less assess their quality. For a while, strategic planning looked like a way to bridge the gap between corporate headquarters and the profit centers, but many chief executives have discovered that they have no way of judging the substance of a proposed

---

* Carter F. Bales, "Strategic Control: The President's Paradox," *Business Horizons*, August 1977. Copyright © 1977, by the Foundation of the School of Business at Indiana University. Reprinted by permission.

business strategy. For its part, division management resents planning as a time-wasting nuisance and scarcely attempts to run the business in accordance with the strategic plan. For many corporations, the strategic planning process is little more than the annual planning ritual of the past, decked out with a new title and new rhetoric. Few large, diversified companies are strangers to the "president's paradox."

Do formal business strategies ever really repay the efforts required to develop them? If so, why are chief executives so often disappointed with their strategic planning efforts? What can corporate management do to promote effective strategies at the business level?

Since definitions of "strategy" are many and various, it is important to be clear about our terms. By strategy, I do not mean broad goals and general policy statements. Rather, I mean the pattern of important decisions by which a general manager and his immediate subordinates actually determine the course of a business. The important decisions are those that measurably affect near-term profitability and risk and the longer-term competitive strength and security of the business. By this definition, every business has a strategy, explicit or implicit, coordinated or not. Indeed, business strategy, as defined here, is the core of the general manager's job.

By an explicit or formal business strategy, I mean a carefully developed and detailed program of future management actions—in essence, a program for managing the business over the next two to five years. An explicit strategy should start with a systematic examination of the industry, the market and the competitive environment in order to identify important threats and opportunities. This should be combined with a careful evaluation of the company's own competitive strengths and weaknesses. On the basis of this situation analysis, strategic objectives are set. Alternative strategies for achieving these objectives are then evaluated, and the one that best meets them at an acceptable level of risk is adopted as the strategy of the business—subject, of course, to change as contingencies may require.

Can Strategies Pay Off?

Going through this process will give management, to begin with, a clear and detailed picture of the latest market and competitive conditions. It may renew confidence in the current business strategy, or it may point to the need for action to correct some unsuspected weaknesses—erosion of product superiority or technological edge, or loss of profitability in some product or customer category. But in many cases the benefits are much more far-reaching, for the outcome of the process may be a fundamentally new strategy that will lead, even in a business that is already turning a respectable profit, to substantially increased earnings. It is this possibility that justifies all formal strategy work, for the payoff can be very large.

Consider the case of a small ($60 million sales), once-profitable maker of industrial plastics. Acquired in 1973 by a giant diversified company, it had suffered a serious downturn in 1974 and was performing well below the corporate target ROI.

The division had never developed a formal strategy, but management cherished ambitions of building the division into a major producer of commodity and specialty plastics. On the commodity plastics side, division management had counted on finding new applications in the construction industry. On the assumption that new Occupational Safety and Health Administration (OSHA) plant regulations would force at least a few of its competitors out of the market, it was planning an aggressive marketing program. In this way, management thought it could enlarge the division's operating base and eventually justify and "base load" a new world-scale plant to replace two older, relatively inefficient facilities. Meanwhile, on the specialty side, sales of the division's 200-odd patented plastics were limping badly, and a score of new items added over the past two years had so far failed to take off as expected.

It is not surprising that corporate headquarters was worried. Top management knew that the profit decline since 1974 was due partly to the rising price of one major raw material, a petroleum derivative, and partly to the deteriorating production economics of their old plants. They were less confident about the division's strategic assumptions. What if customers should begin shifting to substitute materials? And what if the maturation of some commodity plastics markets should lead to a more cyclical pattern of demand? Faced with these questions, corporate management decided to invest in a formal strategy development effort.

The initial situation analysis was an eye opener. First, division management's optimism about the commodity end of the business turned out to be ill founded: the specialty plastics side was clearly more promising. an analysis of end-use markets, coupled with detailed projections of likely profit economics, pointed to a slow-growing but genuine opportunity in selected segments. But to capitalize on that opportunity, the product line and marketing effort would have to be modified.

Accordingly, management decided to convert the division, over a five-year period, from a minor factor in many sectors of the industrial plastics market to a strong competitor on a much narrower front. The speciality product line would be tailored to customer requirements, the sales force upgraded and the marketing approach refocused. As demand for the speciality line grew, the division would gradually withdraw from the commodity business. At the same time, exposure and risk would be reduced by closing the older of the two manufacturing plants, by cutting working capital and by eliminating near-term capital expenditures.

Eighteen months after these decisions were made, the division had already realized profit improvements of better than $4 million, almost doubling its profits and performing well above the corporate ROI target.

It did so well, in fact, that a proposal to replace the remaining manufacturing plant with a modern, efficient facility had already been approved. The division's profitable new strategy had four characteristics that are present in most high-payoff strategies:

It focused on the sectors of highest potential yield. The plastics division concentrated on the most profitable and exploitable product families and types, customer industries and specific customers, and channels of distribution. Analysis showed that well over half of the division's 200 speciality plastics line were making a marginal contribution to fixed costs or actually losing money. Nearly forty had been competing in markets where they were clearly inferior; for example, one that was being pushed for outdoor application did not stand up well to weathering. And the many colors offered often meant short, uneconomic production runs.

By pruning unprofitable products and consolidating product recipes, the division reduced its line to thirty-three items that had above-average performance characteristics and were targeted at end-use markets where competition was not yet severe and demand was likely to grow. Prices were increased, based on the price differential with the nearest competitive material and the calculable effect on the customer's production costs. A special surcharge was instituted on low-volume purchases of nonstandard colors.

It balanced profit payoff and business risk. In its drive for expanded market share in the commodity sector, the plastics division had unwittingly embraced a high-risk strategy. Despite its precarious position as a marginal competitor, it had failed to plan for such contingencies as a proposed federal regulation that could have wiped out one major product application. Moreover, it would have sharply increased its financial exposure had it proceeded with the proposal to replace the two obsolete plants.

Management carefully examined a range of alternatives before settling on the strategy offering the most acceptable combination of risk and payoff. Risk was reduced by withdrawing from the commodity business, while the phaseout of the older factory shrank the asset base and cut working capital. To put the strategy on a pay-as-you-go basis, specific financial and market development objectives were set up for specialty plastics, and replacement of the second plant was tied to their attainment. At the same time, a targeted sales effort and a tough manufacturing cost reduction program were launched.

It emphasized both feasibility and consistency. Surprisingly often, businesses plan market and sales initiatives, product development programs and the like that are unrealistic or incompatible. The plastics division, for example, had been trying to penetrate the specialty market with a sales force that knew how to sell only commodity plastics to a few high-volume customers. Unable to help with new applications, they soon lost the few prospects that turned up for the specialty line. The new strategy, in contrast, explicitly identified target customers and analyzed their potential, and laid out programs for upgrading the sales force and providing applications support.

Again, though the division was plagued with cost problems and loaded with new products it couldn't sell, its R&D staff had been hard at work developing new specialty products. But four out of the twelve new products under development were technological long shots, and the total potential market for the rest was estimated at less than $50 million. Under the new strategy, a watchdog group of managers—from marketing, customer applications assistance and R&D—was set up to keep all new product and applications projects geared to the new market priorities.

It specified tasks, responsibilities, and timetables. Specific goals, responsibilities and completion dates were assigned to each major product group and business function for three years ahead. Volume, profit and market share objectives were translated into specific targets such as the percentage of trial customers to be converted into repeat purchasers and the amount and timing of price increases by product and customer. Performance criteria were established for successive six-month progress reviews, and contingency moves were mapped out, based on the results in hand and the market and competitive situation as each checkpoint was reached.

What Goes Wrong?

In view of the payoff possible from high-quality strategy work, why are so few companies satisfied with the results of their strategic planning efforts? Observation suggests three principal reasons: superficial analysis, monolithic planning and inadequate review.

Superficial Analysis. Like the detective who pursues the most obvious leads and then arrests the butler, when more digging might have led him to Lady Emily, strategic planners are often inclined to be satisfied with superficial answers, especially if these fit in with management's preconceptions. The resulting strategies rarely address the most important opportunities, threats and weaknesses. Often they amount to little more than a warmed-over rationale for maintaining the status quo.

A large manufacturer of office equipment wanted to stop a gradual erosion of market share and profitability in one of its mainstay product lines. Management believed that the market was growing, that market size was sensitive to price and that the company's still strong market position gave it a cost advantage over competitors. By cutting its prices, it reasoned, it could rebuild its market share and eventually lower unit production costs and increase total dollar profits. Accordingly, it cut prices, but the loss of market share continued. The explanation was simple: its competitors' products were more reliable, more easily maintained and backed by better field service.

Meanwhile, small, unsophisticated users and first installations—once the main source of market growth—were thinning out, while in big companies, already used to good service from their copier and computer suppliers, satellite installations were multiplying. These trends called for improvement of field maintenance services and, possibly, the development of adaptation kits that would increase the versatility, reliability and maintainability of the product. But in settling for shallow analysis, management missed the critical factors.

Monolithic Planning. Good strategic planning calls for extensive staff analysis of market and competitive data not generated by the routine information system. It cannot be a spin-off from routine operational planning, which is fundamentally different in nature and purpose. Operational planning is used to establish incremental business objectives and "program" the business toward their achievement. Hence, it needs relatively little analysis and is best done by line management with minimum staff participation.

Failing to appreciate this crucial distinction, many companies make the mistake of yoking strategic planning to the annual planning-budgeting cycle, requiring their managers to write up a "business strategy" as part of the annual planning effort. Since both sets of plans draw on the same data sources and are commonly reviewed together by top management at budget time, routine manipulation of financial data tends to drive out fresh, innovative thinking. Indeed, the strategies may amount to little more than fundraising proposals that highlight the pros and bury the cons of the proposed course of action.

Inadequate Review. Business strategies that have been reviewed by several levels of management are often virtually assured of approval once they get to the top. To be sure, the strategy may be trimmed. A capital project may be turned down or delayed when money is tight, the R&D budget may be cut or not expanded, and the unit may be given a cash bogey to meet. But the planners are rarely sent back to the drawing board.

Many chief executives hardly know what questions to put to their division managers in strategy review sessions, and their staff people are not much better off. In effect, this means that there is no check on empire-building tendencies among division managers—nor, for that matter, is there any real incentive to excellence in staff work. Good strategies cannot be developed without the stimulus of critical challenge and informed counteradvocacy, and these in turn are impossible without superior staff work and the will to use it.

Developing Business Strategies

A growing number of companies have been notably successful in developing business strategies by following an approach that avoids these common mistakes. Every three to five years, a full-time multifunctional team is put together under the guidance of the business unit manager to develop the business strategy. Typically, the project team may comprise half a dozen members: a marketing manager; one representative each from manufacturing, R&D and the controller's office; and, particularly in first-time efforts, one or two experienced strategy analysts perhaps on loan from the corporate planning staff or a sister division. As outsiders to the business, their objectivity and healthy skepticism generally are of great help in problem definition and project planning, and sharpen the focus of the team's data collection and analysis. The process the team follows is carefully structured, and the analytical work is punctuated with regular review meetings to synthesize findings, check progress and refocus work when so indicated. Corporate management as well as corporate staff are deeply involved in the evaluation and approval of the strategies.

Normally, the strategy project will comprise three phases: assessing the current status of the business; generating and evaluating alternative strategies; and developing an action program for the chosen strategy. Let us look at these in turn.

Assessing Current Status. To evaluate the business's competitive standing in view of present and expected market conditions and weigh the opportunities for strengthening or revising its strategy, the team analyzes the attractiveness of the industry, both in total and by market segments. The team also examines the company's strengths and weaknesses as compared to its competitors in each market segment, investigates major opportunities and threats, and estimates the overall opportunity for profit improvement. Typically, it begins by working through a series the questions in order to identify those few issues that will most crucially affect the future of the business. Such questions might include: How mature is each segment of our industry? What new sources of market growth can we foresee? Is the industry becoming more cyclical? Are competitive factors changing (for example, product line elaboration declining and cost control gaining in importance)? Is our industry as a whole likely to be hurt by continuing inflation? Are new regulatory restrictions impending?

Turning from the industry situation to its own competitive position, the team might ask: How mature is our product line? How do our products perform compared with their leading competitors? How does our marketing capability compare? What about our cost position? What are our customers' most common criticisms? Where are we most vulnerable to competitors? How strong are we in our distribution channels? How productive is our technology? How good is our record in new product introduction?

Some critical issues are immediately apparent in many companies. For example, a company in a highly concentrated industry might be unable to hold its market share if a powerful competitor were to mount an all-out marketing effort to launch a low-priced new product. Again, in a capital-intensive industry, the cyclical pattern and possible pressures on pricing are usually critical. If product transport costs are high, preemptive investments in regional manufacturing facilities may be called for. Other obvious key issues may relate to threats of backward integration by customers or forward integration by suppliers, technological upset, new regulatory action, or the entry of foreign competition in the home market.

Most strategy teams supplement this brainstorming exercise with certain basic analyses that often lead to fresh insights and a more focused list of critical business issues. Three of these—profit economics analysis, market segmentation analysis and competitor profiling—deserve attention here.

Profit Economics Analysis. This analysis will show how product costs are physically generated and where the economic leverage lies, details that are usually masked by financial accounting systems. The contributions of individual products to fixed costs and profit are calculated by classifying the elements of cost as fixed, variable or semivariable and subtracting variable cost from product price to yield contribution per item sold. It is then possible to test the sensitivity of profits to possible variations in volume, price and cost elements. Similar calculations can be carried out by manufacturing facility, by distribution channel and by customer.

Calculations by equipment hour are also useful if different product mixes produce different machine yields, or if a manufacturing bottleneck calls for trade-offs in production scheduling. Value-added analysis, showing the relative economic value added at each stage in the processing of a product from raw material procurement to final sale and after-sale maintenance, can also be informative.

Segmenting the Market. Segmenting can be done in various ways: by end-use applications, product performance characteristics, customer industries and customer characteristics (such as buying sophistication), regional markets, channels of distribution and even manufacturing processes. Once the appropriate segmentation has been decided, the team will normally seek to project the determinants of demand (including cyclical factors and any constraints on market size or growth rate) and to explain pricing patterns, relative market shares and other determinants of profitability. Of course, the results may indicate that a different segmentation scheme should be used in developing the market-related elements of the business strategy.

Profiling Competitors. Competitor analysis may involve examining their sales literature, talking with experts or representatives of industry associations, and interviewing shared customers and any known former employees of competitors. If more information is needed, the team may acquire and analyze competing products and perhaps even arrange to have competitors interviewed by a third party. Using these data, competitors are compared in terms of product features and performance, pricing, likely product costs and profitability, marketing and service efforts, manufacturing facilities and efficiency, and technology and product development capabilities. Finally, each competitor's basic strategy is inferred from these comparisons.

A recent example illustrates how a planning team may move from basic analysis to the identification and study of specific strategic issues. A medium-sized manufacturer of preprogrammed control circuitry (I will call it Omicron, Inc.) had made its mark by supplying standardized components to the low end of the manufacturing process control market. Its strategy team began with a market segmentation analysis, listing all the end-use equipment markets for preprogrammed control circuitry and all the manufacturers producing for these markets. It then probed the largest and fastest growing market segments to discover the sources of market growth, the cyclical extent of the market, value added to customers' products by the circuitry component, customers' buying sophistication, likelihood of substitution by more advanced product technologies, the strength and inferred strategies of competitors, and prevalent selling methods.

These market segments, though potentially very profitable, turned out to be highly competitive and dominated by a few technologically rich companies. Moreover, new competitors were likely to move in with well-financed product development programs. Similar probing of several slower growing segments disclosed a slower rate of technological development, less cost and performance pressure by customers, and a mixed pattern of direct selling and selling through manufacturers' representatives and distributors.

Among the issues raised by these findings were the following:

> Should the strategy concentrate on the safer, slow growing market segments, or on the riskier, faster growing ones?
>
> What were the prospects for preprogrammed control circuitry in the high growth market segments? In the slow growth segments? How would heavier investment in product development be likely to pay off in the former? What about heavier spending on sales and customer assistance in the latter?
>
> What future reductions in unit manufacturing costs would be necessary to stay competitive in selected high-growth and low-growth market segments, respectively?
>
> Which market segments might be better exploited by direct selling? Would different incentive arrangements improve sales by manufacturers' representatives?

Having identified the major issues, the strategy team and the business unit manager then framed one or more hypotheses with respect to each and specified what analysis was required to confirm or modify the hypothesis. They then summarized all this in an issue-oriented work plan.

With the work plan in hand, the Omicron team proceeded to analyze six large, slow growing market segments and four smaller but faster growing ones. For each end-use segment, they developed a detailed five-year market projection (both new and replacement volume) by specific application and major prospective customer; investigated the maturity and cost of neighboring technologies, projecting their likely performance advances and reductions in unit costs; and attempted to project their own future unit cost and product efficacy pattern.

This last step took the team deeply into the company's own manufacturing economics to consider supporting issues. Could process improvements reduce the machine-hour time for certain costly components? How would likely increases in material and energy costs affect variable costs and product contribution? Could fixed costs be reduced by replacing some equipment and changing maintenance and repair schedules? Would it pay to cut down on rejected batches and, therefore, reprocessing, by improving the quality of manufacture?

The result of this work was a detailed picture of manufacturing economics showing the real cost and profitability of each product at various production levels, its susceptibility to future cost pressures, and the likelihood of achieving further unit cost reductions. Together with the market analysis and technology assessment, this analysis of profit economics served as the basis for setting marketing priorities, establishing a manufacturing cost reduction program and modifying the product development program. Equally important, it laid the groundwork for framing and evaluating alternative strategies.

For another example of strategic issue analysis, consider the case of an industrial gas manufacturer compelled by soaring electricity costs to raise its prices to its merchant customers at a time when their consumption was rapidly increasing. The strategy team knew that the combination of increased consumption and increased price could push the customers into building their own gas conversion plants. Therefore, they proposed that the company offer to build and operate over-the-fence plants for customers who are approaching the tipover point.

To determine this tipover point as precisely as possible, the strategy team calculated the cost of gas usage in various customers' manufacturing processes, the cost to the customer of buying various sizes of gas conversion plants from a competitor, the likely cost of customer-produced gas under various plant utilization rates, and the availability of regional merchant gas markets to customers wishing to sell off their own excess gas capacity. An economic model constructed with the aid of this information enabled the manufacturer to predict quite accurately when each of its key

FIGURE 1
Alternative Business Strategies

	Thrust	Description	Product Line
"Managed exit" from business	Divest	• Maximize cash flow and earnings • Cut back R&D, sales force, technical service • Sell proprietary technology and specialty business • Minimize EPA/OSHA compliance	• 300MM lbs. of current products (declining to 225MM with loss of productivity)

"Think lean" commodity producer	Harvest	• Operate as "lean" as possible
		  — Reduce R&D, technical service, and sales force to minimum
		  — Sell proprietary technology and specialty business
		• Contract 80+ percent of output
		• Compete as a commodity rather than specialty producer
			• 240MM lbs. Product A
			  190MM lbs. Product B
			  430MM lbs.

"Think small" specialty producer	Selective Investment	• Compete only in those markets with a competitive advantage (e.g., Products B and C)
		• Develop small, specialized sales staff, technical service group, research and development team
		• Expand specialty business on a "wait and see" basis
			• 220MM lbs. Product B
			  135MM lbs. Product C
			  355MM lbs.

"Buy-time" approach	Selective Investment	• Consolidate current product lines at Houston
		  — Maintain current *potential* product mix
		  — Renew all productive capacity
		• Operate small specialty business (25MM-30MM lbs.) at either Newark or Houston plants
		• Selectively trim and add to sales force technical service, R&D, other overhead departments
			• 210MM lbs. Product A
			  180MM lbs. Product B
			  310MM lbs. Product C
			  700MM lbs.

"Consolidate position"/build a flexible three-product plant	Selective Investment	• Load Houston plant with Product A production • Aggressively pursue specialty business at Newark plant • If Specialty Program succeeds, expand Newark plant capacity for specialty products	*At Houston* 250MM lbs. Product A *At Newark* 180MM lbs. Product B 150MM lbs. Product C 330MM lbs.

Manufacturing Facilities Requirements	Capital Costs	Timing
• Patch up Newark and Houston Plants to meet minimum EPA/OSHA regulatory requirements	• $2.0MM-$2.5MM (non-maintenance EPA/OSHA expenditures)	• Shut down both plants in 2½ years (by June 1979)
• Concentrate manufacturing at Houston plant • Close Newark plant by end of 1979 • Finish Houston expansion and open a second line for Product B production	• $14.0MM Houston expansion $ 5.0MM Product B line $3.25MM Refurbish 16th reactor from Newark ―――― $22.25MM	• Houston expansion completed mid-1977 • Product B capacity completed late 1977
• Convert Product A expansion at Houston to Product B • Transfer 16th reactor at Newark to Houston on-line with five small reactors • Locate specialty plant at either plant location	• $14.0MM Houston expansion $3.25MM Refurbish 16th reactor $ 1.0MM Other ―――― $18.25MM	• Product B capacity completed mid-1977 • Product C capacity on-stream in late 1977
• Locate three product lines at Houston — One-line Product A (two 18,000 gal. reactors) — One-line Product B (16th reactor plus five old reactors) — New-line 25,000-gal. reactor for Product C • Shut down Newark plant by December 1977	• $14.0MM Houston expansion $ 5.0MM Product C line $1.25MM Refurbish 16th reactor $ 2.0MM Other ―――― $22.25MM	• Houston Product A capacity on-stream late 1978 • Flexible plant (three lines) on-stream late 1979
• Houston expansion for Product A production • Begin Newark two-product expansion of specialty business in mid 1977 — Product B line — Products C and D line	• $14.0MM Houston expansion $6.0MM-$7.0MM EPA/OSHA $6.0MM Newark revitalization ―――― $26.0MM	• 250MM lbs. Product A capacity at Houston available 1978 130MM-150MM lbs. expansion at Newark available 1981

customers would integrate backward and what size and price for an over-the-fence plant would be most attractive in each case.

As the analysis of critical issues unfolds, the strategy team develops a picture of the growth and earnings prospects of the business over the next several years. The team can then tentatively judge its proper positioning in the company's business portfolio: whether it warrants substantial investment, should be managed mainly for earnings with selective investment, or ought to be considered strictly as a source of near-term cash (or, possibly, as a candidate for divestment). These findings, after review and approval by top management, lay the basis for the next phase.

Evaluating Alternative Strategies. Next, the team begins to define alternative strategies; evaluates them for profit payoff, investment cost, feasibility and risk; and then presents them to top management for decision. This phase is more straightforward than the preceding one, but teams can still easily get off the track.

The most common pitfall is lack of specificity. Broad language such as "maintain low unit cost," "provide high quality service," "identify and serve market segments requiring high quality components," is no substitute for precise description and differentiation of alternatives. If the team has done the proper diagnostic job in the first phase, it should have little difficulty in thinking through concrete strategy alternatives related to the key opportunities and threats before the business. In addition, many teams work with a table of strategies, such as shown in the accompanying table, to find the right level of abstraction in defining alternatives. In setting out these strategy alternatives for evaluation, the team tries to specify the risks and payoff probalities associated with each, so that top management can make a balanced choice.

The most effective teams I have observed try to confine themselves to alternatives which, within the scope of the agreed portfolio category, present management with real choices. Ambitious alternatives are fitting for a business assessed for investment (rapid growth with negative cash flow); but for a business assessed as a candidate for "harvesting" (as a cash source or a divestment candidate), each alternative should combine cash generation with minimum R&D and minimum capital investment.

Initially, a team may come up with a dozen or more strategic alternatives, but informal discussion with management can soon pare these down to a handful. Each surviving alternative is then weighed in terms of projected financial consequences (sales, fixed and variable costs, profitability, investment, return on assets and so on), and relevant nonfinancial measures (market shares, product quality and reliability indices, manufacturing efficiencies) over, perhaps, the coming three to five years. When a large number of product lines are being considered, a simple computer-based financial model can be useful for projecting income and cash flow statements and balance sheets, as well as testing the sensitivity of projected

FIGURE 2
Strategy Implementation Schedule

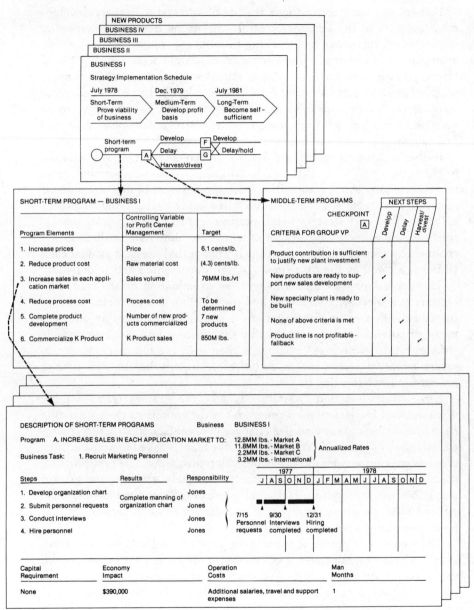

outcomes to reasonable variations in input assumptions, once the basic sales volume, product cost and investment figures have been estimated.

Perhaps the most conspicuous feature of successful strategy development projects is the amount of effort the teams devote to examining important contingencies and thinking through appropriate responses. For example, if product cost reduction programs should achieve only 70% of target, what pricing and distribution actions might be taken? If an over-supplied product pipeline should empty more slowly than predicted, what shifts in marketing expenditures would be indicated? What ought to be done if OSHA or the Consumer Products Safety Commission should promulgate new work safety or product usage controls?

If the business is a cyclical industry, each alternative will also be tested against several market-size scenarios, perhaps incorporating varying assumptions about competitive pricing pressures. In industries dominated by a few competitors, the team will usually evaluate the business's ability to adapt each strategy to competitive actions, such as pricing moves, shifts in advertising strategy or attempts to dominate a distribution channel. As a side benefit, this will help ensure that the case against each strategy, as well as the case for it, is well documented and understood.

This second phase culminates with an examination of the trade-offs between the alternative strategies and the selection of a preferred strategy (together with two or three alternative strategies representing different mixes of potential payoff and risk) by the business unit manager and his strategy team. A progress briefing is then held for top management to secure tentative agreement on a choice of strategy before staff time is invested in implementing it.

Developing an Action Program. Finally, the strategy teams will lay out a detailed implementation program for the chosen strategy including recommendations for any needed changes in organization structure, budgets, staffing or systems. In one company, the team is asked to prepare three consecutive eighteen-month implementation programs. The first program specifies, for each product or product family: sales, earnings and market share objectives; programs, tasks and steps; benefits to the business unit; elapsed time, expected results, responsibility, timetable, capital requirements, operating costs and man-months.

The sequence of product-specific programs is then displayed in network charts. These programs also specify criteria for alternative actions (hold, delay, reduce or divest) to be taken at the end of each eighteen-month period. The accompanying figures give examples of formats used by this particular company in developing action programs. In effect, this approach gives managers at all levels a map with which to monitor the business and enables top management to react faster and more flexibly than ever before to changes in the business environment.

As its final task, the strategy project team may be asked to specify—

based on its fresh knowledge of the business—any new management information requirements. This may well lead to a general upgrading of the business unit's information systems. Management may also decide to institute an overlay information system—in effect, a project status tracking system—to track progress against the strategy and to monitor strategic external variables (for example, competitors' plans to expand capacity).

A New Corporate Federalism?

The approach to developing business strategy described in this article has implications for the corporate form of organization and the relationships between the corporate office and the individual business units. In particular, it challenges decentralization as practiced in many large corporations. Decentralized profit or investment centers are usually the best way to divide large, diversified companies into manageable and accountable portions. But the profit centers may easily gain so much autonomy that chief executives and their corporate management groups become spectators rather than shapers of major strategic decisions.

Clearly, the business unit managers must remain accountable for the profitability of their businesses. Just as clearly, corporate management needs to maintain ultimate operational as well as financial control. In practice, this suggests that strategic decisions might best be made at three levels in a diversified company: by the corporate group alone where portfolio decisions on the strategic thrust of the businesses are at issue; by the chief executive and the business unit manager jointly where the elements of a business strategy are concerned; and by the business unit manager and key subordinates where questions of implementation are at stake. Given real corporate participation in shaping strategy for the business units, day-to-day operating decisions could then be effectively decentralized to the business unit level.

Admittedly, these changes would tend to centralize some of the strategic decisions now normally being made at the individual business level. But they would not reduce the active involvement of the responsible business managers. Indeed, these managers would have a freer hand in executing the strategy and producing bottom-line results. Such a new balance is, I think, consistent with the basic principles of decentralization. And it is probably the best available solution to the "president's paradox."

STRATEGIC EVALUATION
AND STRATEGIC CHOICE

Never follow the crowd.

Bernard M. Baruch

The preceding chapter surveyed the ins and outs of the major strategic alternatives. The task here is to examine some of the analytic considerations which go into the strategy evaluation process and the final selection of strategy. Specifically, we will delve into such questions as: What are the relevant factors to consider in making a strategic evaluation? How can a portfolio of businesses be evaluated? How can the key success factors in a business be identified? How can predictions of trends and economic conditions be factored into strategic analysis? What criteria can be used to separate strong strategic candidates from weak ones? What role does judgment play in finally deciding upon a choice of strategy?

Our discussion of strategy evaluation will be at two levels, corporate strategy and business strategy. Corporate strategy evaluation deals principally with the question of what set of businesses to be in; business strategy evaluation centers around the question of how to compete most effectively in a given line of business. The issues involved are different enough to require different evaluative approaches.

STRATEGY EVALUATION AT THE CORPORATE LEVEL

Approaches to strategy evaluation at the corporate level vary to some extent with the type of company. In a diversified, multiindustry enterprise, the primary task of corporate strategy evaluation is one of (1) working out tentative corporate objectives and the desired portfolio lineup of businesses, (2) determining the relative attractiveness of each of the firm's current businesses, and (3) figuring out how the performance of the total portfolio can be upgraded via better strategic management of existing businesses, further diversification, and/or divestiture. The development and evaluation of *business* strategies in multiindustry companies tend to be delegated to lower-level general managers who have profit-and-loss responsibility for particular divisions and product lines. Corporate and business strategies are then joined and dovetailed by negotiation between corporate managers and business-unit managers, usually according to the priorities and objectives of corporate strategy. Consequently, in a multi-industry enterprise business strategy tends to follow corporate strategy.

In contrast, in single-line or dominant-product-line companies, the strategy of the base business assumes priority, after which diversification and other portfolio questions relating to corporate strategy are addressed. Such firms generally do not divorce corporate strategy evaluation and business strategy evaluation because (1) activities outside the base business contribute minimally to sales and profits and (2) the issue of "which way do we go from here" is so closely related to the main business. Thus in dominant-business companies corporate strategy is heavily keyed to business strategy instead of being the other way around.

In this section we shall concentrate on the portfolio approach to corporate strategy evaluation since it is the prevailing method of strategy analysis at the corporate level in diversified firms and in multi-product firms. In less diversified firms, the portfolio approach is applicable, but requires modification: the issue being not so much how to alter the business portfolio to make it perform better as what kind of new businesses—if any—should the firm attempt to get into to go along with its base business.[1]

The Portfolio Approach to Corporate Strategy Evaluation

One of the simplest and easily visualized ways of making an aggregate assessment of a firm's several lines of business is to construct a *business portfolio* matrix. This type of matrix is useful for comparing different businesses on the basis of such strategically relevant variables as growth rate in sales, relative competitive position, stage of product/market evolution, market share, and industry attractiveness. Any two-variable comparison can be used.

The most publicized business portfolio matrix is a four-square grid pioneered by the Boston Consulting Group (BCG) and depicted in Figure 4–1.[2] Each of the company's businesses is plotted in the matrix according

---

[1] However, the portfolio approach turns out to be just as valid for a multiproduct firm as for a multiindustry firm when the former manages each product and/or market segment as if they were independent businesses.

[2] For a more detailed discussion see Barry Hedley, "A Fundamental Approach to Strategy Development," *Long-Range Planning* (December 1976), pp. 2–11.

FIGURE 4–1
The BCG Business Portfolio Matrix

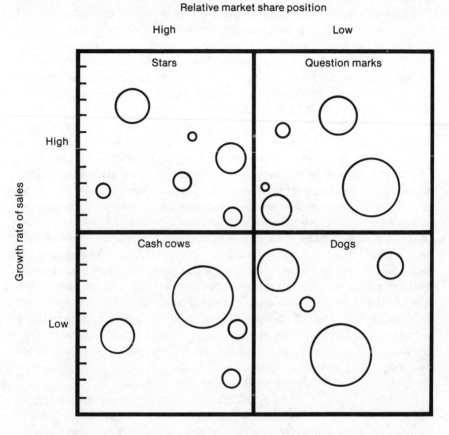

Relative market share position

High | Low

Stars | Question marks

High

Growth rate of sales

Cash cows | Dogs

Low

to its percentage growth rate in sales and its relative market share position.[3] The size of each circle in the matrix is proportional to the sales revenues generated by each business.

Businesses with high growth rates and high market share positions are labeled as "stars" by BCG, because they usually represent the best profit and growth opportunities in the firm's portfolio. As such, they are the businesses that an enterprise needs to nurture and groom for the long-run. Star-type businesses vary as to whether they need heavy infusions of investment funds to support continued rapid growth and high performance. Some stars (usually those that are well-established and beginning to mature) are virtually self-sustaining in terms of cash flow, and little investment will be needed from sources external to the business. Young

---

[3] Relative market share position is measured by the ratio of the business's market share to the market share held by the largest rival firm.

stars, however, often require substantial investment capital beyond what can be generated internally to maintain and secure their high growth/high market share ranking.

Businesses with a high market share in a low growth market are called "cash cows" by BCG because their entrenched position tends to yield substantial *cash surpluses* over and above what is needed for reinvestment and growth in the business. Many of today's cash cows are yesterday's stars. Cash cows, though less attractive from a growth standpoint, are nonetheless a valuable corporate portfolio holding because they can be "milked" for the cash to pay corporate dividends and corporate overhead, they provide debt capacity, and they provide cash flow to make new acquisitions and support investment in the next round of stars. "Strong cash cows" are not "harvested" but are maintained and managed for cash flow. The idea is to preserve market position while efficiently generating dollars to reallocate to business investments elsewhere. "Weak cash cows," however, may be prime candidates for harvesting and, eventually, divestiture.

Businesses with low growth and low market share are referred to as "dogs" by BCG because of their weak competitive position (owing, perhaps, to high costs, low quality products, less effective marketing, and the like) and the low profit potential that can be associated with slow growth and impending market saturation. Another characteristic of dogs is the lack of attractive cash flow on a long-term basis. Sometimes they do not produce enough cash to maintain their existing position, especially if competition is stiff, profit margins are thin, or inflation is causing sharply higher costs. Consequently, except for unusual reasons, BCG recommends that dogs be harvested, divested, or liquidated, depending on which alternative will maximize short-term cash flow.

Businesses falling in the upper right quadrant of the matrix are tagged as "question marks." Rapid market growth makes the business attractive from an industry standpoint, but low market share makes it questionable whether the profit potential associated with growth can realistically be captured; hence, the "question mark" designation. According to BCG, question mark businesses are typically "cash hogs"; so labeled because their cash needs are high (owing to rapid growth) and their internal cash generation is low (owing to low market share). BCG reasons that the most rational strategic options for a question market business are (1) to grow it into a star or, if the costs of strengthening its competitive position do not warrant the effort, (2) to divest it.

For evaluating different businesses and reaching strategic decisions on how to manage the corporate portfolio, the BCG business portfolio has considerable appeal. Yet, several legitimate shortcomings exist:

1. A four-cell matrix based on high-low classifications gives scant attention to the many businesses in varying degrees of intermediate positions. All businesses cannot be neatly and accurately categorized as stars, dogs, cash cows, or question marks.

2.   Other relevant strategic factors exist besides just business growth rate and relative market share position—including stage of product-market evolution, strategic fit among the different businesses, the presence of competitive advantages and distinctive competences, emerging threats and opportunities, vulnerability to recession, market structure, capital requirements, and size of market. The BCG matrix does not give explicit consideration to these factors.

3.   The variables of growth rate and market share are not always good proxies for a business's profitability, cash flow, and overall industry attractiveness. In many industries, companies with a low market share are able to earn consistently high profits and sometimes outperform larger rivals. High market share businesses in low growth industries may not generate cash surpluses since it is to be expected that competition will stiffen and profit margins will shrink during the maturity-saturation stages. In sum, long-run profitability is subject to a variety of influences not directly tied to growth and market share.

In recognition of these difficulties, General Electric, with some help from McKinsey & Co., has developed a nine-cell portfolio matrix based on long-term product-market attractiveness and business strength/competitive position. In this matrix, depicted in Figure 4–2, the area of the circles is proportional to the size of the industry, and the pie slices within the circles reflect the business's market share. At GE, product-market attractiveness is defined as a *composite projection* of market size, market growth rate (units and real dollars), competitive diversity, competitive structure, profitability, and technological, social, environmental, legal, and human impacts.[4] Business strength or competitive position is viewed as a function of market size and growth rate, market share, profitability, margins, technology position, skill or weaknesses, image, environmental impact, and calibre of management.[5]

The strength of the Figure 4–2 approach is twofold. One, it allows for intermediate rankings between high and low and between strong and weak and, two, it incorporates explicit consideration of a much wider variety of strategically relevant variables. However, once each existing business has been evaluated and positioned in the matrix, the prescriptions for what to do with each business to improve the overall portfolio lineup are largely analogous to those for the four-cell matrix. The only difference concerns what to do with those that are "average," and no generalized answers can be given. Here lies the greatest shortcoming of the matrix approach: it provides no real clues or hints as to the right strategy for dealing with the vast number of businesses which, of statistical necessity, are "average" or close to average. Thus, while the business portfolio matrix is insightfully suggestive of the "right" strategies for managing

---

[4] William K. Hall, "SBUs: Hot, New Topic in the Management of Diversification," *Business Horizons*, vol. 21, no. 1 (February 1978), p. 20.

[5] Ibid.

FIGURE 4–2
GE's Nine-Cell Business Portfolio Matrix

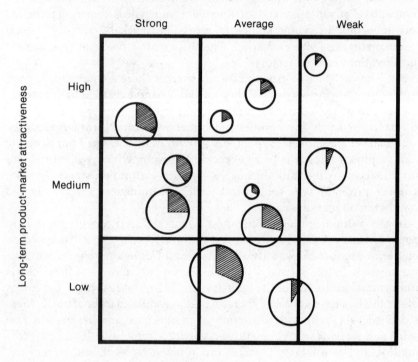

stars, dogs, and cash cows, it suggests virtually nothing about the right strategy selection for average or near-average businesses. This is a very serious weakness given the direction-setting function of corporate strategy and given that every business needs a specific strategy that will lead to the best possible performance, regardless of its attractiveness and competitive position.

Another weakness has been pointed out by Hofer and Schendel: the GE approach does not depict as well as it might the positions of businesses that are about to emerge as winners because the product/market is entering the takeoff stage.[6] To better identify a *developing winner* type of business, Hofer and Schendel propose a 15-cell matrix in which businesses are plotted in terms of stage of product/market evolution and competitive position, as shown in Figure 4–3.[7] Again, the circles represent the sizes of the industries involved and pie wedges denote the business's market share. Looking at the plot in Figure 4–3, business A would appear to be a

---

[6] Charles W. Hofer and Dan Schendel, *Strategy Formulation: Analytical Concepts* (St. Paul, Minn.: West Publishing Co., 1978), p. 33.

[7] Ibid., p. 34. This approach to business portfolio analysis was reportedly first used in actual practice by consultants at Arthur D. Little, Inc.

FIGURE 4–3
A Product/Market Evolution Portfolio Matrix

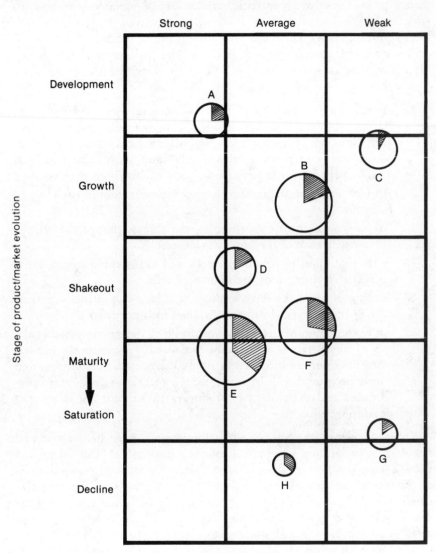

Source: Adapted from C. W. Hofer, "Conceptual Constructs for Formulating Corporate and Business Strategies," (Boston: Intercollegiate Case Clearing House, #9–378–754, 1977), p. 3.

developing winner, business C might be classified as a *potential loser,* business E might be labeled an *established winner,* business F could be a cash cow, and business G a loser or a dog. The power of the Hofer-

Schendel approach is the story it tells about the distribution of the firm's businesses across the stages of product-market evolution.

Actually, there is no need to force a choice as to which type of portfolio matrix to use: several types with various sets of variables can be constructed to gain insights from different perspectives. Each matrix type has its pros and cons. The important thing is not so much methodological procedure as it is completeness of analysis. Thus, whatever approach best fits an organization's own situation, a thorough corporate portfolio evaluation will include:

1. A searching assessment of each industry in which the firm does business to determine key trends and market changes, the nature and direction of competition, important technological developments, cost and raw material supply conditions, labor relations, and, in particular, the key factors requisite for high performance.

2. An identification of the firm's competitive position in each line of business.

3. An identification of opportunities and threats that might reasonably arise in each of the firm's businesses.

4. A consideration of what resources and skills could improve the competitive strength of each business unit.

5. A comparison of the relative short- and long-run attractiveness of each of the different businesses in the firm's portfolio.

6. An examination of the overall portfolio to determine whether the mix of businesses is adequately "balanced"; for example, not too many losers or question marks, not so many mature businesses that corporate growth will be slow, not too few dependable profit performers, and enough cash producers to support the stars and developing winners.

To be successful, this sort of evaluative process must be iterative and ongoing, incorporating reappraisals of each business as it develops and takes a new position in the portfolio matrix. Moreover, reassessments of the mix of businesses in the corporate portfolio should be routinely conducted. At General Electric, reappraisal is initiated not just at regular intervals but also when a strategic "trigger point" (an external development projected to have a significant impact on a business's peformance) occurs.[8] Such an approach is one way of keeping a close watch on whether a business actually contributes its expected weight toward the achievement of corporate objectives.

One final point. Once the portfolio has been evaluated and strategic decisions reached on how to handle each business, the process is not con-

---

[8] William K. Hall, "SBUs: Hot, New Topic in the Management of Diversification," p. 22.

cluded. Simply deciding to manage a business as a star or a cash cow will not make anything happen.[9] Detailed business strategies, functional area support strategies, and operating-level strategies will need to be devised and implemented. And numerous alternatives exist: there is more than one kind of cash cow and more than one way to harvest a dog. It is at this juncture that business strategy and corporate strategy come together and can be dovetailed.

STRATEGY EVALUATION AT THE BUSINESS LEVEL

Most of the action and really hard work of strategy evaluation and strategy selection are at the business-unit level. Also, there are more proven, familiar tools and techniques for analyzing a business, for forecasting such things as market growth, pricing, cost changes, and the impact of government regulations, and for arriving at a strategic plan capable of dealing with the moves of competitors, swings in market volume, and customer wants and needs. This section describes some of the approaches and analyses that can be used to assist in strategy evaluation and strategy selection at the business level.

Developing a Strategic Profile
of an Industry

Perhaps the most important phase of business strategy evaluation is that of analyzing industry attractiveness and the position an organization occupies (or is considering occupying) in that industry. Developing a strategic profile of an industry serves several purposes: (1) to assess future industry attractiveness, (2) to help determine a firm's competitive position in an industry, (3) to identify the key success factors for profitably competing in an industry, and (4) to provide benchmarks for appraising any new business strategy alternatives which a firm has under consideration. For a firm considering entry, the role of an industry profile is to take what seems like a promising strategic alternative and gather the information requisite for adequately assessing whether to get into the business.

Often, there is a temptation to short-circuit this phase of strategy evaluation, especially when the strategic alternatives being considered each involve staying within familiar industry bounds or when the pressures of time and circumstance close in. The managements of some organizations may feel that their longtime industry experiences have programmed all of the key factors into their thinking. Supposedly, the reasoning goes, their administrative experiences have schooled them well in the whys and hows of being systematic in their evaluation of pertinent

---

[9] Ibid.

industry information. But experience can also boomerang. Prior knowledge and a stubborn defensive pride in established ways of doing things may blind management to change; a management may assume knowledge about the industry or the overall environment that is no longer accurate. Therefore, a periodic strategic profile analysis in which "the facts" are updated is well worth doing and certainly so when entry into a new industry, product market, or geographic area is being contemplated.

Figure 4–4 contains a checklist of questions part and parcel of a thor-

FIGURE 4–4
Checklist for Developing a Strategic Profile of an Industry

A. *Product-Market Structure*
   1. Identify the industry's products, their characteristics, and position in the product life cycle.
   2. How big is the market? What are the locations of greatest market concentration? Are there major geographic differences in saturation intensity?
   3. Who are the customers and why do they buy the product? What is the degree of market penetration in terms of per capita usage or the target market (households, age categories, etc.)? What are customers really getting in terms of cost savings and/or better performance? Are there meaningful differences between types of customers?
   4. What are the basic determinants of demand? What is the pattern of repeat business? What new product uses could be promoted to broaden the demand base?
   5. Assess the significant market trends. What is the growth profile of the market? Is the market becoming more specialized? More application-oriented? More diverse in terms of customers or products?
   6. What is the relationship between industry demand and general economic conditions?
   7. Is demand sensitive to price changes? Changes in income?

B. *History of the Industry*
   1. What is the industry's growth and profitability record?
   2. At what stage is the industry in its life cycle—infancy? Growth? Maturity? Steady-state? Decline?
   3. Has the industry been plagued by excess capacity? Have there been severe competitive shakeouts during periods of oversupply?
   4. What are the industry's prospects for the future?

C. *Technology and Cost*
   1. Identify the technologies by which the product is made and ascertain the cost structure of each. If there are wide divergencies in production methods and costs, why do they continue to coexist?

FIGURE 4–4 *(continued)*

2. What is the history of innovation in the industry? Which firms are generally recognized as the leaders in innovation? Has innovation produced major changes in costs and prices?

3. Are there any technological threats or opportunities on the horizon?

4. How crucial is technological proficiency to success? Are patents a significant factor? What is the nature and depth of the R&D effort in the industry?

5. How significant are economies of scale and what is the minimum entry size? How has the size of firms in the industry been changing and what are the underlying causes?

6. What are the key cost variables and cost trends? Have costs been rising or falling? Why? How have these changes affected price?

D. *Financial and Operating Considerations*

1. What sort of capital investment is required for entry? Are there any major barriers to entry and exit?

2. What is the expected life of plant and equipment? What is the chance that manufacturing facilities will be made obsolete by technological change or new forms of competition? How adaptable are manufacturing facilities to other uses?

3. What are the typical financial features in terms of debt vs. equity, working capital requirements, investment payback, cash flow, inventory turnover, liquidity ratios, debt ratios, bond and interest coverages, and so on?

4. How is the industry viewed by the banking industry and by Wall Street?

5. What is the financial condition of firms in the industry?

6. What is the relationship between capacity utilization and profit margins?

7. Evaluate labor supply and raw-material supply conditions. What is the union situation and the history of union-management relations in the industry?

8. How are raw materials and finished goods warehoused and shipped? Given service and cost considerations, how adequate are the available modes of transportation?

E. *Marketing*

1. What are the means and methods of marketing the product? Are market channels well-organized or underdeveloped? Do existing channels need shortening, lengthening or a revised emphasis?

2. What makes a product competitive in the industry? Has the industry evidenced a capacity for exploiting new products and developing new markets?

3. What is necessary in terms of advertising, sales promotion, technical support for sales staff, and sales force organization?

FIGURE 4–4 *(concluded)*

4. What is the role of marketing research? Is the R&D based on needs defined by market research? Is it an integral part of new product development?

5. What sort of marketing mix typifies firms in the industry? What proportion of total costs are marketing and distribution expenses? What are the expenses of adding new customers?

6. How significant is new product R&D? Brand consciousness? Trademarks and copyrights? Reputation? The degree of product differentiation? Product customization? Customer loyalty? Obsolescence factors? Customer turnover?

F. *Competition*

1. Draw up a profile of each firm in terms of products, market shares, market coverage, growth, and competitive strategies. What are the *trends* in market standing among the various firms and how do these vary by area, customer type, and product application? Which firms are considered the industry leaders in price and in the introduction of new products and technologies?

2. What features distinguish the poorly performing firms from the outstanding performers?

3. Are there good substitute products? Are they price competitive? For what reasons might customers turn to substitutes?

4. How strong are competitive pressures in the industry and what form do they take? Are these pressures equally strong in every target market niche?

5. How secure are established firms from entry by new firms?

6. Are there geographic limits to competition? Is the focus of competition local, regional, national, or international? Are there any gaps in geographic coverage?

7. How active are trade associations in promoting or containing increased competition?

G. *Key Success Factors and Strategic Forecasts*

1. What are the keys to being successful in this industry; that is, what does a firm have to be sure of doing right in order to succeed? What particular distinctive competences does it need? Are there different requirements for success from one type of customer to another?

2. Make a strategic forecast; i.e., assess the overall shape of future economic, political, market, technological, and competitive conditions to provide a backdrop for viewing the total picture.

3. What conclusions can be drawn from the above with respect to strategy? What is the range of viable strategic options? How strong are the constraints on strategic flexibility?

ough strategic profile of an industry. All of the topics and questions may not be pivotal in each and every situation, but the list does suggest the range of factors to be considered.

Most of the items on the checklist in Figure 4–4 are self-explanatory and warrant no further discussion. However, the item pertaining to the strategic forecast (G-2) merits elaboration.

The Strategic Forecast. It has been noted on several previous occasions that the general manager conducting a strategic analysis is obliged to assess both present and expected future conditions within and without the industry. Indeed, the nature of tomorrow's environment is of more overriding import than today's. Strategic forecasting, as we shall use the term, refers to the judgmental process of predicting the future course of relevant economic, political, market, technological, and competitive changes in an industry.[10] Strategic forecasting is not to be confused with simply extrapolating past trends into the future. There is more to forecasting than just projecting trends, namely the predicting of turning points and major product/market changes, neither of which are necessarily deducible from trend analysis.

Trend projections are inherently rooted in the past and the past is not always a reliable preview of coming events. Hence, while trends have a valid place in the making of an operational forecast, by themselves they are not a trustworthy basis for predicting the future.

Although the specifics of a strategic forecast are understandably a function of each organization's own business and market situation, the thrust of the general issues to be explored does not vary greatly. Figure 4–5 is illustrative of the kinds of questions which ought to be part and parcel of a strategic forecast.

As with any technique to try to see what lies ahead, strategic forecasting is laden with assumptions and uncertainties. Different people may view the same set of "facts" and reach significantly different judgments about where the industry is headed and why. Nonetheless, judgmental errors based on serious analysis are more tolerable than flying blind with little or no preparation for change. At the very least, the "hard to call" areas can be made explicit and explored fully for the various probable scenarios. Moreover, a set of forecasts can be prepared to test the sensitivity of the predictions to changes in the underlying assumptions, this makes contingency planning for forecasting errors much easier. Consequently, a serious attempt at strategic forecasting is better than no attempt. It beats short-sighted management despite the inaccuracies involved.

---

[10] For a more thorough discussion of strategic forecasting and its role in strategy formulation, see Hugo Uyterhoeven, Robert Ackerman, and John Rosenblum, *Strategy and Organization: Text and Cases in General Management*, Rev. Ed. (Homewood, Ill.: Richard D. Irwin, Inc., 1977), chap. 5; and Francis Aguilar, *Scanning the Business Environment* (New York: Macmillan Co., 1967).

FIGURE 4–5
Elements of a Strategic Forecast

1. *Technology.* What sorts of pertinent new products/services are likely to become technically feasible to produce in the foreseeable future? Will it be economically feasible to sell them at a competitively attractive price?

2. *Customer Needs.* Which customer needs are presently *not* being met by existing products? Why? Are R&D activities under way to develop means for fulfilling these needs? What is their status?

3. *Market Change.* What demographic and population-based changes can be anticipated and what do they portend for the size of the market and sales potentials?

4. *Competition.* How likely are important new competitive pressures to arise from substitute products? Entry of new firms? Strategic moves by existing rivals?

5. *Costs and Supply.* What is the likelihood of incurring major cost increases because of a dwindling supply of natural resource-based raw materials? Will sources of supply be reliable? Are there any other reasons to expect major changes in costs?

6. *The Economy.* What is the probable future course of the economy with regard to rates of inflation, unemployment, economic growth, money supply expansion and capital availability, increases in consumer purchasing power, and so on? Which economic variables have the greatest impact on the organization's business?

7. *Government Policy.* What changes in government policy can be expected regarding environmental controls, product safety, consumer protection, antitrust, foreign trade regulations (tariffs, quotas, trade agreements), tax policy, wage-price controls, energy conservation, transportation, and other pertinent regulations? What course will monetary and fiscal policies take in response to economic change?

What uses can be made of such forecasting techniques as intuitive methods of experts (e.g., the Delphi technique), trend extrapolation, regression and correlation analysis, econometrics, and dynamic predictive models (e.g., simulation) to arrive at quantitative estimates of how the above factors might combine to affect overall market and strategic opportunity?

As an illustration of the relevance of strategic forecasts, consider the following long-range strategic issues raised by dwindling world oil supplies. What is the long-range future for firms in the petroleum industry? What should they be doing *today* to prepare for this future? How soon and how fast can rising crude oil prices and a dependence on foreign oil imports be expected to propel a switch to other forms of energy? When and what kinds of new substitute energy sources are likely? What kinds of cost and supply advantages are they likely to have over currently known energy alternatives? Will the established oil companies have access to these new energy technologies or will antitrust factors make them the exclusive province of new companies? How probable is it that large industrial energy-users will be able to integrate backward and supply their own energy needs? Predictive answers to these questions have obvious strategic value to energy suppliers and major energy users and can scarcely fail to weigh heavily in their strategic investment decisions.

Figure 4–6 provides a rundown of major sources of information for

FIGURE 4–6
Sources of Information for Conducting a Strategic Analysis and Evaluating Companies

---

A. *Population, the Economy, and Current Business Conditions*

1. U.S. Department of Commerce, Bureau of the Census, *Census of Population, Census of Housing, County Business Patterns, Census of Governments*—for periodic, but comprehensive and detailed, data on population characteristics, housing conditions, and various business and governmental statistics.

2. U.S. Department of Commerce, *Survey of Current Business* (monthly), *Business Conditions Digest* (monthly), *U.S. Industrial Outlook, Statistical Abstract of the United States* (annually) —for current and historical statistics on the economy and business conditions.

3. Council of Economic Advisors, *Economic Report of the President* (published annually)—contains a good variety of statistics relating to GNP, income, employment, prices, money supply, and governmental finance.

4. United Nations, *Statistical Yearbook*—for various economic statistics of foreign countries.

5. OECD, *Economic Outlook and Main Economic Indicators*—for international economic data.

6. Board of Governors of Federal Reserve System, *Federal Reserve Bulletin* (monthly)—for data on banking, money supply conditions, interest rates, and credit conditions.

7. U.S. Department of Labor, Bureau of Labor Statistics, *Monthly Labor Review* (monthly), *Employment and Earnings* (monthly), *Handbook of Labor Statistics* (annually)—for data on employment, hours worked and earnings, productivity, wholesale and consumer prices, labor turnover, and area unemployment characteristics.

FIGURE 4–6 *(continued)*

8. Editor and Publisher, *Market Guide* (annually)—contains rankings of cities, counties, and SMSA areas based on individual income population, total retail sales, and food sales as well as pertinent local area information.

9. *Sales Management* magazine's "Annual Survey of Buying Power" —for rankings on the amount spent for selected products/ services by geographical location.

B. *Industry Information*

1. U.S. Department of Commerce, Bureau of the Census, *Census of Manufactures, Annual Survey of Manufacturing, Census of Business, Census of Transportation*—for statistics relating to the volume of manufacturing activity, size and structure of firms, retail and wholesale trade, and transportation.

2. Federal Trade Commission, *Quarterly Financial Report for Manufacturing, Mining, and Trade Corporations* (quarterly)—for sales, profit, balance sheet, and income statement statistics by industry division and size of firm.

3. U.S. Department of the Treasury, Internal Revenue Service, *Business Income Tax Returns* (annually) and *Corporate Income Tax Returns* (annually)—for breakdowns on revenues, operating expenses, and profits by type of business organization and industry division.

4. National Industrial Conference Board: research and statistical reports issued periodically and the *Conference Board Record* (monthly).

5. Securities and Exchange Commission: quarterly reports of finance and capital expenditures.

6. Trade association and industry publications such as *The Commercial and Financial Chronicle, Banking, Advertising Age, Automotive News, Public Utilities Fortnightly, Engineering News Record, Best's Insurance Review, Progressive Grocer,* and *Electronic News.*

C. *Company-Oriented Information*

1. Annual reports of companies.

2. Investment services and directories: Standard and Poor's, Moody's, *Value Line.*

3. Financial ratios: Dun & Bradstreet Annual Surveys, Robert Morris Associates *Annual Statement Studies.*

4. Securities and Exchange Commission, Form 10–K reports.

5. Periodicals: *Fortune, Barron's, Forbes, Wall Street Transcript, Dun's Review, Business Week, Financial World, Over-the-Counter Securities Review.*

Source: C. R. Goeldner and Laura M. Dirks, "Business Facts: Where to Find Them," *Business Topics,* vol. 24, no. 3 (Summer 1976), pp. 23–36.

making strategic analyses and strategic forecasts and for finding out about specific companies.

Assessing Competitive Position

Once the industry profile is complete, the next step in business strategy evaluation is to conduct a thorough audit of the competitive environment, with emphasis on determining the competitive position of the business within the industry or, in the case of markets where entry is being contemplated, on identifying the most desirable competitive position to try to occupy. The following questions suggest the major points to be considered:

❑ How firmly does the business stand with its customers? What do customers think of the company and its product line? How does this compare with what they think of rival firms? What is the company's trend in market standing, e.g., reputation improving or not?

❑ What is the image of each major competitor from the viewpoint of the consumer? What are the distinguishing features of each major competitor's strategy? Why and how are they approaching the market differently? What evaluation should be placed on the competitive programs, policies, and strategy execution of major rivals? How do their strategies compare with the company being studied?

❑ What benefits do customers get by buying from this company? Does it offer more or less value than the competition? What are the pivotal product features that prompt a buyer to purchase from one seller and not another? Does the company's product line have these features and how successful has it been at promoting them?

❑ What are the firm's biggest competitive weaknesses? What is it doing and what can it do about them in terms of competitive strategy?

❑ In what segments of the market is the company strongest? weakest? What potential customers is it missing? What is its record on expanding its customer base and what are the reasons for this record?

❑ Is the firm's market standing one of a leader or a follower? Is this confirmed by its customers' perceptions? When customers have a problem do they look to this company or to its rivals for help?

❑ Where does the company rank in the industry on overall competitive effectiveness? How can this ranking be strengthened?

In most cases, the preceding line of questions, if thoroughly probed, should spotlight what it takes to compete successfully (the strategic advantage factors), thereby revealing why and how firms in the industry occupy their relative competitive positions. But in instances where the product line, the competition, or the market is broadly segmented, it may be necessary to do a separate analysis for each product or brand, or for each identifiable market segment. This means conducting a detailed examination of what the specific dimensions of competition are for the distinguishable product-customer segments, followed by an examination of how rival firms vary in their emphasis on these different segments. Determining what variations underlie the competitive strategies of major firms goes a long way toward accounting for some firms in the industry doing better than others. It also facilitates drawing up a profile of the competitive strategies of the major firms and evaluating their respective strengths and weaknesses.[11]

Once the competitive audit of the industry is complete, an enterprise is ready to decide what its own most advantageous strategy might be for this industry and whether and how its market approach should be segmented to allow for differences based upon product applications, geographical territory, customer category, channels of distribution, or other relevant factors.

The Role of Competition in Strategy Evaluation

The audit of the competitive environment sets the stage for thoroughly analyzing the impact of competition on an organization's choice of strategy. Whenever two or more enterprises sell in the same market, their partially conflicting economic interests become manifested in business rivalry. Each firm is motivated to try to outdo the other to gain a stronger foothold with buyers and thereby reap the rewards of market success. Out of this motivation, together with an awareness of the interactions of their approaches to the market, emerges an ongoing series of competitive strategies and counterstrategies—some offensive, some defensive—on the part of each seller in the market.

Each firm's competitive moves and countermoves are likely to be related to its business strategy for developing a viable business organization and achieving a degree of success sufficient to sustain operations over the long-run. With the passage of time, a firm's corporate strategy and/or its line of business strategies will tend either to be fine-tuned or to undergo major overhaul, according to the firm's market successes (or failures) and the durability of its chosen business strategies in withstanding competitive challenges from rival firms.

When a firm makes a successful competitive move, it can expect increased rewards, largely at the expense of either rivals' market shares or their rates of sales growth. The speed and extent of the competitive en-

---

[11] See Jerry Wall, "What the Competition Is Doing: Your Need to Know," *Harvard Business Review*, vol. 52, no. 6 (November-December 1974), pp. 22 ff.

croachment varies, depending on the product being standardized or differentiated, the initiator's competence and resources to capitalize on the advantage the strategy has produced, how difficult it is to shift buyer loyalties, and the ease with which the strategy can be copied. The pressures on rivals to respond vary with all these factors, together with whether the initiator is (1) a major firm with considerable market visibility, (2) a fringe firm whose efforts can be ignored for some time, or (3) a firm in financial distress whose strategy is predicated on desperation.

For instance, if a firm's strategic offensive is keyed to a low price aimed at quick penetration but with a substantial risk that full costs will not be recovered, rivals may judge the strategy short-lived. They may choose to respond or not, depending on their estimates of whether it will be better to meet the low price on a temporary basis or ride out whatever buyer resistance may be encountered. If the initiating firm finds its move neutralized by rivals' countermoves, it is challenged to seek a better strategy not as easily defeated or else remain content with the stalemate it has encountered.

The ease with which a firm's alternative strategies can be neutralized is a major criterion of business strategy selection; firms will gravitate strongly towards competitive approaches which are not easily imitated or defeated. Such considerations should strongly incline a firm to try to develop a distinctive competence whereby it can differentiate its product in ways not susceptible to successful imitations and acquire a reputation and image on some facet or facets of its product offering that sets its product above and apart from other firms'.

A variety of competitive outcomes may flow from the business strategies of rival firms. The pattern of strategic behavior may range from one of cooperation or collusion to one of highly combative rivalry. Because the best strategy for firm A depends on firm B's choice, and because B in turn must choose its strategy in light of the options open to A, what is optimal fades into a fog of interacting uncertainties. And, except in the case of distressed firms in dire straits, no strategic choice is ever final. The sequence of move and countermove is never-ending.

It may be that only a few firms (large or small) will tend to initiate fresh strategic moves. They may not do it often, but to the extent they do, they set the pace for the others, and the give-and-take of move and response spreads and continues. An initiatory move may come from a firm with ambitious growth objectives, from a firm with excess capacity, or from a firm under pressure to gain added business. More generally, though, the important offensive strategies tend to be made by firms that see market opportunities and a chance to improve their standing. Such firms tend to be aware they are starting a chain of moves and countermoves (if in fact it has not already been triggered by other firms), and they have confidence, one, that they are shrewd enough to keep ahead of the game and, two, that they will be better off than they would be by holding back and letting others take the lead. Often, new marketing moves are undertaken by sales force organizations under pressure from top management to increase market penetration and/or otherwise improve performance, the thesis being that an organization which stands still soon stagnates. The more aggressive firms may well *create* competitive pressures that are sufficiently strong to *compel* responses from other firms and also bankrupt the inefficient and ineffective firms—those which have been unable to build an organization with the distinctive competence to attract buyers and to carve out a market niche for their product.

Although initiatory moves may come from a variety of firms for a variety of reasons, it is not likely that all, or even most, firms will take a turn at starting a fresh round of moves. It is to be expected that some firms will be bolder and more aggressive than others in trying to make an impact with their strategies. The defensive responses which follow will not only reflect time lags and uncertainties but their character will tend to differ if the new offensive consists of a new promotional campaign, introduction of a new product or product variation, a new channel of distribution, or an expansive move towards a new form of horizontal or vertical integration. Furthermore, the strategic process will not generally be so active that the market becomes unstable and chaotic. Short intervals of stabilized product offerings may surface that permit firms to better gauge trends and opportunities. In fact, a rapid-fire pattern of fresh moves may turn out to be counterproductive for all concerned because of the confusion and uncertainty which it generates among customers, suppliers, and rival firms.

However, any stalemates or pauses in moves and countermoves tend to be temporary owing to the continuous stream of strategic opportunities and threats which emerge from the possibilities for product variation, cost-related technological changes, new buyer tastes and preferences, changing demographics and lifestyles, shifts in buying power, new product availability, and on and on. Apart from these market-related variables, ongoing changes can also be expected in the host of complex institutional factors that mold a firm's strategy choices from the outside and the intrafirm considerations which shape strategy from the inside. All these aspects, together with the time-sequence of strategic moves and the information base underlying them, act to shape the evaluation of business strategy alternatives and the final choice of a line of business strategy.

Gearing Business Strategy to the Economic Environment

Once a competitive assessment of the strategic alternatives has been made, a second area for analysis is to determine whether each option under consideration is capable of succeeding in a variety of market situations.

To opt for a strategy which is heavily dependent on general economic prosperity and a "seller's market" is to tempt fate. Inevitably, periods of market slack will create excess capacity problems. When over-supply conditions are compounded by a high ratio of fixed costs to total costs, the outcome is a certain profit squeeze. Furthermore, during a recession competitive pressures typically intensify as firms scramble to maintain or build volume back up. The paper industry provides an excellent example of what can happen when strategy is not closely allied with the realities of the business cycle. Time and again, the paper producers have been lulled into overexpanding when demand was strong only to have their profit margins evaporate at the next cyclical downturn. While this occurred partly because additional paper making capacity comes on stream in big increments, it also resulted from individual firms acting without reference to their rivals' expansion plans and the implications these had for supply-demand equilibrium.

On the other hand, to adopt a cautious, defensive posture that minimizes downside risks may put a company in poor position to ride the waves of a booming market. Getting caught short on capacity means a potential loss of market share and perhaps a weaker competitive edge because production facilities, being relatively older, are less cost effective. Overcoming these disadvantages and trying to make up lost ground can be an expensive and time-consuming task. International Nickel Co. (Inco) found this out after complacently standing by while its share of the free world's nickel market dropped from 85 percent in the 1950's to 40 percent in 1974.[12] Late in responding to challenges from competitors, Inco found itself straining when nickel demand began a steep rise in 1963. A $1.1 billion expansion program was launched in 1966 to increase capacity by 30 percent. But by waiting three years to begin, Inco gave rival producers a golden opportunity. It takes a long time to expand nickel sulfide mines (Inco's principal source of ore), and in the meantime Inco's smaller rivals turned up a cheap and available source of low-grade nickel source called Lateritic ore from which ferro-nickel could easily be made. Inco's market share deteriorated rapidly; then in 1971, just when Inco's new capacity was blossoming, market demand fell by 17 percent. Inco, whose market projections for 1971 had been very bullish, found itself stuck with huge inventories and inventory-maintenance charges. These charges came due precisely when the debt payments on the 1966 expansion program were peaking; during part of 1971 one Inco executive recalled "we were spending a million dollars a day more than we were bringing in."[13] Not until 1974 did a new management team, which took over in 1972, shore up Inco's fundamental market position.

---

[12] See Lansing Lamont, "Inco: A Giant Learns to Compete," *Fortune* (January 1975), pp. 104–16.

[13] Ibid., p. 110.

The Inco example is not unique.[14] As a general proposition, the more volatile the firm's markets are, the more flexible the firm's strategy needs to be for it to be effective. Moreover, the likely prospect of changing market conditions speaks to the desirability of having not only flexible strategies but contingency strategies. *Business Week* in 1975 reported that the top managements of more and more companies were readying a "whole battery of contingency plans and alternate scenarios." According to *BW*, companies are reviewing and revising strategic plans more frequently to stay abreast of changing conditions. Quarterly or even monthly updates are not unusual.

Narrowing Down the List of Alternatives

Once management has identified several alternatives for improving its current business strategy and the information necessary to evaluate them has been gathered in the form of an industry profile and a competitive assessment of the industry, it is time to begin the process of narrowing down the list of candidate strategies. Although there is no set procedure for approaching this phase of business strategy analysis, inquiring into each of the following is likely to be a fruitful way of screening out weaker alternatives:

◻ Which, if any, of the strategic alternatives call for greater competence and/or resources than the organization can muster?

◻ Are any of the candidate strategies less attractive from the standpoint of profit outlook or return on investment criteria, even though they meet minimum standards?

◻ Do any of the alternatives fall short of adequately exploiting the organization's distinctive competence?

◻ Are the relevant market conditions and competitive conditions such that the best strategic advantage is to challenge rival firms where they are strong? or where they are weak?

◻ How do the alternatives rank in terms of offering the best or strongest competitive advantage?

◻ Which alternatives are most vulnerable to an effective strategic counterattack from rivals?

◻ How vulnerable are each of the candidate strategies to environmental threats now existing or on the horizon? How flexible are the alternatives in terms of allowing for responses to unforeseeable events?

◻ Should any of the candidates be ruled out because of a conflict

---

[14] See, for instance, Eleanor J. Tracey, "How A&P Got Creamed," *Fortune* (January 1973), pp. 103–14.

with management's sense of social responsibilities or an incompatibility with personal values?

□   On the basis of the answers to the foregoing questions, which alternatives seem to be inferior?

In all likelihood, a penetrating inquiry into the kinds of questions posed above will result in several of the strategic alternatives being screened out.

Weighing the Strengths and Weaknesses of Leading Candidate Strategies

At this juncture, the strategist's task becomes one of reconciling the pros and cons of the remaining alternatives. Ideally, one would like to assemble a business strategy in which all or most of the vital considerations were simultaneously optimized.[15] In practice, this objective proves much too utopian. Trade-offs are inevitably necessary. Trying to minimize risk exposure, for example, nearly always entails a sacrifice of potential profits. Likewise, strategic attempts to exploit every opportunity to its fullest can mean concomitant increases in the number of failures—the criterion of maximizing organizational strengths can be incompatible with minimizing organizational weaknesses. In addition, compromises are necessary in order to fashion a strategy which meets the needs of various coalition groups in the management hierarchy (marketing, manufacturing, finance) and also is consonant with the interest of exogeneous groups (stockholders, labor, consumers, government, the general public). Hence, which strategy is "best" from one angle seldom turns out to be the "best" from other pertinent angles. Normally, the best one can do is to search out the alternative offering the most satisfactory lineup of advantages and disadvantages. Toward this end, the strategist is forced to scrutinize the set of leading candidates from several perspectives:

□   Which strategic alternative offers the best match with the organization's competence and financial resources?

□   Which strategy promises to make the greatest contribution to overall organizational performance?

□   Which candidate offers the most dominant competitive edge and how vulnerable is it to a strategic counterattack from rival enterprises?

□   Which alternative minimizes the creation of new (and perhaps thorny) operating or administrative problems?

□   Which alternative has the best combination of high expected profitability and low risk exposure?

---

[15] The discussion in this section applies to corporate strategy evaluation as well as to business strategy evaluation.

□ Which alternative offers the most favorable trade-off between maximizing opportunities and minimizing weaknesses?

□ Which strategy appears best suited to management's know-how, philosophy, personality, and sense of social responsibilities?

□ Which of the leading candidate strategies appears most propitious from the standpoint of timing? Is now the opportune time to be bold or cautious, a leader or a follower? Which strategy offers the best tradeoff among near-term, long-term, and flexibility objectives?

□ Which strategy, if successful, would provide the best platform for taking advantage of other opportunities that might present themselves?

When an alternative scores well on some factors but negatively on others, the net effect is not simply a function of there being more pluses than minuses, or vice versa. Some factors are more critical than others, and which ones are the most important vary from case to case. Several quantitative approaches may prove helpful in trying to resolve the conflicts and inconsistencies. For instance, so long as the various factors can be ranked in order of priority or relative importance, the factors can be weighted according to any of several procedures to compute an overall weighted scale for each of the strategic alternatives. The problem here is that different weighting techniques and different numerical weights may result in different strategies being identified as superior or dominant. This can be partly overcome by using several logical weighting schemes and subjecting them to tests for consistency. Comparing their results then gives a systematic basis for judging how the pros and cons of a strategy add up.[16] The important thing for the analyst is to be sure the expected benefits of a strategic alternative represent *solid* prospects and not superficial promise—see Illustration Capsule 10.

STRATEGIC CHOICE: CORPORATE STRATEGY AND BUSINESS STRATEGY

In the final analysis, strategic decisions, both at the corporate level and the business level, boil down to a matter of managerial and business judgment. Even after a lengthy and exhaustive strategic evaluation, management is often confronted with choosing among several close alternatives rather than merely confirming a clearcut choice. Very rarely is the issue of what to do so cut-and-dried as to eliminate the judgment/choice problem. Facts and analysis by themselves usually do not resolve the

---

16 For a discussion of how various quantitative decision rules might be helpful in making a strategic choice, see H. Igor Ansoff, *Corporate Strategy* (New York: McGraw-Hill, 1965), pp. 182–88.

ILLUSTRATION CAPSULE 10
A Failure in Strategy Evaluation

Recently, Greyhound and Trailways took on one another in a fierce and profitless strategic maneuver over passenger bus fares. Greyhound, in an effort to boost passenger traffic on its intercity bus routes, in early 1978 announced a $50 fare applying to all trips extending more than 1,000 miles. Trailways responded with a series of commercials on national television proclaiming the cheapest rates from New York to Los Angeles.

However, the promotional war drew in little new business, mainly because it took no account of the changing market for intercity bus service. The reduced fares were aimed at long-distance travelers—despite the fact that fewer than 5 percent of all bus passengers ride 1,000 miles or more. Most of the passenger market for distances over 500 miles is captured by the airlines. Even though air fares are roughly 50 percent higher than bus fares, the travel time is much less on long trips. For instance, at the height of the Greyhound-Trailways price war, the lowest one-way bus fare from Chicago to Miami was $69 and involved travel time of a day and a half; by airplane the fare was $99 and flight time was two and a one half hours—a comparison which pinpoints the strategic folly of the bus lines' attempt to attract long-distance business.

At the same time, both Trailways and Greyhound failed to focus their business strategy on the short-haul market of less than 200 miles, the segment containing 40 percent of all intercity travel. Moreover, they ignored the airlines' long-standing and successful strategy of structuring their routes into networks of short-haul markets, where each major city serves as the hub for a series of spokes or corridor routes radiating out for 100–200 miles to smaller cities and other key hubs. Instead, buses were often run on a continuing schedule from one end of the country to the other, passing through many metropolitan areas in the middle of the night and not during prime-time travel hours.

SOURCE: Rush Loving, Jr., "The Bus Lines Are on the Road to Nowhere," *Fortune* (December 31, 1978), pp. 58–64.

---

problem of conflicts and inconsistencies. For this reason, intuition, personal experience, judgment, qualitative trade-offs, value preferences, intangible situational factors, and compromise of opinion become an integral part of the process of making a strategic commitment. And no formula or how-to-do-it description is ever likely to take their place.

Three elements of the strategy selection problem frequently assume a pivotal import in reaching a decision:

1. The risk/reward trade-off,
2. Timing the strategic move, and
3. Contribution to performance and objectives.

Risk/Reward Considerations

The first of these has been alluded to previously. It essentially involves the willingness of an organization to assume risk. Risk-averters will be inclined toward "safe" strategies where external threats appear minimal, profits adequate but not spectacular, and in-house resources ample to meet the task ahead. "Conservative" firms will prefer a low debt-to-equity financial structure to a more highly leveraged approach. They will probably opt to defer major financial commitments as long as possible or until the effects of uncertainty are deemed minimal. They may view pioneering-type innovations as "too chancey" relative to proven, well-established techniques. Or they may prefer to be followers rather than leaders. Often, the risk-averter places a high premium on strategies which shore up organizational weaknesses.

On the other hand, eager risk-takers lean more toward opportunistic strategies where the payoffs are greater, the challenges more exciting, and the glamour more appealing—despite the pitfalls which may exist. Innovation is preferred to imitation. Aggressive action ranks ahead of defensive conservatism. A confident optimism overrules pessimism. The organization's strengths, not its weaknesses, serve as a chief criterion for matching strategy and organizational capability.

Timing Considerations

An organization's risk/reward posture also spills over into the way it decides to time its strategic move. Where uncertainty is high, the risk-averter's tendency is to proceed with extreme caution or to stall. A defensive stance is likely to emerge. In contrast, the risk-taker is willing to move early and assume a trail-blazing role. Yet, the timing dilemma goes deeper than the risk/reward trade-off and a preference for an active or reactive style. It also relates to whether market conditions are ripe for the strategies being contemplated. A "good" strategy undertaken at the wrong time can spell failure. Chrysler Corp. had this experience in 1974–75 when it decided to put more emphasis on full-size, family cars and compete head-on with General Motor's Chevrolet Impala and full-sized Pontiacs, Buicks, and Oldsmobiles. Chrysler redesigned its Plymouth, Dodge, and Chrysler cars along the styling lines of GM's medium-priced models but, unfortunately for Chrysler, they had barely hit the market when the Arab oil boycott and the subsequent steep climb in gasoline prices made consumers wary of "big" cars. Chrysler found itself not only stuck with the high costs of having restyled its line of cars but also without any appealing selection of small cars to offer the growing number of small-car buyers.

In addition, there are several other timing-related issues which bear on strategy selection.[17] One pertains to the lead time between action and result and any difficulties which may ensue if this time is "too long" or "too short." In a closely related vein, management's primary concern of the moment being for the short-run or the long-run can prompt the selection of a strategy set which promises to yield the desired results in the desired time interval. Still another involves the magnitude and rate of investment funding required to support a given strategy fitting in with the organization's overall financial structure and cash flow requirements. Inasmuch as strategic investments commonly entail a stream of expenditures rather than a single lump-sum expenditure, the timing of the components may favor the selection of one strategy over another, especially if other factors are not decisive.

Contribution to Performance and Objectives

Frequently, the real problem of strategy selection originates as a response to unsatisfactory performance. Thus it makes sense that as the strategy formulation process approaches the point of strategy selection one of the foremost considerations is the contribution which each of the leading candidate strategies can reasonably be expected to make toward improved performance and achievement of corporate objectives. Plainly, a strategy is more attractive the greater promise it holds for producing the desired performance results.

Consider, for example, the case where a firm is contemplating a new competitive strategy to improve its market position and its profits. One of the most relevant evaluative factors will be the sort of "counterattack" which may be expected from rivals and how this will affect the likely success of each leading candidate strategy. A particular competitive strategy is stronger (1) the less vulnerable it is to the moves and countermoves of rivals and (2) the greater the chance that it will put an enterprise in a superior or at least equal competitive position vis-a-vis the strategies it confronts—see Illustration Capsule 11.

In weighing the competitive interplay of strategic moves and countermoves, several salient points merit consideration. To begin with, the posture of one's own proposed strategy has a bearing on the counter-responses of competitors. Attacking the competition squarely will elicit an almost sure response—and maybe a vigorous one at that, unless the attack is deemed feeble or doomed to failure. But, to choose a strategy that sidesteps direct confrontation stands a fair chance of going ignored for a time period long enough to establish a lead over rivals. The comparative benefits of attacking competitors' strengths or weaknesses war-

---

[17] Seymour Tilles, "Making Strategy Explicit," in H. Igor Ansoff, *Business Strategy* (Baltimore: Penguin Books, Inc., 1970), p. 197.

ILLUSTRATION CAPSULE 11
The Whys and Hows of GE's Strategic Divestment of Its Computer Business

In 1970, General Electric in a surprise move announced the sale of its computer manufacturing assets to Honeywell, Inc. The rationale underlying GE's divestiture of its computer operations recently came to light when highly confidential documents about GE's appraisal of its computer business were introduced as evidence by the Justice Department in its antitrust suit against IBM (alleging that IBM has monopoly power over the U.S. computer-systems market).

Although IBM considered GE as its strongest competitor in the mid-1960s, by 1970 the technical capabilities of GE's computer products were falling behind those of other firms and the company's competitive strength had deteriorated markedly. From 1957–70, GE sustained net losses from its computer operations of $162.7 million. Meanwhile, having just weathered a costly strike and with the nation in a slight recession, GE was under financial strains from short-run losses in two of its biggest product lines—nuclear power plants and jet aircraft engines. Both were deemed vital to GE's overall business in electrical products and were expected to turn profitable in the near future; as a consequence, GE's management felt these two lines had to be supplied with whatever cash was needed.

In contrast, the computer business had never been considered vital to GE and many of GE's top management group were of the opinion that if the company was to salvage anything financially from its venture into computers, it would have to be the first of "the seven dwarfs" (as IBM's main competitors were known) to drop out of the market.

It was, then, in this environment that GE's computer division proposed to corporate headquarters to undertake the manufacture of a broad new computer line that would have 20 to 40 percent better performance than IBM computers, yet sell at about the same price. According to the plan, the new computer line would generate revenue of $8.2 billion and profit before taxes of $2.34 billion in the 13 years 1969–81. However, the program was projected to incur losses through 1973 of $538 million. Profits would begin in 1974, but the cumulative losses would not be offset until 1977. GE's computer heads forecast a net cash drain of $685 million through 1974—a drain which would require GE to borrow at least $500 million to undertake the plan. If the plan succeeded, GE was projected to become a clear second to IBM, with an 8 percent market share by 1975, rising to 10 percent soon thereafter. This compared favorably with the current 4 percent to 5 percent share and was felt to be adequate to keep the division profitable.

However, the plan incorporated some shaky assumptions: (1) that GE could take customers from IBM, (2) that IBM would tolerate a sizable loss in market share without retaliating, (3) that GE could achieve key inventions on schedule and meet developmental deadlines, and (4) that

ILLUSTRATION CAPSULE 11 (continued)

IBM and other computer manufacturers would not leapfrog GE by bringing out still better computer products.

Aside from the fact that the assumptions were questionable and "fraught with risk," it was GE's assessment that IBM would continue to dominate the computer business, owing to its superior sales coverage, low manufacturing costs, and large base of customers—estimated at 72 percent of the market. IBM had steadily improving profit margins, strength in all aspects of computer technology, and overwhelming programming resources (software) to go with its computers. Although IBM was confronted with antitrust suits, some loss of skilled personnel to other companies, increasing specialization by competitors, and some gradual loss of its position in software and peripheral equipment technology, IBM's competitors still were earning only meager profits and were nowhere near as able as IBM to respond to the rapid market growth, rapid technological change, and rapid developments in the use of computers.

Whereas some computer companies were managing to compete on the basis of specialization in certain products for uses, GE was a generalist, attempting to compete across the board with IBM. In the view of GE's top executives, GE did not have a strong basis for specializing. Its major computer products were not as up-to-date and GE was weak in peripheral, mass-storage, and terminal devices—all of which were viewed as key products of the future. GE had limited technical strength in many areas of computer technology and its customer loyalty was reputed to be the lowest of any firm in the market.

Whereas IBM had 210 sales offices in the U.S. and 17,000 salesmen and systems analysts, GE had 38 offices with a staff of 600. To reach its 1975 market share objective, GE would have to increase sales force sizes by 60 to 70 percent per year and, at the same time, develop salesmen who were twice as productive as IBM's. Whereas GE's manufacturing costs were 47 percent of its computer revenue IBM's were estimated at 20 percent. GE's assessments of other firms in the computer market included the following:

Control Data Corporation—4.2 percent of worldwide computer installations; growing faster than the market; specialists in large computer systems and government applications; technically strong but weak in business applications.

Burroughs Corporation—2.4 percent of the market; growing substantially faster than other firms; specialists in banking and some other uses; technically strong.

National Cash Register Corporation—2.2 percent of the market; specialists in smaller systems, banking and first-time users; weak in peripherals and software; unprofitable.

Sperry Rand (UNIVAC)—6.8 percent of the market but losing ground; technically strong except for large-system software but had never fully used its strength; a generalist firm with weak marketing organization.

ILLUSTRATION CAPSULE 11 *(continued)*

Honeywell—3.9 percent of the market; growing slower than the market; technically good but with an incomplete and somewhat out-of-date product line; a generalist firm which had seriously delayed product development in order to be profitable.

RCA Corporation—2.9 percent of the market and losing ground; a generalist firm with no identifiable customer segment; technically poor except in communications; aging and incomplete product line; no real strength; unprofitable.

Finally, GE's management viewed the industry as being on the threshold on a major merger movement. No one of the small-share firms was in a position to seriously challenge IBM or make a lasting impact on the market.

Given these considerations, beset with mounting pressures for immediate profit increases, and facing stringent financial demands from its nuclear power and jet engine businesses, General Electric decided to "disengage" from the industry and sell its computer business. Moving quickly, GE officials approached Control Data, Xerox, and Honeywell about "the structure of the industry" and the hazards posed by "the continuing dominance of IBM"—but without revealing its intention to get out.

Meanwhile, GE explored how well its own operations would mesh with the business of each of its competitors in the event a sale could be worked out and concluded: Honeywell and Burroughs, good; Sperry Rand and NCR, fair; Control Data and RCA, poor; Xerox, unrated. As for their financial capabilities of purchasing GE's computer operations (which had a $176 million depreciated net book value on an original investment of $472 million), GE's assessment was: Xerox, high; Honeywell, RCA, Burroughs, and NCR, medium; UNIVAC, low-plus; Control Data, poor.

GE found Honeywell to be most receptive to taking over GE's computer operations. Honeywell, stronger in the U.S., and GE, stronger in Europe, would together be an undisputed "Number 2" with assets of $1.24 billion, combined 1972 revenues of $932 million, and 12,500 marketing and service employees worldwide. With the elimination of duplicate activities and the adoption of Honeywell's "more liberal" accounting policies, it was estimated that acquisition by Honeywell could produce a pre-tax profit of $66 million. According to a top GE vice-president, such a deal seemed to be "an optimum fit with a well managed and successful growth company."

At GE's urging, negotiations began at once (to minimize the chances for leaks) and within two months of its decision to get out of the industry, GE and Honeywell announced an agreement to combine their computer businesses and create a new company controlled and managed by Honeywell. In return for turning over its computer business assets to the new company, GE received $110 million in Honeywell notes, Honeywell stock valued at $124.5 million, and an 18.5 percent interest in the new company. GE kept its time-sharing service (which allows simultaneous op-

ILLUSTRATION CAPSULE 11 (concluded)

eration of a computer by many users) and its process-control computers for industry, though in 1974 the process-control line was also sold to Honeywell.

Although GE was the first dwarf to get out, about a year later RCA announced it was abandoning its computer business at a net loss of $210 million. Sperry Rand bought some of the RCA assets. In 1975, Xerox also dropped out of the computer industry, taking a loss of $84.4 million and turning over some of its activities to Honeywell.

SOURCE: Adapted from *The Wall Street Journal*, January 12, 1976, p. 26.

rant careful assessment. Challenging rivals where they are strongest carries a higher risk of failure although a greater performance improvement if the strategy succeeds. On the other hand, to attack weakness brings modest gain in overall performance unless competitive weakness is associated with strong market potential, as sometimes it is.

The Act of Strategic Commitment

The final component of strategy selection choice is the commitment decision. In fact, a strategic choice cannot be said to have been made until money and manpower have been committed. The act of commitment is what takes the issue of the strategic decision out of the category of an alternative and activates the chosen strategy to official organizational status. Commitment entails (1) directing some part of the organization to undertake the strategy selected, (2) assigning responsibility for implementing the strategic plan to the appropriate personnel, (3) allocating the resources necessary for implementation, (4) clarifying exactly where and under what circumstances implementation is to be undertaken, and (5) specifying the time interval for implementation. In effect, then, strategic commitment supplies answers to the obvious implementation issues of *who, where,* and *when* and thus lays a foundation for launching the task of putting the chosen strategy into place.

A final point. The process of evaluating strategic alternatives and arriving at a choice of strategy has elements of ambiguity. There are no infallible rules or procedures which, if followed to the letter, will lead to the "right" strategy choice. Strategy selection cannot be reduced to a precise, formula-like, analytic process. Intangible situational factors, astute entrepreneurship, and creativity must be judiciously interwoven with the quantifiable, concrete realities of a competitive market-place. Thus, there is no substitute for the exercise of managerial business judgment and, consequently, no way of posing a strategy formulation methodology that will "guarantee" an effective strategic choice. In short, strategy selection

is a managerial responsibility, not a technique; the process is not susceptible to a step-by-step "how to" set of answers. One can, at most, offer
guidelines, indicate pitfalls, and pose some of the right kinds of questions to ask.

SUGGESTED READINGS

Aguilar, Francis *Scanning the Business Environment.* New York: Macmillan
Co., 1967.

Buchele, Robert B. "How to Evaluate a Firm," *California Management Review,*
vol. 4, no. 1, Fall 1962, pp. 5–17.

Cannon, J. Thomas *Business Strategy and Policy.* New York: Harcourt, Brace,
and World, Inc., 1968, pp. 84–102.

Cohen, K. J., and Cyert, R. M. "Strategy: Formulation, Implementation, and
Monitoring." *Journal of Business,* vol. 46, no. 3, July 1973, pp. 349–67.

Gilmore, Frank "Formulating Strategy in Smaller Companies." *Harvard Business Review,* vol. 49, no. 3, May–June 1971, pp. 71–81.

Hall, William K. "SBUs: Hot, New Topic in the Management of Diversification." *Business Horizons,* vol. 21, no. 1, February 1978, pp. 17–25.

Hedley, Barry "A Fundamental Approach to Strategy Development." *Long-
Range Planning,* December 1976, pp. 2–11.

Hofer, Charles W., and Schendel, Dan *Strategy Formulation: Analytical Concepts.* St. Paul, Minn.: West Publishing Co., 1978, chaps. 2, 4, and 5.

Hussey, David E. "The Corporate Appraisal: Assessing Company Strengths
and Weaknesses." *Long-Range Planning,* vol. 1, no. 2, December 1968,
pp. 19–25.

Lunneman, Robert E., and Kennell, John D. "Short-Sleeve Approach to Long-
Range Planning." *Harvard Business Review,* vol. 55, no. 2, March–April
1977, pp. 141–50.

Mason, R. Hal; Harris, Jerome; and McLoughlin, John "Corporate Strategy: A
Point of View." *California Management Review,* vol. 13, no. 3, Spring
1971, pp. 5–12.

Vancil, Richard F. "Strategy Formulation in Complex Organizations." *Sloan
Management Review,* vol. 17, no. 2, Winter 1976, pp. 1–18.

Wall, Jerry "What the Competition Is Doing: Your Need to Know." *Harvard
Business Review,* vol. 52, no. 6, November–December 1974, pp. 22 ff.

READING

SBUs: Hot, New Topic in the Management of Diversification*

WILLIAM K. HALL

William K. Hall teaches business policy in the Graduate School of Business at the University of Michigan.

It started in 1971 in the executive offices at General Electric, the world's most diversified company. Corporate management at GE had been plagued during the 1960s with massive sales growth, but little profit growth. Using 1962 as an index of 100, dollar sales grew to 180 by 1970; however, earnings per share fluctuated without growth between 80 and 140, while return on assets fell from 100 to 60. Thus, in 1971, GE executives were determined to supplement GE's vaunted system of management decentralization with a new, comprehensive system for corporate planning.

The resulting system was based upon the new concept of strategic business units—SBUs, as they are now commonly called. Not only did this new system change the direction of planning at GE; it subsequently affected the corporate strategies and the planning processes in hundreds of other diversified firms around the world as well.

The SBU concept of planning is an intuitively obvious one, based on the following principles:

> The diversified firm should be managed as a "portfolio" of businesses, with each business unit serving a clearly defined product-market segment with a clearly defined strategy.
>
> Each business unit in the portfolio should develop a strategy tailored to its capabilities and competitive needs, but consistent with the overall corporate capabilities and needs.
>
> The total portfolio of business should be managed by allocating capital and managerial resources to serve the interests of the firm as a whole—to achieve balanced growth in sales, earnings, and asset mix at an acceptable and controlled level of risk. In essence, the portfolio should be designed and managed to achieve the overall corporate strategy.

As might be expected, the successful implementation of this intuitive approach provides a number of complex management choices and challenges. As a result, a heightened understanding of the benefits and costs of the SBU approach to the management of diversification is essential to the practice of general management. The objective of this article is to add to this understanding by summarizing the principles behind the SBU ap-

---

* William K. Hall, "SBUs Hot, New Topic in the Management of Diversification," *Business Horizons*, February 1978. Copyright © 1978, by the Foundation for the School of Business at Indiana University. Reprinted by permission.

proach, and by examining the alternatives, benefits, and problems encountered to date in its successful implementation.

A Look at Traditional Planning

In order to put the SBU concept of planning into a proper context, it is necessary to review briefly the traditional planning and resource allocation processes in large, diversified firms. These traditional processes grew out of the massive movement toward divisionalization and decentralization during the period 1920–65. This movement began as a response to growth, diversity, and overall complexity in the large, diversified firm. In essence, the movement was essential, as one general manager put it, "to tailor responsibilities down to the size where a general manager could get his arms around them."

As the decentralized, divisionalized structure matured in the 1960s, formal planning became a way of life in the well-managed, diversified firm. Typically, the approach was initiated with the delineation of overall corporate mission, objectives, targets, and environmental assumptions. These were disseminated annually to the various divisions, where plans, projections, and sub-unit targets were developed as a response to these guidelines. Then a delicate, iterative process of "bottom up—top down" negotiation and consensus-seeking eventually resulted in an "approved plan" for the upcoming planning period.

This approach to formal planning had a number of advantages:

> It forced divisional managers to be explicit in their target-setting and goal-seeking, often on a profit center or investment center basis.
> It allowed the corporate entity to add up the divisional pieces in advance, adjusting resource allocations and pushing divisions toward different targets when discrepancies against corporate objectives arose.
> It allowed the development of sophisticated control systems to project, measure, and interpret deviations from the planned divisional results.

At the same time, however, this approach to planning and control was not without deficiencies. Divisional plans were frequently either overly optimistic or overly pessimistic. Depending upon the corporate "culture," they typically were based on one of three scenarios: extrapolated results, a philosophy that "next year things will get better," or a philosophy that "it's better to plan things a little conservatively so that we come out looking good at the end." Often, management commitment to plans was incomplete—either at the corporate or divisional level. Variances were frequently explained by unforeseen external factors, inadequate divisional resources, or deficiencies in the target-setting process itself. The total corporate plan, formed by adding up the divisional plans, often left corporate management without a clear grasp of either divisional or corporate strategy. Moreover, division plans were frequently approved (or rejected) without an explicit understanding of the strategy behind the plans or the risks and opportunities associated with this strategy. As one divisional general manager commented, "Planning without an understanding of corporate strategy was a lot like throwing darts in a darkened room."

In short, the traditional corporate plan almost always contained notebooks full of facts, figures, and forecasts, but it frequently failed to digest these in a way that provided key insights into strategies and business success factors at both the divisional and the corporate levels. The result, for many firms, was a decade of "profitless growth."

The SBU Alternative

In an attempt to deal with inadequacies in its traditional planning process, General Electric, guided by a task force of senior general managers and assisted by a team of management consultants, developed the SBU alternative to corporate planning. This process, now applied under a variety of names and in a variety of ways in other diversified firms, is almost always based on four steps:

> identification of strategic business elements, or units
> strategic analysis of these units to ascertain their competitive position and long-term product-market attractiveness
> strategic management of these units, given their overall positioning
> strategic follow-up and reappraisal of SBU and corporate performance

Identifying SBUs. The fundamental concept in the identification of SBUs is to identify the discrete, independent product-market segments served by the firm. In essence, the idea is to decentralize on the basis of strategic elements, not on the basis of size or span of control. This can be accomplished, as one general manager observed, by "identifying natural business units which correspond to the degrees of freedom a manager has available to compete."

Thus, within GE, nine groups and forty-eight divisions were reorganized into forty-three strategic business units, many of which crossed traditional group, divisional, and profit center lines. For example, in three separate divisions, food preparation appliances were merged as a single SBU serving the "housewares" market. A very small part of the Industrial Components Division was broken out as a separate SBU, serving a distinct industrial product-market niche in the machine tool industry. Within Union Carbide, another firm adopting the SBU approach, fifteen groups and divisions were decomposed into 150 "strategic planning units," and these were then recombined into nine new "aggregate planning units."

Ideally, an SBU should have primary responsibility and authority for managing its basic business functions: engineering, manufacturing, marketing, and distribution. In practice, however, traditions, shared facilities and distribution channels, manpower constraints, and business judgments have resulted in significant deviations from this concept of autonomy. In General Foods, for instance, strategic business units were originally defined on a product line basis, even though several products served overlapping markets and were produced in shared facilities. Later, these product-oriented SBUs were redefined into menu segments, with SBUs like breakfast food, beverage, main meal, dessert, and pet foods targeted toward specific markets, even though these, too, shared common manufacturing and distribution resources.

The General Foods example, and examples from many other firms adopting the SBU concept, point out that identification and definition are ultimately managerial decisions reflecting philosophical and pragmatic resolutions of the question: "What are our businesses and what do we want them to be?" As one general manager succinctly put it, "In our company an SBU ultimately becomes whatever subdivision corporate management wants it to be."

Strategic Positioning. The subsequent process of positioning an SBU is typically driven by two criteria: long-term attractiveness of the product-market segment served by the SBU, and the SBU's competitive position (business strength) within that product-market segment. A conceptual 2×2 matrix illustrating this positioning is shown in the accompanying figure:

Competitive position (business strength)

	High	Low
High		
Low		

Long-term product-market attractiveness

Here again, the scales of measurement and the precision of measurement along both scales vary significantly in practice. Since the choice of a measurement scale is more important then the degree of detail in measurement along the chosen scale, it will be discussed in some detail.[1]

---

[1] I have seen primarily 2×2 matrices, although 3×3 and 4×4 matrices are used in some organizations.

Long-Term Product-Market Attractiveness. Two distinctive philosophies have evolved in ranking SBUs on this dimension. The first uses a single measure, almost always defined as the long-term projected real growth rate of the product-market segment.[2] (The split between high and low growth rates is sometimes arbitrarily set at 10 percent; other times it is set at the level of growth of the economy as a whole or at the level of growth of some sector of the economy.) Support for the growth rate definition of product-market attractiveness is clearly based upon a life cycle theory. With such a theory, attractive product-market segments are those in the development or "take-off" stage, and less attractive segments are in maturity or decline. Ideally, the long-term growth rate measures life cycle position and, hence, long-term product-market attractiveness.

The second methodology for assessing product-market attractiveness uses a set of measures, some qualitative and others quantitative. There, the choice of measures and the actual assessment of SBU position against these measures can be made at the SBU level, the corporate level, or jointly. In corporate practice, I have seen all of these possibilities being utilized. At General Electric, for example, SBU product-market attractiveness is determined by examining and projecting ten criteria: segment size, segment growth rate (units and real dollars), competitive diversity, competitive structure, segment profitability, and technological, social, environmental, legal, and human impacts.

Competitive Position (business strength). As in the case of assessing long-term attractiveness, two alternative philosophies have evolved for ranking competitive position. Here again, the first is based on a single measure, generally defined as segment share or as segment share relative to competition.[3] Support for this single factor concept comes from the theory of experience curves, an approach to strategy formulation developed by the Boston Consulting Group.[4]

This theory suggests that the unit costs of production, marketing, and distribution drop proportionately (in real terms) each time total output (experience) doubles. This decrease in unit costs presumably comes from learning effects, scale effects, substitution of lower cost factor inputs, redesign, and technology. Thus, if one believes that costs in an SBU are on an experience curve, it follows that there should be strong relationships between high market share (experience), lower costs, and higher profit-

---

[2] In a few cases, I have also seen projected long-term return on assets used as a measure of segment attractiveness.

[3] Relative share is defined as the ratio of the SBU's dollar sales in the product-market segments to the dollar sales of the SBU's major competitor (or in some cases, competitors).

[4] See, for example, the article by Hedley, "A Fundamental Approach to Strategy Development," *Long Range Planning* (December 1976), pp. 2–11.

ability.[5] In essence, high market share (or relative market share) becomes a surrogate measure of business strength relative to competition within the product-market segment.

In many firms, however, the market-share–experience-curve approach to assessing competitive position is viewed as overly simplistic or even erroneous. In this regard, a number of arguments have emerged:

> The competition with the most experience may be the "oldest" competitor. If this older firm has dedicated plant and equipment, it may not be able to exploit new, cost-reducing technology as rapidly as an emerging competitor.

> Shared experience obtained from other related product-market segments may be as important as accumulated output in lowering costs. (That is, experience cannot be measured independently for each product-market segment).

> External factors, technology breakthroughs, and other events may be as important as accumulated output in lowering (or in raising) costs.

In those firms that have either partially or totally rejected the experience-curve rationale, multiple measures of business strength have emerged. These measures are generally a mixture of qualitative and quantitative factors, and, depending upon the company, they can be defined and assessed either at the corporate or at SBU level. At General Electric, for example, competitive position is evaluated on the following dimensions: segment size and SBU growth rate, share, profitability, margins, technology position, skill or weaknesses, image, environmental impact, and management.

Strategic Handling. The strategic plan for an SBU is ultimately derived from its position with respect to long-term attractiveness (potential) and competitive position. Four combinations are possible.

Low Potential/Low Position. An SBU in this category is clearly an unattractive member of the firm's portfolio for both the short run and long run. Furthermore, an infusion of resources to improve position will still leave the SBU in a low-potential segment. In essence, the SBU in this category is unworthy of major future commitments.

In the evolving jargon of the field, this "low/low" SBU is typically given the title of "cash trap," "mortgage," or "dog." Regardless of the title, the recommended strategic handling is always the same—manage the SBU to maximize short-term cash flow. In some cases this strategy can be accomplished through closing the SBU down or through rapid divestiture. In other cases, it can be handled by "harvesting" cash from the operation through ruthless cost cutting, short-term pricing policies, and sometimes

---

[5] See Buzzell, "Market Share: Key to Profitability," *Harvard Business Review* (January-February 1975), for an empirical study lending some support to this hypothesis.

through giving up market share and growth opportunities that absorb short-term cash.

Low Potential/High Position. Here an SBU is serving an unattractive product-market segment from a position of strength. Typically called a "bond" or "cash cow" in SBU parlance, the recommended strategic handling is to "milk" the entity for cash, although without the aggressiveness with which one would handle a "dog." The idea of selective cash "milking" is to preserve market position while generating dollars in an efficient fashion to support other, growth-targeted elements of the portfolio. Carefully targeted growth segments, stabilized pricing, differentiated products, selective cost reduction, less creative marketing, and selective capital investment are all means of achieving this goal.

High Potential/Low Position. SBU elements in this category are typically termed "question marks," "problem children," or "sweepstakes" competitors. These elements are in an awkward position, for if they do not strengthen their competitive position, someone will almost certainly attack their product-market segment aggressively. Yet, the costs of strengthening their competitive position may not warrant the effort.

Thus, these elements are in a "get up or get out" strategic handling situation. Rigorous planning alternatives must be generated, evaluated, and costed. And then, the SBUs in this category must be moved, either upward or out of the firm's portfolio through divestiture or consolidation.

High Potential/High Position. SBUs in this category would seem to have the best classification. As "stars" or "savings accounts," these represent the businesses that must be groomed for the long run. As such, they should be given the resources and corporate support to grow faster than the market segment in sales, profits, and cash flow.

The recommended strategic handling of portfolio SBU elements can be summarized as follows:

> Dogs and cash cows are managed for short-term cash flow. Over the long run, dogs are divested or eliminated, while cash cows ultimately become dogs as their competitive position declines.
>
> Question marks must either get into the star category or get out of the portfolio. In the first case, they should make the move with carefully developed strategic plans so that major risk elements are identified and contained.
>
> Stars are short-run cash consumers and are managed for long-term position. Over the long run, as their segment attractiveness ultimately declines, they will become cash cows, generating cash to support the next round of stars.

Strategic Follow-Up and Reappraisal. In most explanations of the SBU process, the typical discussion stops after an explanation of SBU identification, classification, and handling. Unfortunately, failure by corporations to exploit the last element—follow-up and reappraisal—has probably resulted in most of the frustrations and failures encountered with the SBU process to date. To be successful, the SBU process must be iterative and ongoing, incorporating strategic planning and reappraisal, as well as managerial control.

Strategic Planning. Simply saying that a business is a star or cash cow will not make anything happen. Once a decision on strategic handling has been reached in this regard, detailed strategic goals and action plans must be evaluated and implemented. Such planning clearly offers alternatives; as one manager put it, "Some companies forget that there's more than one kind of cow." Detailed analysis and conceptual thinking are both required here, focusing on key success factors and major risk elements apt to be encountered along the way.

Strategic Reappraisal. A one-time evaluation and strategic positioning are also insufficient. In most companies in which SBUs are successful, strategic reappraisal is routinely conducted on an annual or biannual basis. In one large company, for instance, each SBU manager must completely reassess his competitive position and strategy in an annual presentation before corporate management. Simultaneously, a staff review group will present and evaluate alternatives to this positioning on a total portfolio basis.

In other organizations, such as GE, reappraisal is initiated when a strategic "trigger point"—an external factor projected to have a significant impact on SBU performance—occurs. One GE manager described this system as follows: "For each business unit we require that management identify the sensitivity to these key external factors. These sensitivities must be identified in advance, and specific contingency plans must be ready in advance. Thus, we at least face the future with our eyes open!"

Managerial Control. Senior managers in many large firms also argue that the SBU approach to the management of diversification requires major changes in systems for budgeting, capital appropriation, measurement, reward, and managerial development. One general manager described the problem in his firm as follows: "To me it makes little sense to go through a sophisticated SBU analysis and then continue to allocate capital simply on discounted rate of return. Moreover, it makes even less sense to continue to measure and reward SBU management on annual performance against a profit budget."

Very little information is available on the modifications in managerial control that accompany the SBU concept.[6] However, General Electric has provided some interesting information on their systems in public sources.

SBU control systems with GE are based on key success indicators (called business screens). For each SBU, performance measurements are monitored

---

[6] Recently, Richard Bettis and I initiated a research project at the University of Michigan on these issues.

on five broad criteria: market position, competitive position, profitability/ cash flow, technological position, and external trigger points. Standards for each criteria are set and weighted differently, depending upon how the SBU is categorized. In addition, a "quality of performance" ranking is maintained as a measure of how well individual SBU managers have attained their standards of performance. As one GE manager put it, "the maturity of our SBU planning process could be measured when we began to bridge the gap between budgeting and the strategic plan."

The measurement and reward of managerial performance was perhaps the biggest shift in the revised GE system. Under the previous system of reward, GE had compensated key managers on the basis of residual earnings—controllable profits during the planning period less a charge for corporate services and capital. Under the SBU system, however, SBU managers in different sectors of the matrix are measured and compensated differentially according to a bonus schedule, as shown in the table.

SBU Classification	Current Performance (residual income)	Future Performance (strategy)	Other Factors
Invest/Grow	40%	48%	12%
Selectivity	60	28	12
Harvest/Divest	72	16	12

Clearly, SBU elements with an invest-and-grow classification are being rewarded on the basis of long-term (strategic) contributions. While GE has recognized the difficulty of such a long-term appraisal, key managers in the company agree that an invest-and-grow manager can be evaluated and rewarded on the quality of his long-run strategy through a careful appraisal of his manpower plans, facilities plans, action programs, and competitive evaluation. As one GE manager described the system, "Of course, it has measurement problems, but so do most good compensation systems. In the end, I'm convinced that our revised executive incentive compensation system is the key that will make the SBU process work."

Management development in GE has also shifted to reflect differential needs in differential business elements. Invest-and-grow business managers are developed to foster entrepreneurial characteristics. Cash cow (selectivity) business managers are developed to take sophisticated and hard looks at their businesses, and harvest and divest managers are developed with a heavy orientation toward experience, operations, and cost-cutting.

The philosophy behind the GE management systems is a classical one: Effective strategy implementation decisions will be made only if managerial selection, appraisal, and incentives are consistent with the strategy and with the planned results. As one manager in a large, diversified company recently observed, "Most firms have gone only half way with the SBU concept—they position their product-market segments and then go right on rewarding and promoting managers on traditional criteria. In the end the companies which make the SBU concept work will be those which change all management systems; developing and rewarding SBU managers differentially depending upon their SBU position and the strategic handling which is appropriate for their element of the portfolio."

Pitfalls in SBU Analysis

Failure to Go All the Way. As discussed above, the failure to tie all management systems to the SBU approach is frequently a key pitfall in SBU analysis. In addition, there is the ever-present danger that short-term perturbations in the economy may drive invest-and-grow managers away from the long-term orientation required by the SBU approach. One senior manager commented on this problem as follows: "The 1974–75 recession came when many companies were moving onto the SBU system. Unfortunately, indiscriminate cost cutting and cash conservation caused many of these firms to cover their heads with a blanket, going back to the 'good old ways' of doing business. In the end, the good companies of the 1980s will be those that stayed with their strategies during the recession—repositioning themselves in the short run to strengthen themselves for the long run."

Doctrinaire Approaches. There is a wide variety of alternatives for identifying product-market segments, for evaluating these segments, and for developing an SBUs strategy vis-à-vis competition. The application of a single methodology in a doctrinaire fashion is likely to create dissension, confusion, and misleading results. SBU-based planning, even more than traditional corporate planning, must be conducted to generate "multibusiness insights"—that is, to learn more about one's businesses than the competitor knows about his. As one manager succinctly observed, "The real payback from SBU planning is an intangible one—it comes slowly as you develop a strategic understanding of your businesses and your portfolio."

Transition Costs. Both the measurable and the hard-to-measure costs of moving from the traditional corporate planning process to the portfolio planning process must also be considered. Managers who have risen through the ranks of a firm to positions of leadership in groups and divisions are not apt to "jump for joy" when they are reorganized and retitled "dogs," "cows," or "question marks." Moreover, their subordinates are apt to be even more unsure as they assess their future employment, career development, and promotion prospects. One middle manager in a business redefined as a cash cow commented on this problem:

> I spent two years in an MBA program learning how to run a business as a profit/investment center. Now, suddenly I'm told to manage my department as a cash center.

Then the corporation turns down a major expansion proposal from our division, reallocating investment funds to another set of businesses. I don't understand it, I don't like it, and I really wonder what my future looks like with the XYZ company.

In addition to these costs of managerial adjustment, there is some question as to whether traditionally trained managers can manage cows or dogs at all. A related question is whether or not a firm can develop and keep the diversified managerial talent necessary for managing diversified portfolio elements. And finally, "going all the way" with SBU implementation involves the high costs of adding new managerial systems or organization, planning, and control.

Transition costs can (and are) being handled in part by executive development programs within companies and within management education institutions. While these programs are useful—perhaps even essential—to a company shifting to the SBU philosophy, management transition takes time and involves some painful reallocations. It remains to be seen how much time and pain will be incurred as organizations shift and how many of these organizations will be able to endure these transition costs. The key issue, as one middle manager put it, will be "to convince managers that there are other ways to heaven than a star."

New Ventures and R&D.   A fourth unresolved problem with the SBU approach to date involves corporate strategies toward new ventures and research and development—that is, toward the businesses of the future.

In theory, it would appear that R&D in a cash cow should be eliminated or restricted to short-term projects generating cost reductions. It is possible that a major R&D effort in a cow could result in major new markets or products that could ultimately turn the cow into a star (or lengthen the life during which the cow continues to generate cash). However, failure to maintain a competitive advantage in R&D within a cow could give competitors market leadership, accelerating, in effect, the cow's movement toward the dog category.

SBU theory would also seem to indicate that new ventures, R&D, and acquisition-merger policies should be directed at potential stars. The question is, how does one identify future stars in business segments where the firm has little or no experience, and should one develop these business segments internally or through acquisition-merger?

Determining the role of new technology and searching for stars of the future that are outside of the firm's existing portfolio are difficult—in theory and in practice. In essence, while the SBU philosophy has provided new insights into the management of existing businesses, new concepts are needed for managing additions to the portfolio effectively.

SBUs in Nondiversified Firms.   It is obvious that SBU analysis has evolved as a powerful concept in the management of diversification. Still, while diversification has been a major trend throughout world corporations for the past quarter-century, many large, nondiversified businesses—even entire corporations—remain, in effect, single SBUs.

The question must be asked: Are there any concepts that would aid in strategy formulation within a nondiversified firm? Clearly there are some:

> . . . consideration of resegmenting the existing single product-market segment into new segments to gain improved competitive position and segment attractiveness.
>
> . . . consideration of using cash flow from the existing single product-market segment to develop new stars—either through acquisition or through internal development (that is, manage the base business as a cow to feed the stars of the future).

While these ideas have conceptual merit, they are not without problems. Resegmentation takes time, money, and managerial skill. Diversification does also, and diversification raises the additional question of direction. Unfortunately, it is uncommon for the nondiversified firm to possess simultaneously all three elements—time, money, and skill in shifting strategies. Even when these three factors are present to some degree, reinvestment decisions in the base business tend to claim priorities on these scarce resources.

This strategic dilemma of the maturing, nondiversified firm is a major challenge to management and to society. While SBU analysis aids in understanding the dilemma, it has not as yet provided the conceptual framework to aid in the resolution.

There is little question that formal SBU analysis—identification, positioning, handling, and follow-up—provides new insights into the management of diversification. While the total number of diversified firms adopting some variant of this approach is unknown, one estimate is that 20 percent of the "Fortune 500" manufacturing firms are utilizing the concept. And while after only five years of experience it is too early to assess its impact, some testimonials provide a feel for preliminary management reaction:

> *General Electric:* "GE is growing rapidly as a result of its strong financial controls and marketing strategies. . . . Two basic failures—an absence of strategic planning and a dearth of financial controls have brought [their major domestic competition] to an [unfortunate] pass."[7]
>
> *Mead Paper:* "Our track record for earnings won't validate it, but we will make this thing (SBU analysis) work. You can't help but improve a company if you get rid of the losers and step up the winners. Our program is the common thread running through the company."[8]

---

[7] "The Opposites: GE Grows While Westinghouse Shrinks," *Business Week* (January 31, 1977), pp. 60–66.

[8] J. W. McSwiney, Chairman, in "Mead's Technique to Sort Out the Losers," *Business Week* (March 11, 1972), pp. 124–27.

Union Carbide: "Business strategies that reflect the category assigned to the business have been developed for each strategic planning unit. . . . At present, about 60 percent of Union Carbide's total sales is concentrated in businesses in growth categories. For the period 1975 to 1979, about 80 percent of forecasted (capital) expenditures has been allocated to these businesses."[9]

Armco Steel: "We [now] know the businesses we should pursue aggressively, those to maintain at the current level, and those to deemphasize or phase out. We can set goals that are reasonable . . . as they are attractive. And, importantly, we can have confidence in achieving our goals."[10]

However, the concept of portfolio management, like any other concept, must continue to evolve and mature as a philosophy for the effective management of diversification. And this evolution must come to grips with a number of issues that still are not fully resolved: tailoring and restructuring planning and control systems, avoiding doctrinaire approaches, and effectively managing transition costs. In addition, the handling of research and development and new ventures, as well as the application of the SBU concept to the nondiversified firm, provide major challenges to both business and business research.

There is little question, however, that the SBU approach to the management of diversification will leave a major mark—just as the movement to divisionalization and decentralization did twenty-five years ago. As one senior executive put it, "SBU analysis makes planning discontinuous. . . . It forces general managers to develop competitive and multibusiness insights at a strategic level. . . . And in the uncertain, rapidly changing world of the 1980s, this kind of strategic planning will become a way of life."

---

[9] *1975 Annual Report,* Union Carbide Corporation, p. 6.

[10] C. W. Verity, Chairman, in "Why a Portfolio of Businesses?" *Planning for Corporate Growth,* Planning Executives Institute (December 1974), pp. 54–60.

5

STRUCTURING A STRATEGICALLY EFFECTIVE ORGANIZATION

It doesn't matter what you do, just so long as you do it well.

J. Galbraith and D. Nathanson

. . . the purpose of formal organizations is to provide a framework for cooperation and to fix responsibilties, delineate authority, and provide for accountability. . . .

Edmund P. Learned

Strategy implementation is fundamentally different from strategy formulation. The latter is largely intellectual and requires the abilities to conceptualize, analyze, and evaluate; it requires shrewd judgment as to what constitutes an entrepreneurially effective strategy and what does not. But a general manager has to be much more than a good paper strategist. He must be able to convert plans into effective action. It is, in fact, on matters of strategy implementation that a general manager spends most of his time and energy.

The tasks of strategy implementation bring to the forefront the whole gamut of policy issues as to exactly *how* the chosen strategy will be carried out. Ongoing enterprises will have to determine whether they have the right organization to implement the chosen strategy and, if not, what changes need to be made. A new organization will have to decide how to build from the ground up. Next, internal operating policies and procedures will have to be developed to guide strategy implementation. This includes figuring out how to develop a distinctive competence, allocating resources to the various subunits, setting performance standards, and devising an effective reward structure. Later, management will have to assess the progress being made in the implementation process and how well the strategy is working out. This chapter and the next focus on these aspects of the general manager's job.

Strategy and Organization

It goes almost without saying that one of the highest priorities of strategy implementation is building an organization capable of effective strategy execution. Accomplishing the strategic mission requires that organization be consciously structured rather than allowed to evolve. As Drucker says, "the only things that evolve in an organization are disorder, friction, malperformance."[1]

A number of distinct subactivities are involved in conceiving and putting in motion an organization capable of seeing the chosen strategy through to a successful conclusion. The key tasks to be performed— those activities that have to be done right and on time if the strategy is to succeed—must be identified and responsibility for them assigned to individuals or groups having the appropriately specialized skills. A review of the formal organization structure, together with its informal relationships, will be needed to assure coordinated integration of separately performed functions. This entails not only assessing various supervisory and line-staff relationships but also making use of project staffs, task forces, teams, committees, and other *ad hoc* units. Ways must be found to communicate and instill organizational objectives in all subunits, while at the same time allowing room for the satisfaction of individual aspirations. An information system must be made operational to keep each subunit posted on what it must know about other subunits and to let those in positions of authority know what is going on so the task sequence can proceed without delay. As for in-house concerns, efforts must be made to contain interdepartmental rivalries, interpersonal conflicts, and the maneuvers of subunits with vested interests to protect, lest too much energy be spent on internal politics and playing the power game.

There are no hard and fast rules for building a strategically effective organization. However, a strong case can be made that the pivotal consideration for all decisions on organizational structure and processes should be the extent to which each organizational alternative contributes to the accomplishment of strategy. In other words, the choice of structural form and process should be closely aligned with the needs of strategy.[2] The logic behind the view that structure should follow strategy is relatively

---

[1] Peter Drucker, *Management: Tasks, Responsibilities, Practices* (New York: Harper and Row Publishers, Inc., 1974), p. 523.

[2] Research evidence also supports the structure follows strategy thesis. The landmark study is Alfred Chandler's, *Strategy and Structure*. According to Chandler, changes in an organization's strategy bring about new administrative problems which, in turn, require a new or refashioned structure if the new strategy is to be successfully implemented. In more specific terms, Chandler found that structure tends to follow

simple: organization is (or should be) a means to an end—not an end in itself. The most appropriate end is the purpose for which the organization exists in the first place, as revealed by its strategy. Without coordination between strategy and structure, the most likely byproducts are confusion, misdirection, and splintered efforts within the organization. Hence the task of organization-building is most properly conceived as one of figuring out *strategically effective ways* of structuring the total work effort.

DuPont's experience offers a classic example of the rationale for strategy determining structure:

> The strategy of diversification quickly demanded a refashioning of the company's administrative structure if its resources, old and new, were to be used efficiently and therefore profitably; for diversification greatly intensified the administrative load carried by the functional departments and the central office. Once the functional needs and the activities of several rather than one product line had to be coordinated, once the work of several very different lines of businesses had to be appraised, once the policies and procedures had to be formulated for divisions handling a wide variety of products, and, finally, once the central office had to make critical decisions about what new lines of business to develop, then the old structure quickly showed signs of strain. To meet the new needs, the new organizational design provided several central offices, each responsible for one line of products. At the new general office, the Executive Committee and staff specialists concentrated on the over-all administration of what had become a multi-industry enterprise. And in transforming the highly centralized, functionally departmentalized structure into a "decentralized," multidivisional one, the major achievement had been the creation of the new divisions.[3]

The lesson of this example is that the choice of organization structure does make a difference in how an organization performs. All forms of organization structure are not equally effective in implementing a given strategy. In the remaining sections of this chapter we will explore aspects of structuring a strategically effective organization.

Stages of Organizational Development

In a number of respects, the strategist's approach to organization-building is governed by the size and growth stage of the enterprise, to-

---

the growth strategy of the firm; but often not until inefficiency and internal operating problems provoke a structural adjustment. His studies of seventy large corporations revealed a sequence consisting of new strategy creation, emergence of new administrative problems, a decline in profitability and performance, a shift to a more appropriate organizational structure, then recovery to more profitable levels and improved strategy execution. Chandler found this sequence to be oft-repeated as firms grew and modified their corporate strategies. For more details see Alfred D. Chandler, *Strategy and Structure* (Cambridge, Mass.: The M.I.T. Press, 1962).

[3] Chandler, *Strategy and Structure*, p. 113.

gether with the key strategic characteristics of the organization's business. For instance, the type of organization structure that suits a small specialty steel firm relying upon a concentration strategy in a regional market is not likely to be suitable for a large, vertically-integrated steel producer doing business in geographically diverse areas. The organization form that works best in a multiproduct, multitechnology, multibusiness corporation pursuing a conglomerate diversification strategy is, understandably, likely to be different yet again. Recognition of this characteristic has prompted several attempts to formulate a model linking changes in organizational structures to changes in the stage of an organization's strategic development.[4]

The underpinning of the stages concept is that enterprises can be arrayed along a continuum running from very simple to very complex organizational forms, and that there is a tendency for an organization to move along this continuum toward more complex forms as it grows in size, market coverage, and product line scope and as the strategic aspects of its technology-product-market relationships become more intricate. Four distinct stages of organization development have been singled out.

Stage I. A Stage I organization is typified by one-person management: the owner-entrepreneur has close daily contact with each employee and each phase of operations. Most employees report directly to the owner, who makes all the pertinent decisions as to finance, marketing, manufacturing, and so on. As a consequence, the organization's strengths, vulnerabilities, and resources are closely allied with the entrepreneur's personality, management ability and style, and personal financial situation. Not only is a Stage I enterprise an extension of the interests, abilities, and limitations of its owner-entrepreneur; its activities often are concentrated in just one line of business that emphasizes one processing level (say, manufacturing or distribution) more than others. For the most part, today's Stage I enterprise is epitomized by small firms run by "independent businesspersons" who are "their own bosses," and which have a strategy focused on a single product, market, technology, or channel of distribution.

Stage II. Stage II organizations differ from Stage I enterprises in one essential respect: an increased scale and scope of operations create a pervasive need for management specialization and force a transition from one-person management to group management. However, a Stage II enterprise, although run by a team of managers with functionally specialized

---

[4] See, for example, Malcolm S. Salter, "Stages of Corporate Development," *Journal of Business Policy*, vol. 1, no. 1 (Spring 1970), pp. 23–27; Donald H. Thain, "Stages of Corporate Development," *The Business Quarterly* (Winter 1969), pp. 32–45; Bruce R. Scott, "The Industrial State: Old Myths and New Realities," *Harvard Business Review*, vol. 51, no. 2 (March-April 1973), pp. 133–48; and Alfred D. Chandler, *Strategy and Structure*, chap. 1.

responsibilities, remains fundamentally a one-unit operation dealing in a limited line of technologically related products sold through one major distribution channel to one end market. This is not to imply, though, that the categories of management specializations are uniform among Stage II enterprises. In practice, there is wide variation. Some Stage II organizations prefer to divide responsibilities along classic lines: marketing, production, finance, personnel, control, engineering, public relations, procurement, planning, and so on. Of course, in infant Stage II companies several of these functions may be assigned to a single person. But in the largest Stage II enterprises, most notably big banks and certain of the oil, steel, aluminum, tire, and farm implement corporations, functional responsibilities are highly developed and specialized, even to the point of having numerous functional subunits. The marketing department of a major tire manufacturer, for example, might well be large enough to include subunits for sales, dealer relations, advertising, product development, market research, and product management.

In other Stage II companies functional specialization is keyed to the particular operating problems of the business; for example, the organizational building blocks of a vertically-integrated oil company may consist of exploration, drilling, pipe-lines, refining, and marketing. In a process-oriented Stage II company, the functionally sequenced units aim primarily at synchronizing production with the next unit in line, as opposed to engaging independently in buying and/or selling in the open market. External market transactions are by no means precluded but, normally, in Stage II companies transactions between internal operating units dominate each sequence of the manufacturing process.

Alfred Chandler cites the experience of Goodyear and Firestone to exemplify how vertical integration tends to lead to a process-oriented form of organization in companies concentrating on a single product line:

> Where Goodrich and United States Rubber considered all areas of rubber and rubber chemistry as their domain, Goodyear and Firestone until the 1930's focused the attention of their whole organization in a single line of products for the volume market. They integrated vertically more than either of their major competitors. Besides the extensive rubber fields, both had their own cotton plantations as well as textile mills for their tire cord and fabricating mills for their rims. Both gave much more attention to creating their own retail outlets. This concentration made development of new and diversified lines much more difficult. The two had had their chemical laboratories and development departments almost from the very beginning but their efforts were devoted almost entirely to designing better tires and finding more efficient ways to make them.[5]

---

[5] Alfred D. Chandler, "Development, Diversification and Decentralization," *Postwar Economic Trends in the United States*, R. E. Freeman, ed. (New York: Harper and Brothers, 1960), p. 263.

Stage III. Stage III includes those organizations whose operations, though concentrated in a single field or product line, are large enough and scattered over a wide geographical area to justify having geographically *decentralized* operating units. These units all report to corporate headquarters and conform to corporate policies but they still have the freedom to develop their own channels of distribution and to buy and sell on their own behalf on the open market. Each of the semi-autonomous operating units of a Stage III organization tends to be structured along the lines of functionally oriented Stage II companies or, more rarely, like Stage I enterprises (when the independent units are small and take on an entrepreneurial character). The key difference between Stage II and Stage III, however, is that while the functional units of a Stage II organization stand or fall together (in that they are built around one business and one end market), the operating units of a Stage III firm can stand alone (or nearly so) in the sense that the operations in each geographic unit are not rigidly tied to or dependent on those in other areas. Characteristic firms in this category would be breweries, cement companies, and steel mills having production capacity and sales organizations in several geographically separate market areas. Corey and Star cite Pfizer International as being a good example of a company whose business in 1964 made geographic decentralization propitious:

> With sales of $223 million in 1964, Pfizer International operated plants in 27 countries and marketed in more than 100 countries. Its product lines included pharmaceuticals (antibiotics and other ethical prescription drugs), agriculture and veterinary products (such as animal feed supplements and vaccines, and pesticides), chemicals (fine chemicals, bulk pharmaceuticals, petrochemicals and plastics), and consumer products (cosmetics and toiletries).
>
> Ten geographic Area Managers reported directly to the President of Pfizer International and exercised line supervision over Country Managers. According to a company position description, it was "the responsibility of each Area Manager to plan, develop, and carry out Pfizer International's business in the assigned foreign area in keeping with company policies and goals."
>
> Country Managers had profit responsibility. In most cases a single Country Manager managed all Pfizer activities in his country. In some of the larger, well-developed countries of Europe there were separate Country Managers for pharmaceutical and agricultural products and for consumer lines.
>
> Except for the fact that New York headquarters exercised control over the to-the-market prices of certain products, especially prices of widely used pharmaceuticals, Area and Country Managers had considerable autonomy in planning and managing the Pfizer International business in their respective geographic areas. This was appropriate because each area, and some countries within areas, provided unique market and regulatory

environments. In the case of pharmaceuticals and agriculture and veterinary products (Pfizer International's most important lines) national laws affected formulations, dosages, labeling, distribution, and often price. Trade restrictions affected the flow of bulk pharmaceuticals and chemicals and packaged products, and might in effect require the establishment of manufacturing plants to supply local markets. Competition, too, varied significantly from area to area.[6]

Stage IV. Stage IV is typified by large, multiproduct, multiunit, multimarket enterprises decentralized along product lines. Their corporate strategies emphasize diversification, concentric and/or conglomerate. As with Stage III companies, the semi-autonomous operating units report to a corporate headquarters and conform to certain firm-wide policies, but the operating units pursue their own respective line of business strategies. Typically, each separate business unit is headed by a general manager who has profit and loss responsibility and oversees the entire unit with all its functions except, perhaps, accounting and resource allocation (which traditionally are corporate functions). Decision-making power for the unit's operations are thus concentrated in the unit's management rather than at the corporate level. The organizational structure of the business unit may be along the lines of Stage I, II, or III types of organizations. Characteristic Stage IV companies include General Electric, ITT, Exxon, Uniroyal, Textron, and DuPont.

Movement through the Stages. The stages model illustrates well how structure follows strategy and why there is a tendency of organization structure to change in accordance with product-market-technology relationships. As firms have progressed from small, entrepreneurial enterprises following a basic concentration strategy to the next phases of volume expansion, vertical integration, geographic expansion, and product diversification, their organizational structures tend to follow a pattern of change from unifunctional to functionally centralized to multidivisional decentralized organizational forms. Firms that remain single-line business will almost always have some form of a centralized functional structure. Dominant-product-line enterprises typically have a hybrid structure; the dominant business is managed via a functional organization and the diversified activities are handled through a divisionalized form. Companies that diversify along either concentric or conglomerate lines overwhelmingly choose some form of decentralized divisional structure.

However, it is by no means imperative that all organizations begin at Stage I then move sequentially toward Stage IV.[7] As Chandler has noted,

---

[6] E. Raymond Corey and Steven H. Star, *Organization Strategy: A Marketing Approach* (Boston: Division of Research, Harvard University Graduate School of Business Administration, 1971), pp. 23–24.

[7] For a more thorough discussion of this point see Salter, "Stages of Corporate Development," pp. 34–35.

U.S. Rubber moved from a Stage II organization to a Stage IV form without ever passing through Stage III. Nor is there any compelling reason why some organizations might not exhibit characteristics of two or more stages simultaneously. Sears, at one time, was decentralized geographically for store operations, personnel, sales promotion, banking, inventory and warehousing, and maintenance, yet centralized for manufacturing and procurement of goods, thus overlapping the organization structures of Stages II and III. Furthermore, some companies have found it desirable to retreat into prior stages after entering a particular stage. For example, the DuPont Textile Fibers Department originated out of five separate, decentralized, fully-integrated fiber businesses: rayon, acetate, nylon, "Orlon," and "Dacron."[8] Many weavers and other industrial users bought one or more of these fibers and used them in significantly different ways that also required different application technologies. According to Corey and Star:

> Customers objected to being solicited by five DuPont salesmen each promoting a different type of synthetic fiber and each competing with the others. Users of synthetic fibers wanted sales representatives from DuPont who understood their product lines and production processes and who could serve as a source of useful technical ideas.[9]

As a consequence, DuPont consolidated all five units into a Textile Fibers Department in an effort to deal more effectively with these customers. The new department established a single multifiber sales force and set up market programs for four broad market segments—men's wear, women's wear, home furnishings, and industrial products—each of which had a potential demand for all five fibers.

In general, then, owing to the several ways which product-market relationships and strategy may turn, the paths along which an organization's structure may develop are more complex and variable than suggested by the stages model. Still, it does appear that as firms move from small, single-product businesses to large, single-product companies then on to concentric or conglomerate diversification, their organizational structure evolves, in turn, from one-man management to large group functional management to decentralized, divisional management. This is substantiated by the fact that about 90 percent of the *Fortune 500* firms (nearly all of which are to some degree diversified) have a divisionalized organizational structure.

Guidelines for Linking Structure to Strategy

In evaluating whether an enterprise is organized and staffed to meet the needs of its strategy, two questions can usefully be posed: "What

---

[8] Corey and Star, *Organization Strategy*, p. 14.
[9] Ibid.

functions and activities must be performed excellently for the organization's strategy to succeed?" and "In what areas would malperformance seriously endanger or undermine strategic success?"[10] The answers to these two questions should point squarely at the basic functions essential to strategic success. In general, an activity's contribution to strategy should determine its rank and placement in the organizational hierarchy. Key activities should never be subordinated to non-key activities. Revenue-producing or results-producing activities should never be subordinated to support activities. By making success-causing factors the major building blocks for organizational structure, the chances are greatly improved that strategy will be effectively executed. Toward this end, a reassessment of organization structure is always useful whenever strategy is changed.[11] A new strategy is likely to entail modifications in key activities, which if not formally recognized and properly restructured, could leave strategic performance unnecessarily short of its potential.

A second strategy-structure linkage concerns the ability of the organization to react to and cope with new external developments of either a threatening or opportunistic nature. Is the organization structure adaptable to the pressures of a recession? stiffer competitive forces? rapid expansion? Is the organization's structure appropriate for dealing with future challenges and developments as revealed in the strategic forecast? Do the predictions contained in the strategic forecast imply that the organization structure will be outgrown in the near-term?

Guidelines for Assessing Structural Efficiency

In deciding whether an organization's structure is efficient, several points need to be considered. Do decisions often have "to go looking for a home" or do people know where within the organization the decision belongs? Does the organization structure put the attention of key people on the right things—major decisions, coordination of essential activities, performance, and results? Are the inherent and inevitable conflicts among (1) the production manager for lower manufacturing costs, (2) the product engineer for designing a product that meets the engineering standards of simplicity and economy, (3) the inventory manager with holding down carrying costs, (4) the credit officer with minimizing bad debts, and (5) the marketing manager with improving quality, adding sales features, eliminating stockouts, and adding more customers all resolved in a timely and effective fashion? Are the firm's R&D activities attuned with the marketplace and with customer needs? Are the various dimensions of supplier-customer relationships (such as technical assistance, product

---

[10] Drucker, *Management*, p. 530, 535.

[11] For an excellent documentation of how a number of well-known corporations revised their organization structure to meet the needs of strategy changes and specific product/market developments, see Corey and Star, *Organization Strategy*, chap. 3.

ILLUSTRATION CAPSULE 12
Restructuring the World's Largest Corporation

In February 1979, American Telephone and Telegraph (AT&T), the world's largest privately-held corporation, announced a massive reorganization to follow a major refocusing of its corporate strategy. At the time of reorganization, AT&T had operating revenues of $40 billion on an asset base of $103 billion.* AT&T employs 985,000 people and has more than 650 million shares of stock outstanding, making AT&T also the largest company in terms of individual stockholders with 3 million owners.

Service Is Our Business

Theodore Vail, the first president of AT&T, was responsible for making the Bell System's corporate strategy one of service. Vail felt that since AT&T was a nationally regulated monopoly the company's long-range business success depended upon rendering good service. Service was defined by Vail as high reliability along with low cost to the telephone customer.

The functional organizational structure that followed the corporate strategy of service is shown below:

AT&T's Functional Organization

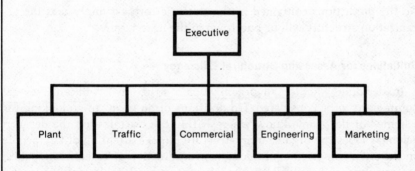

The headquarters as well as the 23 operating companies all were organized in the same fashion. Vail felt that the functional structure best allowed the implementation of the service strategy.

While the functional organization changed from time to time to accommodate new technology and more efficient managerial methods, the operating departments (both at AT&T and the operating companies) were organized according to the tasks performed: Plant (installation and maintenance of equipment), Traffic (operator handling of telephone calls), Commercial (business office dealings with customers), Engineering, and Marketing. Marketing was distinct from operations, as shown in the diagram.

* Exxon Corporation, by comparison, has less than one half the assets of AT&T.

ILLUSTRATION CAPSULE 12 *(continued)*

The functional structure was well-suited to the times. For most of AT&T's 90-year history, the concept of providing universal, high quality, readily affordable telephone service was the focal point around which AT&T's business was built. But if universality of service was the hallmark of the first 90 years, diversity of products, technology, services, and customers is the new hallmark.

During the last year of leadership of John D. deButts as Chairman of the Board of AT&T, the corporate strategy of the company made a dramatic shift to recognizing this diversity of service—orienting the organization structure to fit the growing diversity of products and customers. For many years, the company was comfortable with its simple business concept of providing universal telephone service; now the hallmark became marketing a diverse group of products and services to meet specific needs and expectations of both business and residential customers.

A New Strategy

To identify and anticipate the unique needs of particular kinds of business and residential customers, to assure the development of products and services to meet these market-specific and customer-specific needs, and to furnish and maintain a broad group of products and services as effectively as possible, AT&T moved to implement its new strategy by reorganizing the marketing of the company's products and services through newly formed customer divisions (business and residential) rather than through the traditional functional divisions which grouped all customer marketing together in one organization unit.†

The structure that followed the new corporate strategy is shown below:

AT&T's Market Channel Organization

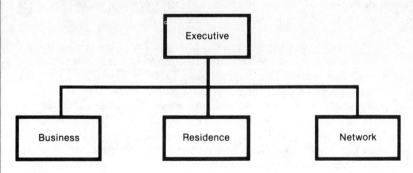

The new market channel organization represented a more specialized marketing approach to the business and residential customer segments of

† The Carterfone decision in 1968 by the Federal Communications Commission, which was the first of many decisions allowing more direct competition in the communications field is considered by many as the impetus for the shift by AT&T strategy aimed at more aggressive marketing of a full range of communication services.

ILLUSTRATION CAPSULE 12 *(continued)*

AT&T's business. At AT&T headquarters, each organization segment was headed by an Executive Vice President. The network division is the nationwide telecommunications system which serves all types of the company's customers.

The New Residential Division has the responsibility of marketing residential services to the individual home or apartment. New products—such as designer phones, conferencing, call forwarding, and automatic callback when lines are busy—will allow the individual to make many new choices about residential services. This represents a vast change from the standard black telephone.

The new Business Division spans an even greater degree of product diversity and service for business customers because of the multiplicity of ways business firms can utilize telecommunications technology. The approach is one of organizing in such a way to allow AT&T greater ability to tailor market products and services. The company is using market specialists to custom design total communications systems for each individual business AT&T serves. For example, the new Enhanced Private Switched Communications Service, which utilizes electronic switching, will enable business customers to monitor their own telecommunications network, rearrange the network to meet changing needs, and receive detailed accounting of the calls made from each telephone. The new Advanced Communications Service (ACS) aims to provide computer users with data transmitting capability as accessible as the long distance network is to the telephone user. ACS will offer to business customers the prospect of more efficient use of existing equipment, ease in adding more sophisticated equipment, and the ability to exchange data with suppliers, customers, and others without concern about compatability.

Charles L. Brown, the new Chairman of the Board, having replaced John deButts in the Spring of 1979, made the following comments about the massive reorganization:

> There is an old Chinese saying: "May you live in interesting times." It is, of course, a curse. AT&T lives in interesting times. But somehow, I don't feel cursed. On the contrary. To be involved in developing corporate policy for this company in this time of transition—as we are—is one of the most satisfying and most memorable professional adventures any of us will ever experience. I believe that this generation of AT&T managers has the chance to shape the future of this business more profoundly than has any generation since the first. Many people spend their lives wishing they were in the right place at the right time. We are there and it is up to us to make the most of it.

Implementation

The implementation of the new structure was particularly interesting in that there were 23 operating companies involved. The implementation strategy revolved around the following guidelines:

ILLUSTRATION CAPSULE 12 (concluded)

☐   Each operating company was to designate a separate executive vice president responsible for each of three segments: business, residence, and network.

☐   These officers were to report directly to the president or a chief operating officer.

☐   In multistate companies, state-level segment managers reported to the state general manager or to the segment officer at headquarters. In the former case, a strong dotted-line relationship continued to exist with the headquarters segment officer.

☐   Directory and public communications were discrete organizational modules.

Coordinating the implementation of the operating companies was the task of William M. Ellinghaus, who replaced Charles Brown as president. Ellinghaus estimated that it would take 18 months to complete the reorganization.

Each operating company developed its own specific implementation plan and timetable. The original plan was for each company to implement the new structure one organization layer at a time starting with the top. However, as word got out about the new structure, entire operating companies began to informally restructure prior to the official word. The results were some misunderstandings as well as some hasty revisions in the premature restructuring once the formal word came down from headquarters. Just how much difference the new organization will actually make in executing the shift in AT&T's corporate strategy remains to be seen.

---

service, delivery, allocation in periods of short supply, negotiation on price and other conditions of sale) being handled consistently among geographic territories? Are there too many people not doing enough things? Are there too many meetings attended by too many people?

Approaches to Organizational Diagnosis

Several diagnostic approaches have evolved regarding the adequacy of an organization's structure. The three which will be described briefly here are (1) the problem approach, (2) the process approach, and (3) the results approach.[12]

The Problem Approach. The problem approach to organization diagnosis and organization-building is used in many management consultant studies and follows the sequence of defining the problems of the business,

---

[12] The following is drawn from J. Thomas Cannon, *Business Strategy and Policy* (New York: Harcourt, Brace, & World, Inc., 1968), pp. 314–17.

identifying their causes, appraising the various alternatives for problem solution, and recommending a course of action and an implementation plan. The problems examined thus include, but by no means are limited to, those of organization structure. The whole enterprise is checked out much like a doctor giving a patient a thorough annual physical examination. Hence changes in organization structure may turn out to be a part of the overall recommendations and implementation plan or they may be diagnosed as not needed at all. This puts organization structure into its proper perspective of being one of a number of things to consider in evaluating an organization's situation. It also has the advantage of endeavoring "to fix first things first." The problem approach works less effectively when the needed emphasis is not so much on solving problems as on integrating organization functions and on bettering performance.

The Process Approach. The process approach to appraising organizational adequacy focuses on improving the coordination of functions that cut across departmental lines and areas of responsibility. It looks at whether the overall tone and conduct of activities is as sharp as it should be—irrespective of an apparent lack of organizational problems. In this sense its thrust is expeditive rather than curative and the objectives are simplification, efficiency, economy, and integration into a unified whole. A principal strength of the process approach is the contribution it makes to understanding the operating sequences and dynamics of the organization. This, in turn, makes it easier to design structural modifications aimed at reducing coordination problems, streamlining the layers of management, facilitating communication flows, and deciding where to delegate authority (or withdraw it) in order to strengthen organization cohesion and unification.

The Results Approach. The unique feature of the results approach is not so much technique of diagnosis as a more concentrated emphasis on the ultimate objective—the accomplishment of strategy. It picks up on "the structure follows strategy thesis" and advocates an organizing-for-results approach keyed directly to the product-market-customer needs aspects of strategy. Thus the results approach suggests five steps in addressing what structure is best suited to the achievement of strategy:

1. Delineate as precisely and clearly as possible the relationships of customer needs and product-market aspects to the organization's strategy, objectives, and goals.
2. Identify the key activities and functional skills requisite for strategic success.
3. Classify each of the key activities and skills according to (a) whether they are unique to the product/market being considered or analogous to those needed for other of the organization's product/markets and (b) their priority of contribution to strategic success.
4. Determine the degrees of authority and responsibility required to manage

both the key and non-key functions, keeping in mind two factors: (a) economy and (b) the degree of decentralization of decision-making best suited to each.

5. Design organizational ties around these principal building blocks to ensure adequate coordination and integration.[13]

Step 4 is a crucial one. The economy factor is the basis for deciding whether to provide a major product/market subunit with the services it needs from other existing functional units or letting it be self-sufficient and install its own duplicate set of functions. The decentralization factor, while partly economic, is mainly a matter of determining the appropriate managerial level at which to make the principal decisions that will confront the product/market subunit and figuring out how to align corporate strategy and line of business strategy. Once steps 1–4 have been completed, the framework of a results-oriented structure should be in focus, and organizing around key building blocks can proceed accordingly.

ALTERNATIVE FORMS OF ORGANIZATION

In trying to relate structure to strategy, management confronts a wide range of choices. The basic structural forms include organizing on the basis of (1) functional specialties, (2) geographic location, (3) process or production, market channel, or customer class, (4) decentralized product divisions, (5) strategic business units, and (6) a matrix form featuring dual lines of authority. These basic forms can, in turn, be combined in varying proportions and formats to generate an almost endless variety of mixed organization structures. The rationale and features of both basic and mixed organization forms warrant brief examination.

The Functional Organization Structure

Dividing key activities according to functional specialization takes as its premise the value of combining related effort and segregating unrelated effort. The resultingly deeper specialization and focused concentration on functional problems can then enhance both efficiency and the development of distinctive competence. Generally speaking, organizing by function promotes full utilization of the most up-to-date technical skills and makes it more possible to capitalize on the efficiency gains to be had from using specialized manpower, facilities, and equipment. Organizations that depend upon a single product line and/or are vertically integrated tend to be organized in a centralized, functionally departmentalized structure.

However, the way an organization chooses to segment its major functions depends on its strategy and the nature of the work activities in-

---

[13] Ibid., p. 316.

voled. Thus, a large, technically-oriented manufacturing firm may be organized around research and development, engineering, materials management, production, quality control, marketing, personnel, finance and accounting, and public relations; further, some of the departments may be line and others staff—as shown in Figure 5–1. A municipal government, on the other hand, may be departmentalized according to purposeful function—fire, public safety, health services, water and sewer, streets, parks and recreation, and education. A university may divide its organi-

FIGURE 5–1
A Functional Organization Structure (manufacturing company)

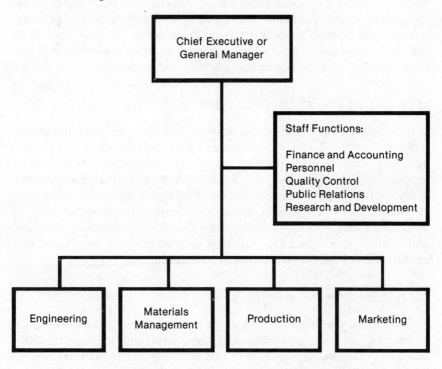

Advantages	*Disadvantages*
Produces excellent results where tasks are routine and repetitive.	Poses problems of functional coordination.
Preserves centralized control.	Can lead to interfunctional rivalry and conflict.
Allows benefits of specialization to be fully exploited.	May promote overspecialization and narrow management viewpoints.
Simplifies training of management specialists.	Limits development of general managers.
Promotes development of a distinctive competence in functional areas.	Forces profit responsibility to the top.
	Not well-suited to situations requiring cross-functional problem solving.
	Conducive to empire building.
	More difficult for functional subunits to relate their tasks to the task of the whole.

zational units into academic affairs, student services, alumni relations, athletics, buildings and grounds, institutional services, and budget control. The Achilles heel of a functional structure is proper coordination of the separated functional units. Functional specialists, partly because of their training and the technical nature of their jobs, tend to develop characteristic patterns of behavior and goal-orientation. The more that functional specialists differ in their patterns of behavior and their approach to task accomplishment, the more difficult it becomes to achieve effective coordination between them. They neither "talk the same language" nor have an adequate understanding and appreciation of one another's problems and approaches. As a consequence, while there may be a free flow of communication and ideas up and down functional units, there often emerges a strong built-in bias against horizontal movements—a bias which plainly can not only impede coordination but also engender conflict and rivalry. This, in turn, can create an excessive decision-making burden at the top of the management hierarchy where much time is spent resolving cross-functional differences, enforcing joint cooperation, and opening lines of communication.

Geographic Departmentation

Organizing according to geographic areas or territories is a rather common structural form for physically dispersed enterprises. The thesis here is that performance in a given territory, branch, district, or region is significantly improved by grouping all activities under the responsibility of a general manager. A geographic organization is especially attractive to enterprises whose operations are essentially similar from area to area since this facilitates holding general managers accountable for results in their assigned territories. In the private sector, a territorial structure is typically utilized by chain store retailers, cement firms, railroads, airlines, the larger paper box and carton manufacturers, and large bakeries and dairy products enterprises; for example, the member companies of American Telephone and Telegraph which make up the Bell Telephone System all represent geographically decentralized units. In the public sector, such organizations and agencies as the Internal Revenue Service, the Small Business Administration, the federal courts, the U.S. Postal Service, the state troopers, the Red Cross, and religious denominations have adopted territorial departmentation in their efforts to provide like services to geographically dispersed clienteles. Figure 5–2 illustrates geographic departmentalization.

Process, Market Channel, or Customer Departmentation

Grouping an enterprise's activities around its several production stages, market channels, or customer groups is often employed where there are important manufacturing or market advantages to be gained from a specialized approach. A metal parts manufacturer may find it operationally effective to subdivide in series, forming foundry, forging, machining, finishing, assembly, and painting departments. A large office may be departmentalized into batteries of machines doing similar work: typing, duplicating, card punching, accounting, labeling, and collating. Firms

FIGURE 5–2
A Geographic Organizational Structure

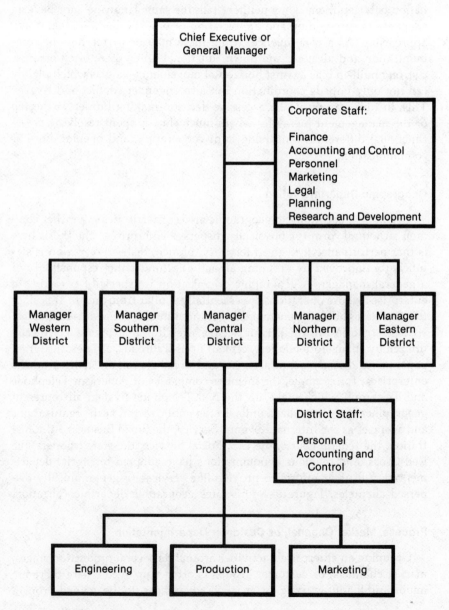

FIGURE 5–2 (continued)

Advantages	Disadvantages
Allows more aggressive development of area markets.	Greater difficulty in maintaining consistent and uniform companywide practices.
Delegates profit/loss responsibility to lowest competent level.	Requires a larger management staff, especially general managers.
Improves functional coordination within the area.	Leads to duplication of staff services.
Takes advantage of economies of local operations.	Poses a problem of headquarters control over local operations.
Allows closer adjustment to specific needs of local markets and customers.	
Area units make an excellent training ground for general managers.	

selling an essentially uniform product to widely diverse customer groups may orient their marketing activities to cater to the requirements of each buyer segment. For example, some years ago Purex Corporation decided that neither product nor territorial departmentation was as well-suited to their operations as a market channel departmentation which allowed it to focus separately on selling to supermarket chains and drug chains. Local United Fund drives are typically organized into a number of individual solicitation units each assigned to canvas a particular segment of the community—commercial establishments, industrial plants, unions, local schools, county government, city government, hospitals, and agriculture. There are various departments of the federal government set up expressly for veterans, senior citizens, the unemployed, small businessmen, widows and dependent children, the poor, and others. Figure 5–3 illustrates departmentation by process, by market channel, and by customer category.

Decentralized Product Divisions

Grouping activities along product lines has been a clear-cut trend among diversified enterprises for the past half-century, beginning with the pioneering efforts of DuPont in the 1920s. Separate product divisions emerged because diversification made a functionally specified manager's job incredibly complex. Even with many immediate subordinates, a production executive could not effectively oversee the production of a large number of different items being produced at many different plant locations. For similar reasons, the jobs of engineering, sales, and R&D executives were also unwieldy. Product decentralization thus aimed at creating *manageable* organizational subunits that were responsive to customer needs, competitive behavior, and emerging market opportunities.

Organizing on a divisional or product group basis permits top management to delegate to a single executive extensive authority over key operating and staff functions for specific products or product families. New semiautonomous divisions can then be created for each substantially dif-

FIGURE 5-3

A. Process departmentation

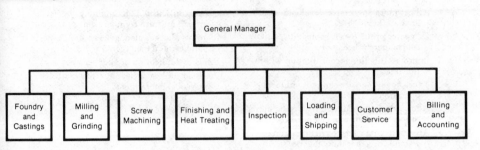

B. Market channel departmentation

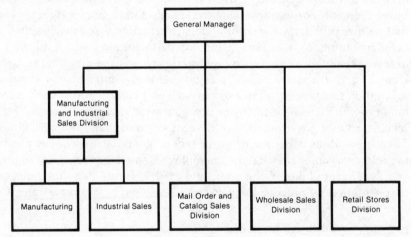

C. Customer departmentation

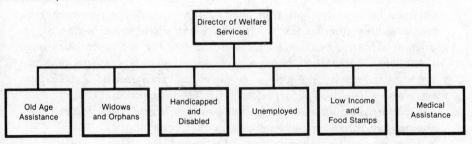

FIGURE 5–3 (continued)

Advantages	Disadvantages
Structure is tied to performance of key activities.	Encourages pressure for special treatment.
Facilitates achievement of operating economies derived from use of specialized facilities and labor force.	Poses problems of how to coordinate interdepartmental activities.
May allow more opportunity for deeper market penetration.	May lead to uneconomically small units or underemployment of specialized facilities and manpower as nature of demand from unit-to-unit changes.

ferent product-market grouping. By and large, the general managers of these divisions are given profit responsibility (which explains why such units are often called "profit centers") and are held accountable for short-run results and long-run market development. They determine the appropriate tradeoffs in allocating resources between current operations and efforts for future growth. Within limits, they develop their own divisional staffs. The effect is to make the division general manager more like a semi-independent entrepreneur.

Figure 5–4 illustrates a typical divisionalized organization structure. One of the most well-known product division structures is that of the Chevrolet, Oldsmobile, Cadillac and other divisions of General Motors.

Strategic Business Units

Sometimes an enterprise's product divisions and interindustry units are so numerous and diverse that the span of control is too wide for a single chief executive. Then it may be useful to group those which are related and assign responsibility for them to a senior executive who reports directly to the chief executive officer. While this imposes another layer of management between the divisional general managers and the chief executive, it may nonetheless improve strategic planning and top management coordination of diverse activities. This explains both the popularity of the group vice president concept among conglomerate firms and the recent trend toward the organization of diverse products into *strategic business units.*

A strategic business unit can be thought of as a clustering of discrete, product/divisional units based on some important strategic element common to each. The idea is to group an organization's activities according to strategically relevant criteria rather than size or span of control. At General Electric, a pioneer in the concept of decentralized strategic business units (SBUs), 48 divisions were reorganized into 43 SBUs; in one case, three separate divisions making various food preparation appliances were combined as a single SBU serving the "housewares" market.[14] This re-

---

[14] William K. Hall, "SBUs: Hot, New Topic in the Management of Diversification," *Business Horizons*, vol. 21, no. 1 (February 1978), p. 19.

230

FIGURE 5–4
A Typical Divisionalized Organization Structure

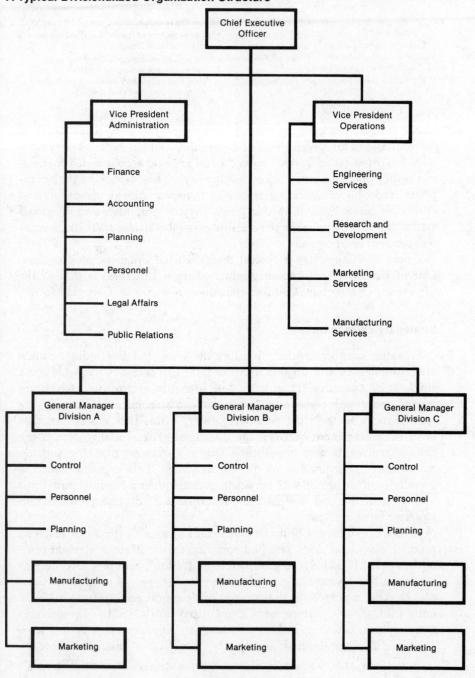

FIGURE 5–4 *(continued)*

Advantages	*Disadvantages*
Offers a logical and workable means of decentralizing responsibility and delegating authority in diversified organizations.	Leads to proliferation of staff functions, policy inconsistencies between divisions, and problems of coordination of divisional operations.
Reduces layering of management.	Poses a problem of how much authority to centralize and how much to decentralize.
Improves coordination of functional activities for a specific product or product family.	
Allows better measurement of specific product performance.	

flects the general guideline to include within a single SBU all those product/market activities which are closely related in terms of technology, use of common manufacturing facilities, use of the same distribution channels, customer base, or target market.

The managerial value of the concept of SBUs is that it provides diversified companies with an attractive rationale for organizing what they do and for reviewing the strategic performance of diverse operating units. It is particularly helpful in reducing the complexity of dove-tailing corporate strategy and business strategy and in developing focused product/market business strategies on a decentralized basis. Figure 5–5 illustrates the SBU concept of organizing diversification where each SBU is headed by a "group" vice president—see also Illustration Capsule 13.

Matrix Forms of Organization

A matrix form of organization is a structure with two (or more) lines of authority, two systems for budgeting, two measures of performance and reward, and so forth. The key feature of the matrix is that product and functional lines of authority are overlaid (to form a matrix or grid) and managerial authority over the employees in each unit/cell of the matrix is shared between the product manager and the functional manager—as shown in Figure 5–6. In a matrix structure, subordinates have a continuing dual assignment: to the product and to their base function.[15]

A matrix type organization is a genuinely different structural form that represents a "new way of life." One reason is that the unity of command principle is broken; two reporting channels, two bosses, and shared authority create a new kind of organizational climate. In essence, the matrix is a conflict resolution system through which priorities are negotiated,

---

[15] A more thorough treatment of matrix organizational forms can be found in Jay R. Galbraith, "Matrix Organizational Designs," *Business Horizons*, vol. 15, no. 1 (February 1971), pp. 29–40.

232

FIGURE 5–5
A Product Group/SBU Type of Organization

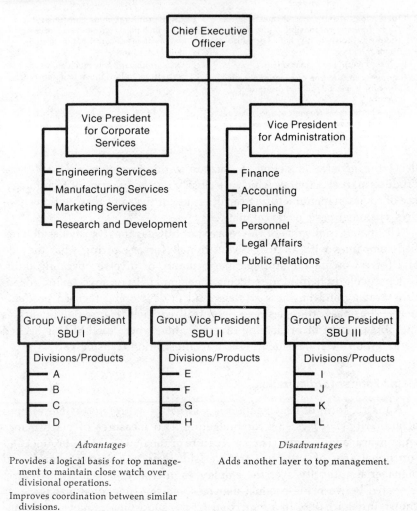

Advantages	Disadvantages
Provides a logical basis for top management to maintain close watch over divisional operations.	Adds another layer to top management.
Improves coordination between similar divisions.	

power is shared, and resources are allocated internally on a "strongest case for what is best overall for the unit" type basis.[16]

The list of companies using some form of a matrix includes General Electric, Texas Instruments, Citibank, Shell Oil, TRW, Bechtel, and Dow Chemical. Its growing popularity is founded on some solid business trends.

---

[16] An excellent critique of matrix organizations is presented in Stanley M. Davis and Paul R. Lawrence, "Problems of Matrix Organizations," *Harvard Business Review*, vol. 56, no. 3 (May–June 1978), pp. 131–42.

FIGURE 5–6
Matrix Organization Structures

A. Defense contractor

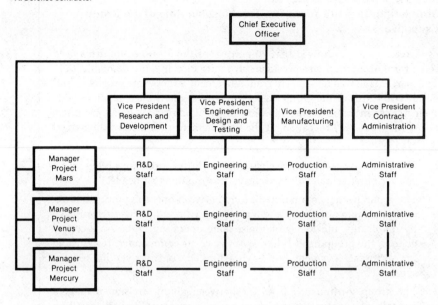

B. College of business administration

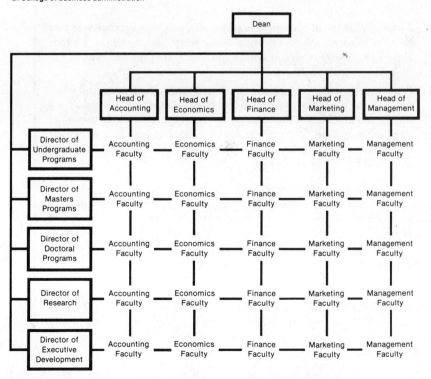

ILLUSTRATION CAPSULE 13
Structuring Diversification: The Troublesome Role of the Group Executive

A recent survey showed that 70 percent of the *Fortune 500* firms used some form of a group vice president structure in managing diversification. This percentage was up sharply from 39 percent a few years previous. Yet, nearly two thirds of the group executives working in these companies view their jobs as more or less a "can of worms." The reasons given are interesting for what they reveal about the management problems of diversified organizations:

1. Some group v-ps find themselves as being little more than a high-priced courier between the chief executive and the division heads.

2. The group head is in a no-man's land between operating units that expect maximum autonomy and a president who judges his performance by the profits and losses of those same operating units. As a consequence, the group head is like an army corps commander, responsible for sector achievement but having limited control over limited resources.

3. The group v-p must walk a line between giving division managers enough elbow room to be effective entrepreneurs and maintaining enough control to keep corporate headquarters comfortable. The manager who is not politically expert at walking this line tends to be regarded as "the gestapo" by the divisions and "a nursemaid" by the CEO.

4. Although the job of group v-p is often seen as a logical progression on the way to corporate president, in many companies a group v-p either moves up, sideways, or out within five years. It is not the type of job that many people make a career out of.

5. For executives who enjoy "doing" rather than "coordinating and overseeing," the nebulous role of a group head is frustrating. It requires a low profile and behind the scenes influence, as opposed to being in the thick of the action. Recognition for performance gets blurred; credit for success tends to go first to the chief executive, then to the division head, and last to the group v-p.

From a corporate perspective, having a layer of group vice-presidents to help the CEO direct and coordinate a growing, diversified company is almost a creation of necessity. The more operating divisions an enterprise has, the more important it becomes to have them report to someone besides the chief executive. So far, no more logical way has been devised than a group structure.

While it is generally agreed that there is a legitimate need for a group v-p type structure in diversified companies, there are wide differences on what the group v-p position should be like. At Textron group managers are regarded as "counselors" while at AMF a group head is held totally

ILLUSTRATION CAPSULE 13 *(continued)*

responsible for division performance. The prevailing view seems to be that, as a minimum, the group v-p should (1) have heavy line responsibility for allocating financial resources within his group, (2) be brought into corporate operating committees, and (3) exercise primary responsibility for defining and directing the group's marketing, sales, and advertising priorities. This means that the chief executive must be willing to relax his own supervision over the divisions and to delegate a meaningful role to the group executive. In addition, it is important for the CEO to not deal directly with the divisions in a manner which undercuts the group manager's role and authority.

The key to making the job of group vice president both attractive and effective is in finding the middle ground in terms of delegating power to the divisions while at the same time fully utilizing the talents and energies of senior executives at the group level. The right balance needs to be found between the desire for autonomy at the division level and a need to hold the group v-p at least partly accountable for division performance and group performance.

SOURCE: "The Frustrations of the Group Executive," *Business Week*, September 25, 1978, pp. 102 ff.

Firms are turning more and more to strategies that add new sources of diversity (products, markets, technology) to its range of activities. Out of this diversity are coming product managers, functional managers, geographic area managers, division managers, and SBU managers—*all* of whom have important strategic responsibilities. When product, technology, geography, and business groups all have strategic importance and their respective strategic priorities are roughly equal, a matrix organization can be an effective structural form. A matrix form of organization allows for the management of multiple sources of diversity by creating multiple dimensions for strategic management, with each dimensional manager being responsible for one source of strategic diversity. The matrix approach thus allows each point of strategic initiative to be managed directly and represented in higher level discussions about how the total enterprise (or business unit) can best be managed. In this sense, it helps middle managers make trade-off decisions from a general management perspective.[17] Further, because a manager is assigned line responsibility for attending to an explicit area of strategic concern, a matrix organization can facilitate rapid management recognition of and response to new strategic product-market-technology developments.

---

[17] Ibid., p. 132.

Supplemental Methods of Organization

The foregoing structural designs have not proved sufficient to meet completely the diversity of strategic situations confronting contemporary organizations. Many enterprises have responded not only by mixing the basic forms in varying combinations but also by introducing some novel features that effect interesting compromises between the pros and cons of the primary organizational forms. Among these are:

1. The *project manager* or *project staff* concept, whereby a separate, largely self-sufficient subunit is created to oversee the completion of a new activity (setting up a new technological process, bringing out a new product, starting up a new venture, consummating a merger with another company, seeing through the completion of a government contract, supervising the construction of a new plant).[18] Project management has become a relatively popular means of handling "one-of-a-kind" situations having a finite life expectancy and the normal organization is deemed unable or ill-equipped to achieve the same results in addition to regular duties. On occasions, however, "temporary" projects have proved worthy of becoming "ongoing," resulting in either the elevation of the project unit to "permanent" status or a parceling out of the project's functions to units of the regular organization.

2. The creation of *cross-functional teams* or *task forces* to work on unusual assignments of a problem-solving or innovative nature where a need exists for a pooling of talent and tight integration among specialists. Special task forces provide increased opportunity for creativity, open communication across lines of authority, expeditious conflict resolution, and common identification for coping with the problem at hand, while at the same time facilitating intensified access to the requisite expertise. However, according to Drucker, team organization is more than a temporary expedient for dealing with nonrecurring special problems. He argues that the team is a genuine design principle of organization and is especially good for such permanent organizing tasks as top-management work and innovative work.[19]

3. The *venture team* concept whereby a group is brought together specifi-

---

[18] For a more complete treatment of project management, see C. J. Middleton, "How to Set Up a Project Organization," *Harvard Business Review*, vol. 45, no. 2 (March–April 1967), pp. 73–82; George A. Steiner and William G. Ryan, *Industrial Project Management* (New York: MacMillan Co., 1968); Ivar Avots, "Why Does Project Management Fail," *California Management Review*, vol. 12, no. 1 (Fall 1969), pp. 77–82; C. Reeser, "Human Problems of the Project Form of Organization," *Academy of Management Journal*, vol. 12, no. 4 (December 1969), pp. 459–67; R. A. Goodman, "Ambiguous Authority Definition in Project Management," *Academy of Management Journal*, vol. 10, no. 4 (December 1967), pp. 395–407; and D. L. Wilemon and J. P. Cicero, "The Project Manager-Anomalies and Ambiguities," *Academy of Management Journal*, vol. 13, no. 3 (September 1970), pp. 269–82.

[19] Drucker, *Management*, pp. 564–71.

cally to bring a specific product to market or a specific new business into being. Dow, General Mills, Westinghouse, and Monsanto have used the venture team approach as a regenesis of the entrepreneurial spirit. One difficulty with venture teams is if and when to transfer control of the project back to the regular organization and the problems of discontinuity and shifting purpose which result.[20]

Perspectives on Organization Design

Organization theorists agree on two points: (1) there is no such thing as a perfect or ideal organization design and (2) there are no universally applicable panaceas for structuring an organization. Studies of organizations confirm that the same structural design which works well in one organization may not work well in another. What suits one type of strategy can be totally wrong for another. Structures that worked well in the past may not be as suitable for the future. Indeed, firms have a habit of regularly outgrowing their existing organizational form: either an internal shakeup is deemed periodically desirable or else changes in the size and scope of product-market-technology relationships make the firm's structure strategically obsolete. An organization's structure thus is dynamic—changes are not only inevitable but proper.

There is less agreement whether organization design should commence with a conceptual framework or with a pragmatic consideration of the realities of the situation at hand—the special needs, the constraints imposed by the personalities involved, and the way things have been done before. By and large, agonizing over which approach is best is counterproductive; both approaches should be used in parallel. A conceptual framework is essential if structure is to be firmly rooted in the organization's mission, objectives, strategy, and activities. But it must be adapted to the circumstances of the situation.

Yet, there is no one indisputably *best* structure or overriding principle of design—even for a particular organization at a single moment of time. All of the basic organizational forms have their strengths and weaknesses. Moreover, use of one organizational form does not preclude simultaneous use of others. Many organizations are large enough and diverse enough to employ departmentalization by functional specialty, by geographical area, by process sequence, by market channel, by customer type, and by product group at the same time. Therefore, there can be ample rhyme and reason in organization-building to depart from a slavish adherence to a basic conceptual framework and, thus, accommodate tailoring to the inevitable internal/external exceptions and special situations. Depending on an organization's strategy and stage of development, the general manager is

---

[20] Philip Kotler, *Marketing Management: Analysis, Planning, and Control*, 3d ed. (Englewood Cliffs, N.J.: Prentice-Hall, Inc., 1976), pp. 200–201.

confronted with different sorts of organizational problems and with a need to design a different sort of organizational structure. The critical element of organization building is figuring out how to support the execution of corporate and business strategies with an organization structure that is workable, efficient, pragmatic, but not just "theoretically sound" in terms of its strategy-supporting features.

The prevailing view about the strategic aspects of organization structure is basically a *contingency approach.*[21] Contingency theory states that choice of structure is dependent on the external/internal aspects of the environment in which the firm is operating. The greater the diversity among an organization's products-markets-technologies, the greater the likelihood that the most effective form of organization will be decentralized and multidivisional, as opposed to centralized and functional. Moreover, if an organization uses a continuous process or assembly-line type of technology, the contingency approach would suggest a larger dose of functionally oriented, centralized principles of organization since common standards of performance as well as tightly sequenced integration are crucial. To use a more decentralized, "free form" organization style in which highly interdependent subunits are individualized in their approaches to task-accomplishment can make it more difficult to achieve a desirable degree of coordination and integration. Similarly, close and strict government regulation may prompt use of a more mechanistic organization structure, since there necessarily are more rules and procedures which must be observed and, consequently, less room for individualized discretion. On the other hand, if a firm's products are mostly custom-made, the day-to-day work routine varies widely, or the production process is almost completely automated, then a heavier mix of decentralized and individualized techniques can be advantageous. From another view, the more uncertain and diverse the organization's product-market environment, the more likely a firm will utilize a discretionary, "organic" type approach, the logic being that it is more conducive to adapting organizational subunits to the unique features of their respective sub-environments.[22]

Drucker has summed up the intricacies of organization-building well:

> The simplest organization structure that will do the job is the best one. What makes an organization structure "good" are the problems it does not create. The simpler the structure, the less that can go wrong.

---

[21] The contingency approach to organization-building has been pioneered by Jay Lorsch and Paul Lawrence of the Harvard Business School. See, for example, P. R. Lawrence and J. W. Lorsch, *Organization and Environment: Managing Differentiation and Integration* (Boston: Division of Research, Harvard University Graduate School of Business Administration, 1967).

[22] Gene W. Dalton, Paul L. Lawrence, and Jay W. Lorsch, *Organization Structure and Design* (Homewood, Illinois: Irwin-Dorsey, 1970), p. 6.

Some design principles are more difficult and problematic than others. But none is without difficulties and problems. None is primarily people-focused rather than task-focused; none is more "creative," "free," or "more democratic." Design principles are tools; and tools are neither good nor bad in themselves. They can be used properly or improperly; and that is all. To obtain both the greatest possible simplicity and the greatest "fit," organization design has to start out with a clear focus on *key activities* needed to produce *key results*. They have to be structured and positioned in the simplest possible design. Above all, the architect of organization needs to keep in mind the purpose of the structure he is designing.[23]

NONSTRUCTURAL CONSIDERATIONS IN ORGANIZING FOR STRATEGIC ACCOMPLISHMENT

There are other organizational considerations besides structure which affect the success of strategy implementation. Two of the more important ones are the development of a distinctive competence and focusing organizational resources on achieving strategic objectives.

Building a Distinctive Competence

The strategic importance of deliberately trying to develop a distinctive competence within an organization stems from the extra contribution which special expertise and a competitive edge make both to performance and to strategic success. To the extent an organization can build and nurture an astutely conceived distinctive competence in its chosen business domains, it creates a golden opportunity for achieving a competitive advantage, gaining market share, and posting a superior record of performance.

In the vast majority of strategically successful enterprises, management will be found to have worked hard at figuring out how to make the organization not just good at what it does but *better* than its rivals. This may be accomplished by making special efforts to be more proficient in product development, quality of manufacture, calibre of technical services offered to customers, speed of response to changing customer requirements, or any other strategically relevant factor. The point is that in building and staffing the organization, management should make a concerted effort to focus time and money on creating high-performance skills and capabilities in those few select internal areas and activities in which superiority can make a real difference to strategic success. Once developed, these strengths become logical cornerstones for successful strategy implementation. Moreover, really distinctive internal skills and capabilities are not easily duplicated by other firms; this means that any differential

---

[23] Drucker, *Management*, pp. 601–2.

advantage so gained is likely to have a lasting strategic impact and pave the way for above-average performance over the long-term. Conscious managerial attention to the task of building strategically relevant internal skills and strengths into the overall organizational scheme is therefore a major element of organization building and effective strategy implementation.

Focusing Organizational Resources on Strategic Objectives

For management to keep an organization results-oriented and pointed in the direction of strategy accomplishment, organizational objectives should become the basis for work and for assignments. In a very real way, strategic objectives help identify the organization's key activities, they set forth organizational priorities, and, thus, are suggestive of how funds should be allocated and where work efforts should be directed.

One of the guidelines a general manager can follow in determining who should do what is to define jobs and tasks in terms of the desired strategic results and performance rather than simply in terms of the functions to be performed. Specific objectives should be developed not only for the organization as a whole but for each major organizational subunit and, through the efforts of subordinate managers, for each job. Every manager in the organization all the way down to the first-level supervisors needs to have his or her job spelled out in terms of expected results and the objectives to be achieved. While the objective/results setting process need not be an exclusively top-down approach, it is important that there be an emphasis on each person and each organizational unit doing their part to achieve strategic success. Such an approach has the advantage of putting the organizational spotlight on accomplishment of strategy and achieving the intended performance. It makes clearer the kind of work and effort that can be strategically productive. It relates jobs to the needs of the organization as a whole. Further, it lets people know what is expected of them—from a results perspective instead of a functional effort perspective.

Using strategic objectives as the focal points for work and assignments therefore begins with the question "What sort of performance and results do we want to generate?" Next to ask is "What key activities, organizational units, tasks, and jobs need to be set up and organized to produce these results?" The answers should suggest the kinds of skills, expertise, staffing, and funding which will be needed to allow the various organizational units to accomplish the designated results. The advantage of a results-oriented approach to the design of organizational tasks and assignments is it keeps the whole organization trained on implementing and executing strategy. It draws organization-wide attention to the right things to shoot for, rather than risking inadvertent drift and diversion to non-strategic concerns.

In the final analysis, though, the test of whether an organization is strategically effective is not revealed by astuteness of structure and design, the care with which the total work effort has been subdivided into jobs then recombined into coordinated action, the degree of reliance on managing by objectives, or by the efficiency of internal resource allocation. These things are important but not sufficient. The sufficient condition is that the organization is able to perform up to potential and expectations. This alone is the most telling measure of effective strategy implementation —for the simple reason it portends strategic success.

SUGGESTED READINGS

Ansoff, H. Igor, and Brandenberg, Richard   "A Language for Organizational Design: Part II." *Management Science*, vol. 12, no. 12, August 1971, pp. B-717–31.

Chandler, Alfred D.   *Strategy and Structure*. Cambridge, Mass.: The M.I.T. Press, 1962.

Corey, E. Raymond, and Star, Steven H.   *Organization Strategy: A Marketing Approach*. Boston: Division of Research, Harvard University Graduate School of Business Administration, 1971, chaps. 2, 3, 4, and 5.

Daniel, D. Ronald   "Reorganizing for Results." *Harvard Business Review*, vol. 44, no. 6, November-December 1966, pp. 96–104.

Drucker, Peter   *Management: Tasks, Responsibilities, Practices*. New York: Harper and Row Publishers, Inc., 1974, chaps. 41–48.

Lawrence, Paul R., and Lorsch, Jay W.   *Organization and Environment: Managing Differentiation and Integration*. Boston: Division of Research, Harvard University Graduate School of Business Administration, 1967.

Lorsch, Jay W., and Walker, Arthur H.   "Organizational Choice: Product versus Function." *Harvard Business Review*, vol. 46, no. 6, November-December 1968, pp. 129–38.

Rumelt, Richard   *Strategy, Structure, and Economic Performance*. Cambridge, Mass.: Harvard University Press, 1974.

Salter, Malcolm S.   "Stages of Corporate Development." *Journal of Business Policy*, vol. 1, no. 1, 1970, pp. 23–37.

Scott, Bruce R.   "The Industrial State: Old Myths and New Realities." *Harvard Business Review*, vol. 51, no. 2, March-April 1973, pp. 133–48.

READING

Problems of Matrix Organizations*

STANLEY M. DAVIS and PAUL R. LAWRENCE

Stanley Davis is professor of business administration at Columbia University Graduate School of Business and at Boston University School of Management.

Paul Lawrence is Wallace Brett Durham Professor of Organizational Behavior at the Harvard Business School.

No organization design or method of management is perfect. And any form can suffer from a variety of problems that develop because of the design itself. This is particularly true when a company tries a new form. In this article we look at one relatively new organization form—the matrix —which has gained considerable popularity in recent years but which has some significant pathologies. Before discussing its ills, however, let us look for a moment at matrix management and organization (see boxed item below) and at how widespread the matrix is in U.S. industry today.

The list of well-known companies that are using some form of a matrix is becoming long and impressive. Take, for example, a company that has annual sales of $14 billion and employs about 400,000 people in scores of diverse businesses—General Electric. For decades, despite the diversity of its businesses, GE used one basic structure throughout its organization: five functional managers reporting to one general manager. Employing the logic that a company must organize to meet the particular needs of each business, some GE groups, divisions, and departments, which have found the pyramid form cumbersome, have turned to the matrix as a fundamental alternative.

In projecting its organization over the next ten years, GE management states in its Organization Planning Bulletin (September, 1976):

> We've highlighted matrix organization . . . not because it's a bandwagon that we want you all to jump on, but rather that it's a complex, difficult, and sometimes frustrating form of organization to live with. It's also, however, a bellwether of things to come. But, when implemented well, it does offer much of the best of both worlds. And all of us are going to have to learn how to utilize organization to prepare managers to increasingly deal with high levels of complexity and ambiguity in situations where they have to get results from people and components *not* under their direct control. . . .

---

* Stanley M. Davis and Paul R. Lawrence, "Problems of Matrix Organizations," *Harvard Business Review*, May-June 1978. Copyright © 1978 by the President and Fellows of Harvard College; all rights reserved.

Successful experience in operating under a matrix constitutes better preparation for an individual to run a huge diversified institution like General Electric—where so many complex, conflicting interests must be balanced—than the product and functional modes which have been our hallmark over the past twenty years.

Other major corporations, in diverse activities, such as Bechtel, Citibank, Dow Chemical, Shell Oil, Texas Instruments, and TRW, to mention a few, have also turned to the matrix. Based on our studies of the matrix in these companies, we believe that while some of the matrix's popularity is simply a passing fad, most uses of it are founded on solid business reasons that will persist. The matrix's most basic advantage over the familiar functional or product structure is that it facilitates a rapid management response to changing market and technical requirements. Further, it helps middle managers make trade-off decisions from a general management perspective.

Because the matrix is a relatively new form, however, the companies that have adopted it have of necessity been learning on a trial and error basis. The mistakes as well as the successes of these pioneers can be very informative to companies that follow their lead. Here, we present some of the more common problems that occur when a company uses a matrix form. For the sake of easy reference, we diagnose each pathology first, then discuss its prevention and treatment. By using this format, however, we do not mean to suggest that simple first-aid treatment of pathologies will cure them.

ILLS OF THE MATRIX

Many of the ailments we discuss do arise in more conventional organizations, but the matrix seems somewhat more vulnerable in these particular ones. It is wise, therefore, for managers thinking of adopting a matrix to be familiar with the diagnoses, prevention, and treatment of nine particular pathologies: tendencies toward anarchy, power struggles, severe groupitis, collapse during economic crunch, excessive overhead, sinking to lower levels, uncontrolled layering, navel gazing, and decision strangulation.

Tendencies toward Anarchy

A formless state of confusion where people do not recognize a "boss" to whom they feel responsible.

Diagnosis. Many managers who have had no firsthand familiarity with matrix organizations tend to have half-expressed fears that a matrix leads to anarchy. Are these concerns based on real hazards? Actually today, a considerable number of organizations are successfully using the matrix form, so we need not treat anarchy as a general hazard of the matrix. However, there are certain conditions or major misconceptions that could lead a company into the formless confusion that resembles anarchy.

Through firsthand experience we know of only one organization that, using a "latent" matrix form, quite literally came apart at the seams during a rather mild economic recession. Following a fast-growth strategy, this company used its high stock multiple to acquire, and then completely assimilate, smaller companies in the recreation equipment field. Within a period of about six months the company changed from an exciting success to a dramatic disaster. Its entire manufacturing, distribution, and financial systems went out of control leaving unfilled orders, closed factories, distressed inventories, and huge debts in their wake.

Of course, there are many possible reasons why this might have happened, but one perfectly reasonable explanation is that the organization design failed under stress. What was that design?

Essentially, the organization used a functional structure. As it acquired each small company, top management first encouraged the owners and general managers to leave, and then it attached the company's three basic functions of sales, production, and engineering to their counterparts in the parent organization. Within the parent marketing department, a young aggressive product manager would be assigned to develop for the acquired product line a comprehensive marketing plan that included making sales forecasts, promotion plans, pricing plans, projected earnings, and so forth. Once top management approved the plan, it told the selected product manager to hustle around and make his plan come true. This is where the latent matrix came in.

The product manager would find himself working across functional lines to try to coordinate production schedules, inventories, cash flow, and distribution patterns without any explicit and formal agreements about the nature of his relationships with the functional managers. Because he was locked into his approved marketing plan, when sales slipped behind schedule, his response was to exhort people to try harder rather than to cut back on production runs.

But once one or two things began to crumble, there was not enough reserve in the system to keep everything else from going wrong. As the product manager lost control, a power vacuum developed, into which the functional managers fell, each grabbing for total control. The result was that a mild recession triggered conditions approaching anarchy.

Prevention. We believe the lesson of this experience is loud and clear. Organizations should not rely too much on an informal or latent matrix to coordinate critical tasks. Relationships between functional and product managers should be explicit so that people are in approximate agreement about who is to do what under various circumstances. Properly used, a matrix does not leave such matters in an indefinite status; it is a definite structure and not a "free form" organization.

A useful "anarchy index" is how many people in an organization do not recognize one boss to whom they feel responsible for a major part of their work. In a study of five medical schools, which are notoriously anarchical,

---

WHAT IS A MATRIX?

The identifying feature of a matrix organization is that some managers report to two bosses rather than to the traditional single boss; there is a dual rather than a single chain of command.

Companies tend to turn to matrix forms:

1.   When it is absolutely essential that they be highly responsive to two sectors simultaneously, such as markets and technology;

2.   When they face uncertainties that generate very high information processing requirements; and

3.   When they must deal with strong constraints on financial and/or human resources.

Matrix structures can help provide both flexibility and balanced decision making, but at the price of complexity.

Matrix organization is more than a matrix structure. It must be reinforced by matrix systems such as dual control and evaluation systems, by leaders who operate comfortably with lateral decision making, and by a culture that can negotiate open conflict and a balance of power.

In most matrix organizations there are dual command responsibilities assigned to functional departments (marketing, production, engineering, and so forth) and to product or market departments. The former are oriented to specialized inhouse resources while the latter focus on outputs. Other matrices are split between area-based departments and either products or functions.

Every matrix contains three unique and critical roles; the top manager who heads up and balances the dual chains of command, the matrix bosses (functional, product, or area) who share subordinates, and the managers who report to two different matrix bosses. Each of these roles has its special requirements.

Aerospace companies were the first to adopt the matrix form, but now companies in many industries (chemical, banking, insurance, packaged goods, electronics, computer, and so forth) and in different fields (hospitals, government agencies, and professional organizations) are adapting different forms of the matrix.

the one with the most explicit matrix structure was also the one with the least number of "bossless" people.[1]

Treatment. Should the worst happen and a company plunge into anarchy, true crisis management would be the best response. The crisis response is really no mystery. The CEO must pull all key people and critical information into the center. He or she must personally make all important decisions on a round-the-clock schedule until the crisis is over. Then and only then can he undertake the work of reshaping the organization so that it can withstand any future shock such as a minor recession.

Power Struggles

Managers jockey for power in many organizations, but a matrix design almost encourages them to do so.

Diagnosis. The essence of a matrix is dual command. For such a form to survive there needs to be a balance of power, where its locus seems to shift constantly, each party always jockeying to gain an advantage. It is not enough simply to create the balance, but there must also be continual mechanisms for checking the imbalances that creep in.

In business organizations that operate with a balance of power form, there is a constant tendency toward imbalance. As long as each group or dimension in an organization tries to maximize its own advantage vis-à-vis others, there will be a continual balancing struggle for dominant power. A power struggle in a matrix is qualitatively different from that in a traditionally structured hierarchy because in the latter it is clearly illegitimate. In the matrix, however, power struggles are inevitable; the boundaries of authority and responsibility overlap prompting people to maximize their own advantage.

Prevention. Most top managers will find it exceedingly difficult to forestall all power struggles. Equal strength on the part of the two parties, however, will prevent struggles from reaching destructive heights. Friendly competition should be encouraged, but all-out combat severely punished. Managers in a matrix should push for their advantages but never with the intention of eliminating those with whom they share power, and always with a perspective that encompasses both positions.

Treatment. The best way to ensure that power struggles do not undermine the matrix is to make managers on the power axes aware that to win power absolutely is to lose it ultimately. These managers need to see that the total victory of one dimension only ends the balance, finishes the duality of command, and destroys the matrix. They must see this sharing

---

[1] From the forthcoming article by M. R. Weisbord, M. P. Charns, and P. R. Lawrence, "Organizational Dilemmas of Academic Medical Centers," *Journal of Applied Behavioral Science*, vol. 14, no. 3.

of power as an underlying principle, before and during all of the ensuing and inevitable power struggles.

Matrix managers have to recognize that they need worthy adversaries, counterparts who can match them, to turn the conflict to constructive ends. For this successful outcome three things are necessary.

First, matrix managers always have to maintain an institutional point of view, seeing their struggles from a larger, shared perspective. Second, they have to jointly agree to remove other matrix managers who, through weakness or whatever inability, are losing irretrievable ground. And, third, that they replace these weak managers with the strongest available people —even if to do so means placing very strong managers in weakened parts of the organization and reversing their power initiatives.

Another key element in stopping power struggles before they get out of hand and destroy the balance is the top level superior to whom the dueling managers report. Because of this element, the matrix is a paradox —a shared-power system that depends on a strong individual, one who does not share the authority that is delegated to him (say by the board), to arbitrate between his power-sharing subordinates. The top manager has many vehicles for doing this: the amount of time he spends with one side of the matrix or the other, pay differentials, velocity of promotion, direct orders issued to one dimension and not to the other, and so forth. What he must do above all, however, is protect the weak dimension in the organization, not necessarily the weak manager in charge of that dimension.

Severe Groupitis

The mistaken belief that matrix management is the same as group decision making.

Diagnosis. The confusion of matrix behavior with group decision making probably arises from the fact that a matrix often evolves out of new project or business teams, which do suggest a group decision process. Under many circumstances, of course, it is perfectly sensible for managers to make decisions in groups. But managers should expect difficulties to arise if they believe group decision making to be the essence of matrix behavior.

We have seen one matrix organization that had a severe case of "groupitis." This multiproduct electronics company had a product manager and a product team, comprised of specialists drawn from the ranks of every functional department, assigned to every product. So far so good. But somehow the idea that the matrix structure requires that *all* business decisions be hammered out in group meetings became prevalent in the organization. To make decisions in other ways was considered illegitimate and not in the spirit of matrix operations.

Many of the decisions that had to be made about each product involved detailed matters with which only one or two people were regularly conversant. Yet all team members were constrained to listen to these issues being discussed until a decision was made, and were even expected to participate in the discussion and influence the choice. Some individuals seemed to enjoy the steady diet of meetings and the chance to practice being a generalist.

However, a larger number of people felt that their time was being wasted and would have preferred leaving the decisions to the most informed people. The engineers, in particular, complained that the time they were spending in meetings was robbing them of opportunities to strengthen their special competence and identities. As well as noting these personal reactions, senior managers reported a general disappointment with the speed and flexibility of organizational responses.

Prevention. Because the whole idea of a matrix organization is still unfamiliar to many managers, it is understandable that they confuse it with processes such as group decision making. The key to prevention is education. Top managers need to accompany their strategic choice to move toward a matrix with a serious educational effort to clarify to all participants what a matrix is and what it is not.

Treatment. In the case of the multiproducts electronics company, the problem came to light while we were researching the matrix approach. Once senior people had clearly diagnosed the problem, it was 90% cured. Top management emphatically stated that there was nothing sacred about group decisions and that it was not sensible to have all product team members involved all the time. Once the line between individual and group matters was drawn according to who had information really relevant to a decision, meetings became fewer and smaller and work proceeded on a more economical and responsive basis. The concept of teamwork was put in perspective: as often as necessary and as little as possible.

Collapse during Economic Crunch

When business declines, the matrix becomes the scapegoat for poor management and is discarded.

Diagnosis. Matrix organizations that blossom during periods of rapid growth and prosperity sometimes are cast away during periods of economic decline. On reflection, we can understand this. In prosperous times, companies often expand their business lines and the markets they serve. The ensuing complexity may turn them toward matrix management and organization.

However, if these companies follow the normal business cycle, there will be a period of two to five years before they experience another economic crunch which is more than enough time for the matrix concept to spread throughout a company. By that time the matrix occupies a central place in company conversations and is a familiar part of these organizations. Although there may still be some problems, the matrix seems there to stay.

When the down part of the economic cycle begins, senior management in these companies may become appreciably bothered by the conflict between subordinates as well as by the apparent slowness with which they respond to the situation. "We need decisive action" is their rallying cry.

In an authoritarian structure top management can act quickly because it need not consider the spectrum of opinion. Thinking there is no time for organizational toys and tinkering, the top level managers take command in an almost, but not quite, forgotten way, and ram their directives down the line. The matrix is "done in."

Prevention. Top management can prevent this kind of collapse of the matrix by employing general managerial excellence, independent of the matrix, long before the crunch arrives. Good planning, for example, can often forecast downturns in the economic cycle. Corporate structures such as the matrix should not have to change because of standard changes in the business cycle. When management planning has been poor, however, the matrix is a readily available scapegoat.

Companies that experience severe economic crunches often make drastic changes in many directions at once: trimming product lines, closing offices, making massive personnel and budget cuts, and tightening managerial controls. The matrix is often done in during this period for several reasons: it represents too great a risk; "it never really worked properly" and giving it the coup de grace can disguise the failure of implementation; and the quality of decision making had not improved performance sufficiently to counterbalance the hard times. Measures management can take to prevent this pathology do not lie within the matrix itself, as much as with improvements in basic managerial skills and planning.

A real estate and construction company provides an example of how a company can anticipate and flexibly respond to an economic crunch that demonstrates the strength rather than the weakness of the matrix. The company has developed a structure as well as procedures that are especially well suited to the economic uncertainties of the business. These include a set of fully owned subsidiaries each the equivalent of a functional department in a manufacturing company and each the "home base" for varied specialists needed to execute all phases of a major building project. The heads of the subsidiaries act as chief salesmen for their various services, and often head up the bidding teams that put together sophisticated proposals.

As a proposal project proceeds, the selected project manager is drawn into the team in anticipation of securing the contract. This ensures an orderly transition to the project management phase. The project office is given first-line responsibility for control of costs, schedules, and quality of the project, but the top management team from the parent company reviews the project regularly as a backup.

The company has used the matrix to advantage in weathering major shifts in both the availability of business by market segment, for example, from schools to hospitals, and the level of construction activity. It maintains a cadre of professional specialists and project managers, who can be kept busy during the lows of the cycle, which it rapidly expands during the highs by subcontracting for temporary services.

Treatment. This is one pathology that requires preventive treatment; we do not know of any cure. When the matrix does collapse during an economic crunch, it is very unlikely that it can be resurrected. At best, the organization will go back to its pendulum days, alternating between the centralized management of the crunch period and the decentralized freedoms of more prosperous times. Even if top management should try again, it is likely to get a negative response from lower level managers. "They said they were committed to the matrix, but at the first sign of hard times all the nice words about the advantages of the matrix turned out to be just that—nice words." If a company's conditioned response to hard times is to retrench, it should not attempt a matrix in the first place.

Excessive Overhead

The fear of high costs associated with a matrix.

Diagnosis. On the face of it, a matrix organization would seem to double management costs because of its dual chain of command. This issue deserves thoughtful consideration.

The limited amount of research on matrix overhead costs indicates that in the initial phases overhead costs do in fact rise, but that, as a matrix matures, these extra costs disappear and are offset by productivity gains.[2] Our experience supports this finding. In a large electronics company we observed in some detail how initial overhead increases not only necessarily occur in a matrix but also how they can inflate unnecessarily. In this case, the company decided to employ the matrix design from the outset in setting up its new operating division at a new plant site.

This unique organizational experiment had a number of positive attributes, but one of its problems was with overhead costs. In staffing the new division, top management filled every functional office and every product manager's slot with one full-time person. This resulted in a relatively small division having top level managers as well as full-time functional group and full-time product managers. Within months, however, this top heavy

---

[2] C. J. Middleton, "How to Set Up a Project Organization," HBR March-April 1967, p. 73.

division was pared down to more reasonable staffing levels; by assigning individuals to two or more slots, management got costs under control.

Prevention. The division's problem was caused by top management's assumption that each managerial slot requires a full-time incumbent. Overstaffing is much less liable to occur when an organization evolves gradually from a conventional design into a matrix, and managers perform as both functional and product managers. While this technique can be justified as a transition strategy, it also has its hazards. A safer route is to assign managers roles on the same side of the matrix (i.e., two functional jobs or two product management jobs).

As a final argument against the fear of overhead costs, consider that no well-run organization would adopt a matrix structure without the longer run expectation that, at a given level of output, the costs of operations would be lower than with other organizational forms. In what way can such economies be achieved?

The potential economies come from two general sources: fewer bad decisions and less featherbedding. First and most important, the matrix can improve quality of business decisions because it helps bring the needed information and emphasis to bear on critical decisions in a timely fashion. The second source, less featherbedding, is not so obvious, but potentially of greater significance. How can it work?

Treatment. Perhaps the clearest example of the matrix's potential to reduce redundancies in human resources is the way some consulting organizations employ it. These firms usually set up a matrix of functional specialists against client or account managers. The body of other consultants are grouped with their fellow specialists but are available for assignment to projects under the leadership of account or client managers.

From an accounting standpoint, therefore, consultants' time is directly billed to clients' accounts when they are working for an account or engagement manager. Otherwise, their time is charged against the budget of their function manager. The firm's nonbillable costs are, therefore, very conspicuous—both by department and by individual consultant. Of course, some time charged to functional departments, such as background study, research work, and time between assignments should by no means be thought of as wasted. But management can budget such time in advance so that it can scrutinize the variances from the budget.

As one senior manager in a consulting firm put it, "There is no place to hide in a matrix organization." This fact makes clear-cut demands on middle level people and consequently puts pressure on them to produce. For the long-term good of both the people involved and the organization, top managers need to keep such pressures from becoming too strong. Because it is perfectly possible to get too much as well as too little pressure, a creative tension is sought.

Sinking to Lower Levels

The matrix has some difficulty in staying alive at high levels of a corporation, and a corresponding tendency to sink to group and division levels where it thrives.

Diagnosis. Sinking may occur for two reasons. Either senior management has not understood or been able to implement the matrix concept as well as lower level managers, or the matrix has found its appropriate place. For example, if a company sets up a matrix between its basic functional and product groups, the product managers never truly relinquish their complete control, and the matrix fails to take hold at the corporate level.

But, say, one or two of the managers find the idea to be useful within their divisions. Their own functional specialists and project leaders can share the power they delegate and the design can survive within subunits of the corporation. For example, Dow Chemical's attempt to maintain the product/geography balance at the top failed, but the function/product balance held within the geographic areas for several years.

When sinking occurs because of top management misunderstanding, it is likely to occur in conjunction with other pathologies, particularly power struggles. For instance, if many senior executives consider adopting the matrix idea, but only one or a few really become convinced of its worth, there is a danger: those at the top who espouse a philosophy and method they did not employ themselves will be pitted against those who are able to show that it does work.

Prevention. If the corporate top management thinks through which dimensions of the company it must balance, and at what level of aggregation, it can keep the matrix from sinking. For example, top managers should ask themselves if all the business units need to be balanced by central functional departments. If the answer is no, then some business units should operate as product divisions with the traditional pyramid of command, while others share functional services in a partial matrix. However, sinking is not always bad and should be prevented only when it indicates that an appropriate design is disintegrating.

Treatment. Before matrix management can run smoothly, it must be in the proper location. As often as not, when a matrix sinks, it may simply be experiencing a healthy adjustment, and ought to be thought of as settling rather than as sinking. Settling is likely to occur during the early stages of a matrix's evolution and leads to manageable matrix units.

The question of size is a great concern for many managers who ask, in effect, "That sounds great for a $250-million company with a few thousand employees, but can it work for a $2-billion or $3-billion company with 50,000 employees? Its entire company is the size of one of our divisions." Our experience indicates that matrix management and organization seems to function better when no more than 500 managers are involved in matrix relationships. But that does not rule out the $2-billion to $3-billion company. In a company of 5,000 only about 50 managers are likely to be in the matrix, so in a company with 50,000 employees only about 500 may need to be involved in dual reporting lines. With that number, the people who need to coordinate regularly are able to do so through communication networks that are based on personal relations.

Whatever the size unit in which the matrix operates the important thing is for management to have reasoned carefully from an analysis of the task to the design of the organization. Then, if settling occurs, it should be seen not as a pathology but as a self-adjustment that suggests the organization's capacity to evolve with growth.

Uncontrolled Layering

Matrices which lie within matrices which lie within matrices result frequently from the dynamics of power rather than from the logic of design.

Diagnosis. Sometimes matrices not only sink but also cascade down the organization and filter through several levels and across several divisions. This layering process may or may not be pathological. In fact, it may be a rational and logical development of the matrix, but we include it briefly here because it sometimes creates more problems than it solves. In terms of the metaphor we have used in this article, layering is a pathology only if the matrix begins to metastasize. When this occurs, organization charts begin to resemble blueprints for a complex electronic machine, relationships become unnecessarily complex, and the matrix form may become more of a burden than it is worth.

Prevention and Treatment. The best remedies for uncontrolled layering are careful task analysis and reduced power struggles. We have seen a few cases where one dimension of a matrix was clearly losing power to the other, so, adapting an "if you can't beat 'em, join 'em" philosophy, it created a matrix within its own dimension. A product unit, for example, developed its own functional *expertise* distinct from the functional *units* at the next level up. The best defense was a good offense, or so it seemed.

In two other cases, the international divisions of two large companies each created its own matrix by adding business managers as an overlay to its geographic format, without reconciling these with the managers who ran the domestic product/service groups. In each case, adequate conceptualization by top managers would probably have simplified the organization design and forestalled the layering, which occurred because of power maneuvers. Management can treat this unhealthy state best by rebalancing the matrix so that no manager of one dimension is either too threatened or pushed too hard toward a power goal.

Matrix design is complex enough without the addition of power struggles. A well-conceptualized matrix is bound to be less complex and easier to manage than one that is illogically organized.

Navel Gazing

Managers in a matrix can succumb to excessive internal preoccupation and lose touch with the marketplace.

Diagnosis. Because a matrix fosters considerable interdependence of people and tasks and demands negotiating skills on the part of its members, matrix managers sometimes tend to get absorbed in internal relations at the expense of paying attention to the world outside the organization, particularly to clients. When this happens, an organization spends more energy ironing out its own disputes than in serving its customers. The outward focus disappears because the short-term demands of daily working life have yet to be worked through.

The navel gazers are not at all lethargic; rather they are involved in a heated fraternal love/hate affair with each other. This inward preoccupation is more common in the early phases of a matrix, when the new behaviors are being learned, than in matrices that have been operating for a few years.

Prevention. Whatever other pathologies develop in a matrix, attention to their cure is bound to increase the internal focus of the members; so prevention of other pathologies will certainly reduce the likelihood of this one occurring. Awareness of the tendency will also help. Since the product dimension of the organization generally has a more external focus than the resource dimension, the responsibility for preventing an excessive introspection is not equally distributed. The product dimension people can help the others keep perspective; but a strong marketing orientation is the best preventative of all.

Treatment. If the managers in the matrix are navel gazing, the first step in the treatment is to make these managers aware of the effects. Are customers complaining a lot, or at least more than usual? Managers need to confront internal conflict, but also to recognize that confrontation is secondary to maintaining effective external relationships. Navel gazing generally occurs when the matrix has been fully initiated but not yet debugged. People accept it, but they are engrossed in figuring out how to make it work.

The second step is to treat the inward focus as a symptom of the underlying issue: how to institutionalize matrix relationships so that they become familiar and comfortable routines, and so that people can work through them without becoming obsessed by them. Finally, it must always be remembered that any form of organization is only a means and should never become an end in itself.

Decision Strangulation

Too much democracy, not enough action!

Can moving into a matrix lead to the strangulation of the decision process, into endless delays for debate, for clearing with everybody in sight? Will decisions, no matter how well thought through, be made too late to be of use? Will too many people have power to water down all bold initiatives or veto them outright? Such conditions can arise in a matrix. We have in mind three situations—constant clearing, escalation of conflict, and unilateral style—each calling for slightly different preventive action and treatment.

Constant Clearing. In one company we know of, various functional specialists who reported to a second boss, a product manager, picked up the idea that they had to clear all issues with their own functional bosses before agreeing to product decisions. This meant that every issue had to be discussed in at least two meetings, if not more. During the first meeting, the specialists and the product manager could only review the facts of the issue, which was then tabled until, at the second meeting, the specialists cleared the matter with their functional bosses—who by this process were each given a de facto veto over product decisions.

This impossible clearing procedure represented, in our view, a failure of delegation, not of the matrix. One needs to ask why the functional specialists could not be trusted to act on the spot in regard to most product decisions in ways that would be consistent with the general guidelines of their functional departments? Either the specialists were poorly selected, too inexperienced and badly informed, or their superiors were lacking in a workable degree of trust of one another. Regardless, this problem, and its prevention and treatment, needs to be addressed directly without making a scapegoat of the matrix.

Escalation of Conflict. Another possible source of decision strangulation in matrix organizations occurs when managers frequently or constantly refer decisions up the dual chain of command. Seeing that one advantage of the conventional single chain of command is that two disagreeing peers can go to their shared boss for a resolution, managers unfamiliar with the matrix worry about this problem almost more than any other. They look at a matrix and realize that the nearest shared boss might be the CEO, who could be five or six echelons up. They realize that not too many problems can be pushed up to the CEO for resolution without creating the ultimate in information overload. So, they think, will not the inevitable disagreement lead to a tremendous pileup of unresolved conflict?

Certainly, this can happen in a malfunctioning matrix. Whether it does happen depends primarily on the depth of understanding that exists about required matrix behavior on the part of managers in the dual structure. Let us envision the following scene: a manager with two bosses gets sharply conflicting instructions from his product and his functional bosses. When he tries to reconcile his instructions without success, he quite properly asks for a session with his two bosses to resolve the matter. The three people meet, but the discussion bogs down, no resolution is reached, and neither boss gives way.

The two bosses then appeal the problem up a level to their respective superiors in each of the two chains of command. This is the critical step. If the two superiors properly understand matrix behavior, they will first ascertain whether the dispute reflects an unresolved broader policy issue. If it does not, they know their proper step is to teach their subordinates to resolve the problem themselves—not to solve it for them. In short, they would not let the unresolved problem escalate, but would force it back to the proper level for solution, and insist that the solution be found promptly.

Often, conflict cannot be resolved; it can, however, be managed, which it must be if the matrix is to work. Any other course of action would represent management's failure to comprehend the essential nature of the design.

Unilateral Style. A third possible reason for decision strangulation in a matrix system can arise from a very different source—personal style. Some managers have the feeling they are not truly managing if they are not in a position to make crisp, unilateral decisions. Identifying leadership with decisive action, they become very frustrated when they have to engage in carefully reasoned debates about the wisdom of what they want to do.

Such a manager is likely to feel frustrated even in regard to a business problem whose resolution will vitally affect functions other than his own, such as in a company that is experiencing critical dual pressure from the marketplace and from advancing technology. A matrix that deliberately induces simultaneous decision making between two or more perspectives is likely to frustrate such a person even further.

If managers start feeling emasculated by bilateral decision making, they are certain to be unhappy in a matrix organization. In such cases the strangulation is in the eye of the beholder. Such people must work on their personal decision-making style or look for employment in a nonmatrix organization.

AT LAST, LEGITIMACY

We do not recommend that every company adopt the matrix form. But where it is relevant, it can become an important part of an effective managerial process. Like any new method it may develop serious bugs, but the experiences that many companies are acquiring with this organization form can now help others realize its benefits and avoid its pitfalls.

The matrix seems to have spread despite itself and its pathologies: what was necessary was made desirable. It is difficult and complex, and human flexibility is required to arrive at organizational flexibility.

But the reverse is also true; success has given the form legitimacy, and, as the concept spreads, familiarity seems to reduce the resistance and difficulties people experience in using the matrix. Managers are now beginning to say, "It isn't that new or different after all." This familiarity is a sign of acceptance, more than of change or moderation of the design.

For generations, managers lived with the happy fiction of dotted lines, indicating that a second reporting line was necessary if not formal. The result had always been a sort of executive ménage à trois, a triangular arrangement where the manager had one legitimate relationship (the reporting line) and one that existed but was not granted equal privileges (the dotted line).

As executives develop greater confidence with the matrix form, they bring the dotted line relationship out of the closet, and grant it legitimacy.

Each time another organization turns to the matrix, it has a larger and more varied number of predecessors that have chartered the way. The examples of wider applicability suggest that the matrix is becoming less and less an experiment and more and more a mature formulation in organization design. As more organizations travel the learning curve, the curve itself becomes an easier one to climb. Similarly, as more managers gain experience operating in matrix organizations, they are bound to spread this experience as some of them move, as they inevitably will, into other organizations.

We believe that in the future matrix organizations will become almost commonplace and that managers will speak less of the difficulties and pathologies of the matrix than of its advantages and benefits.

MANAGING ORGANIZATIONAL PROCESSES

Nothing makes a prince so much esteemed as the undertaking of great enterprises and the setting of a noble example in his own person.

N. Machiavelli

Given that the organization's structure is suitably keyed to the needs of strategy, the general manager's priorities tend to focus on seeing that prescribed activities and processes are effectively carried out. This means motivating people, overseeing and coordinating day-to-day tasks, creating a timely flow of the right information to the right people, instituting controls to contain deviations from plan, and exercising appropriate leadership and communication skills. All of these functions are important and pose tests of the manager's basic administrative abilities. This chapter highlights how managerial performance of these functions relates to successful strategy formulation and implementation.

MOTIVATIONAL CONSIDERATIONS

Motivation is a key ingredient of strategy implementation. Obviously, it is important for organizational subunits and individuals to have a reasonably strong commitment to the achievement of the enterprise's goals, objectives, and overall strategy. Motivation is brought about most fundamentally by the organization's reward-punishment structure—salary raises, bonuses, stock options, fringe benefits, promotions (or fear of demotions), assurance of not being "sidelined" and ignored, praise, recognition, criticism, tension, fear, more (or less) responsibility, increased (or decreased) job control or autonomy, the promise of attractive locational assignments, and the bonds of group acceptance. As the foregoing suggests, motivational incentives can be positive or negative in nature. They may also be intrinsic, as in the case of the increased self-respect and gratification which comes with achieving a goal or solving a tough problem.

The prevailing view is that a good motivational system allows for blended fulfillment of both organizational goals and personal goals. No doubt this is a useful guideline. But, in practice, it is a ticklish task to gear the size of an individual's rewards to a corresponding contribution to organization objectives; rewards may be excessive, target achievement levels set too low, or contributions unrecognized and mismeasured. More often, though, the opposite is true, as suggested by the way Harold Geneen, former president and chief executive officer of ITT, allegedly motivated his subordinates through the combined use of money, tension, and fear:

> Geneen provides his managers with enough incentives to make them tolerate the system. Salaries all the way through ITT are higher than average—Geneen reckons 10 percent higher—so that few people can leave without taking a drop. As one employee put it: "We're all paid just a bit more than we think we're worth." At the very top, where the demands are greatest, the salaries and stock options are sufficient to compensate for the rigors. As someone said, "He's got them by their limousines."
>
> Having bound his men with chains of gold, Geneen can induce the tension that drives the machine. "The key to the system," one of his men explained, "is the profit forecast. Once the forecast has been gone over, revised and agreed on, the managing director has a personal commitment to Geneen to carry it out. That's how he produces the tension on which the success depends." The tension goes through the company, inducing ambition, perhaps exhilaration, but always with some sense of fear: what happens if the target is missed?
>
> The price in human terms is very high. "Geneen wants us all to be as gung-ho as he is," one manager said, "but somehow it isn't as much fun for the rest of us." The sense of strain is very noticeable in the Park Avenue skyscraper: not only the tension of worry and work, but the lack of the satisfaction of personal achievement.[1]

It goes without saying that if and when an organization's structure of rewards and punishments induces too much tension, anxiety, and job insecurity, the results can be counterproductive. Yet, it is doubtful whether it is ever useful to completely eliminate tension, fear, anxiety, and insecurity from the motivational system; there is, for example, no evidence that "the quiet life" is highly correlated with superior performance. On the contrary, high-performing organizations usually require an endowment of ambitious people who relish the opportunity to climb the ladder of success, who have a need for stimulation (or who want to avoid boredom), and who thus find some degree of position anxiety useful in order

---

[1] Anthony Sampson, *The Sovereign State of ITT* (New York: Stein and Day, Publishers, 1973), p. 132.

ILLUSTRATION CAPSULE 14
The Mysteries of Motivation

The eminently successful Paul W. Bryant, head football coach at the University of Alabama, tells of the time he unwittingly motivated a team just prior to game time:

> When I was at Kentucky I got booed one night by a group of students who came to the train to see us off for a game with Cincinnati. I had fired some of our star players and they didn't like that. And we'd lost three of our first five games and they didn't like that either, which I can understand. I didn't like it myself. In fact, I hated it. For a young coach —which I was then—so keyed up I couldn't get to work in the morning without vomiting along the way, it was not exactly heaven on earth. The Cincinnati game took on added importance.
>
> Cincinnati had fine teams then, coached by Sid Gillman, who has been a big name in the pros and is with the Houston Oilers now. What I'm about to say should not be taken as a lack of respect for Sid. You have to appreciate that my collar was tighter than it is now.
>
> We got to the stadium at Cincinnati and I sensed something was wrong. When we went out to warm up for the game there was nobody in the stands. Just a few handfuls scattered around. I thought for a minute I was in the wrong place. When we finished our warm-up and the Cincinnati team still hadn't made an appearance, I said to Carney Laslie, one of my original assistant coaches, "What's that no-good conniving smart-aleck"—meaning the eminent Coach Gillman—"up to now? What the hell is that damn thief trying to pull?"
>
> Carney just shook his head. He was as dumbfounded as I was.
>
> I ordered the team back into the locker room—and then it dawned on me. I'd screwed up the schedule. We were an hour early.
>
> I was too embarrassed to tell what I knew. I just walked around, up and down the aisles where the players sat waiting, my big old farmer's boots making the only noise in there. I couldn't think of anything to say, so I didn't say a word. For an hour I clomped up and down. Finally, when I'd used up enough time I delivered a one-sentence pep talk, the only thing I could think to say:
>
> "Let's go."
>
> They almost tore the door down getting out. Cincinnati was favored that day, but it was no contest. We won, 27–7.

Bryant tells of a second instance when coaching at Texas A&M where an approach he tried worked on one occasion but apparently failed when someone else tried it.

> They'd been dead all week in practice before the SMU game, and I wondered, what could we do? What was left to try? I'd run out of ways to motivate them. Elmer Smith, one of my assistants, said he remembered one time when he was playing for Ivan Grove at Hendrix College.

ILLUSTRATION CAPSULE 14 *(continued)*

Grove woke him up at midnight and read him something about how a mustard seed could move a mountain if you believed in it, something Norman Vincent Peale, or somebody, had taken from the Bible and written in a little pamphlet. It impressed me.

I didn't tell a soul. At 12 o'clock on Thursday night I called everyone on my staff and told them to meet me at the dormitory at 1 o'clock. When they got there, I said, OK, go get the players real quick, and they went around shaking them, and the boys came stumbling in there, rubbing their eyes, thinking I'd finally lost my mind. And I read 'em that little thing about the mustard seed—just three sentences—turned around, and walked out.

Well, you never know if you are doing right or wrong, but we went out and played the best game we'd played all year. SMU should have beaten us by 40 points, but they were lucky to win, 6–3. In the last minute of play we had a receiver wide open inside their 20-yard line, but our passer didn't see him.

Several years after that, Darrell Royal called me from Texas. He was undefeated, going to play Rice and worried to death. He said he'd never been in that position before, undefeated and all, and his boys were lazy and fatheaded, and he wanted to know what to do about it.

I said, "Well, Darrell, there's no set way to motivate a team, and the way I do it may be opposite to your way but I can tell you a story." And I gave him that thing about the mustard seed. He said, by golly, he'd try it.

Well, I don't know whether he did or not, but I remember the first thing I wanted to do Sunday morning was get that paper and see how Texas made out. Rice won, 34–7.

Source: Paul W. Bryant and John Underwood, *Bear: The Hard Life and Good Times of Alabama's Coach Bryant* (Boston: Little, Brown and Company, 1974), pp. 3–4, 6–7.

to satisfy their own drives for personal recognition, accomplishment, and self-satisfaction.

INSTILLING A SPIRIT OF PERFORMANCE

One test of administrative effectiveness lies in management's ability to perceive what each employee can do well and what he or she cannot. A good manager works at developing employees' strengths, neutralizing their respective weaknesses, and building on and blending the individual skills of employees in ways that cause employees to perform consistently at or near peak capability. When successfully done, the outcome is a spirit of high performance and an emphasis on excellence and achievement.

Such a spirit of performance, sometimes referred to as "morale," should not be confused with whether employees are "happy" or "satisfied" or whether they "get along well together." An organization whose approach to "human relations" and "dealing with people" is not grounded in high standards of performance actually has poor human relations and a management that is liable to produce a mean spirit.[2] Certainly, there is no greater indictment of an organization than that of allowing or fostering an atmosphere in which the outstanding performances of a few people become a threat to the whole group and a source of controversy, back-stabbing, and attempts to enforce safe mediocrity.

For an organization to be instilled with and sustain a spirit of performance, it must maintain a focus on achievement and excellence. It must strive at developing a consistent ability to produce results over prolonged periods of time. It must be alert to opportunities and seek to capitalize on them. It must succeed in utilizing the full range of rewards and punishment (pay, promotion, assignments, tension, pressure, job security, and so on) to establish and enforce standards of excellence.

Particularly management must have the courage and willingness to remove people who consistently render poor or mediocre performance. Such people should, if for no other reason, be removed for their own good since people who find themselves in a job they cannot handle are usually frustrated, anxiety-ridden, harassed, and unhappy.[3] One does not do a person a favor by keeping him in a job he is not equal to. Moreover, subordinates have a right to be managed with competence, dedication, and achievement—unless their boss performs well, they themselves cannot perform well.[4] In general, then, an organization should not have to tolerate managers who fail to perform; they should be "sidetracked," or in extreme cases dismissed, so not to undercut either the implementation of strategy or the careers of subordinates. One well-known proponent of this approach was General George C. Marshall, chief of staff of the U.S. Army in World War II.[5] Marshall reportedly said, "I have a duty to the soldiers, their parents, and the country, to remove immediately any commander who does not satisfy the highest performance standards." He repeatedly upheld this duty, actually removing a number of commanders from assignments. But when he did, he followed it up with the recognition that, "It was my mistake to have put this or that man in a command that was not the right command for him. It is therefore *my* job to think through where he belongs."

The toughest cases, of course, concern the need to reassign people who have given long and loyal service to the organization but who are past their

---

[2] Peter F. Drucker, *Management: Tasks, Responsibilities, Practices* (New York: Harper & Row, Publishers, Inc., 1974), p. 455.

[3] Ibid., p. 457.

[4] Ibid.

[5] As cited by Drucker, *Management*, p. 459.

prime and unable to deal effectively with demanding situations. The decision in such cases should be objectively based on what is best for the company, which usually means removing the person from his or her job. Yet, it can be done in a compassionate and human fashion. When Henry Ford II was trying to revive Ford Motor Company after World War II, he felt that none of the nine top-management people in one key division were competent enough to handle new jobs created by reorganization.[6] Not one was appointed to the newly created positions. But while their incompetence was undisputed and it would have been easy to fire them, the fact remained that they had served loyally through trying periods. Ford took the position that while no one should be allowed to hold a job he or she could not perform in superior fashion, neither should anyone be penalized for the mistakes of the previous regime. So, the nine men were assigned as experienced technicians and experts to jobs they could be expected to do well. As things turned out, seven of the men did well in their new assignments—one so well that he was later promoted into a more important job than originally held. The other two failed: the older one was given early retirement and the younger one was dismissed. A management that is concerned with building excellent organization spirit takes the cases of loyal nonperformers seriously because, while they are (or should be) few in in number, they have a major impact on morale, and how their cases are handled tells others in the organization much about management's character and respect for its employees.

Two additional considerations weigh heavily on whether an organization attains a high spirit of performance in implementing the chosen strategy.[7] The first concerns the extent to which an organization is pointed toward capitalizing on opportunity as opposed to solving existing problems. An organization is prone to have higher morale and an acceptance of challenge when top priority is given to converting opportunities into results. Concentrating on solving problems tends to detract from an organization's momentum and to put it on "hold" until the problems at hand are solved or else brought under control. In contrast, an attitude of "damn the torpedoes, full steam ahead" works to keep the attention of the organization focused on generating the greatest impact on results and performance—an orientation which, in many circumstances, acts to enhance strategy implementation.

The second consideration which affects an organization's spirit of performance is the reward-punishment structure. Decisions on pay, on assignments, and on promotion are management's *foremost* "control" device. These decisions signal who is getting ahead and who is not, who is climbing up the ladder fastest, and who is perceived as doing a good job.

---

[6] This example is drawn from Drucker, *Management*, p. 459.
[7] Ibid., pp. 460–61.

They signal what sort of behavior and performance management wants, values, and rewards. Such decisions seldom escape the closest scrutiny of every member of the organization. If anything, an organization will over-react to these kinds of management decisions. What management may view as an innocuous move to solve an interpersonal conflict or to bypass an organizational obstacle may be interpreted as a sign that management wants wants one kind of behavior while preaching another. Hence, a good manager must be ever alert to his or her decisions on placement, pay, and promotion. They should be based on a factual record of performance as measured against explicit standards—never on "potential" or friendship or expediency or casual opinions. They should reflect careful thinking, clear policy and procedures, and high standards of fairness and equity.

Drucker offers a number of personal characteristics in a manager which can undermine a spirit of high performance:

□   A lack of integrity.

□   A lack of character.

□   Cynicism.

□   Emphasizing the negative aspect of what subordinates cannot do (their weaknesses) rather than the positive aspects of what they can do (their strengths).

□   Being more interested in "who is right?" than "what is right?"

□   Being afraid of strong (high-performing) subordinates.

□   Not setting high standards for one's own work.

□   Valuing intelligence more highly than integrity.[8]

Obviously a management interested in nurturing a spirit of high perform-ance and accomplishment should endeavor to weed out managers and candidate managers who display such characteristics.

LEADERSHIP

According to an old proverb, "Trees die from the top"—the implication being there is no substitute for leadership. The litany of good leadership is simple enough: plan, decide, organize, direct, control, *win!*[9] Obviously, any organization benefits from having people who are able to "take charge" and serve as both "spark plug" and "ramrod" in implementing strategy. Leadership is exemplified by those who are known as "the movers" and "the shakers" in the organization. But at the same time, the ability to exercise extraordinary leadership is rare—not many managers are skilled in the art of inducing subordinates to accomplish their assign-

---

[8] Ibid., p. 462.

[9] Jay Hall, "To Achieve or Not: The Manager's Choice," *California Management Review*, vol. 18, no. 4 (Summer 1976), p. 5.

ments with eagerness, enthusiasm, and to the maximum of their ability. Moreover, an effective leadership style in one setting may be ineffective in another.

To lead is to initiate, guide, direct, facilitate, change, and inspire; it entails lifting aspirations, raising performance to higher levels, and developing people to their fullest. It may involve great personal or career risk. The leader is part of the group, yet distinct from it. His skills revolve mostly around the art of inventing and using motivators to effect high performance. His role exists because of the need of people for someone to follow. Indeed, one of the most fundamental tenets of leadership concerns the tendency of people to follow those in whom they see a means of satisfying their own personal goals: hence *the more a manager understands what motivates his subordinates and the more he uses these motivations in carrying out his managerial activities, the more effective as a leader he is likely to be.*[10]

It is equally important to understand what leadership is not. It is not *necessarily* having a magnetic personality or charisma. It is not winning friends and influencing people. It is not being likable, loved, and well thought of. On the contrary, history describes a number of renowned leaders as demanding, arrogant, obstreperous, or hard to get along with— Napoleon, Patton, and Queen Elizabeth I serve as examples. A study of noted business leaders would, no doubt, yield similar conclusions. The key to understanding leadership seems to hinge more on what leaders do rather than on their personal traits.

In general, four leadership patterns stand out: autocratic, participative, instrumental, and "great person." The autocratic leader tends to command, to be dogmatic, positive, and confident, and to rely upon authority and discipline. He or she leads through his control over rewards and punishment. The participative leader believes that people will work hard and accomplish their assignments best when supervised in a manner that lets them use their own initiative, be independent, contribute their ideas, and participate in decisions. Participative leaders act as "coordinators" instead of bosses and endeavor to treat subordinates as "self-starters." The instrumental type leader is perceived as a manager who must plan, organize, direct, and control in whatever way best gets the job done. The instrumental leader may use autocratic or participative approaches but the emphasis is on the central task of allocating human and organizational resources in the most effective, efficient manner. The instrumental leader is skillful in arousing support and developing a consensus, in working with people, in achieving objectives and results on schedule, and in making the right things happen. The essence of the instrumental approach is that those who manage well are also effective as leaders. The "great person"

---

[10] Harold Koontz and Cyril O'Donnell, *Principles of Management: An Analysis of Managerial Functions* (New York: McGraw-Hill Book Company, 1972), p. 559.

concept of leadership is a combination instrumental-participative pattern whereby the leader exhibits balanced concern both for people and for production, but does so in ways which exemplify vision, a grand design, and innovative plans calling for major changes and progress. The great person pattern is a heroic leadership style and suggests that such persons are "natural" or "born" leaders who most likely will be successful leaders in any situation.

Although the historical position of most behavioral scientists has been anti-authoritarian and pro-participative management, the increasingly widespread view is that for managers, as leaders, to be effective they should utilize whatever leadership posture or style is best for them in that situation, quite irrespective of whether it is strongly authoritarian or strongly participative or somewhere in between.[11] More specifically, it is held that effective managers will tend to vary their leadership techniques as people, tasks, organization environment, and the requirements of strategy vary. This "contingency approach" to leadership is based on growing research evidence (as well as intuitive management opinion) that different kinds of organization groups, given their different tasks and staffing

---

[11] Drucker, for one, has launched a powerful attack on some of the psychological aspects underlying participative management styles (represented most prominently by McGregor's Theory Y) and suggests that managers are correct in being leery of it. Drucker describes Theory Y management as "enlightened psychological despotism" and a "repugnant form of tyranny." According to Drucker,

> Most, if not all, of the recent writers on industrial psychology profess allegiance to Theory Y. They use terms like "self-fulfillment," "creativity," and "the whole man." But what they talk and write about is control through psychological manipulation. They are led to this by their basic assumptions, which are precisely the Theory X assumptions: man is weak, sick and incapable of looking after himself. He is full of fears, anxieties, neuroses, inhibitions. Essentially he does not want to achieve but wants to fail. He therefore wants to be controlled. Indeed, for his own good he needs to be controlled—not by fear and incentive of material rewards but through his fear of psychological alienation and the incentive of "psychological security." . . . The manager, if one listens to the psychologists, will have to have insight into all kinds of people. He will have to be in command of all kinds of psychological techniques. He will have to have empathy for all his subordinates. He will have to understand an infinity of individual personality structures, individual psychological needs, and individual psychological problems.

Such an approach, Drucker alleges, supposedly makes psychological control by the manager "unselfish" and in the worker's own interest but, more importantly, by becoming his workers' psychological servant the manager retains control as their boss. The effect, says Drucker, is to substitute persuasion for command, psychological manipulation for the carrot of financial rewards, and empathy for the fear of being punished.

Drucker maintains that such an approach is not only contemptuous but also will cause the manager-psychologist to undermine his own authority. Why? Because the integrity of the manager stems from his commitment to the work of the organization and any manager who pretends that the personal needs of subordinates, rather the objective needs of the task, determine what should be done is apt not to be believed and, therefore, risks losing his integrity and his subordinates' respect. See Drucker, *Management*, pp. 243–45.

"personalities," function best when they are structured, managed, and led in quite different and distinct ways.[12] For example, it makes sense that a manager's leadership behavior in implementing organization strategy will be influenced by whether:

□ He feels strongly that individuals should have a voice in making decision which affect them.

□ He has confidence in subordinates' qualifications to handle the problem issue on their own.

□ He fells more comfortable functioning in a directive role or in a team role.

□ Subordinates exhibit relatively high needs for independence.

□ Subordinates are experienced enough to make responsible decisions.

□ Subordinates prefer to be given clear-cut directives or whether they wish to have wider areas of freedom.

□ Subordinates are interested in the problem and wish to have a voice in solving it.

□ Subordinates expect to share in decision making.

□ Subordinates work together as a unit effectively.

□ There is severe time pressure for immediate action.

□ The size of organizational subunits, their geographical distribution, and the degree of intraorganizational cooperation required to attain goals and objectives are such as to preclude use of authoritarian (or participative) practices.

□ There is a need for confidentiality.

□ The organizational climate is flexible enough to allow for deviation from what higher-ups have established as approved behavior.[13]

In deciding what kind of leadership pattern to employ in strategy implementation, the manager may find it useful to ask two questions of himself: (1) Have I gotten the ideas and suggestions of everyone who has the necessary knowledge to make a significant contribution to the solution of the problem? and (2) What can the organization do and what can I do to help my subordinates the most in doing a superior job? He may also find it useful to ask subordinates what *they* can do to help him, as their manager, do the best job for the organization.

INSTITUTING MANAGEMENT CONTROLS

The role of management controls is to provide systematic verification of whether strategy implementation is proceeding in accordance with plan.

[12] E. P. Learned and A. T. Sproat, *Organization Theory and Policy* (Homewood, Ill.: Richard D. Irwin, Inc., 1966), p. 61.

[13] Robert Tannenbaum and Warren H. Schmidt, "How to Choose a Leadership Pattern," *Harvard Business Review*, vol. 36, no. 2 (March-April 1958), pp. 98–100.

Is the strategy being put in place on schedule? Are goals and objectives being met? Are the established policies being followed and are they effective? Have appropriate standards of performance been set? What sorts of deviations from these standards are being experienced? Is the strategy (and its accompanying set of policies) working?

The purpose of management controls is to provide feedback on the accomplishment of strategy: pointing out weaknesses in standards (whether they are clear and realistic), uncovering and correcting negative deviations from agreed-upon standards, and preventing their recurrence. The desired effect is to carry out organizational activities smoothly, properly, and according to high standards. The whole concept of management control is therefore normative and concerned with what ought to be.

Controls are necessary because the structure of an organization, by itself, is never "tight" enough to ensure the proper commitment to and execution of organization strategy and policy. Organizational subunits have their own substrategies which are at least slightly deflected from the overall organizational strategy. Moreover, individuals have their own career goals and needs, as well as their own perceptions of strategy. Internal politics and rivalry among subunits and professional groups introduce still other possibilities for misdirection. Such happenings and considerations are all quite normal—even in high-performing organizations manned by people of competence and goodwill who are informed of strategy and policy. As a consequence, the performance of individuals and subunits cannot be left to chance. And, understandably, the thrust of the control process is on goal-setting, standard-setting, measuring, comparing, and taking corrective action.

In designing a set of control devices, the manager should keep one principle firmly in mind—*controls follow strategy.* Unless controls are means to strategy accomplishment, there is undue risk of wrong action and "miscontrol." In addition, controls should satisfy seven other specifications:

1. Controls should be economical and involve only the *minimum* amount of information needed to give a reliable picture of what is going on. In general, the less effort and fewer control devices which have to be created to maintain the desired standards, the better and more effective the control design; too many controls create confusion.

2. Controls should seek to measure only meaningful events (sales volume, product mix, market standing, productivity rates) or symptoms of potentially significant developments (lower profit margins, higher rates of turnover, and absenteeism). Controls should relate to key objectives, key activities, and priority considerations rather than the mass of trivia and events which are marginal to strategic performance and results.

3. Controls should report the variables being measured in ways which reveal the real structure of the situation and which are grounds for action. For example, reporting the *number* of grievances per thousand employees does not indicate the *importance* of the grievances in terms of the impacts on morale and performance.

4. Controls should be geared to provide information on a timely basis —not too late to take corrective action nor so often as to confuse and over-burden.

5. Controls should be kept simple. Voluminous control manuals and complicated reports are likely to misdirect and obscure because of the attention that has to be paid to mechanics, procedures, and interpretive guidelines instead of to what is being measured. Moreover, the measures reported should be in a form that is suitable for the recipient and tailored to his needs.

6. Controls should be oriented toward taking corrective action rather than just providing interesting information. It is debatable whether reports or studies should receive wide distribution ("for your information"), but they should without fail reach the persons who can take action by virtue of their position in the decision structure.

7. Controls should, for the most part, aim at pinpointing the "exceptions"; this allows management to zero in on the significant departures from norm.[14]

When corrective action is required, care should be taken to act in ways which do not dampen initiative and spirit of performance. For a manager to dwell on finding errors and mistakes in subordinates' work encourages them to play it safe, "cover up" difficulties, and use political tactics to stay on the boss's good side. Attention shifts from doing things better to avoiding doing things wrong. One approach to get around this pitfall is to give as much attention to favorable variances as to unfavorable variances in control reviews. In other words, positive reinforcement, incentives, and rewards for performance above standards may in some situations be as effective in reducing negative deviations as are various forms of criticism, punishment, and disciplinary action. This gets back to the most fundamental control device of all—management's use of the reward-punishment structure.

COMMUNICATION AND MANAGEMENT CONTROL

It is management's job, of course, to communicate the organization's strategy and the plans and policies for implementing it to all members of

---

[14] Drucker, *Management*, pp. 498–504; Harold Koontz, "Management Control: A Suggested Formulation of Principles," *California Management Review*, vol. 2, no. 2 (Winter 1959), pp. 50–55; William H. Sihler, "Toward Better Management Control Systems," *California Management Review*, vol. 14, no. 2 (Winter 1971), pp. 33–39.

ILLUSTRATION CAPSULE 15
United Airlines' System of Management Controls

As early as the mid-1950s, United Airlines had a computer-assisted system of reporting and controls which resulted not only in the chief executive officer having a profit and loss statement every 24 hours but also provided operating heads with up-to-the-hour information on how to respond to weather and passenger load patterns. According to an article in *Nation's Business* by Philip Gustafson:

> The statement has its birth every day in the statistical production room at United's Denver operating base. Passenger and cargo volumes, collected from each flight, are combined at the end of the day. The results are wired to United's Chicago offices ready for processing at 8:30 A.M. Economic research employees apply revenue rates predetermined by experience and expense rates based on current operating budget requirements to the previous day's volume appearing on the wire. Within an hour, an operating profit or loss is estimated and passed on to top management.
>
> The daily report shows the day's operating profit or loss along with a month and year to date accumulation. Also, daily revenue passenger-miles and the passenger load factor are given. Data are broken down in such a way as to give the passenger department information on which to decide whether to put more planes on the Chicago to San Francisco run or advertise to get additional passengers.
>
> An intrinsic part of United's reporting system is what company executives like to call "the room with the 14,000-mile view." This is an information and planning center at Denver which is the business world's equivalent of the military briefing room. Facts funneled daily into this center present a clear picture of operations throughout United's 80-city system.
>
> In keeping with the idea of expansive vision, the room has glass walls on one side. Modern white plastic chairs are grouped before a map of the United States, 8 feet high and 20 feet wide, on which United's routes are outlined. Colored lights (red for weather, green for maintenance, and white for passengers) at major terminals show current operating conditions. If the red light glows steadily, for example, it means adverse weather; if it is flashing, the weather is marginal. Electric clocks above the map show the time in each zone through which United operates.
>
> The room is designed to provide management with operational facts in the most convenient form. Data, such as mileage flown, delays at terminals by type of plane and total number of departures, are posted on lucite panels, flanking the map. Dozens of supplementary charts deal with payload volumes and load factors, weather, actual performance as compared with schedule and related information.
>
> Daily at 8:30 A.M., MST, United's operations executives meet in the room for a 14,000-mile view. Four briefing specialists review operations of the past 24 hours and outline what the next 24 are expected to bring.

ILLUSTRATION CAPSULE 15 *(continued)*

The opening summary is presented by a meteorologist who analyzes the decisive factors in yesterday's weather conditions from the Atlantic seaboard to the Hawaiian Islands. He then gives his forecast for the next 24 hours, accenting developments which may affect operations.

A mechanical specialist follows with information on the status of the company's fleet. He reports the number and types of aircraft withdrawn from service for overhaul and comments on the progress of various engineering projects at the San Francisco base.

A traffic specialist then gives a resumé of the previous day's performance in terms of any customer service problems which arose. Approximately 750 plane departures are scheduled daily. Those which deviate from schedule are spotlighted for management study to prevent possible recurrence.

The remaining gaps in the 14,000-mile view are filled in by a flight operations specialist who discusses the availability of equipment, and weather outlook on the line. The session then adjourns. Immediately afterwards, some department chiefs may call their staffs together to act on particular facets of the day's operating plan.

SOURCE: Philip Gustafson, "Business Reports: How to Get Facts You Need," *Nation's Business*, vol. 44, no. 8 (August 1956), pp. 78–82.

the organization. That this must be done and done effectively requires no further elaboration. But it is worth noting that the control process provides a way of thinking about and approaching the task of informing members of the organization of their unit's objectives, how these objectives relate to overall corporate objectives and strategy, and the relative priorities that various tasks should have. Control devices should clearly signal the kinds of results and behavior expected. And periodic reviews of the organizational unit's performance, together with the manager's periodic reviews of individual job performance with his or her subordinates, offer a golden opportunity to (a) evaluate standards of performance with employees, (b) review results on the job, (c) analyze the reasons for these results, (d) discuss plans for increasing on-the-job effectiveness, (e) consider each job incumbent's potential for advancement, (f) prepare plans, programs, and budgets for the coming year, and (g) agree on specific standards and objectives for periods ahead.

PROBLEM AREAS IN MANAGING PEOPLE

How well or how poorly a manager manages people is a major factor in the implementation of strategy and, ultimately, in the strategy's success. Unfortunately, there is no neat formula of "five steps to follow" in managing people. Proper motivation and effective leadership, as discussed above, are plainly important. But during the course of strategy implementation there are also a number of questions relating to organization personnel and management which need to be asked regularly and the current practices reevaluated:

1. What type and quality of personnel does the organization now have and how does this compare with what it will need in the future? Is management competent to meet the challenges ahead? What are management's strengths and weaknesses? What are the ages of key executives and personnel? Will there be adequate replacements at retirement?

2. How and from where will the organization recruit new personnel? Is the organization attracting the right kinds of people to fill entry level positions? Is the organization attracting and keeping qualified personnel? Is there a high turnover rate among good employees at lower levels? To what extent should the organization promote from within or recruit from the outside?

3. Does the organization have a "key executive" problem; i.e., an executive without a replacement? To what extent would operations be impaired if something happened to the key executive?

4. Are the organization's personnel adequately trained? Is formal on-the-job training needed? Do new employees have trouble understanding what is expected of them?

5. How well are employees, including managers, performing? Does the appraisal system really measure performance or is it simply an exercise which management goes through to comply with organization procedures? Are promotable persons being identified through the appraisal system? Are those who need more training or better training being identified?

6. In what ways should people be compensated? Is the compensation structure adequate? Are compensation rewards correctly geared to the sought-for results and performance? Are those employees (and managers) perceived as "high-performing" or as "key executives" better compensated than other employees at their level? Are material rewards relied upon too heavily as the main (or only) positive motivator?

7. How should the performance of managers be evaluated? (This is not a small matter when one considers that the manager's job description includes such phrases as "maintaining relationships with," "supervising the operation of," "having responsibility for," and such activities as coordinating, problem solving, and administering—all of which lack concreteness and ready measurement.) To what extent should complexity of the work, general education and technical training re-

quired, the scope of responsibility for people and property, and the effect of the manager's decisions and activities upon profits (or other desired outcomes) be balanced against performance in determining the manager's compensation package? What relationship should the compensation of managers and executives have with the monetary reward paid to others in the organization?

8. To what extent should the general manager manage his subordinates through personal contact and direct intervention, offering his own ideas and inputs and getting involved in day-to-day matters? Or, should he reject the "playing coach" approach and place greater reliance on instituting the necessary guidelines via formal planning, budgeting, control, and compensation systems? How far should he go in staying out of daily operating activities by delegating authority to subordinates?

PLAYING "THE POWER GAME"

All organizations are political. The drives and ambitions to climb the ladder of career achievement and success, the conflicts and coalitions that evolve in translating goals into action and on into results, and the hierarchical divisions of responsibility and authority combine to guarantee the existence of a political atmosphere. Positions of power and weakness are inevitable and the people involved are neither likely to be indifferent to power relationships nor passive in their own maneuvering and use of power. Jockeying for position is a normal activity. After all, careers, prestige, and egos are at stake, not to mention material rewards.

On occasions, therefore, ambition, personal biases, and favoritism may overrule "objective" analysis; conceivably, unscrupulous actions and unethical behavior may arise, together with selfish attempts to "feather one's own nest." One cannot assume that virtue guarantees rewards nor that doing a good job suffices for promotion. This is not to say that organizations are a political jungle with much effort put into political maneuvering and thinking up new power plays. Such can occur, but it is the exception not the rule. Usually, organizational politics is kept within bounds and does not deteriorate into wholesale plotting and schemes, backstabbing, and dissension. Yet, it would be naïve to presume that a manager can be effective and get ahead without being perceptive about internal politics and being adept at playing the power game. Like it or not, managers need to be sensitive to the political environment in the organization.

Middle-level managers are particularly susceptible to political considerations. Higher level executives measure success in terms of results; they tend to be less interested in how the results are produced. The middle manager's performance thus often hinges on how well the results of his or her actions match the general directives from above to get the job done.[15] But in the course of translating these general directives into concrete action to be followed by first-level managers and technical unit heads, middle managers are vulnerable to heavy flak from both sides. They are caught between pressure from above for results to make their bosses look good and the need for the goodwill and cooperation of their own subordinates (plus other organizational subunits on which they must rely for support) to carry out their assignments. It is difficult for middle managers to shift blame or make excuses when things do not work out well. Hence, they are thrust into walking a political tight-rope, seeking compromise and workability between the objectives of subordinates (whose cooperation is required) and the objectives of superiors (whose approval is needed to get ahead). If they want to maintain the loyalty and respect of subordinates, middle managers must represent their interests and be willing "to go to bat" for them when the occasion demands. Middle managers must understand the organization's power structure and be sensitive to the direction of political winds. They need to ask themselves a series of questions: Who are my friends and who are my enemies? Who can I count on in a showdown or when the going gets tough? Whose opinions really count and whose can be ignored? Which department and division heads have the most influence and the most clout in shaping decisions? With whom should I develop strong alliances? On what issues do I need to take a stand and be willing "to rock the boat" if necessary and on what should I accept the status quo? Given the way the system works, am I better off with a job assignment in a non-key activity where I can be a "star performer" (perhaps outshining a weak boss) or with a job assignment in an area "where the action is" (perhaps working directly for someone who is reliably reported to be "on their way up")?[16] To what extent should I strive for positions with high visibility and exposure to higher level executives?

---

[15] Middle managers are seldom told how to get their jobs done in specific terms. The guidelines they receive from higher-ups regarding increasing sales or profits, carving out a bigger market share, or getting by on a smaller budget are mostly general and, so long as organizational policies are observed, the boss's attitude is most likely to be "I don't care how you do it, just get it done—and on time." In other words, the specifics are delegated to the next level down, and it ends up the middle manager's job to figure out what plans and concrete actions will be needed to generate the desired results. It is the middle manager, more than anyone else, who translates financial, sales, production, and strategic objectives into a day-to-day operating plan, then communicates it in functional-specialist language to the technical, detail-oriented, first-line supervisors.

[16] For a discussion of how to climb to higher ranks in an organization, see Ross A. Webber, "Career Problems of Young Managers," *California Management Review*, vol. 18, no. 4 (Summer 1976), pp. 19–33.

ILLUSTRATION CAPSULE 16
Playing the Power Game the Machiavellian Way

Niccolo Machiavelli, in his classic *The Prince*, presented a manual of methods and tactics in the acquisition and use of power. *The Prince* is full of straightforward, bitter truths about the drive for power and the realities of human motivation. Some say that *The Prince* is diabolical; others call it insightful and utterly realistic in its portrayal of human nature. Whatever adjectives one chooses to apply, there is no denying it as one of the most influential books ever written.

Although Machiavelli's study of power politics was addressed specifically to political rulers, the lessons apply equally well to management. Indeed, if in reading the excerpts below one will simply substitute "manager" for "prince" (or its equivalent), then the relevance of Machiavelli to modern management can be readily approached:

. . . men must either be cajoled or crushed; for they will revenge themselves for slight wrongs, while for grave ones they cannot. The injury therefore that you do to a man should be such that you need not fear his revenge.

. . . in taking possession of a state the conqueror should well reflect as to the harsh measures that may be necessary, and then execute them at a single blow, so as not to be obliged to renew them every day; and by thus not repeating them, to assure himself of the support of the inhabitants, and win them over to himself by benefits bestowed. . . . Cruelties should be committed all at once, as in that way each separate one is less felt, and gives less offence; benefits, on the other hand, should be conferred one at a time, for in that way they will be more appreciated.

. . . he who, contrary to the will of the people, has become prince by favor of the nobles, should at once and before everything else strive to win the good will of the people, which will be easy for him, by taking them under his protection.

. . . it is much more safe to be feared than to be loved, when you have to choose between the two.

. . . there are two ways of carrying on a contest; the one by law, and the other by force. The first is practiced by men, and the other by animals; and as the first is often insufficient, it becomes necessary to resort to the second. . . . It being necessary then for a prince to know well how to employ the nature of the beasts, he should be able to assume both that of the fox and that of the lion; for while the latter cannot escape the traps laid for him, the former cannot defend himself against the wolves. A prince should be a fox, to know the traps and snares; and a lion, to be able to frighten the wolves; for those who simply hold to the nature of the lion do not understand their business.

. . . a prince should seem to be merciful, faithful, humane, religious, and upright, and should even be so in reality; but he should have his mind so trained that, when occasion requires it, he may know how to change to the opposite.

ILLUSTRATION CAPSULE 16 *(continued)*

. . . For the manner in which men live is so different from the way in which they ought to live, that he who leaves the common course for that which he ought to follow will find that it leads him to ruin rather than to safety. For a man who, in all respects, will carry out only his professions of good, will be apt to be ruined among so many who are evil. A prince therefore who desires to maintain himself must learn to be not always good, but to be so or not as necessity may require. . . . For all things considered, it will be found that some things that seem like virtue will lead you to ruin if you follow them; while others, that apparently are vices, will, if followed, result in your safety and well-being.

. . . the dispositions of peoples are variable; it is easy to persuade them to anything, but difficult to confirm them in that belief. And therefore a prophet should be prepared, in case the people will not believe any more, to be able by force to compel them to that belief.

. . . The worst that a prince may expect of a people who are unfriendly to him is that they will desert him; but the hostile nobles he has to fear, not only lest they abandon him, but also because they will turn against him. For they, being more farsighted and astute, always save themselves in advance, and seek to secure the favor of him whom they hope may be successful.

We must bear in mind . . . that there is nothing more difficult and dangerous, or more doubtful of success, than an attempt to introduce a new order of things in any state. For the innovator has for enemies all those who derived advantages from the old order of things while those who expect to be benefited by the new institutions will be but lukewarm defenders. This indifference arises in part from fear of their adversaries who were favored by the existing laws, and partly from the incredulity of men who have no faith in anything new that is not the result of well-established experience. Hence it is that, whenever the opponents of the new order of things have the opportunity to attack it, they will do it with the zeal of partisans, while the others defend it but feebly, so that it is dangerous to rely upon the latter.

. . . a prince cannot depend upon what he observes in ordinary quiet times, when the citizens have need of his authority; for then everybody runs at his bidding, everybody promises, and everybody is willing to die for him, when death is very remote. But in adverse times, when the government has need of the citizens, then but few will be found to stand by the prince. And this experience is the more dangerous as it can only be made once.

A wise prince, therefore, will steadily pursue such a course that the citizens of his state will always and under all circumstances feel the need of his authority, and will therefore always prove faithful to him.

A prince . . . should always take counsel, but only when he wants it, and not when others wish to thrust it upon him; in fact, he should rather discourage persons from tendering him advice unsolicited by him. But he should be an extensive questioner, and a patient listener to the truth

ILLUSTRATION CAPSULE 16 *(concluded)*

respecting the things inquired about, and should even show his anger in case any one should, for some reason, not tell him the truth.

It is obvious from the above quotations that a practicing Machiavellian divorces morals from power politics; indeed, moral considerations have no place in the Machiavellian system of power politics except where an evil reputation would be a political detriment. To many people, this is shocking if not abhorrent. But even if your own moral code totally rejects a Machiavellian use of power, the issue still remains what to do in your dealings with people who are Machiavellian in their attempts to acquire and use power. How would you deal with such a person? Do you not, in fact, know people who in your own experience are Machiavellians? What would your strategy be if you were one of the intended "victims?"

CONCLUSION

To sum up, making work productive and the worker achieving is a major dimension of strategy implementation. Personal satisfaction of the worker without productive work is failure. But then so is productive work that undercuts individual achievement. The former blocks strategic success and the latter destroys morale and a high spirit of performance. Neither is tenable for very long.

Hence, in translating strategy into action it is extremely important that management strive to develop administrative policies that on the one hand are conducive to strategic success and on the other allow workers to achieve and realize appropriate nonmaterial satisfaction from their work. This means, in part, identifying all operations that are necessary to strategic achievement, rationally organizing the sequence of these operations to reflect a smooth, economical flow of work, and integrating these operations into individual jobs in ways that will ensure high organizational performance and individual opportunities for creativity, personal development and meaningful work.

SUGGESTED READINGS

Adizes, Ichak "Mismanagement Styles." *California Management Review*, vol. 19, no. 2, Winter 1976, pp. 5–20.

Drucker, Peter *Management: Tasks, Responsibilities, Practices.* New York: Harper & Row, Publishers, 1974, chaps. 16–19 and 33–39.

Fiedler, Fred E. "The Contingency Model—New Directions for Leadership Utilization." *Journal of Contemporary Business*, vol. 3, no. 4; Autumn 1974, pp. 65–80.

Hall, Jay "To Achieve or Not: The Manager's Choice." *California Management Review,* vol. 18, no. 4, Summer 1976, pp. 5–18.

Herzberg, Frederick "One More Time: How Do You Motivate Employees." *Harvard Business Review,* vol. 51, no. 3, May-June 1973, pp. 162–80.

Koontz, Harold "Management Control: A Suggested Formulation of Principles." *California Management Review,* vol. 2, no. 2, Winter 1959, pp. 50–55.

McClelland, David C., and Burnham, David H. "Power Is the Great Motivator." *Harvard Business Review,* vol. 54, no. 2, March-April 1976, pp. 100–110.

Machiavelli, N. *The Prince.* New York: Washington Square Press, 1963.

Morse, John J., and Lorsch, Jay W. "Beyond Theory Y." *Harvard Business Review,* vol. 48, no. 3, May-June 1970, pp. 61–68.

Robbins, Stephen P. "Reconciling Management Theory with Management Practice." *Business Horizons,* vol. 20, no. 1, February 1977, pp. 38–47.

Roche, W. J., and MacKinnon, N. L. "Motivating People with Meaningful Work." *Harvard Business Review,* vol. 48, no. 3, May-June 1970, pp. 97–110.

Tannenbaum, Robert, and Schmidt, Warren H. "How to Choose a Leadership Pattern." *Harvard Business Review,* vol. 51, no. 3, May-June 1973, pp. 162–80.

Tosi, Henry L.; Rizzo, John R.; and Carroll, Stephen J. "Setting Goals in Management by Objective." *California Management Review,* vol. 12, no. 4, Summer 1970, pp. 70–78.

Webber, Ross, A. "Career Problems of Young Managers." *California Management Review,* vol. 18, no. 4, Summer 1976, pp. 19–33.

Zalenik, Abraham "Power and Politics in Organizational Life." *Harvard Business Review,* vol. 48, no. 3, May-June 1970, pp. 47–60.

READING

Mismanagement Styles*

ICHAK ADIZES

Ichak Adizes is associate professor of management studies in the Graduate School of Management, University of California, Los Angeles.

According to the Peter Principle,[1] individuals in organizations tend to be promoted to their level of incompetence. This means that people mount the ladder of promotion until they fail because they have achieved a position that is beyond their capacities. Yet while author Peter Laurence presents a vivid description of corporate reality, he does not provide a theoretical explanation of this phenomenon. The purpose of this article is to analyze the ways in which some people become managerially incompetent as they climb the organizational ladder and to provide a profile of an effective managerial process.

My research on styles of management shows that four roles must be performed; whenever one of those roles is not performed, a certain style of mismanagement can be observed. It is suggested that the Peter Principle phenomenon occurs because people are promoted on the basis of excellent performances in one or more of these roles, but they become incapable, at a certain stage of their ascent up the hierarchy, of performing the additional roles that are required. As a result they become "organizationally incompetent." They become *mismanagers*.

In this article I will first present the four roles and then describe the several styles of mismanagement that can be discerned in the extreme cases in which one or more, but not all, of the roles is performed. It is my conclusion that managers who excel in all four roles are extremely rare and that this fact accounts for the prevalence of the Peter Principle phenomenon. Several recommendations are made on how to use these findings in organizational staffing and in carrying out organizational change. These recommendations are based on my own experiences, which are reported at the end of this article. This report is based on six years of systematic observations of managerial behavior and experience in effecting organizational change in a variety of organizations and cultures.

---

* Ichak Adizes, "Mismanagement Styles," *California Management Review*, Winter 1976, pp. 5–17. © 1976 by the Regents of the University of California. Reprinted by permission.

[1] Laurence Peter and Raymond Hull, *The Peter Principle* (New York: W. Morrow, 1969).

The Managerial Function

A manager is one who manages, and managing is getting the job done by working with or through people or by managing the process necessary for accomplishment. Thus, while the production manager is engaged in achieving tangible results working with and through people, the staff specialist can also be considered a manager attending to the intangible processes. This report, however, is concerned only with the managers who work with and through people.

First of all a manager is expected to achieve results equal to or better than those of the competition. The principal qualification for an achiever is the possession of a functional knowledge of his field, whether marketing, engineering, accounting, or any other discipline. But being individually productive, and having the functional knowledge of a particular discipline or technology, does not necessarily enable one to produce commensurate results in working with a group of people.

A manager should thus have more than functional knowledge. He should be more than an individual producer. He should be able to administer the people with whom he works and to see that they also produce results. In this role he schedules, coordinates, controls, and disciplines. He is an implementor: he sees to it that the system works as it was designed to work. "Administration" consists mainly of implementation; "management," on the other hand, entails a higher degree of discretion, as in the setting of goals, strategic planning, and policy making. Discretionary decision making, however, involves entrepreneurship.

In a changing environment a manager must use his judgment and have the discretion to change goals and change the systems by which they are implemented. To perform this role he must be an organizational entrepreneur and an innovator, since, unlike an administrator who is given certain plans to carry out and certain decisions to implement, an entrepreneur has to generate his own plan of action. He has to be a self-starter. A manager who performs the entrepreneurial role has to be sufficiently creative to identify possible courses of action, and he should be willing to take risks. If he is not creative, he will be unable to perceive new possibilities. If he cannot take risks, he may not be able to take advantage of them.

A manager is thus expected to be a producer, for which he must have the functional and technical know-how necessary to turn out maximal results. He is, furthermore, expected to implement a system designed to achieve those results in the short run and to initiate new directions whenever opportunities or threats arise in order to maximize those results. He should be a producer (P), an administrator (A), and an entrepreneur (E). The roles that must be performed are those of *producing, implementing, and innovating*. But these three roles in combination are also insufficient for adequate managerial functioning. Many an organization that had been managed by an excellent achiever-administrator-entrepreneur (usually their founder) nose-dived when this key individual died or for some reason was replaced. For an organization to be continuously successful, an additional role must be performed.

The fourth essential role of management is that of *integration* (I). This is the process by which individual strategies are merged into a group strategy; individual risks become group risks; individual goals are harmonized into group goals; and ultimately individual entrepreneurship emerges as group entrepreneurship. When a group can operate on its own with a clear direction in mind and can choose its own directions over time without depending on any one individual for its successful operation, then we know that the integrating role has been performed adequately. It requires an individual who is sensitive to people's needs. Such an individual unifies the whole organization behind goals and strategies. If he has been a good integrator, he makes himself dispensable; the strategies which he helped the organization to identify will survive his death. True integrators can thus be measured by the persistence of their unifying process, and this depends on how well they performed the integrating role.

Mismanagement Styles

These four roles of management enable us to construct a typology of incompetence in organizations according to the Peter Principle. Consider, for example, the case of an employee who is a competent individual producer but who, once promoted to a managerial position, fails as a manager because he cannot administer other people. He has difficulty in relating to subordinates; he cannot delegate tasks, coordinate tasks, or follow up on subordinates' accomplishments. Another example is the case of a good technician and administrator who, when further promoted, fails to innovate. He can accomplish what is being delegated to him and he can work with others, but he does not initiate new activity on his own, either because he is not creative or because he is incapable of taking risks. So the entrepreneuring role is not performed, and in the long run the organization stagnates. Even a person who can perform all three of these roles—producer, administrator, entrepreneur—will be an incompetent manager unless he can function as a group integrator and can develop group cohesion around group activity. If he cannot do this, the organization will be too dependent on him; he will be the focal person who makes all crucial decisions by himself and the organization will become too centralized to function well. Also, an organization which has become too dependent on one individual may face major difficulties when that person leaves. Many management-owned companies have failed after the death of the founder because of this deficiency in management.

Let us now describe the styles of mismanagement exhibited in those extreme cases in which a manager (or rather a mismanager) performs only one role, whether that of an individual producer (PXXX), an administrator (XAXX), an entrepreneur (XXEX), or an integrator (XXXI). From these "pure" cases, mixed types of mismanagement can be identified subsequently.

Mismanagement Style PXXX: The Exclusive Producer (the "loner"). The loner is himself very industrious and knowledgeable about his task, but he is neither an administrator, nor an entrepreneur, nor an integrator. He mismanages because he does not administer his staff, initiate systematic change, or mobilize the group with which he works to make the necessary change.

His main fault as a manager is the compulsion to do everything himself. One would think that he carries the whole plan of action in his inner coat pocket, usually on the back of an old envelope.

He sees every task as *his* personal responsibility, rather than as the responsibility of his department. He resists delegating authority to his subordinates, even though they may be underutilized, understimulated, and hungry for more responsibility. When he is forced to delegate, he feels highly uncomfortable and quickly finds reasons to take the authority back into his own hands. He does not allow the delegation process to take root. "They don't do it right" he will say as a pretense for reversing a delegation process or a defense for not performing it.

In an organization that is mismanaged by the loner there is a significant imbalance in the work load; while he is overburdened, the rest of the organization is underworked. In visiting his organization one notices the lack of tension in the atmosphere; people seem to have all the time in the world for the visitor. But when one enters the office of the manager, the contrast is conspicuous. The atmosphere is tense, he speaks rapidly and disjointedly, the phone rings constantly, and secretaries come and go with decisions that have to be implemented. The subordinates are hardly more than spectators to his performance. Still, since he cannot do everything personally, he makes extensive use of "expeditors," persons who assist him with errands or short-term assignments but who have no permanent long-term responsibilities. Most of their time is spent waiting for the next errand or task, which will be assigned in the form of a crisis that should have been handled "yesterday," for which they often have had no previous training, and which is usually presented as a request to "Please help *me*...."

This mismanager does not acknowledge the value of systematic training of subordinates. He prefers the apprenticeship approach, in which they have to learn by actually performing all duties in the organization, and by emulating him. "Why don't they show motivation, take initiative, show me what they can do?" he usually complains. "Who trained me? I learned by myself! Why don't they learn? In this business there are no secrets; just get the job done. . . ."

The loner resents subordinates who do not look industrious and come up with results—he considers it their fault, and he will not listen to their complaints that there was no systematic support for their efforts. Furthermore, he resists advice on how to manage. Consultants who try to change his attitude and behavior are labeled "academicians" who "can't do," and he usually has neither the time nor the patience to listen. "There is too much to do," is his usual defense mechanism. His second line of defense is, "We cannot worry about the long run; if we do not produce results today there might be no tomorrow."

This mismanager is always busy, running from crisis to crisis; his secretary, if he has one, is usually burdened with a work load she cannot meet. But in spite of his constant complaining that he is overburdened, he is happiest when he is busiest. He suffers from anxiety if he does not feel productive and to him being productive does not mean getting others to work, but being personally involved in performing the task. He measures his productivity by how hard *he* works. When you ask him, "Well, how are you doing?" his typical answer will be, "We sold (or produced, or whatever)" or "I am working very hard—I stayed last night until midnight. . . ."

So he usually refuses to accept additional tasks because he always feels he must give the impression that he is overburdened with work. However, when new tasks seem crucial to him he will take them on even though he feels he is already overburdened. When it is suggested that he reduce his work load he has many excuses at hand to show that this would be impossible; it seems that he perceives a reduction in his own work load as a threat to his self-esteem. If he does accept additional tasks, one can safely assume that he will fail in something, since he will try to do everything himself and some tasks will have to be ignored.

In one company I have worked with, one of the vice presidents was a typical loner. He worked longer hours than anyone else; his subordinates were underutilized and undertrained; and he was always immersed in some crisis solution. While I was working on budgetary procedure with one of his subordinates (since he had no time for that), he stuck his head in the door and asked, "So, what are you doing?" "We are preparing a budgetary procedure," we answered, "How about you?" "I was making sales to pay for all of this," he replied sarcastically.

Mismanagement Style XAXX: The Exclusive Administrator Implementor (the "bureaucrat"). By the XAXX style of mismanagement I mean the exclusive performance of the implementing role. This manager acts exclusively as an administrator. He is a manager who knows by heart the standard operating procedures in the organization and manages by means of directives that are usually presented in writing. In contrast to the loner, who is a hyperbusy achiever and performer, concerned with *what* is achieved rather than *how* it is achieved, the bureaucratic mismanager spends inordinate amounts of time worrying about administrative details. He is more concerned about *how* things are done than about *what* is being done. He rebukes his subordinates if they do not follow standard operating procedures, even when this was necessary to achieve results; he always has arguments to show why the system must be left intact. His arguments are usually legalistic and unrelated to the missions and objectives of the organization. He considers himself the guardian of the system, rather than of the mission which the system is designed to achieve. His primary and often exclusive commitment is to the implementation of a plan regardless of its wisdom or even its ethics. Over a period of time, the department will perform the same duties, but with more and more complex procedures to assure maximum conformity and minimum uncertainty. This behavior actually hinders changes, because the mushrooming bureaucracy will make change more and more expensive. Thus, both the loner and the bureaucrat inhibit the effective growth of the company. The loner resists new tasks because he accepts only the amount of work *he* can perform alone. The bureaucrat does not allow for effective changes if he perceives them to be a threat to his ability to control.

The bureaucrat abhors ambiguity; he insists that everything be in writing and that all spheres of responsibility be clearly demarcated. He is meticulously organized and has a fantastic memory for details. He is very loyal and does not change organizations easily; he avoids all change as much as possible. His ingenuity in finding reasons to discourage new projects makes him an obstructionist. The organization has to achieve its goals in spite of him, and persons in the organization who are committed to getting things done learn to bypass him.

While the loner evaluates himself by how hard he works, and by the results he achieves, the bureaucrat evaluates himself by *how well he controls* the system and by his success in eliminating digressions from standard procedure and minimizing uncertainty. Because of this, he is prone to the abuse of Parkinson's Law: he gets increasing numbers of subordinates to perform the same job, without achieving any apparent increase in productivity; the only apparent change is that more people are involved in more systems and procedures designed to control even more what appears to be already overcontrolled!

Mismanagement Style XXEX: The Exclusive Entrepreneur (the "crisis maker"). This mismanagement style is exhibited when an individual performs exclusively the innovating role. This person charges ahead at almost any target that appears on his organizational horizon. He attempts to exploit all opportunities simultaneously, whenever they arise, regardless of the repercussions for the organization. He is on several frontiers at the same time, spreading himself thin. He comes into an organization with new ideas and new ways of accomplishing tasks and tries to change the methodology and the tasks simultaneously.

The true entrepreneurial manager must be both a creative person and a risk taker. We can, of course, conceive of both a creative person who does not take risks, and a risk-taking person who is not creative. Although they are complementary, creativity and risk taking are independent, individual personality characteristics. We maintain that these personality types, by themselves, are less commonly found in managers.

The archetypal creative person is usually treated as a bohemian or reclusive inventor, while the archetypal risk taker is, of course, the compulsive gambler. As a pure type of manager of the entrepreneurial sort, an equal combination of these attributes must be present.

The perspective of the entrepreneur is not limited by the organization with which he is associated. For him creative ideas are as applicable to the problems of the organizations in the environment as they are to those within his organization. This manager is neither local nor cosmopolitan— perhaps he is both.

Subordinates avoid the crisis maker just as they avoid the bureaucrat, but for different reasons. Subordinates of the bureaucrat who wish to be effective avoid him because he is constantly telling them what they should not do, while the subordinates of the crisis maker avoid him because he is always assigning new tasks, forgetting about the old tasks that have been earlier assigned and that already fully occupy the subordinates' time.

The crisis maker has little sense of what people can accomplish. He usually gets upset when objectives are not achieved. He is so excited about his own creative capabilities that he is impatient with limited achievements. He expects instantaneous accomplishment of his ideas and when that is not forthcoming, instead of trying to identify the barriers that prevented effective accomplishment, he changes the assignment altogether and thus ends up loading new assignments on his subordinates. They soon learn not to ask for help.

While the bureaucrat may achieve goals in spite of his mismanagement (because people learn how to bypass him), the harder the crisis maker tries to manage, the further behind he gets; while he is busy making everyone else busy, the organization gets nowhere because he changes directions too often and because his subordinates do not actually cooperate: they always have a reason why tasks couldn't have been done rather than why they shouldn't be done. This behavior might be attributed to their ambiguity as to what to do and how to do it. They have learned that the crisis maker is not to be taken too seriously. No task that he delegates is really intended to be accomplished; in a very short time he will change his mind. But they have also learned not to reject these tasks outright, because the crisis maker identifies himself with the task to the point where rejection of the tasks seems to him a personal rejection. So the subordinate is trapped: on one hand, there is no use in trying to achieve the task since it will be changed; on the other hand, he cannot refuse the task outright. The only way out is to accept the task but to do very little about it and to come up with creative excuses as to why the task could not have been accomplished—to appear cooperative without actually being so.

The crisis maker has many complaints about his subordinates. He keeps them busy, but he complains that they are inefficient. He refuses to see that he is responsible for their ineffectiveness because of his constant changes in goals. As long as they appear to have tried hard to accomplish his plan, however, he is satisfied.

This mismanager has little use for systems. He perceives planning procedures as unwanted constraints because they require him to commit himself to some direction. He likes to change directions. He is an optimist at heart; he believes that there are no barriers to what people can do in spite of the fact that he constantly fails himself and others.

This person is usually very personable and likable, since he is stimulating, enterprising, and full of energy. Working for him can be exciting for a while, until one learns that no matter what one does, the crisis maker will be dissatisfied because he always has new projects and new ideas to achieve before the old ones have been accomplished. He is unrealistic and often vague about his demands; his entrepreneuring, creative mind has no patience for detail.

The crisis maker is not himself a performer. He is not really concerned about results, although he is highly critical of the failures of his subordinates. If the loner appraises himself by how hard he works, and by the results he produces, and the bureaucrat by the control he feels he has, the crisis maker appraises himself by how hard his subordinates *appear* to work. He gets his reinforcement from the appearance of productivity, the beehive atmosphere of activity that attests to the influence of his creative ideas.

The differences among mismanagement styles can be exemplified by describing the different reactions of mismanagers to an office where all subordinates seem to be working peacefully at their desks. The loner, in passing through the office, won't notice it; he is too busy with his own work. The bureaucrat notices it but since no one is asking him to solve any problem he will assume everything is going according to plan and will be satisfied. The crisis maker will be upset; the order, the peacefulness, the lack of tension will disturb him. If there is no crisis in the air, he will produce a new project like a magician in order to prod the organization into frantic activity.

Subsequently, the subordinates of the loner learn that they can take long breaks so long as they are available on short notice to "help get things done." The subordinates of the bureaucrat learn that so long as they come on time, leave on time, comply with all regulations, and don't ask too many questions, their jobs are secure. The subordinates of the crisis maker learn quickly that they have to look busy whenever he is in sight, and preferably pretend to be busy on his latest pet project.

The easiest way to summarize the characteristics of the crisis maker is to present an authentic description of such a mismanger given by one of his subordinates in an interview (somewhat abridged and paraphrased here):

> I hate to see him go on vacation, and Monday mornings are just as bad. I know that as soon as he comes back we will have a new set of priorities. . . . We are always in a state of flux. My title, position, and responsibilities change too frequently for me to take hold. If you try to dispute any of his ideas he will produce information, figures, quotes—you name it—to prove he is right. He is a fantastic juggler, throwing out this evidence like a magician to prove that his new pet project is absolutely the best, and that it's your fault if you don't understand how it is related to the previous project. Later on, after we fail, it becomes our fault that we didn't understand him, and before you know it he is presenting all the arguments against it that you presented to him when he first suggested the project. The worst thing that you can do is to remind him that that's what you said in the first place. Even if he doesn't fire you right then, he will keep a grudge. . . . If you suggest a project of your own, he will have a hundred reasons why it cannot be done. But a week later, he will be back with the same idea. This time he will present it as *his*, and as a top priority which should have been done yesterday; he will be angry that no one thought of this before. . . .
>
> He likes to have people around him to listen sympathetically to his ideas, and if they leave he gets hurt. He always has to have an audience, whether it's his secretary or his executive vice-president. He will keep his audience long after the working day is over. This is the price we have to pay to show we take his ideas seriously. Many of his subordinates have gotten divorced or soon will be, because the sort of unequivocal loyalty he demands competes with family life.
>
> Every so often he comes up with five or six new ideas and starts making the rounds of the offices presenting them to people. You have to decide which ones you're going to fight and how. After a while he's left with two ideas, which he pushes through. Then one gets a few memos out to show that one has tried to do something about it, and then one gets ready for the next week and the next bag of ideas. You always have to show token attention and follow-up on his requests. Do not get over-enthusiastic and excited though, when he shows up the next day with the next idea he might be highly upset if he finds that you are too busy to get involved with the latest project.
>
> He is very charismatic. Makes you feel at odds with yourself. If you fail in a task he can show you how you misunderstood his genius. It is always you who were dumb . . . his ideas was really so simple.
>
> You must keep him out of details. The details bore him; and if he does make suggestions that he thinks deal with details, he is likely to turn

the system upside down . . . you ask him what time it is and he gives you a lecture . . .

You should always tell him about successes. If you tell him you have a problem he will listen, but by the time he is done with helping you out, you will have ten projects ten times more problematic on your hands.

Mismanagement Style XXXI: The Exclusive Integrator (the "superfollower"). By the XXXI style, I mean the mismanager who, while not an entrepreneur or an administrator or an individual producer, is involved in uniting people behind a cause. I call him a superfollower because he tries to find out what plan will be acceptable to the largest number of people and then tries to unite them behind that plan. He has no ideas of his own that he would like to implement. There is nothing he wants to achieve except the position of a conflict resolver. Like the bureaucrat who does not care what he produces as long as it is well implemented, the superfollower is little concerned about what or how he integrates, so long as there is an appearance of consensus, a united front.

This manager is an integrator who deals exclusively with the interactions of others. As such, he is not bound by the limits of his own organization unit. If he is sincerely interested in others, he is likely to exhibit this behavior with others in (and outside) the organization as well as with his own subordinates. On the other hand, if he is a manipulator of others, he is likely to exhibit this kind of behavior outside as well as inside his unit. This type of manager "gets things done through people," whether he cares for people or not. He is not necessarily a local or a cosmopolitan; his perspective is in effect boundless. Like the entrepreneur, we cannot predict from this, his dominant management style, whether or not he will take an open systems perspective.

The superfollower enjoys being instrumental in solving conflicts; but unfortunately, not all conflict resolutions are functional. A course of action that seems adequate in terms of resolving a short-term need might not be beneficial to the organization in the long run. A consensus among members of an organization at a particular time may satisfy their immediate interest at the expense of the total organization. The total interest of an organization includes groups that are not always represented in its decision-making bodies. While the role of the manager is also to represent future interests, the superfollower is less interested in these than in his immediate constituency.

Short-range interest groups flourish under the superfollower because he does not identify corporate goals for them but rather considers a goal to be that which is desired at a particular moment by a consensus of those participating in the decision-making process. The superfollower does not attempt to lift himself above the temporary interests of the organization and to decide the direction which the organization should take. He will not threaten an already existent consensus. He does not like to confront subordinates. He will not absorb the aggression created when a course of action offends a powerful group. In other words, he does not really lead— he follows. He tries to identify himself *with* a direction which is already acceptable to the organization rather than to identify a direction for the organization which will be the best one to take in the light of all the conditions the organization faces. He is always asking, "What do we agree about. . . ." He hardly ever makes his own suggestions. Instead, he quotes others: "So and so said that . . . and so and so agrees that. . . ."

He will not volunteer to tell you what is going wrong although he is looking for what people worry about in order to work on it. While the loner complains that he never has enough time, the bureaucrat complains that people are late or are spending too much, and the crisis maker complains that nothing ever gets done. If the superfollower complains at all, it is usually that someone did not understand him correctly about something.

The reaction of subordinates to this type of mismanagement is mixed; it can range from enthusiasm through apathy to rebellion. If one happens to belong to a group which gets all it wants from the organization, one will accept him. On the other hand, rebellion can be aroused when the company is following a direction that a minority knows to be disastrous.

In the case of a power struggle among members of the organization this type of mismanager will assess the struggle in order to determine which side is likely to win and then will jump on the bandwagon and try to lead it. He will try to be the focal person who achieves unity by extracting compromising commitments from the various parties involved. He will not mobilize for a controversial alternative, especially not one which requires the dominant group to make concessions, even when such an alternative can provide a unity based on consensus rather than on compromise.

Power struggles under a superfollower can be very dysfunctional. People turn against each other while he maneuvers around them all. Power struggles under the loner are minimal, since most of the time he struggles with himself; and if such struggles exist he is too busy to get involved with them. The crisis maker will manipulate the power struggle, either by introducing it or by channeling it into his latest project. The bureaucrat will fight it zealously if it poses a threat to his control. The superfollower will thrive on it, and never really resolve it. Since he does not present a long-term uplifting and unifying alternative, but advocates the dominant short-term acceptable alternative, people turn against each other rather than uniting against the alternative which the superfollower should have provided if he were capable of entrepreneurial behavior. He does not really unite, but he integrates; and since it is intended only for the short run it provides only an apparent unity. In the long run the group never becomes united. To provide long-term unity we need not only an integrator, but an entrepreneur. The true leader and statesman, who leads rather than follows, is the entrepreneuring integrator: one who can offer alternatives which unite, rather than integrating existing alternatives.

The mismanagement of the superfollower has other long-term repercussions. Since the organization changes directions according to the power shifts within it, it lacks a unified and consistent long-term policy. The organization finds itself oscillating from one direction to another, and these frequent changes are costly.

Mismanagement Style XXXX: Does Not Excel in Performing Any Role ("deadwood"). Another pure type of mismanagement is one in which the person in question performs no role well. He is not an integrator because he does not have the social sensitivity and the capacity for communication to perform this function. He cannot perform the entrepreneuring role because he is neither creative nor capable of taking risks. He cannot be an administrator because he is incapable of delegating, coordinating, motivating, or whatever else is necessary in order to carry out a predetermined task. But what is more surprising is that he is not even an individual producer: he is not even technically competent to produce results. He is managerially incompetent, hence I label him deadwood. This type of mismanager can develop when an organization is changing rapidly either in its markets or in its technology. Without an adequate attempt to provide for the development of human resources and to retrain people, the loners of yesterday become the deadwood of today. This can also happen to the bureaucrat and the crisis maker if they lose power because of changes introduced over their heads and if they also lack the psychological energy necessary to reestablish their positions and to perform their roles in a functional way. They accept the enforced change, drift away, and become deadwood.

The deadwood is apathetic. He waits to be told what to do. He does not produce; he does not administer others zealously; he does not worry about power intrigues; and obviously he does not provide sparks like the crisis maker. If he has any "sparking" ideas he keeps them to himself. He is mostly worried about how to survive until retirement and how to keep intact the little he has. In his ample free time he looks for successes that he can take the credit for, a strategy intended to improve his chances of survival. Change is a serious threat to him. He knows that in any change he is the one whose position is most threatened. In order to maximize his chances for organizational survival he resists change, attributes successes to himself, and avoids starting or even joining new projects: his hiring practices also reflect the strategy of survival. He favors the not-so-bright and not-so-aggressive subordinate, the one even less productive than himself, who can pose no threat to him.

He has no complaints about anything. He fears that any complaint will reflect on him; so it is always "Everything is going well, we are making excellent progress," while the company is actually going bankrupt. He trains, but his heart is not in it once he has become deadwood. Why should he train his own replacement? What is the hurry? Hence, he will only go through the motions of training.

This mismanager is afraid of conflict. Conflict may mean change, and change threatens his survival. So he tries to cover up conflicts and explain them away as mere misunderstandings. Planning, organizing, controlling are to him only words that mean more work. Since he is neither a producer, an implementor, an entrepreneur, nor an integrator, the process of management is to him a mere ritual, acted out religiously but only for the sake of survival.

As far as his personality traits are concerned, he might have been any one of the other mismanagers. One can still see, from time to time, traces of the enthusiastic crisis maker or the meticulous bureaucrat that he once was. But by the time he has become deadwood, his main characteristic is a "low metabolism." He smokes or drinks a lot; he coughs, nods, hums, nods his head in agreement; he confides in you about how well he is doing, or did in the past, or will do; but one senses that there is not much to be expected from him.

This person is usually out of the information network. If he does get access to any information he cherishes it and uses it whenever possible, however remotely relevant; this proves to the rest of the organization that he is still plugged in and still kicking.

Comparative Analysis

Identification of Mismanagement Styles by Nature of Misinformation. Subordinates, if they misinform a mismanager, will misinform him on different subjects, depending on the type of mismanager he is. The loner will be misinformed about how much free time his subordinates have, the bureaucrat about transgressions and violations in the organization, the crisis maker about the limits to what can be done, for his subordinates will accept any assignment and then come up with excuses for not accomplishing it. But deadwood is not misinformed; he is simply ignored. He is not sufficiently threatening so that anyone has to misinform him so as to protect himself.

Identification of Mismanagement by Promotion Criteria. How do employees get promoted in a mismanaged organization? Under a loner, one must always be present to carry out any errand with minimal fuss. Under a bureaucrat, one must always be organized and informed, and never doubt or question the validity of what is being done and how. Under the crisis maker, the prescription for success is to show enthusiasm, listen carefully, support all the ideas of the boss and agree with all his criticisms of the current situation. With deadwood, there is no sure way to succeed and get promoted. If anyone is really successful, deadwood will be threatened and will find ways to discount the successes of the subordinate and discreetly magnify his own contribution. The only way to succeed is to leave the unit that deadwood mismanages, if possible. Otherwise, all one can do is to lie low and wait for his retirement or replacement, while slowly losing one's own creative capacity.

Identification by Creative Processes.   It is possible to identify the type of mismanagement being practiced by the location of the creative processes in the organization. Under the loner, people can be creative if they have the inclination. He does not feel threatened by it, and he will notice and encourage it if it produces results. The bureaucrat ignores creativity so long as it does not challenge his system of controls. So if there are any creative people they can operate without inhibition. The crisis maker monopolizes creativity. He exhibits anxiety when those around him challenge his creativity with theirs. He could accept them if they would channel their creativity so as to augment his own project, but otherwise he perceives it as a threat. The superfollower does not like creative people who question his leadership either. But in all these cases, creativity is exhibited somewhere. If a creative individual finds himself under the deadwood, he will quit and go elsewhere, or else lose his creative needs because there is no way to express them.

Identification by Subordinates' Behavior.   The kind of dysfunctional behavior exhibited by subordinates of the various kinds of mismanagers also differ. The loner's subordinates learn how to waste time in a creative and enjoyable fashion. Those of the bureaucrat derive their intrinsic rewards from trying to beat the system, and they can be highly creative in thinking of ways to turn the system to their advantage. The subordinates of the crisis maker learn to produce excuses. Those of the deadwood, if they do not leave, find the unchallenging environment congenial, in which case deadwood accumulates. The dysfunctional behavior in this case produces low results, for there will either be high turnover or no turnover at all.

The Mismanagement Mix

Mixed Mismanagement Style XAEI: The "Zealous Newcomer."   So far we have described and analyzed five pure styles of mismanagers. There are additional styles of mismanagement that are less acute, which occur when more than one role is performed well but still all four are not included. If only one role of management is missing, we can identify a mixed style of mismanagement. Here we will limit ourselves to describing one prominent example of a "mixed" type. The XAEI style, the zealous newcomer, is an individual who is an administrator and an entrepreneur and an integrator, but he is not a producer. An example is the highly respected manager from one industry who is hired by a failing firm in another industry. They expect him to produce instantaneous results. Under pressure he introduces new procedures, penetrates new markets, generates new products, and unifies the organization behind these new directions. He does not exhibit any of the pure styles of mismanagement presented above. He is working hard in "catching up with the industry." He appraises how well he does by "how fast we are moving." If he has any time left he attacks new problem areas; he recognizes the indispensability of change and he hires those who can most quickly bring about change and "get us out of the jam." He is open-minded and does not necessarily hire the people who agree with him. He listens. He acts. He will try to solve conflicts by providing alternatives of his own and he will take the risk of confronting power centers. Nor is he misinformed. But in time losses start pouring in. The organization and its board of directors realize that crucial mistakes were made; the realities of the market were not properly understood. The mismanager simply did not know the technology and the environment of the organization well enough to be able to innovate successfully and to actually understand what he was told. He did not have enough time to learn all that he had to learn. He was a great administrator, entrepreneur, and integrator; but unfortunately, he just didn't understand what he was doing.

The "Textbook Manager" (PAEI). How does a manager behave, as opposed to a mismanager? The "textbook manager" is a producer of results, an excellent administrator, entrepreneur, and integrator (PAEI). He initiates action systematically, integrating the human resources to that end. He delegates, develops the organization continuously and systematically in its markets, production facilities, finances, and human resources. Unlike the mismanager, he appraises himself by how well *the group* that he manages performs; by how well, together and individually, they achieve their respective goals, and by how instrumental and supportive he was in facilitating this goal achievement. He listens carefully whenever time allows to what is being said and to what is not being said. He is aware of the need to change. He cautiously, selectively, and systematically introduces it in a planned fashion. In his hiring practices, he is not threatened by a prospective subordinate who is bright and challenging; he looks for potential and is able to identify it. He is sufficiently self-confident and self-realized that he can respect people who act like himself. He manifests anxiety not by complaining but by constructive criticism. He trains systematically. He resolves conflicts in a statesmanlike manner, seeking consensus by elevating people's aspirations and expectations and appealing to their social consciences.

This manager is at once analytic and action-oriented, sensitive but not overly emotional. He seeks maximal integrity in the process, but not at the expense of the necessary short-term results. He does not monopolize information and use it as a source of power. His subordinates are not afraid to report failures; they know that he can be reasonable and supportive. He promotes those with managerial potential and encourages constructive creativity. Overall one finds a well-integrated, goal-seeking organization whose members fully cooperate and fully accept one another and the judgment of their manager. No dysfunctional behavior on the part of subordinates is easily observable. I have labelled this manager the textbook manager because one usually finds him in textbooks; in real life he is rare. The reasons for this rarity will be explained in the following paragraphs.

Is Mismanagement Avoidable?

Does the reader know a manager who fills perfectly all four of these roles and thus exhibits no mismanagement style since he is a manager who is at once an excellent technician, administrator, entrepreneur, and integrator? Probably not. At least such managers are rarely encountered, by comparison with the number of mismanagers. To perform all these roles equally well requires too many different personality traits, some of which are incompatible. To understand why this is so, it is necessary to work out a typology of decision making.

A Typology of Decision Making in Management. It is important to realize that the four roles of management involve different kinds of decision-making processes. Producing results and administering involve programmed decisions—those that are made in advance for predetermined cases. Producing is mainly a matter of programmed decisions. Whether the task is producing shoes, making sales, or raising funds, there is a particular sequence that will be most efficient and a particular technology that must be used. There are some nonprogrammed decisions that occur in performing these tasks but management tries to minimize these in order to achieve maximum predictability of outcome. Administrative decisions are also mostly programmed, for the same reasons. Administrators are expected to keep to standard operating procedures as closely as possible.

On the other hand, entrepreneuring and integrating do not involve programmed decisions. There is no program that can tell an integrator or an entrepreneur what to initiate or when and how to do it. One can be taught skills that will be useful for dealing with people, but whether those skills will actually be put into action depends on the individual's personality. Entrepreneuring and integrating are self-starting, discretionary processes which entail creativity and require willingness to take risks.

The four roles of management presented above can be arranged into a hierarchy with the most completely programmable kind of decision-making at the bottom and the least programmable at the top.

Role	Least
Integrating	
Innovating (entrepreneuring)	Decision
Implementing (administering)	Programmability
Producing (doing)	
	Most

The higher one ascends in this hierarchy the more creativity is required, since decisions have to be made from a more diffused and less structured data base. I propose that integrating is less programmable than entrepreneuring because the last does not necessarily deal with people while integrating by my definition involves uniting individuals behind a group decision. If one has to unite a group of individual entrepreneurs, there is a greater degree of creativity required than in making a decision for oneself.

I suggest that in the typical corporate hierarchical organization the higher one ascends, the more nonprogrammed decision making is required and that the Peter Principle phenomenon derives from the fact that at certain levels of promotion the individual finds himself incapable of being as creative as the position requires. Also, entrepreneurship and innovation affect a larger organizational area the higher one moves in the hierarchy; so the higher one ascends, the greater is the risk involved in making decisions. In these circumstances some managers will fail not only because they are deficient in creativity but also because they are unwilling to undertake risk.

Prevalence of Mismanagement Styles. Since the roles of a manager require both programmed and nonprogrammed decisions, a manager is required to be a "realistic dreamer." He is expected to plan for the future, to initiate change, to take risks; but at the same time he must have both his feet on the ground and must understand the practical consequences of his dreams.

It is hard to find managers who perform all four roles. That requires being highly critical and detail-oriented (administrator) and at the same time highly creative and daring (entrepreneur). Thus qualities that make a manager an outstanding entrepreneur may preclude him from being an outstanding administrator. Furthermore, the qualities that make a good process facilitator and integrator may inhibit entrepreneurship; the entrepreneur is likely to find the process of making plans acceptable to everyone a painful and frustrating one, since it usually involves compromising his own ideas.

Certain characteristics of the individual performer are also incompatible with the other roles of the manager. A manager who is extremely excited about his functional performance might resent being taken away from them in order to administer, innovate and integrate. I have interviewed many artistic directors who would rather direct themselves than hire other directors to do the job. Several architect-partners whom I interviewed expressed to me their anguish that they had no time to design; since the company grew they had to administer, to solicit new projects, and to motivate others to do what they would love to do themselves. The best example is the closest to home: getting to be chairman of one's department in a university is gratifying but it has its costs, and those who love research resent the task and usually mismanage it. On the other hand, those who love administration have "reentry blues" when the mandate expires. They have a very difficult time getting back into research after they have experienced the gratification of administering others.

The most common combinations in my research are the productive entrepreneur (PXEX) (doing and innovating) and the compromising bureaucrat or the nondirective administrator (XAXI) (integrating and administering). These combinations are not "pure," since in these cases the mismanager makes both programmed and nonprogrammed decisions. But he will still mismanage. The PXEX will change directions and try to do everything himself. The XAXI will be a participative administrator but will still provide little direction himself and remain excessively detail-oriented. The combinations most rarely met with are producer-administrator (PAXX), the entrepreneurial-integrator (XXEI), and the producer-administrator-entrepreneur-integrator (the textbook manager) (PAEI).

It does appear that a capacity for one role may inhibit performance in another role. The individual performer who likes functional involvement will resent the time he has to spend in administration. The administrator who feels rewarded by bringing the system under control will feel threatened by change and will therefore not function well as entrepreneur. The innovator's personality traits make him very creative and he is unlikely to cherish the role of integrator, which necessarily means compromising his own ideas to make them acceptable to others.

So it is highly improbable that an individual will have all the qualities that enable him to excel in all four roles. This brings me to the conclusion that most organizations are necessarily somewhat mismanaged. If a manager attempts to perform all four roles by himself, he will probably not excel in any of them.

Certain styles of mismanagement are more prevalent in some types of organization than in others. The loner is prevalent in small, rapidly growing, management-owned companies, and more prevalent in developing countries than in highly industrialized countries. The bureaucrat is prevalent in government agencies and in organizations that operate in secure, noncompetitive environments. The crisis maker is readily found in recently established, owner-managed organizations and in artistic organizations (on the artistic rather than the managerial side, such as the artistic director), while the superfollower is common in political and educational organizations in which decision-making power is vested in the members and the manager is mainly a coordinator. Deadwood can be found in any organization, technology, or culture. What makes it more prevalent in one organization than in others is the rate of change the organization experiences and the capacity of its members to adapt systematically to it. So it appears that organizational goals, technologies, and climates may affect the distribution of these styles; though each style can appear in many different types of organizations.

READING

A Framework for Management Control Systems*

PETER LORANGE and MICHAEL S. SCOTT MORTON

Peter Lorange and Michael S. Scott Morton are assistant and associate professor respectively at the Sloan School of Management, Massachusetts Institute of Technology.

Introduction

The process of control and the application of control system concepts to *management* control has been discussed at great length in the literature over the past twenty years. In its practical form control in organizations today is synonymous with financial control and, in particular, with budgets and the budgeting process. This will continue to be extremely important for all organizations. However, it is apparent from the recent increase in pressure from outside the organization that existing views of control systems will have to be modified if organizations are to continue to run effectively. There already is ample evidence of this shift in the control practices of many organizations, and these changes are taking place in three major areas:

1.   The need for control systems to be modified to reflect the evolution from traditional organizational patterns (such as divisionalized organizations) to more complex patterns (such as multidimensional structures).

2.   The use of non-dollar variables as a regular part of the formal control system.

3.   The linkage between planning and control and between control and operations.

Management Control: Purposes and Steps in the Process

Many reasonable definitions of management control systems have been suggested over the years.[1] Admittedly, some of these are so general that they yield less than desirable guidance for the researcher or the practitioner. Other definitions tend to be too partial by focusing on narrower aspects of what seems to be a broader management control process. Nevertheless, a number of useful definitions of management control exist. We propose that the *fundamental purpose* for management control systems

---

* Peter Lorange and Michael S. Scott Morton, "A Framework for Management Control Systems," *Sloan Management Review*, Fall 1974, pp. 41–56. Reprinted by permission.

[1] See, for instance, Anthony [3], Jerome [22], Anthony, Dearden and Vancil [4] Horngren [20] and [21], Welsch [33], Emery [14] and Dearden [11].

is to help management accomplish an organization's objectives by providing a formalized framework for (1) the identification of pertinent control variables, (2) the development of good short-term plans, (3) the recording of the degree of actual fulfillment of short-term plans along the set of control variables, and (4) the diagnosis of deviations.

An overall illustration of the management control process model is given in Figure 1. The figure indicates the interrelationship between management control and the long-range planning process (A). The management control process is split into the control variable identification process (B), the short-term direction setting process (C), and the short-term plan accomplishment tracking process (D). The linkage between planning and control is illustrated by arrow (a). The relationship between the two control subprocesses is illustrated by arrows (b) and (d). The tracking of deviations between actual performance and budget may lead to a number of actions, arrows (c), (d), and (e).

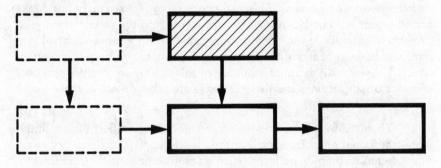

Identification of Control Variables. Control variables form the content of the short-term plan. They are the items that represent the goals of the organization, and they determine what is to be tracked. One of the central activities of management control is to identify what these control variables should be. In the following discussion it will be shown that control variables come from two major sources:

1. The goals and objectives.
2. The situational setting, particularly the organization structure, the people in the organization, the technology available, and the external environment.

The choice of control variables is partially dependent on the choice of key variables in the long-range plans. This is indicated in Figure 1 by the arrow linking the key variable identification and the control variable identification processes. Key variables are operational measures that reflect the goals of the organization. For example, change in market share might be a key variable used to reflect the organization's goal of growth.

FIGURE 1
Interrelationship between the Components of the Long-Range Planning and Management Control Processes

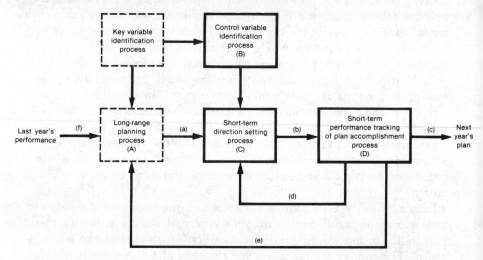

Some key variables cannot be used as control variables, because they are virtually uninfluenced by the organization. For instance, new product innovations by competitors could be a key variable but could not be a control variable. Nevertheless, the goals and objectives of the corporation, as represented by the key variables, are a major source for the determination of control variables.

The actual choice of control variables also will depend critically on each given corporate setting. Leavitt's work will be used to indicate the aspects of an organizational setting that should be considered in developing a situationally tailored set of control variables.[2] Leavitt argues that a particular task interacts strongly with three other sets of variables: the organizational structure in which the task is taking place, the people that are in the organization, and the technology that is available to support the task. He finds that these factors have to be in a state of dynamic equilibrium if an organization is to remain healthy. For the purposes of this article the external environment will be added as a fourth major independent variable. Each force will be discussed in detail in order to indicate the impact it has on the choice of control variables.

Organization Structure. The type of control system to be used is partially dependent on the organization structure that exists in the company. The generally accepted contingency theory of organizational design suggests that the choice of a structure depends on the company's situational

---

[2] See Leavitt [26].

setting. Since virtually all companies differ in this respect, there will be no one best way of designing the organization.[3]

Every corporation consists of a number of more or less autonomous decision-making units known as cost centers, investment centers, departments, divisions, areas, etc. Although there are many different types of responsibility center units, it will be claimed here that each center has several common features of the management control process. However, the control variables to be tracked through plans and budgets will differ, depending on the type of responsibility center that is involved. Further, an analysis of the common elements of management control with the responsibility center helps the exploration of management control for various combinations of centers, such as functional, divisional or matrix organizations. Thus, a management control problem is encountered at two levels: for individual responsibility centers and for combinations of centers.

People. The type of control variables and the nature of the control process may be significantly affected by several sets of variables that characterize people in organizations. The first of these might be labeled "style." The style of the managers and the style of the organization with respect to conflict resolution, attitudes toward risk, and the way decisions are made, often vary between organizations. Some organizations have a well-documented, bureaucratic approach toward each decision. Others tend to be more informal with largely verbal conversations and little or no documentation. The control system will obviously be different in these two types of organizations. The control system will also be affected by the educational levels and the degree of professionalism of the managers and by the history of the organization. These factors of style, education, and history are augmented by the "political science" of the organization. The importance of the informal power structure and the informal communication network of organizations has been well-documented elsewhere.[4] Although the control systems design cannot take all these factors into account explicitly, it is crucial for the designer to recognize that the people in the organization will determine in large measure what kind of control system is possible.

There is an important reverse effect of the control system on the people in the organization. Not only do the people affect the kind of control systems possible, but there often is a strong effect of the control system on the individuals involved. The question of the motivational impact of tight versus loose budgets is merely one example of this effect. The early work by Stedry and others attempted to illustrate some of the behavioral effects

---

[3] For a review of empirical studies on contingency theory, see Galbraith [15] and Lorsch and Allen [28]. For some viewpoints critical to the contingency theory school of thought, see Christenson [9].

[4] See Lorange [27] and Bower [6].

of the budgeting process.[5] Although this research focused largely on dollar budgets or on single dimensional budgets, it is clear that it had an impact.

Technology.   There are at least three important aspects of technology with respect to control systems. The first and most prevalent is the management information system necessary to support the control system. A simple example of this is the computer-based information system which allows a much more elaborate and detailed budgeting system to be maintained than would be possible manually.

A second aspect is the problem of measurement techniques. In addition to the developments in cost measurement systems, there is a technology involved in tracking non-dollar key variables such as employee morale, market share, productivity, and product quality. If the measurement technology is not adequate to track these variables, it becomes impossible for them to form a robust part of the control system.

A third component of technology involves the mathematical techniques that allow us to make trade-offs between different objectives based on multi-attribute preference theory.[6] For instance, if the system requires tracking a series of control variables and each is measured on a different scale, it becomes necessary to find a way of assessing the status with respect to the combination of these objectives. Evaluating a division that is ahead on market share, behind in quality, and above inventory target levels is an example of such a problem. Further, a given course of action may have different effects on the various attributes and it may become difficult, or even impossible, to assess which action strategy would give the best results.

The reverse effect of the impact of the control system on technology probably is most significant in the information systems area. In many instances the information systems ought to be designed to support the control system and should not be built as ends in themselves. This view of subordinating information systems to the purposes of the control system is not widely shared by professionals in the field.[7]

Environmental Forces.   The fourth set of forces that help determine the control system are those external to the organization. It might be more accurate to show a planning function between the environment and the control system since it is a purpose of the planning activity to assess the environment and its implications for the organization. As was argued at the beginning of the article, changes in the external environment may indicate that a shift in emphasis in the control system is appropriate. For example, the environment is exerting pressure for product quality or product safety. It is raising the costs of production due to energy shortages and is

---

[5] See Stedry [31] and Becker and Green [5].

[6] See Keeney [24] and [25].

[7] See Gorry and Scott Morton [19].

304

causing shifts in raw material supplies and their costs. The environment also is placing requirements on the organization from governmental authorities and is exerting competitive pressures due to shifting technology. It seems reasonable that the control system should change to include an expanded set of variables which will enable the organization to respond to these external forces.

Setting Short-Term Direction. From Figure 1 it follows that the next step in the control process is to set short-term goals. A major objective of management control is to provide a vehicle for systematically narrowing down the wide number of business opportunities immediately facing the corporation into a single set of proposed business actions. Initially, the primary participants in the process will be top management, but as the control process proceeds, more of the organization's managers become involved. This procedure leads to the adoption of a course of action by a gradually increasing set of managers, and culminates in an agreement on a near-term plan to which all management should be committed.

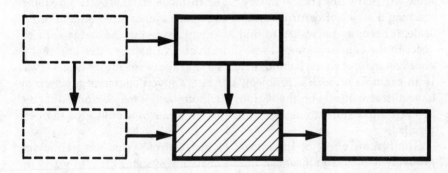

One purpose of management control is to arrive at a "smart" set of short-term goals which may be specified in dollar numbers (as exemplified by the budget) or in non-monetary terms. Each responsibility center will attempt to develop its own short-term goals. There will be a number of inputs from the preceding planning, such as the responsibility center's charter, objectives, goals, and strategy. Also, a relatively broad and tentative resource allocation to the unit's overall programs typically will exist. The task of the short-term planning process is to further narrow down the span of immediate opportunities so that a good near-term plan will result. In case of little or no previous long-range planning or in case of loose linkage between the long-range and short-term planning parts of the process, much less narrowing down of strategic options will have taken place. Thus, at the short-term planning stage, more dramatic narrowing down will then be needed in order to arrive at the same near-term plan. In practice, this may jeopardize the quality of the short-term plan, since usually there is insufficient time to complete this more extensive procedure.

For a functionally organized combination of responsibility centers, the steps in the short-range, strategic goal-setting process may be that the corporate president's office states the overall corporate goals, based on a summary of the inputs from the preceding planning cycle. The departments then develop their short-range plans and submit them for coordination, review, and approval by the corporate headquarters. Approval implies allocation of funds to the short-range plans.

For a divisionalized organizational structure, each division proceeds in essentially the same way as a functionalized corporation. The most significant difference seems to be in the role of corporate headquarters which in this case requests each division to initiate the development of its short-term goals, operationalized by its short-term plans. Corporate headquarters and the division level responsibility centers will have agreed previously on both corporate and divisional long-range goals. This agreement, involving all three hierarchical levels of the divisionalized organization (corporate, divisional, and departmental), will be based on planning at earlier stages. Headquarters also will have made tentative allocations of available resources to the program "packages" of each division. In other words, it will have indicated how much will be allocated to each segment of the company so that the desired balance of profits, growth, and risk properties can be attained for the corporation overall.[8] Within the constraints imposed by this specification of linkage to long-range plans, the divisions will be asked to formulate their short-term plans.

A number of characteristics of this process should be pointed out. First, close coordination often will be required between the functional departments; they are not developing their short-term plans in isolation. Second, the process is iterative. Typically, the short-term planning cycle will go through a number of "spins" before the budget is finalized. Third, the budgeting process is hierarchical. This implies that the higher organizational level will review the plans of the level underneath as a portfolio. Thus, each responsibility center plan at the lower level will be reviewed in terms of its effect on all the other responsibility center plans at that level.

The Performance Tracking and Diagnosis Steps.   The third purpose of management control, as indicated by (D) in Figure 1, is to serve as a "tracking function" for measuring performance and as a basis for diagnosis of performance deviations. It provides a vehicle for systematically learning how to adjust to one's business environment by attempting *ex post facto* to determine why plans and budgets were not fulfilled. By making use of plans and budgets as benchmarks for reference in analyses of why the company did not realize its plans, important understanding about future direction-setting can be gained. In fact, since the management control process monitors both long-range and short-range plans, the tracking

---

[8] See Vancil and Lorange [32] and Carter and Cohen [8].

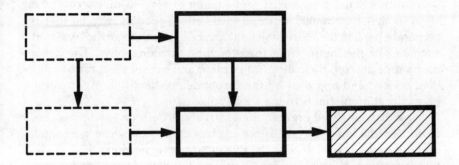

function will be essential for effective planning in both the long term and the short term.

The ability of an organizational unit to fulfill its short-term plans depends not only on its own performance but on the performance of other organizational units as well. For instance, a division's ability to realize its short-term plan depends considerably on how well its departments are attaining their short-term goals. Consequently, the tracking function must provide for signaling performance deviations to those organizational units for which such information is relevant. At this point, however, the tracking process will be discussed in terms of a single responsibility center. The tracking functions may be divided into two subfunctions: the recording of deviations from short-term plans and the diagnosis of deviations, hopefully leading to a determination of their causes.[9]

The first of the two subfunctions, the recording function, can in turn be separated into three components: the measurement of each control variable, the determination of the extent to which deviations are due to controllable factors and whose responsibility it is,[10] and the determination of the extent to which deviations are due to uncontrollable events in order to then initiate the proper adjustments. The control variable measurement function consists of measuring the progress over time of the short-term goal attainment. Since not all goals can be quantified in monetary terms, a measurement is needed for control variables that are expressed in non-dollar terms or in qualitative terms. A number of criteria have been proposed for judging the appropriateness of control measures; many of them originate from financial accounting.[11] The measures may have to satisfy criteria such as objectivity, reliability, and verifiability. But it is most important that the data being monitored are useful for decision making and management control.

---

[9] See Zannetos [34].

[10] See Kaplan [23], Dyckman [13], and Demski [12].

[11] See, in particular, American Accounting Association [1] and American Institute of Certified Public Accountants [2].

The second subtask of the tracking function is the diagnosis of variances which involves applying analytical tools to understand what caused the deviations. Since different types of variations are being analyzed for a variety of control variables, a number of analytical tools may have to be used. The diagnosis of a variance may lead to three different actions:

1. The performance deviation may trigger a corrective action process which could involve some alteration of the previous resource allocation. This is illustrated by arrow (d) in Figure 1.

2. In cases of serious deviations, corrective measures may be taken regarding the overall resource allocation pattern. This will be evidenced by a revision of the long-range plans and will be followed by a revision of the short-term goals. Arrow (e) illustrates this relatively rare effect.

3. In some cases no immediate corrective actions are taken, but the deviations may have an impact on next year's plan, as evidenced by arrow (c). (Of course, deviations in last year's performance similarly led to impacts on this year's plan, as illustrated by arrow [f].)

Complicating issues of tracking arise when working with hierarchical combinations of responsibility centers. In the case of a functionally organized company, performance measurements typically are for cost centers and/or discretionary expense centers. Diagnosis also focuses heavily on costs and expenses. These problems shall not be explored in detail, but reference is made to a relatively well-developed body of literature.[12] For the divisionalized corporation the performance tracking focuses not only on cost and expense centers, but also on profit and investment centers. Many difficult measurement problems arise when attempting to determine profits and even more arise when attempting to estimate an asset base. The various arguments within this field will not be discussed, but again reference is made to the literature.[13]

There is a danger that the performance tracking process will lead to decision-making behavior which violates the overall organizational goal congruence requirement. This is partly due to the "technical" measurement problems just referred to. These often stem from a desire to capture complex and multifaceted phenomena by means of a few variables, usually expressed in dollar terms. Oversimplification, leading to impossible measurement tasks, could be the result. Also, lack of goal congruence may arise due to inconsistencies between the time span used for control purposes and the time span that is appropriate for the business. For instance, a research laboratory organization would experience severe problems with a one-year time horizon for its control system when a five-year plan would be more appropriate.

---

[12] See Horngren [20], Gordon and Shillinglaw [18], and Dearden [11].
[13] See, for instance, Solomons [30] and Dearden [10].

The preceding discussion has attempted to synthesize the current view of management control systems. The literature contains a variety of views and most of them can be summarized by Figure 1. However, the literature does not emphasize three emerging areas of control which will be discussed in the next section.

Emerging Issues

The three emerging areas of management control are linkage to planning, use of non-dollar control variables, and impacts from the added complexity of multidimensional organizational structures.

Control Implications of Multidimensional Organizational Structures. A result of the increasing complexity of today's technology is a greater interdependency between many intermediate production processes. This may lead to a considerable penalty in terms of diseconomies of scale in corporations that are divisionalized. Much duplication of effort may be taking place. Similarly, a company that is expanding multinationally may be too small to set up separate production facilities in each geographical area. In both instances, a matrix-type organizational structure may be adopted to achieve both production economies and business/area effectiveness. Given the trends toward increased complexity of technical processes and toward increased internationalization, multidimensional organizational structures probably will become more common.

For a company with a matrix structure key decision-making activities are carried out in committees made up of managers who represent diverse task backgrounds. Consequently, within part of such organizations, unidimensional hierarchical responsibility center patterns no longer exist. The managers on the matrix boards will represent one of the following three task types:[14]

1. *Business units:* These will have performance responsibility for a business family, similar to a divisional organization along business areas, and typically will be profit centers.
2. *Geographical units:* These will have performance responsibility for a geographical area, e.g., a country, and also will typically be profit centers.
3. *Functional units* (e.g., manufacturing, marketing, R&D): These will have performance responsibility for the functional services they render to each business or area unit, and typically will be cost centers.

Not all matrix organizations will have a three-dimensional structure; they may not have all three task types represented on the group decision-making matrix boards. For instance, a company that operates only on the domestic market may be matrix-organized only along the business and functional dimensions. A company which is manufacturing essentially one

---

[14] See Galbraith [15] and [16], and Goggin [17].

class of products world-wide may adopt a two-dimensional matrix with geographical and functional elements. Thus, only multinational, multi-product corporations typically will adopt the more complex three-dimensional structure.

It should be stressed that a relatively small proportion of a company's decision makers will be directly involved in committee decision-making. The functional organizational hierarchies, such as marketing or production, will still exist, and unidimensional responsibility patterns will be evident within these hierarchies. However, at one level fairly high up in the organization each function will be coordinated with the other functions, and with the business and/or the area dimensions. A corporation may consist of a few or many matrix groups at this level.

Three distinctive types of control tasks emerge from such a matrix structure:

1. Control within each of the three task dimensions (i.e., the business, geographical and functional tasks). Particularly for the functional responsibility centers elaborate control similar to that found in unidimensional structures typically will be instituted.

2. Control of each matrix committee effort. The multidimensional responsibility and reporting patterns are a distinctive feature.

3. Control of the overall corporation. The major task is to control the overall portfolio of matrix team efforts.

For a matrix structure the steps in the short-term planning process will be much more complicated. A high level of interaction among many executives and substantial interrelationships between sub-plans and sub-tasks will be necessary. The need for a formal system of management control becomes greater in such a setting in order to ensure proper timing, proper formats, and coordination of many diverse control activities.

One might speculate that in order to initiate the planning and control process, one of the three task dimensions should be given a more dominant role than the others. For instance, when developing the long-term plans, the business or geographic task units may be more involved than the functional dimensions. However, when options have been narrowed down and short-term budgeting is to take place, the functional units may play the more dominant role.

As a further illustration of the complexity of matrix structures, one can look at the measurement and diagnostic step. In multidimensional organizations the problem is compounded because of the multiple responsibility for tasks among decision makers. One implication is that costs and incomes must be tracked so they are assignable to matrix responsibility units as well as to functional, area, and/or business responsibility centers. A given income figure may be credited to two functional responsibility centers or to a functional unit and an area unit. Hence, income and cost figures normally will have to be divided and accounted for by more than one unit of the organization. Measuring costs and incomes so they can be divided in other than an arbitrary manner becomes a major task of performance tracking in matrix organizations.

A second implication of the complexity of matrix structures is the substantial increase in the volume of internal reporting that is needed. Because of the more complex patterns of interdependencies, the minimum time requirements for updating and revising plans must be expanded. A computer-based management information system could be cost-benefit advantageous for organizations of this type.

A third implication is the necessity to ensure consistency of formats for short-term plans and for procedures of calculating and reporting deviations.

The internal information-handling tasks become quite complex in a matrix organization. Consequently, the choice of a formal structure for the management control system becomes crucial, and the potential increases for utilization of advanced information-handling techniques.

Non-Dollar Variables. An emerging issue from the discussion of the identification of control variables was that many of the variables will not be measured in monetary terms. The inclusion of these control variables reflects the added importance of environmental pressures and suggests a fundamental shift from the traditional control systems.

It is implied here that the control systems design process should be adapted to reflect the need for an environmental diagnosis and to decide which control variables should be used. The shifting environment does not suggest that the fundamental nature of the control process should change. However, it does suggest that the kind of variables that are in the control system, the way they are derived, and the people, structure and technology that are employed may have to be changed. In particular, if the external environment is shifting as suggested, then the control system will require different control variables.

An example of this situation is the attempt by a furnace manufacturer to track dealer inventory levels in order to reduce hoarding. Dealer stock-outs were occurring frequently because of a scarcity of parts at the factory which was caused by the energy shortage. Similar examples are easy to find. However, there does not exist a good statement of what such control variables should be or a well-understood methodology by which they can be derived. It is suggested that analysis of the five forces reflected in the list at the outset of the discussion on the identification of control variables is an effective first step which can be done readily by any organization.

Linkage of the Control System. The discussion outlining the steps in the management control process emphasized the linkage to planning. In addition, there are linkages between control and the action programs that are designed to correct the operations of the organization based on the diagnosis stage. A third linkage is caused by the need to connect control across the hierarchical levels of an organization.

The Linkage between Management Control and Planning. It has been indicated that the linkage between the long-range planning phase and the control phase is critical for the characterization of the control process. This is because the way and extent to which business opportunities have been previously narrowed down will largely dictate the activities of the control phase. Two aspects of this linkage, content and timing, will be discussed.[15] It has been suggested that content linkage between the long-range plan and the budget can be judged by comparing the two in terms of (1) comparability of the level of financial detail, (2) agreement between the plan and budget at a given time, (3) agreement of this year's budget with last year's plans and (4) the extent to which differences at a given time and over time are reconciled. Given the different purposes of planning and control, an alternative way to look at these linkages will be suggested. Although the key variables may be entirely compatible, the figures of the plan and budget need not coincide. Thus, situations with tight content linkage may exist despite this compatibility.

In cases with loose content linkage, little "narrowing down" of options occurs in the planning stage. This implies that most of the narrowing down is done at the short-term planning/budgeting stage. Consequently, heavier requirements will be placed on this process stage in order to arrive at a "smart" plan. It is important to realize that loose content linkage implies a shifting of the narrowing down from planning to control.

There may be several reasons for a rational choice of a specific degree of tightness or looseness of content linkage. During some stages of an organization's evolution, the linkage may be loose by default rather than by design. Typically, most companies have had much longer experience with budgeting than with long-range planning. When planning is initiated, it often will be difficult to integrate it with the mature control process. In effect, this means loose linkage, accompanied by the implications just discussed.

The time schedule for the completion of the planning and budgeting task also becomes important. If relatively little time elapses between the execution of the long-range planning tasks and the short-range planning (budgeting) tasks, a tighter *de facto* substance linking is indicated. However, because of the longer elapsed time between completion of the budget and the beginning of next year's planning, the outputs of this year's control process will have a looser impact on next year's plan. But the timing linkage question may be less significant than perceived by many because of the continuous nature of the processes and the necessity to perform them on a continual basis all year.

Linkage to Action Plans. The signals from the control system generate a diagnostic activity as part of the management control process. This diagnosis is used by the responsibility center manager to help establish an

---

[15] See Shank et al. [29] and Camillus [7].

action plan to solve, or mitigate, the existing variances. Such action plans may be more or less successful in curing the fundamental cause. The effectiveness of the existing signals in helping the manager to solve problems is an important consideration in redesigning the control system. This linkage between action and control has severe implementation problems and, judging from the existing literature, seems almost nonexistent. Measurement of cause and effect in these situations is difficult, but such a linkage is desirable if the control system is to be usefully modified over time.

Organizational Linkage. As many as three types of organizational levels must be considered. At the corporate level there is a linkage problem between the corporate long-term and short-term plans; at the division level there is a linkage problem between the division's business plan and its business budget. At the departmental level there is a linkage problem between the functional plan program and the functional budget. Further, there is the problem of linking each level's plans and budgets with those of the levels above and below. In dealing with a three-level interdependent linkage a number of issues are raised. Should the degree of content linkage be the same at the three levels? If corrective actions are taken at one organizational level, how are the other levels' long-range and/or short-range plans affected? Will the effect be the same under patterns of tight linkage and loose linkage?

This suggests that the planning/budgeting process model portrayed in Figure 1 should be expanded into a multi-level model in order to cope with these organizational linkage problems.

Implications

The above view of control systems has been designed to emphasize the implications of three emerging evolutionary trends for management control.

1. The increasingly unstable external environment necessitates a tighter linkage of the management control system to the formal planning system.
2. The instability of the external environment causes a need for a more robust set of control variables than exists with the current dollar-based budget.
3. The increasing diversification of large corporations often creates more complex organizational forms (at the extreme, the matrix structure) which operate in varying environments (the multidimensional corporation) and in different businesses (the conglomerate).

Even for small or medium-sized organizations these three factors are changing, and similar changes can be identified for public sector organizations. As a result, a clear view of control systems and their basic purposes is needed; without such a view it is difficult to build or run one effectively in an organization.

The framework suggested here is a first step in trying to build a structure which is useful for diagnosing existing control systems. Is there an agreement between this "normative" view and the descriptive model of the organization's existing control system? In particular, it would be argued that the framework presented here is useful for making changes in the management control system to reflect the continuing changes in the external environment, changes which exert considerable pressure on the corporation.

REFERENCES

[1] American Accounting Association *A Statement of Basic Accounting Theory.* Evanston, Ill.: American Accounting Association, 1966, chap. 4.

[2] American Institute of Certified Public Accountants *Objectives of Financial Statements.* (Trueblood Committee Report). New York: AICPA, 1973.

[3] Anthony, R. N. *Planning and Control Systems: A Framework for Analysis.* Boston: Division of Research, Graduate School of Business Administration, Harvard University, 1965.

[4] Anthony, R. N.; Dearden, J.; and Vancil, R. F. *Management Control Systems.* Homewood, Ill.: Richard D. Irwin, Inc., 1972.

[5] Becker, S., and Green, D., Jr. "Budgeting and Employee Behavior." *Journal of Business,* October 1962, pp. 392–402.

[6] Bower, J. *The Resource Allocation Process.* Boston: Division of Research, Graduate School of Business Administration, Harvard University, 1970.

[7] Camillus, J. C. *Formal Planning Systems: The Control Considerations in Design.* Unpublished D.B.A. Thesis, Graduate School of Business Administration, Harvard University, 1972.

[8] Carter, E. E., and Cohen, C. "Portfolio Aspects of Strategic Planning." *Journal of Business Policy,* Summer 1972.

[9] Christenson, C. "The Contingency Theory of Organization: A Methodological Analysis." Harvard Business School Working Paper, 1973.

[10] Dearden, J. "The Case Against ROI Control." *Harvard Business Review,* September-October 1966.

[11] ——— *Cost Accounting and Financial Control Systems.* Reading, Mass.: Addison-Wesley, 1973.

[12] Demski, J. "Optimal Performance Measurement." *Journal of Accounting Research,* 1971.

[13] Dyckman, T. R. "The Investigation of Cost Variances." *Journal of Account Research,* 1969.

[14] Emery, J. C. *Organizational Planning and Control Systems.* New York: Macmillan, 1969.

[15] Galbraith, J. *Organization Design: An Information Processing View.* Sloan School Working Paper, M.I.T., 1969, pp. 2–5.

[16] ——— "Matrix Organization Design" *Business Horizons,* February 1971.

[17] Goggin, W. C. "How the Multidimensional Structure Works at Dow Corning." *Harvard Business Review,* January-February 1974.

[18] Gordon, M. S., and Shillinglaw, G. *Accounting: A Managerial Approach.* Homewood, Ill.: Richard D. Irwin, Inc., 1964.

[19] Gorry, A., and Scott Morton, M. S. "A Framework for MIS." *Sloan Management Review,* Fall 1971.

[20] Horngren, C. *Cost Accounting: A Managerial Emphasis.* Englewood Cliffs, N.J.: Prentice-Hall, 1972.

[21] ——— *Accounting for Management Control.* Englewood Cliffs, N.J.: Prentice-Hall, 1974.

[22] Jerome, W. T., III *Executive Control—The Catalyst.* New York: Wiley, 1961.

[23] Kaplan, R. S. "Optimal Investigation Strategies with Imperfect Information." *Journal of Accounting Research,* 1969.

[24] Keeney, R. L. "An Illustrated Procedure for Assessing Multiattributed Utility Functions." *Sloan Management Review,* Fall 1972.

[25] ——— "A Decision Analysis with Multiple Objectives: The Mexico City Airport." *Bell Journal of Economics and Management Science,* Spring 1973.

[26] Leavitt, H. *Managerial Psychology.* Chicago: The University of Chicago Press, 1972.

[27] Lorange, P. *Behavioral Factors in Capital Budgeting.* Bergen, Norway: Universitetsforlaget, 1973.

[28] Lorsch, J. W., and Allen, S. A., III *Managing Diversity and Interdependence: An Organizational Study of Multidivisional Firms.* Boston: Division of Research, Graduate School of Business Administration, Harvard University, 1973.

[29] Shank, J. K.; Niblock, E. G.; and Sandalls, W. T., Jr. "Formal Planning Systems: Getting Creativity and an Action Orientation." *Harvard Business Review,* November-December 1972.

[30] Solomons, D. *Divisional Performance.* New York: Financial Executives Institute, 1965.

[31] Stedry, A. C. *Budget Control and Cost Behavior.* Englewood Cliffs, N.J.: Prentice-Hall, 1960.

[32] Vancil, R. F., and Lorange, P. *Steps in the Long-Range Planning Process.* Sloan School Working Paper, M.I.T., 1974.

[33] Welsch, G. *Budgeting: Profit Planning and Control.* Englewood Cliffs, N.J.: Prentice-Hall, 1972.

[34] Zannetos, Z. S. "On the Theory of Divisional Structures: Some Aspects of Centralization and Decentralization of Control and Decision-Making." *Management Science* 12 (1965).

CASE ANALYSIS:
ITS ROLE AND METHOD

Management is an action-oriented activity. It requires doing to achieve proficiency. Managers succeed or fail not so much because of what they know as because of what they do. A person cannot expect to succeed as a manager and become a "professional" simply by studying excellent books on management—no matter how thoroughly the text material is mastered nor how many As are earned at exam time. Moreover, just like a golfer needs to practice at being a better golfer, a person who aspires to become a manager can benefit from practicing at being a manager.

PRACTICING MANAGEMENT VIA CASE ANALYSIS

In academic programs of management education, students practice at being managers via case analysis. A *case* sets forth, in a factual manner, the conditions and circumstances surrounding a particular managerial situation or series of events in an organization. It may include descriptions of the industry and its competitive conditions, the organization's background, its products and markets, the attitudes and personalities of the key people involved, production facilities, the work climate, the organizational structure, marketing methods, and the external environment, together with whatever pertinent financial, production, accounting, sales, and market information upon which management had to depend. It may concern any kind of organization—a profit-seeking business, or a public service institution.

A good case offers about as live and effective a practice situation as can be achieved short of "the real thing." It puts the readers at the scene of the action and familiarizes them with the situation as it prevailed. As such, it is well suited as a pedagogical device for students practicing what they, as managers, would do if confronted with the same circumstances—and to do so without having to worry about inexperience and making amateurish or costly mistakes.

315

The essence of the student's role in the case method is to diagnose and size up the organization's situation and to think through what, if anything, should be done. The purpose is for the student, as analyst, to develop answers to a number of questions, the gist of which include: What factors have contributed to the organization's success (or failure)? What problems are evident? How would I handle them? What managerial skills are needed to deal effectively with the situation? How should they be applied? What actions need to be taken?

In some cases the managerial issue or problem is readily apparent and the thrust of the case is to develop the analysis and propose a plan of action. In others, however, the point of the case is to sift through clues, symptoms, and conflicting opinions to figure out what the root problems are, as well as to conceive workable solutions.

The subject matter of cases is as varied as the uncertainties and problems confronting managers. Cases may concern areas as diverse as (1) starting a new venture, (2) implementing management by objectives, (3) evaluating corporate strategy, (4) establishing new financial policies, (5) revamping the product line and the marketing mix, (6) shifting to a divisionalized organization structure, (7) setting up employer stock options and bonus plans, (8) entering the market for a new product, (9) determining performance standards and control procedures, (10) evaluating personnel practices, (11) improving employee motivation and morale, (12) assessing the adequacy of distribution channels, (13) revising depreciation and inventory valuation practices, or (14) replacing key management personnel. A case may encompass one or a series of problems—either related or unrelated.

Some cases consist of only a brief one to three page description that is sharply focused upon a specific event or problem. Other case descriptions are more detailed and some are very detailed, offering a wealth of information about the organization and its situation. The short cases, however, are not necessarily the easiest to analyze nor are longer cases indicative of complexity. On occasions, the situation described in the case is disguised to preserve a firm's anonymity or to avoid disclosing competitively sensitive information. This is usually accomplished by using fictitious names for the companies and people involved, changing locations or products, and altering the nature of quantitative data. Nonetheless, any modifications in a disguised case can be counted upon to preserve key relationships and be true to life in its essentials.

It should be emphasized that most cases are *not* intended to be examples of right and wrong, or good and bad management. The organizations concerned are selected neither because they are the best or the worst in their industry nor because they are average or typical. The important thing about a case is that it represents an actual situation where managers were obligated to recognize and cope with the problems as they were.

WHY USE CASES TO PRACTICE MANAGEMENT?

A student of business with tact
Absorbed many answers he lacked.
But acquiring a job,
He said with a sob,
"How *does* one fit answer to fact?"

The foregoing limerick was offered some years ago by Charles I. Gragg in a classic article, "Because Wisdom Can't Be Told," to illustrate what might happen to students of management without the benefit of cases.[1] Gragg observed that the mere act of listening to wise statements and sound advice about management does little for anyone's management skills. He contended it was unlikely that accumulated managerial experience and wisdom could effectively be passed on by lectures and readings alone. Gragg suggested that if anything has been learned about the practice of management, it is that a storehouse of ready-made answers does not exist. Each managerial situation has unique aspects, requiring its own diagnosis and understanding as a prelude to judgment and action. In Gragg's view and in the view of other case method advocates, cases provide aspiring managers with an important and valid kind of daily practice in wrestling with management problems.

The case method is, indeed, *learning by doing.* The pedagogy of the case method of instruction is predicated on the benefits of acquiring managerial "experience" by means of simulated management exercises (cases). The biggest justification for cases is that few, if any, students during the course of their college education have an opportunity to come into direct personal contact with different kinds of companies and real-life managerial situations. Cases offer a viable substitute by bringing a variety of organizations and management problems into the classroom and permitting students to assume the manager's role. Management cases therefore provide students with a kind of experiential exercise in which to test their ability to apply their textbook knowledge about management.

OBJECTIVES OF THE CASE METHOD

As the foregoing discussion suggests, the use of cases as an instructional technique embraces four chief objectives:[2]

---

[1] Charles I. Gragg, "Because Wisdom Can't Be Told," in M. P. McNair, ed., *The Case Method at the Harvard Business School* (New York: McGraw-Hill Book Company, 1954), p. 11.

[2] Ibid., pp. 12–14; and D. R. Schoen and Philip A. Sprague, "What Is the Case Method?" in M. P. McNair, ed., *The Case Method at the Harvard Business School* (New York: McGraw-Hill Book Company, 1954), pp. 78–79.

1. Helping you to acquire the skills of putting textbook knowledge about management into practice.

2. Getting you out of the habit of being a receiver of facts, concepts, and techniques and into the habit of diagnosing problems, analyzing and evaluating alternatives, and formulating workable plans of action.

3. Training you to work out answers and solutions for yourself, as opposed to relying upon the authoritative crutch of the professor or a textbook.

4. Providing you with exposure to a range of firms and managerial situations (which might take a lifetime to experience personally), thus offering you a basis for comparison when you begin your own management career.

If you understand that these are the objectives of the case method of instruction, then you are less likely to be bothered by something that puzzles some students: "What is the answer to the case?" Being accustomed to textbook statements of fact and supposedly definitive lecture notes, students often find that discussions and analyses of managerial cases do not produce any "answer." Instead, issues in the case are discussed pro and con. Various alternatives and relevant aspects of the situation are evaluated. Usually, a good argument can be made for one decision or another, or one plan of action or another. When the class discussion concludes without a clear consensus, some students may, at first, feel cheated or dissatisfied because they are not told "what the answer is" or "what the company actually did."

However, case descriptions of managerial situations where answers are not clear-cut are quite realistic. Organizational problems whose analysis leads to a definite, single-pronged solution are likely to be so oversimplified and rare as to be trivial or devoid of practical value. In reality, several feasible courses of action may exist for dealing with the same set of circumstances. Moreover, in real-life management situations when one makes a decision or elects a particular course of action, there is no peeking at the back of a book to see if you have chosen the best thing to do. No book of provably correct answers exists; in fact, the first test of management action is *results*. If the results turn out to be "good," the decision may be presumed "right"; if not, then, it was "wrong." Hence, the important thing for the student to understand in a case course is that it is the exercise of managerial analysis and decision making that counts rather than discovering "the right answer" or finding out what actually happened.

To put it another way, *the purpose of management cases is not to learn authoritative answers to specific managerial problems but to become skilled in the process of designing a workable (and, hopefully, effective) plan of action through evaluation of the prevailing circumstances.* The aim of case analysis is not for you to try to guess what the instructor is thinking or what his solution is. Rather, it is to see whether you can support your views against the counterviews of others in the group or, failing to do so, whether you can accept the merits of the reasoning underlying the approaches of others. Therefore, *in case analysis you are expected to bear the strains of thinking actively, of making managerial assessments which may be vigorously challenged, and of defending your analysis and plan of action.* Only in this way can case analysis provide you with any meaningful practice at being a manager.

In sum, the purpose of the case method is to initiate you and encourage you in the ways of thinking "managerially" and exercising responsible judgment. At the same time, you should use the cases that follow to test the rigor and effectiveness of your own theories about the practice of management and to begin to evolve your own management philosophy and management style.

PREPARING A CASE FOR CLASS DISCUSSION

Given that cases rest on the principle of learning by doing, their effectiveness hinges upon *you* making *your* analysis and reaching *your* own decisions and then in the classroom participating in a collective analysis and decision-making process. If this is your first experience with the case method, you may have to reorient your study habits. Since a case assignment emphasizes student participation, it is obvious that the effectiveness of the class discussion depends upon each student having studied the case *beforehand.* Consequently, unlike lecture courses where there is no imperative of specific preparation before each class and where assigned readings and reviews of lecture notes may be done at irregular intervals, *a case assignment requires conscientious preparation before class.* You cannot, after all, expect to get much out of practicing managing in a situation with which you are totally unfamiliar.

Unfortunately, though, there is no nice, proven procedure for studying cases which can be recommended to you. There is no formula, no fail-safe step-by-step technique that we can recommend. Each case is a new situation and you will need to adjust accordingly. Moreover, you will, after a time, discover an approach which suits you best. Thus, the following suggestions are offered simply to get you started.

A first step in understanding how the case method of teaching/learning works is to recognize that it represents a radical departure from the lecture/discussion/problem classroom technique. To begin with, members of the class do most of the talking. The instructor's role is to solicit student participation and guide the discussion. Expect the instructor to begin the class with such questions as: What is the organization's strategy? What do you consider to be the real problem confronting the company? What factors have contributed most to the organization's successes? Its failures?

Which manager is doing a good job? Are the organization's goals and strategies compatible with its skills and resources? Typically, members of the class will evaluate and test their opinions as much in discussions with each other as with the instructor. But irrespective of whether the discussion emphasis is instructor-student or student-student, members of the class carry the burden for analyzing the situation and for being prepared to present and defend their analysis in the classroom. Thus, you should expect an absence of professorial "here's how to do it," "right answers," and "hard knowledge for your notebook"; instead, be prepared for a discussion involving what do *you* think, what would *you* do, and what do *you* feel is important.[3]

Begin your analysis by reading the case once for familiarity. An initial reading should give you the general flavor of the situation and make possible preliminary identification of issues. On the second reading, attempt to gain full command of the facts. You may wish to make notes about apparent organizational goals, objectives, strategies, policies, symptoms of problems, problems, root causes of problems, unresolved issues, and roles of key individuals. Be alert for issues or problems which are not necessarily made explicit but which nevertheless are lurking beneath the surface. Read between the lines and do not hesitate to do some detective work on your own. For instance, the apparent issue in the case might be whether a product has ample market potential at the current selling price while the root problem is that the method being used to compensate salespeople fails to generate adequate incentive for achieving greater unit volume. Needless to say, a sharp, clear-cut "size-up" of the company and its problems is an essential function of management: one cannot devise sensible solutions to an organization's troubles until the troubles have first been correctly identified. In short, before a company's problems can be solved, they must be understood; they must be analyzed; they must be evaluated; and they must be placed in proper perspective.

To help gain this perspective, put yourself in the position of some manager or managerial group portrayed in the case and get attuned to the organizational environment within which the manager or management group must make decisions. Try to get a good feel for the "personality" of the company, the management, and the organizational climate. This is essential if you are to come up with solutions which will be both workable and acceptable in light of the prevailing environmental constraints and realities. Do not be dismayed if you find it impractical to isolate the problems and issues into distinct categories which can be treated separately. Very few and significant real-world management problems can be neatly sorted into mutually exclusive areas of concern.

Most important of all, you must arrive at a solid evaluation of the com-

---

[3] Schoen and Sprague, "What Is the Case Method?" p. 80.

pany, based on the information in the case. Developing an ability to evaluate companies and size up their situations is *the key* to case analysis. How do you evaluate a company? There is no pat answer. But there are some guidelines—as specifically outlined in Figure A–1. In general, the financial position of the firm must be scrutinized closely, the firm's external opportunities and internal resources compared and evaluated, and an assessment of its future potential made. Decide how urgent the organi-

FIGURE A–1
Checklist for Evaluating a Company's Present Position and Future Potential

A. *Product Lines and Competitive Position*

1. How do the firm's products (or services) stack up against those of rival firms? Has the firm been successful in differentiating its products from those of its rivals and in carving out a viable market niche for itself? Does the firm enjoy a position of market advantage and, if so, what is the basis for this advantage?

2. How do customers and potential customers regard the company's products? What market shares does it have and how firmly does it hold them? Have market shares been increasing or decreasing? Is the company dependent on a few large customers for the bulk of its sales?

3. What are the firm's profit margins? Have these been increasing or decreasing? Are the firm's margins above or below those of the industry? Is the firm in a position to be competitive on price?

4. Where do the company's chief products stand in the life cycle? Is the industry young or mature? Are the markets for the firm's products expanding or contracting, and at what rates? How is the company's business affected by upswings and downswings in the economy? Is the firm's target market big enough to generate the revenues needed to be profitable?

5. Is the company confronted with increasing competition? What is the nature of this competition and how vulnerable is the firm's strategy to new competition? Is entry into the industry easy or hard? Has the firm demonstrated an ability to compete effectively?

6. Is the company a leader in its market area? Is the company being forced into head-to-head competition with proven leaders? If so, does the company have the competitive artillery it needs or is it trying to go to war with a popgun? Is the firm relying on a "me too" or "copycat" strategy?

7. What are the strengths and weaknesses of the company's marketing strategy? How well do its marketing efforts compare with those of rival firms? Is there a capability for exploiting new products and developing new markets? Does it have the necessary distribution channels or the ability to develop them?

FIGURE A–1 *(continued)*

8. If the firm is diversified, then are its product lines compatible? Is there evidence of strategic fit? Is the diversification plan well thought-out or has the company been seduced by the illusions of glamour products and glamour technology?

What is your summary evaluation of the firm's product line and competition position? What are its particular strengths and weaknesses and how important are these to the firm's ultimate success or failure?

B. *Profitability and Financial Condition*

1. What is the trend in the firm's profitability as concerns total profits, earnings per share, return on sales, return on assets, return on total capital investment, and return on equity investment? How does the firm's profitability compare with that of other firms in the industry? What is the "quality" of the firm's earnings?

2. How is the company viewed by investors? What is the trend in the company's stock price, its price-earnings ratio, dividend payout, and dividend yield on common stock?

3. Is the firm liquid and able to meet its maturing obligations? What trends are evident in the firm's current ratio and quick (or acid test) ratio?

4. To what extent is the firm leveraged? What are the trends in the firm's debt ratios, its time-interest-earned coverages, and its fixed charge coverages? Has the firm exhausted its debt capacity? Does it have the ability to raise new equity capital?

5. How effectively is the firm employing the resources at its command? What problems are revealed by such ratios as inventory turnover, accounts receivable turnover, fixed asset turnover, total asset turnover, and average collection period?

6. Is cash flow adequate to supply the company with working capital? Is the company (or some of its businesses) a "cash hog" or a "cash cow?" (A "cash hog" business uses more cash than it generates, whereas a "cash cow" business generates more cash than is required to finance working capital and expansion needs.)

7. Is the company well-managed from a financial standpoint? Does it have adequate financial controls and careful cash planning? Have capital investment decisions been based on thorough calculations?

What strengths and weaknesses are evident in the firm's overall financial condition? How do these relate to the company's present competitive situation and strategy?

C. *Operations and Internal Organization*

1. How well do the firm's resources and capability match its strategy in the marketplace? Does the firm have the talent, the know-how, and the financial strength to succeed in executing its strategy? Does

FIGURE A–1 *(continued)*

the company have the resources to make a commitment to see its strategy through to a successful implementation?

2. To what extent is the firm's manufacturing strategy, marketing strategy, R&D strategy, and financial strategy integrated, coordinated, and compatible? Are the organization's objectives and strategies suited to its skills and resources?

3. Is the firm threatened by new technological developments? Does it have enough R&D capability? What is its track record in innovation?

4. Is the firm large enough to take advantage of economies of scale? Is it efficient in its manufacturing and production activities? Are its equipment and facilities modern? Have capital expenditures been either inadequate or excessive with regard to ensuing future operating efficiency?

5. How vulnerable is the company to adverse shifts in raw material supply and labor supply conditions? Is there a major problem with unions or a history of poor union-management relations?

6. Is the firm developing the kinds of information it needs to solve its problems? Do operating-level managers have solid, pertinent, and timely data on the status of current operations? Is too much reliance placed on unsupported opinion or management hunch or seat-of-the-pants guestimates?

7. Does the firm have adequate knowledge about costs? Do its costs appear to be in line with other comparable firms? Is it generating the right kind of cost information?

8. How strong is the company's financial management? Are its inventory controls adequate? Are its purchasing procedures adequate?

9. Is the organization adequately staffed? Do key personnel appear knowledgeable and capable in performing their jobs?

10. Are the firm's pay scales and overall reward structure adequate? Is motivation a problem? Is there ample opportunity to promote good people? Are performance appraisals made on a regular basis? Does the company appear to treat employees fairly?

What distinctive competence(s) has the firm developed? How important has this been in accounting for the firm's success (or failure)? What distinctive competence(s) is it missing?

D. *Management Capability*

1. Is the firm well-organized? Is the organization structure supportive of strategy?

2. Does the firm's present management have a good track record? How well has it handled past problems and crises? Have previously set objectives been achieved on schedule?

FIGURE A–1 *(continued)*

3. How capable are each of the firm's key management personnel? Do they have the necessary qualifications and experience? Do they appear to know their jobs well and are the areas for which they are responsible functioning smoothly?

4. Are policies and control procedures in the various departments adequate? Is the organization efficient? Does it take too long for key decisions to be made?

5. Is the organization overly dependent on one person? Is there enough management depth for the type of business being run?

6. How good a job has top management done in selecting, training, and developing lower level management personnel? Have the right kinds of people been selected to fill new or vacant positions?

7. Is top management's leadership style adequate for the firm's situation and needs? Do the firm's managers know how to manage people? Do the managers have the respect of the people they supervise?

8. Does the extent to which the firm has diversified present undue problems of coordination and control to the present management?

9. Has management given evidence of an ability to adapt the firm and the organization structure to meet changing needs, priorities, and competitive conditions?

10. Does management have the respect of the financial community?

What is your summary evaluation of the company's management? What are its strengths and weaknesses and how do these weigh upon the firm's performance?

E. *Prospects for the Future*

1. Has the firm developed (or is it in a position to acquire) the technological proficiency it needs to remain competitive over the long run?

2. If the firm's competitive position is weak or is slipping, is it in a position to "play catch-up"? What are the chances that it can make up lost ground?

3. What is the future market potential for the firm's chief products? Will it need to diversify in the near future and, if so, does it have the financial and organizational strength to make new acquisitions or to build new businesses from the ground up?

4. What are the basic "facts of life" about product-market-technology and competitive trends in the firm's industry over the next decade? Will the company need to make fundamental revisions in its strategy in the near future?

5. What do the trends in the firm's profitability and overall financial condition suggest regarding the firm's prospects for growth and success? Does the firm have adequate long-range financial plans?

FIGURE A-1 (concluded)

6. How adequate is management for coping with the challenges of the future?

7. Which factors have contributed most to the organization's successes? Its failures? How will these factors affect the firm in the future?

8. In view of the firm's overall strengths and weaknesses, and the challenges it faces, what are the odds that it will survive? At what level of success? Will it have to succeed by diversifying out of its present lines of business?

SOURCE: Adapted with major revisions and additions by the authors from Robert B. Buchele, "How to Evaluate a Firm," *California Management Review*, vol. 5, no. 1 (Fall 1962), pp. 5–17.

zation's difficulties are and weigh the probable impacts upon performance and capability. Pinpoint the key factors which are crucial to success or failure. Uppermost in your efforts, strive for defensible arguments and positions. Do not rely upon just your opinion; support any judgments or conclusions with evidence! Use the available data to make whatever relevant accounting, financial, marketing, or operations analysis calculations are necessary to support your assessment of the situation.

Lastly, be wary of accepting *everything* stated in the case as "fact." Sometimes, information or data in the case will be conflicting and/or opinions contradictory. For example, one manager may say that the firm's organizational structure is functioning quite effectively, whereas another may say it is not. It is your task to decide whose view is more valid and why. Forcing you to make judgments about the validity of the data and information presented in the case is both deliberate and realistic. It is deliberate because one function of the case method is to help you develop your powers of judgment and inference. It is realistic because a great many managerial situations entail conflicting points of view.

Once you have thoroughly diagnosed the company's situation and weighed the pros and cons of various alternative courses of action, the final step of case analysis is to decide what you think the company needs to do to improve its performance and to set forth a workable plan of action. This is a crucial part of the process of case analysis since diagnosis divorced from corrective action is sterile; but bear in mind that making a decision and jumping to a conclusion are not the same thing. One is well-advised to avoid the infamous decision-making pattern: "Don't confuse me with the facts. I've made up my mind."

On a few occasions, some desirable information may not be included in the case. In such instances you may be inclined to complain about the lack of "facts." A manager, however, uses more than facts upon which to base his or her decisions. Moreover, it may be possible to make a number of inferences from the facts you do have. So, be wary of rushing to include as part of your recommendations "the need to get more information." From time to time, of course, a search for additional facts or information may be entirely appropriate but you must also recognize that the organization's managers may not have had any more information available than that presented in the case. Before recommending that a final decision be postponed until additional facts are uncovered, be sure that you think it will be worth while to get them and that the organization could afford to wait. In general, though, try to assess situations based upon the evidence you have at hand.

Again, remember that rarely is there a "right" decision or just one "optimal" plan of action or an "approved" solution. Your goal should be to find a practical and workable course of action which is based upon a serious analysis of the situation and which appears to you to be right in view of your assessment and weighing of the facts. Admittedly, someone else may evaluate the same facts in another way and thus have a different "right" solution, but since several good plans of action can normally be conceived, you should not be afraid to pursue your own intuition and judgment. One can make a strong argument for the view that the "right" answer for a manager is the one which he or she can propose, explain, defend, and make work when it is implemented.

THE CLASSROOM EXPERIENCE

In experiencing class discussions of management cases, you will, in all probability, notice very quickly that you will not have thought of everything in the case that your fellow students think of. While you will see things others did not, they will see things you did not. Do not be dismayed or alarmed by this. It is normal. As the old adage goes, "two heads are better than one." So, it is to be expected that the class as a whole will do a more penetrating and searching job of case analysis that will any one person working alone. This is the power of group effort and one of its virtues is that it will give you more insight into how others view situations and how to cope with differences of opinion. Second, you will see better why sometimes it is not managerially wise to assume a rigid position on an issue until a full range of views and information has been assembled. And, undoubtedly, somewhere along the way you will begin to recognize that neither the instructor nor other students in the class have all the answers, and even if they think they do, you are still free to present and hold to your own views. The truth in the saying that "there's more than one way to skin a cat" will be seen to apply nicely to most management situations.

For class discussion of cases to be useful and stimulating you need to keep the following points in mind:

1. The case method enlists a maximum of individual participation in class discussion. It is not enough to be present as a silent observer; if every student took this approach, then there would be no discussion. (Thus, do not be surprised if a portion of your grade is based on your participation in case discussions.)

2. Although you should do your own independent work and independent thinking, don't hesitate to discuss the case with other students. Managers often discuss their problems with other key people.

3. During case discussions, expect and tolerate challenges to the views expressed. Be willing to submit your conclusions for scrutiny and rebuttal. State your views without fear of disapproval and overcome the hesitation of speaking out.

4. In orally presenting and defending your ideas, keep in mind the importance of good communication. It is up to you to be convincing and persuasive in expressing your ideas.

5. Expect the instructor to assume the role of discussion leader; only when the discussion content is technique-oriented is it likely that your instructor will maintain direct control over the discussion.

6. Although discussion of a case is a group process, this does not imply conformity to group opinion. Learning respect for the views and approaches of others is an integral part of case analysis exercises. But be willing to "swim against the tide" of majority opinion. In the practice of management, there is always room for originality, unorthodoxy, and unique personality.

7. In participating in the discussion, make a conscious effort to *contribute* rather than just talk. There *is* a difference.

8. Effective case discussions can occur only if participants have "the facts" of the case well in hand; rehashing information in the case should be held to a minimum except as it provides documentation, comparisons, or support for your position.

9. During the discussion, new insights provided by the group's efforts are likely to emerge, thereby opening up "the facts" to reinterpretation and perhaps causing one's analysis of the situation to be modified.

10. Although there will always be situations in which more technical information is imperative to the making of an intelligent decision, try not to shirk from making decisions in the face of incomplete information. Wrestling with imperfect information is a normal condition managers face and is something you should get used to.

11. Ordinarily, there are several acceptable solutions which can be proposed for dealing with the issues in a case. Definitive, provably correct answers, rarely, if ever, exist in managerial situations.

12. In the final analysis, learning about management via the case method is up to you; just as with other learning techniques, the rewards are dependent upon the effort you put in to it.

PREPARING A WRITTEN CASE ANALYSIS

From time to time, your instructor may ask you to prepare a written analysis of the case assignment. Preparing a written case analysis is much like preparing a case for class discussion, except that your analysis, when completed, must be reduced to writing. Just as there was no set pattern or formula for preparing a case for oral discussion, there is no ironclad procedure for preparing a written case analysis. With a bit of experience you will arrive at your own preferred method of attack in writing up a case and you will learn to adjust your approach to the unique aspects that each case presents.

Your instructor may assign you a specific topic around which to prepare your written report. Common assignments include (1) identify and evaluate company X's corporate strategy; (2) in view of the opportunities and risks you see in the industry, what is your assessment of the company's position and plan? (3) how would you size up the strategic situation of company Y? (4) what recommendations would you make to company Z's top management? and (5) what specific functions and activities does the company have to perform especially well in order for its strategy to succeed?

Alternatively, you may be asked to do a "comprehensive written case analysis." It is typical for a comprehensive written case analysis to emphasize:

1. Identification of key issues and problems confronting management,

2. A thorough analysis and evaluation of these issues and problems,

3. An assessment of action alternatives, and

4. Presentation of a plan of action.

You may wish to consider the following pointers in preparing a comprehensive written case analysis.[4]

Issues and Problems. As the checklist in Figure A–1 suggests, there are five vital areas in an organization which form an integral part of any com-

---

[4] For some additional ideas and viewpoints, you may wish to consult Thomas J. Raymond, "Written Analysis of Cases," in M. P. McNair, ed., *The Case Method at the Harvard Business School* (New York: McGraw-Hill Book Company, 1954), pp. 139–63. In Raymond's article is an actual case, a sample analysis of the case, and a sample of a student's written report on the case.

prehensive analysis: (1) its product line and basic competitive position, (2) its profitability and financial conditions, (3) its operations—production, personnel, organization structure, controls, and so on, (4) the caliber of top management, including not only management's past record but also its adequacy to cope with what lies ahead, and (5) the company's prospects for the future. A comprehensive analysis must survey all five of these areas, with a view toward identifying the key issues and problems which confront the organization. It is essential that your paper reflect a sharply focused diagnosis of these key issues and problems and, further, that you demonstrate good business judgment in sizing up the company's present situation. Make sure you understand and can identify the firm's corporate strategy. You would probably be well advised to begin your paper by sizing up the company's situation, its strategy, and the significant problems and issues which confront management. State the problems/issues as clearly and precisely as you can. Unless it is necessary to do so for emphasis, avoid recounting facts and history about the company (assume your professor has read the case and is familiar with the organization!). Consider when and why each problem arose, who is involved, and how critical the situation is. Indicate, where appropriate, the interrelationships between problems/issues. Be careful to distinguish between symptoms and root causes.

Analysis and Evaluation.   Very likely you will find this section the hardest part of the report. Analysis is hard work! Study the tables, exhibits, and financial statements carefully. Check out the firm's financial ratios, its profit margins and rates of return, its capital structure, and decide how strong the firm is financially. Similarly, look at marketing, production, managerial competences, and so on, and evaluate the organization's strengths and weaknesses in each of the major functional areas. Identify the factors underlying the organization's successes and failures. Decide whether it has a distinctive competence and, if so, whether it is capitalizing upon it. Is the firm's strategy working? Why or why not? Assess opportunities and threats, both internally and externally. Determine whether objectives, strategies, and policies are realistic in light of prevailing constraints. Look at how the organization is hedging its risks. Evaluate the firm's competitive position. Establish a hard-nosed perspective view of each problem-issue and indicate problem linkages and interrelationships. Formulate a judgment as to the organization's future prospects. (Review the checklist in Figure A–1 to see if you have overlooked something.)

In writing up your analysis and evaluation, bear in mind that:

1. You are obliged to offer supporting evidence for your views and judgments. Do not rely upon unsupported opinions, overgeneralizations, and platitudes as a substitute for tight, logical argument backed up with facts and figures.

2. You should indicate the key factors which are crucial to the organization's success or failure; i.e., what must it concentrate on and be sure to do right in order to be a high performer. Is manufacturing efficiency the key to profitability? Or is it high sales volume? Or convincing customers that the product is of high "quality?" Or is it rendering good service? Or what?

3. While some information in the case is established fact, other evidence may be in the form of opinions, judgments, and beliefs, some of which may be contradictory or inaccurate. You are thus obligated to assess the validity of such information. Do not hesitate to question what seems to be "fact."

4. You should demonstrate that your interpretation of the evidence is both reasonable and objective. Be wary of preparing an analysis which omits all arguments not favorable to your position. Likewise, try not to exaggerate, prejudge, or overdramatize. Endeavor to inject balance into your analysis. Strive to display good business judgment.

Assessing Alternatives. In dealing with this facet of the written report, you may wish to start with a brief account of the areas or categories where action needs to be initiated. Then, you will need to consider the various ways of undertaking each of the *action priorities*. Be sure to keep the focus on what can and should be done to solve the organization's problems. Decide what is feasible in light of the constraints involved. Weigh the risks that attach to each alternative, as well as the pros and cons. If there are important compromises or trade-offs, identify them.

The Plan of Action. The final section of the written case analysis should consist of a plan of action (or alternative plans, if contingencies may arise). The action plan should follow directly from the analysis. If it comes as a surprise, because it is logically inconsistent with or not related to the analysis, the effect of the discussion is weakened. Obviously, any recommendations for action should offer a reasonable prospect of success. *Be sure that the company is financially able to carry out what you recommend;* also your recommendations need to be workable in terms of acceptance by the persons involved, the organization's competence to implement them, and prevailing market and environmental constraints. Unless you feel justifiably compelled to do so, do not qualify, hedge, or weasel on the actions that you believe should be taken. Furthermore, state your recommendations in sufficient detail to be meaningful. Avoid using panaceas or platitudes such as "the organization should implement modern planning techniques" or "the company should be more aggressive in marketing its product." State *specifically* what should be done and *make sure your recommendations are operational.* For instance, do not stop with saying "the firm should improve its market position," continue on with exactly *how* you think this should be done. And, finally, you should indicate how your plan should be implemented. Here, you may wish to give some attention to leadership styles, psychological approaches, motivational aspects, and incentives that may be helpful. You might also stipulate a timetable for initiating actions, indicate priorities, and suggest who should be responsible for doing what. For example, "Have the manager take the following steps: (1) _____, (2) _____, (3) _____, (4) _____.

In preparing your plan of action, remember that there is a great deal of difference between being responsible, on the one hand, for a decision which may be costly if it proves in error and, on the other hand, expressing a casual opinion as to some of the courses of action which might be taken when you do not have to bear the responsibility for any of the consequences. A good rule to follow in designing your plan of action is to *avoid recommending anything you would not yourself be willing to do if you were in management's shoes.* The importance of learning to develop good judgment in a managerial situation is indicated by the fact that while the same information and operating data may be available to every manager or executive in an organization, it *does* make a difference to the organization which person makes the final decision.[5]

It should go without saying that your report should be organized and written in a manner that communicates well and is persuasive. Great ideas amount to little unless others can be convinced of their merit—this takes effective communication.

---

[5] Gragg, "Because Wisdom Can't Be Told," p. 10.

LIST OF SUGGESTED CASES

$$\overline{}$$

The following is a list of cases that can be used to supplement and illustrate the material found in this book. All the cases can be ordered[1] through the Intercollegiate Case Clearing House (ICCH) by listing the name and case number and sending to:

> Intercollegiate Case Clearing House
> Soldiers Field Post Office
> Boston, MA   02163

Chapters 1 and 2

City Hardware (A) (B) (C) (D), 32 pp.   9–378–957, 958, 959, 960
The case allows the student to formulate new objectives for a small business that is having management planning and control problems. (TN [Teaching Note] 5–378–961)

Hasket Computer Services, 34 pp.   9–378–221
The president of a computer service company is attempting to formulate a corporate strategy for his firm. Major issues are management of change, growth strategy, and organizational structure.

Home Box Office, 17 pp.   9–676–150
A new employee is charged with the responsibility of developing a growth strategy for the new Home Box Office (HBO) satellite-transmission pay TV network.

Ohio State University, 28 pp.   9–378–648
Case concerns the difficulty of Ohio State in balancing the athletic budget in light of a desire to spend more money on the women's sport program. User can formulate strategies where limited resources is a prime factor.

Patio Time, Inc., 9 pp.   9–378–223
The case is about a manager who is having great difficulty in managing a small furniture business from a distance. Management control and strategy implementation are major issues.

---

[1] Examination copies can be obtained for a very reasonable price.

Crown Cork and Seal Co., Inc., 27 pp.   9–378–024

The case concerns the formulation of corporate policy and strategy for a firm that is facing immediate threats from competition and the environmentalists. The user can formulate new objectives for the company. (TN 5–378–108)

University of Virginia, 21 pp.   9–378–650

The case concerns whether the university should spend $3 million to enlarge its football stadium. The role of intercollegiate athletics in a large university is discussed.

Chapters 3 and 4

Bradley's Bakery, 14 pp.   9–278–721

The case concerns the possibility of acquiring ownership of a small retail bakery. Significant factors addressed include financial and managerial problems associated with the acquisition. (TN 4–278–721)

Chinon, S.A., 13 pp.   9–278–157

A loan officer in a Paris bank is considering an increase in the credit limit for a French firm. The case allows for considerable contingency planning analysis.

Campbell Soup Co., 10 pp.   9–578–123

The case describes an antitrust suit brought against the company by a former competitor, H. J. Heinz. Heinz charges that Campbell Soup is guilty of unfair competition.

Mary Carter Paint Co., 15 pp.   9–578–142

The company's pricing practices are found to be deceptive by the Supreme Court. The case allows a discussion of business ethics and pricing strategies.

Homestake Mining Co., 33 pp.   9–378–627

The case explores the corporate strategy of the Homestake Mining Co., which is the largest gold producer in the United States. The concept of a multinational corporate strategy is discussed.

Kroehler Manufacturing Co., 34 pp.   9–378–860

The case concerns the decision to divest the office furniture subsidiary and close or sell marginal manufacturing plants. The issues of the case center around divestment, vertical integration, and marketing strategy formulation.

Portland's Stadium Decision, 51 pp.   9–178–239

A complex case exploring the decision to expand the existing stadium or build a new stadium. The case describes the many positions of the protagonists. The case provides an excellent vehicle for discussion of strategy implementation.

Southeastern Steel Co., 26 pp.   9–277–068

A large steel company located in the Sunbelt is considering a capital expansion program. The issues of the case are expansion and financial planning.

Vermillion Municipal Liquor Store, 20 pp.   9–578–650

The city council is concerned with whether to make extensive changes in the methods of operation of the city owned liquor store. The issue of formulating a pricing strategy is central to the case. (TN 5–578–651)

Victoria Station, 30 pp.   9–378–981

The company is looking at various strategies that will assure the company maintaining its market leadership position in the industry. Strategy formulation and strategic planning are the major issues covered in the case.

Disposable World, Inc., 34 pp.   9–378–690

The case traces the start up of a new business and its subsequent failure. The case allows the user to analyze where the strategy went wrong. (TN 5–378–691)

Watson's Landscape and Gardening Center, 23 pp.   9–378–658

A young couple is considering starting a new business where there is a great amount of uncertainty. The case allows an analysis of horticultural services and the start-up problems of a new business.

Chapters 5 and 6

Artisan Industries (B), 22 pp.   9–378–733

The case concerns a company with $10 million in sales that manufactures wooden toys. The company is family-owned and operated. Currently very successful, the management is looking at future opportunities. The case issues center on how to formulate strategy when the management organization is controlled by one family whose ideas differ. (TN 5–378–733)

Concrete Masonry Corp., 9 pp.   9–578–632

A company with an established business philosophy is threatened by changing market conditions. The case looks at various approaches to project management.

Continental Telephone Co., 18 pp.   9–378–689

The case traces the growth of a firm that has grown to $2 billion in sales in less than 15 years. The issues of the case are acquisition analysis, formulating growth strategies, and organizational change.

Clark Equipment, 27 pp.   9–676–052

The case looks at the problems of interfacing new technologies with managerial and production control systems. Production planning is the main issue.

Mead Corp. (A) (B), 29 pp.   9–377–183, 184

The company forms a corporate responsibility committee of the board of directors. The committee looks at affirmative action, policies for helping workers affected by plant closings, and so on. The case concerns the role of corporate responsibility in a profit-making organization.

United Way of Warren County, 15 pp.   9–378–853
The decision of who should be the chairman for the 1977 campaign is the central
issue of the case. The case examines the role of a board of directors, financial
management, and business ethics in a nonprofit organization. (TN 5–378–854)

Bishopric, Inc., 28 pp.   9–378–025
A large manufacturer of storage tanks has ambitious plans to diversify into
nuclear power and food-processing equipment. The major issues are acquisition,
diversification, and organizational structure. (TN 5–378–279)

Modern Machines Works–1977, 25 pp.   9–678–678
Case looks at the continuing problem of an organization that faces changing
markets. Issues of the case are strategic planning, organizational structure, and
dealing with plant layout.

Megalith, Inc. (A) (B), 28 pp.   9–476–107, 108
The case is about a company that has centralized its financial and control functions. Two young "stars" have recently resigned and the senior vice president is
convinced that salary is the reason.

Multi-products, Inc. (A) (B) (C), 10 pp.   9–378–074, 075, 076
The motivation of the president, who has taken over an unspecified business, is
discussed. The president's action plans and values are discussed.

INDEX

338

*This book has been set in 10 and 9 point Pala-
tino, leaded 2 points. Chapter numbers are 36
point Palatino and chapter titles are 18 point
Palatino. The size of the type page is 27 by 45½
picas.*